The Handbook of Writte

Unprovided with original learning, uninformed in the habits of thinking, unskilled in the arts of composition, I resolved – to write a book.

Edward Gibbon 1737–1794, English Historian,
author of *The Decline and Fall of The Roman Empire.*

The Handbook of
Written English

John G. Taylor

howtobooks

Published by How To Books Ltd,
3 Newtec Place, Magdalen Road,
Oxford OX4 1RE. United Kingdom.
Tel: (01865) 793806. Fax: (01865) 248780.
email: info@howtobooks.co.uk
http://www.howtobooks.co.uk

First edition 2002
Second edition 2005

British Library Cataloguing in Publication Data
A catalogue record for this book is available from the British Library

Cover design by Baseline Arts Ltd, Oxford
Produced for How To Books by Deer Park Productions, Tavistock
Typeset by PDQ Typesetting, Newcastle-under-Lyme, Staffs.
Printed and bound by Bell & Bain Ltd, Glasgow

NOTE: The material contained in this book is set out in good faith for general
guidance and no liability can be accepted for loss or expense incurred as a result
of relying in particular circumstances on statements made in the book. The laws
and regulations are complex and liable to change, and readers should check the
current position with the relevant authorities before making personal
arrangements.

Contents

About the Author

John Taylor was born in London in 1937. Originally destined for a career in music, he studied piano, timpani and double bass at the Royal Academy of Music. His first degree, a BA at the University of Reading incorporated music and economics. He then became a professional jazz musician, but discovered that economics was more lucrative. He became a teacher of English as a Foreign Language while studying at the London School of Economics. Studies at LSE led to an MSc (Econ.) and involved research, and ultimately a post in Norway. In Norway, he lectured in local government economics and later engaged in further research at Odense University in Denmark. But the mountains beckoned and he returned to take up a position at a county planning office in western Norway. He returned to Oslo to a new teaching post, this time in statistics and computing. His familiarity with economics and local government resulted in commissions for proofreading and translation for government departments, research institutions and local authorities – something which had occupied his spare time from 1973. This became a full-time occupation in 1989, one that enables a seasonal migration of work place to his summer cottage in the forests of eastern Norway. He is also a court interpreter and translator for the Oslo City Justices and the Norwegian Directorate of Immigration. In 2004 he was appointed as a lay judge. Musically, he prefers Mahler to Grieg, but still turns out an acceptable blues on the piano!

Preface

This was originally intended to be the 'Preface to the Second Edition' of my book *A Handbook for Writers of English: Punctuation, common practice and usage.* In the opening paragraph I explained that the intention of the book was indeed to be a 'handbook' – something to have at hand. But a survey of my clients revealed that they had indeed ordered a copy, which was now conveniently placed in the reference section of the library, which in turn was located in the basement. Now, no-one but no-one goes down five floors to find out the use of the semicolon, only to be told by the librarian 'sorry, reference books can't be taken out of the library'. I had toyed with the idea of calling this a 'Deskbook for writers', but are potential purchasers going to consider whether space on their desks is actually available when glancing at this book?

Nevertheless, this is more than a revised edition. It *is* fully revised, but there are major additions. I think it worth repeating a couple of things I said in the preface to the first edition. Much information for which I have frequent use *is* available, but in a number of different handbooks. This publication aims at providing all *essential* information in a single handbook. You will find that certain points are repeated in several places. The colon, for example is treated under that section, but also under 'dates and time'. This emphasises the point that a handbook is not intended to be read from cover to cover; rather, it should be consulted as the need arises. Even then, do not look for rules. Common practice and usage relate to custom. Custom changes rapidly from time to time and from place to place.

In the above paragraph I mentioned *essential* information, but I find that some less essential information is also of interest, as my mailbox revealed. I had a surprising response to the former book. How kind people were about some abysmal errors (moral: do the proofreading yourself); how generous they were with ideas: in sum, the inspiration to make amends for my faults and to make it bigger and better. I apologise not. Bigger *is* Better.

Consequently, I have added more notes and examples throughout, but deleted information which was clearly outdated, the chapter on Reference books, for example. New ones appear as regularly as *Newsweek* (a clear inspiration to some). This chapter has been swept clean. Web sites such as Amazon, Barnes and Noble etc., provide absolutely the latest information. I have therefore included more information on useful sites. Even these, however, seem to disappear and re-emerge under new site names. The best advice is to use search words. I find *Google* very good here, even in foreign languages.

The chapter on Tables has been supplemented with one on diagrams. It is a simple matter to transform data from a table into an impressive diagram using a spreadsheet (I use Excel). I am sure that this will enable the visual presentation of many works to be improved. Remember that readers of your thesis or article may not study a statistical table in great detail, but may well become absorbed in a pie chart.

This brings us to statistical analysis. A course in statistical method is an integral part of virtually all courses in the humanities, social and natural sciences, not to mention medicine, at university and college levels. Such courses were few prior to the era of computerised statistical programs. SPSS, Minitab and SAS changed all that. Many of yesterday's 'SPSS students' are the professors of today, and so armed, are more critical of their own students, scrutinising tables for choice of statistical test, probability and significance. There are still many who cringe at this terminology, but it all boils down to which statistical test to employ, and what to look for in the results. Now this is not anything like as difficult as it sounds. We do not have to have a degree in mechanical engineering to realise that the car exhaust pipe needs replacing. We analyse the situation (the 'popping' sound), formulate a theory (needs replacing), make a test (give the exhaust pipe a tap with the hammer), analyse the results (rust fell off), and reach a conclusion (it'll probably last another month). Statistical analysis does not differ so much from this procedure. Of course, you are sweating with the thought of making a decision; was it correlation or regression we should have used? Chapter 7 will help you; here is a quick guide to selecting the appropriate test and what to look for in the results.

Many of my clients still treat the PC like a typewriter. Help Menus assist with the basic refinements, but I would be surprised if as much as a half of them know how to compile a macro. While the Help Menu does offer much assistance in compiling a macro, among other things, I often find the 'bibles' confusing. An index is essential but compilation is not really as demanding as many of the bibles would have us believe. In a dozen or so pages I introduce some aids, including index – and macro – compilation, which are destined to become vital elements in the preparation of your manuscript.

One critic of my original text made the comment that I covered quite a lot of material that was of only limited interest. I agree! Certainly, the chapter on punctuation may well be the reason why 80% of readers purchased this book. But they could have chosen from a couple of dozen excellent punctuation books. So why choose mine?

Do we have to include *everything* in which the writer may be interested? It is true that nobody reads a reference book from cover to cover, but if we reduce a book to the lowest common denominator, then there is not really much originality. We arrive back at the situation where we need to buy several reference books, one each for punctuation, abbreviations, metric conversions, style, and an introduction to statistical method (among others).

Typical questions which confront authors and students are: The population increased from 10 million to 20 million over ten years. What was the average annual growth rate? Is it boat race, boat-race or boatrace? Is there an abbreviation for 'The Convention of Scottish Local Authorities'? In troy weight, how many grains are there in an ounce? Do I use chi-square or Pearson's correlation coefficient in this analysis? Of course this is not everybody's cup of tea, but for the few pages this takes to supply information concerning each of these questions, I think that many readers will appreciate the time saved by finding this information between two covers rather than two dozen.

There are certain subjects which are of interest to the majority to which many books are devoted to the subject. Here, I am thinking particularly of style, of which there are probably around thirty – some excellent, many mediocre. One which I purchased a few years ago was described as a 'manual of style', but had little to do with style as such. It contained largely lists – lists of automobiles, labour organisations, nobility titles and even team names. Although I now know that Boston Red Sox is a baseball team I am not confident that my literary style will be greatly improved armed with this knowledge. Nevertheless, I feel that there is room for a brief discussion on *style*. What is it that gives an article or a thesis *style*? I considered that a chapter providing us with food for thought had a place in this book

After all this, if you don't find a particular chapter interesting, well at least you might find the heading material amusing. I admit to drawing this matter from three excellent books of quotations (see References). All of them are well worth purchasing – they are the sort of books one buys as Christmas presents for friends but to which the personal attachment becomes too great so that a pair of socks is substituted. And during the final throes of self-pity, I happened to come across a book in Vilnius, published in Moscow, but printed in English, with the title *Oscar Wilde. The Aphorisms*. Now I had always thought that these were some sort of stick-insect, but the *COD* definition is 'a pithy observation which contains a general truth'. What a pithy I didn't know that, but neither was I clear what a pithy observation was. Anyway, I have included a number of the pithiest aphorisms to entertain and enlighten. By way of example:

> *If you want to get rich from writing, write the sort of thing that's read by persons who move their lips when reading.* – Don Marquis (1878–1937)

I also considered the idea of including Bushisms to add some lighter material, but after a while these become more pathetic than amusing. (I have just eliminated half of my U.S. market.)

Comments are still welcome. I do not intend to rewrite the book again, but expect and hope that there will be an opportunity to make improvements to any subsequent reprint. In the meantime I will make available any goodies brought to my attention on my web page: www.jgtaylor.com So don't hesitate to embarrass me.

John Taylor, Oslo 2005

john@jgtaylor.com

Acknowledgements

As stated in the original edition, this book is the result of the inspiration of many of my clients. Who are these? Mostly people who have the courage to admit that their English needs a bit of polishing. Now, I am not a polisher by profession, but I have suffered from the professorial comment that my style needs to be improved. Professor Wise (how appropriate the name) shocked me into submission when he said that we all need to improve our style of writing, but some of us needed to learn to write first. I accepted his challenge. That was forty years ago. I pledged that no postgraduate should ever again be subjected to the pains I had to suffer. I would become a proofreader, a language advisor, a consultant, whatever, at a salary no more than a pittance: I was committed and devoted.

My work as a proofreader and translator soon brought me into contact with a wide range of subjects and papers written by an even wider variety of authors.

In the first edition I paid tribute to my clients who had encouraged me to write a handbook. I also acknowledged several colleagues who had offered advice and encouragement, including author/translator Bill Mulholland.

I am deeply indebted to a number of readers of that book for comments and suggestions – as well as pointing out some errors. These include Gordon and Mary Snow, Peter Carney, Satu and Jacob Jørgensen, and in particular Janet Calderbank who offered constructive comments to the first draft and to Beth Anne Crocket for meticulous proofreading.

My appreciation also to Nikki and her colleagues at How To Books for their encouragement and professional advice.

1
Introduction

Punctuation – The Devil's Own Rules?

John where James had had had had had had had had had had had the teacher's approval.[1]

Remember this schoolboy howler? With appropriate punctuation this forms a logical sentence. I remember my teacher taunting us with a similar one. Apparently a sign-writer had been employed to paint a sign for 'Smith and Jones Ltd'. Upon completion the boss had one small criticism: *'There's too much space between Smith and and and and and Jones.'*

I have deliberately not punctuated this and place the ball in your court. However, the footnote provides the solutions. I am sure the point about punctuation will be readily appreciated.

The Archbishop of York once said: 'Intellectually, spelling – English spelling – does not matter ... Intellectually, stops [the period] matter a great deal. If you are getting your commas, semicolons and full stops wrong, it means that you are not getting your thoughts right, and your mind is muddled.' (*Observer*, 23 Oct. 1938.) In support of his argument the Archbishop also pointed out that Shakespeare spelt his own name at least four different ways (but he always got his punctuation right!).

Nowhere does the Archbishop, and certainly not Shakespeare, mention the *rules* of punctuation. Neither, to my knowledge, is there to be found a book with such a title. Rather than rules as such, punctuation reflects the traditions of style. But even that is to simplify. Can we talk about a single style of academic writing, or the style of paperback writers? To each his own! Robert Benchley once said: 'It took me fifteen years to discover I had no talent for writing, but I couldn't give it up by that time as I was too famous.' Most of us can't afford to wait that long to find out.

---

1   John, where James had had 'had', had had 'had had'. 'Had had' had had the teacher's approval. 'There's too much space between "Smith" and "and", and "and" and "Jones".'

Article or Lecture?

'Drawing on my fine command of language, I said nothing.' Robert Benchley (1889–1945), American humorist.

I have become increasingly aware of the qualities of the different types of articles and papers I am required to read. Some are clearly designed as a lecture, implicitly if not explicitly. There is a difference between the spoken word and the written word. This also implies that when *reading* a text which is to be *spoken*, the punctuation may have to be adjusted accordingly. In **contrast** to the written text, the delivered lecture is history as soon as a statement is proclaimed. The listener is rarely taken up with what *has been* said, rather, with what is *currently* being declared. Tone and emphasis readily replace many punctuation marks, but it is here that the reader of literature requires assistance. Consider the following:

Mr Smith said Mr Jones is a master of English.

'Mr Smith,' said Mr Jones, 'is a master of English.'

Mr Smith said: 'Mr Jones is a Master of English.'

The latter example also emphasises the point that Mr Jones (and not Mr Smith) is an academic, as well. I will not dwell on this point, but the three examples illustrate the need for clear punctuation.

However, punctuation is only a part of the story. The ultimate aim of most authors is not to present a thesis on the English language: it is to present an article which stimulates and retains the interest of the reader in the subject matter. That occasional missing comma, that amusing tie-pin error, will all be overlooked if the article is structured and presented in such a way as to clearly convey a message.

We have all read articles which are profusely punctuated. These may well leave no doubt as to what the author is saying. But could he have retained the message with fewer commas, fewer – or even more – sentences, and a glut of exclamation marks? Look through your own work and you may realise (as I did) that typing within the 30 mph limit (or should that be wpm – words per minute?) results in more gear changes. We are writing as we speak, so to say, where the pause for breath is required, a little more emphasis is laid on that special term, and where we suspend our delivery for that nano-second awaiting the acclaim of the audience.[2]

---

2   If you are preparing a speech then you might find *How to Make Your Point in Just a Minute*, Phillip Khan Panni (How To Books) a useful aid.

But for the writer there is no audience, no collective gathering of admirers eagerly hanging on every utterance. If you are lucky there are a few thousand individuals widely dispersed, of diverse backgrounds, varied intellect, and with the ability to absorb anything from two to ten pages per hour. How are these reacting to your written words of wisdom? The answer is that you just don't know. But credit them all with an IQ considerably above the mean and an ability to readily grasp your point (and your commas). Most will be able to absorb phrases at a time, and many will readily grab the sentence, chew it and swallow it all in one gulp. Don't give them indigestion with a peppering of unnecessary punctuation.

All this may seem to suggest that I am advising you to be a minimalist. Not at all. Common practice and usage changes over time. What may be favoured by one teacher may be frowned upon by another. But there are certain accepted standards in abbreviations, addresses, in dates, placement of the final inverted commas and so forth which all publishers use. We need to know these, or at least be able to look them up. But where punctuation is used so as to mark the style and preference of the author, then we would expect to encounter differences.

My examples are drawn from a wide range of texts – books (fiction and non-fiction), articles and magazines. As such they will show a variety of uses and styles. Many of those indicated as wrong (read unacceptable) are from articles which I have proofread. In most cases I have changed the text slightly: the object is to provide an illustration, not a quotation.

The American journalist and raconteur Irvin Cobb (1876–1944) once said: 'Learn all the rules, every one of them, so that you will know how to break them.' But we are not in the business of breaking rules, or even making them: we are looking at common usage. Even that does not mean that you have to be as common as the next bloke. If you really consider there is a preferred way to punctuate a sentence in order to convey a specific meaning, then I would not dispute your judgement. English is a living language. If it was not then we would be speaking the language of the Pilgrim Fathers on both sides of the Atlantic today. Or as George Bernard Shaw (1856–1950) observed: 'England and America are two countries divided by the same language.' (See also page 345.)

2
The Basic Elements

It is all very well being able to write books, but can you waggle your ears? – J.M. Barrie (1860–1937) Scottish playwright. To H.G.Wells.

When we are writing something, a letter, an article, a thesis, perhaps a note or a description, we are communicating *something* to someone. Even if it is a reminder to ourselves, the message has to be clear and incontrovertible. Three elements of writing help us to achieve this aim: punctuation, grammar and syntax.

Punctuation is more easily understood when the function of the sentence construction is appreciated. The way in which your sentence is constructed and punctuated, the manner in which sentences are grouped into paragraphs and so forth, are some of the elements of style. If the sentence is grammatically correct, the meaning will become clearer. The way in which the words of the sentence relate to each other – the syntax – (in other words, the logical structure of the sentence), is an integral part of grammar.

The first draft of this book included a number of grammatical terms which were questioned by the proof editor. Using the search words 'grammar' and 'glossary', I discovered how much has changed since my school days! The adjectival noun (the 'poor' get poorer) is rarely mentioned as such in the standard texts. But then, I cannot recall learning about phrasal verbs either. A colleague at the University of Sheffield maintained that the development of the language was being accompanied by the development of the grammatical glossary. Witness indeed: comma splice, dangling modifier, fused sentence, trite expression (all from the Internet). I will refer just to the basics – and only where absolutely necessary.

It may be appropriate to emphasise that the material here is not only the result of experience in correcting manuscripts but also the study of the material given in the references. Of course, no two books are the same, not even when issued by the same publishing house. One example is the abbreviation for Reverend. The modern style is to drop the full point after Mr and Dr, for example. So why not Rev? The *Oxford Dictionary for Writers & Editors* gives Revd – no full point. The *Oxford Dictionary of Abbreviations* gives Rev or Rev. (with or without a full point). *Collins*

Electronic Dictionary gives Rev. (with a full point) whereas *Collins Abbreviations* (paperback) gives Rev (without). The same applies to *Cambridge International Dictionary* and *Cassells Dictionary. Chambers* allows Rev or Rev. When we look at the 'Right Reverend', both *Collins* and *Chambers* give Rt Rev.; Cambridge uses Rt. (full point) as does *Cassells.* I haven't even begun on the US dictionaries.

I should add a note here about the use of the term 'full point'. *The Oxford English Dictionary*, no less, defines a full stop as follows: The end of a sentence; the single point or dot used to mark this; a period, full point.

We note that alternative terms are 'period' – now mainly US English, and 'full point'. I wonder if Carey (1976) whose book *Mind the Stop* was first published in 1939, would have given it the title *Mind the Full Point* if he had written it today. Roberts (1987) apparently prefers just 'point'. Another term is 'end stop' (Burt, 2000) and which applies to the full stop, exclamation mark and question mark. This omits the full stop used for abbreviations although Phythian (1980) refers to the full stop in connection with abbreviations. The *New Oxford English Dictionary* states 'full point' to be another term for 'full stop' (although it is not given in the *Oxford Dictionary for Writers & Editors*). However, *Hart's Rules for Compositors and Readers at the University Press Oxford* does use this term, also in conjunction with abbreviations. So I am in good company when I select this option.

If you are intending to have your work published, check the *Guidelines for authors* issued by the publishing house. They will prefer certain uses of punctuation signs and format for references. This book is very largely based on actual examples, even though the text may have been changed. The variety of usage suggests a choice; it also emphasises the need for consistency. Oscar Wilde once said: 'Consistency is the last refuge of the unimaginative', and in the words of the parodist, Horace Smith (1779–1849), 'Inconsistency is the only thing in which men [subst. writers] are consistent'. Most publishers would probably agree with Wilde, while simultaneously nodding their heads resignedly at Smith's comment.

And so! This book will hopefully assist you in certain aspects of preparing your manuscript but you may well profit from an excellent book in the *How To* series: *Improving your written English* by Marion Field. If you are a bit 'rusty' on grammar, you will certainly find some gems in the references in this publication.

Before considering the basic elements of our manuscript a few words on planning the paper.

'A bad book is as much of a labour to write as a good one.' – Aldous Huxley (1894–1963). English novelist and essayist.

The Title

The title of your paper says everything about the subject. The fact that this contains a limited number of words necessitates careful thought. Do not think that a subtitle will suffice to provide details. This may not always appear on the cover, and even if does may hardly be readable if a small font is used. The casual visitor to the bookshop will be captivated by the main title before he even glances at the contents. By way of example, I have no less than four books on my shelf with the plain title *Punctuation*. I have another four: *Plain English Guide, Plain English – a user's guide, Guide to Plain English, The Complete Plain Words*. Encountering all these in a bookshop I am hardly likely to examine all four of either group. But when, on the same shelf, I see *Eats, shoots and leaves*, my curiosity is aroused. Glancing at the front cover, I read: *The Zero Tolerance Approach to Punctuation.*[3]

The same applies to your thesis or article, although a light-hearted title might not be particularly appropriate for the former. Nevertheless, the title of a research study such as I have encountered, *Solidarity – a historical overview*, could well have been *What solidarity? Workers and politicians unite!* I am inclined to think that more readers (potential purchasers) would glance at a book with the latter title. But it may be that you come across the appropriate title during the course of preparing your paper.

Structuring Your Paper

We all work best according to our own scheme. The trouble is that we are not always sure of the scheme until we are halfway through the book. A constructive approach is to compile a list of titles of chapters. The PC is the easiest method as we can then delete, change and sort titles as required. Having made a preliminary list I then use a filing unit. Many of us will not have a filing cabinet as such, but simple plastic frames with hanging files are perfect. The files are the chapters in my book into which I slip notes, photocopies, newspaper extracts, and so forth. The fact that these are 'hanging' enables me to rearrange the files (chapters) as required. For this reason I would avoid these so-called 'home archives' with fixed compartments.

---

3 Little wonder that this was a best seller. *Eats, shoots and leaves*, by Lynne Truss. Profile Books, 2003. [Drop the comma in the title and you might expect to find this on the natural history shelf.]

We can now commence writing!

The Sentence

The major error made by most authors is making a sentence too long. Indeed, in one of the books listed in the references, I read that the full point is the only punctuation sign which is not over-used! The occasional short snappy sentence rouses our senses; the abnormally long one dulls our concentration. If your sentence is more than three lines on an A4 manuscript page, look at it and check for punctuation. If it is more than four lines, look at it even more closely and check for punctuation and argument. If it is more than five lines, check for punctuation, argument and logic. More than six lines? Well, you should probably rewrite it.

I could have written the above paragraph as one sentence using commas, semicolons and colons. It is all based on the same subject so that would not have been difficult. But try reading the following:

> The major error made by most authors is a sentence which is too long: if your sentence is more than three lines, then look at it and check for punctuation; if it is more than four lines, look at it even more closely and check for punctuation and argument; if it is more than five lines, check for logic as well, and if it is more than six lines then you should probably rewrite it.

We have probably just about reached all a reader can absorb in one breath.

I have mentioned the number of lines rather than the number of words. Most texts recommend an *average* of 14 to 18 words per sentence, even up to 20 in non-fiction. (This chapter has a mean of 15 words per sentence.) But that does not say much about the length of the longest sentences. Some texts recommend a maximum of 30 words but, as the above example shows, it is erroneous to think that a long sentence may be broken up by the use of a colon. The subject of the sentence may get lost in a myriad of separators. The colon and semicolon, and also the dash, have specific functions and should be used with discretion.

Sometimes a sentence can become too 'wordy'. Frequently the phrase containing 'of' may be rewritten. 'Lots of' may (should) be replaced by 'many', for example. Other expressions may also be written more concisely:

> Considerable doubt has been expressed concerning whether the Minister's series of fiscal actions during the crisis actually had the level of public support that he vociferously maintained to be the case!

– meaning:

The economic situation raises questions concerning support for the Minister's actions.

We appear to have lost reference to *the level* of support. But that is surely implicit in the rewritten sentence. Thomas Jefferson once said: 'The most valuable of all talents is that of never using two words when one will do.' This does not mean to say we should seek out every phrase or clause and reconstruct it with fewer words. As the author, you should ask yourself whether you feel that you have managed to convey precisely what you intended. Now put yourself in the place of the reader and ask what the written word conveyed to you.

It is not always the length of a sentence but the variation that gives style. That long, demanding sentence, the short, sharp witticism, that arresting punctuation mark! This is the stuff of the novel, the drama – and the academic thesis. At least, it ought to be. Here is an extract from Kingsley Amis's[4] book, *The King's English*:

> There is a feeling here and there that the spelling of such words with an *x* is somehow classier, richer in history, *better* than the spelling with *ct* that everybody naturally adopts. Pfui! Everybody is often wrong, but not this time. The philological evidence is dubious and no one has yet succeeded in introducing even the ghost of an *x* into important by-forms like *connecting, connective* and indeed *connect*. Go on writing *connection* and the rest and treating *connexion* and the rest with the tolerant indifference they deserve.

Now, there is no doubt that Amis is a bit long-winded here. But he intends to be. The longer sentences demand concentration. The short sentence or fragment (see below) arouses it. Here are 87 words, 5 sentences; mean 17.4 words. The distribution is 31, 1, 8, 28, 19. The Mean Deviation (an expression of the variation or spread about the mean) is 10.3 words. (See Chapter 7, Statistical measures and statistical tests)

It is, of course, hardly necessary to statistically analyse a work in this way. The essential question is 'Does the text flow?' It is the variety of short and long sentences which assists in keeping the reader's mind focused on the content. A mean length of 14 to 18 words per sentence seems to be acceptable, but bear in mind the significance of the short sentence in arresting the reader's attention. If 95% of all sentences were in this range for the mean, then the style would be cramped.

Modern word processors provide a character and word count, and even the mean length of sentence. One or two professional programs give a detailed

---

4   The 'pronunciation rule' prompts me to write Amis's book rather than Amis' book! In fact, the former is correct, I have since found out.

analysis as above. Rather than analysing the material *post facto*, your reader's interest will be sustained by the considered use of connectors, fragments, and, not least, the terminology.

Sentence Connectors

Sentence connectors assist the flow of an argument, but terms such as 'however', 'nevertheless', and others, are frequently overdone. There are quite a number of alternatives to these, which are discussed further under Sentence connectors (see page 138).

The Fragment

A fragment is an incomplete sentence. Amis's exclamation, 'Pfui!', is a good example. Used with discretion the fragment is a useful element in style – something to arrest the reader's attention. Overdone, it destroys the essence of style. Even the most 'academic' articles can easily become 'dry' with such phrases as:

> It was hardly surprising that the fifth congress failed once again to reach an agreement on CO_2 gases since the agenda did not explicitly refer to these.

But a fragment can rouse the drooping reader.

> The fifth congress failed once again to reach any decision on CO_2 gases. Hardly surprising! The agenda did not specifically refer to these.

The (very) occasional *pièce de résistance* in French or Latin perhaps, gives a little resuscitation to a tired text. (See Chapter 20, Foreign terms and phrases)

Paragraphs

Whereas the sentence is a statement, the paragraph is a connected train of thought related to a single idea or set of ideas. Normally, the subject of the matter under debate will be mentioned or implied in the first sentence of the paragraph. In other words, the first line should not employ 'he', 'they' or other pronoun, unless it is absolutely clear from the last few lines of the previous paragraph who is being referred to. It is disconcerting for the reader to have to glance back to see who 'it' or 'these' are.

There is no prescribed minimum or maximum number of sentences, or indeed lines, which may comprise a paragraph. Even if the same theme is under discussion for a page or more, it is often convenient to provide occasional breaks in the text. This improves the visual appearance and enables the reader to consolidate his thoughts and comprehension. The end of the sentence provides space to breathe: the paragraph provides a stage where one may collect one's thoughts. Generally, a maximum of 10–12 lines is to be recommended.

The paragraph extending over half a page or more has the psychological effect of warning the reader that he had better have his wits about him to follow the line of argument which will occupy the next few minutes of his time. The occasional short paragraph of three or four lines also provides variety to the layout. Even so, too many short paragraphs can hinder the absorption of an argument and can give the impression of too many ideas being juggled. The reader will have to sort these out in order to establish some sequence in the train of thought (either the author's or his own). On the other hand, the occasional lengthy paragraph of 15–20 lines provides some 'body' to the text.

It is possible to calculate the mean number of lines per paragraph from the word-count feature. But this is of little importance. Take the psychological approach and look at the visual presentation. Are you satisfied? Then the reader probably is too.

A typographical point. Double line spacing between paragraphs can give the appearance of a disjointed style. Try with the 1.5 line spacing or even set your word processor to 1.3 line spacing. This gives a pleasing effect. In Word this spacing between paragraphs is achieved by using the 'Format' command on the menu bar, and selecting 'Paragraph'. Set 'Spacing before' to 0, and 'Spacing after' to half of the point size used. For example, if you are using Times Roman 12, set the 'Spacing after' to 6. You may set this as the default.

Many printed publications do not use a blank line between paragraphs but require the first word of each paragraph to be indented two spaces. This does not apply to the leading paragraph at the commencement of a chapter which is flush with the left margin. Nor does it apply to the first paragraph immediately following a table or diagram. A table or diagram should preferably be placed at the end of a paragraph and not in the middle unless the page layout really forces this. In other words, a large amount of 'white space' would result because there was not sufficient room on the rest of the page for the placement of the table.

Spelling

Frequent surprises will be revealed by the spellchecker. First, the spellchecker is not without its faults. Even so, think twice before dropping the unusual word straight into the waste bin. But beware! The spellchecker will detect that *airmailletter* was misspelt (should be *airmail letter*), but will fail to detect *air mail letter, air-mail letter*, and *airmail-letter* as being erroneous.

Neither will it detect that *air-ship* should be *airship*, nor that *air strip* should be *airstrip* and *air conditioning* should be *air-conditioning*. Hyphenated words can be a headache (or should that be head-ache?). A discussion of these is given in Chapter 15, Hyphenated, conjoined and compound words. There are a number of electronic dictionaries available (See Chapter 24) which are useful aids. We can state here that use of the hyphen will vary from one dictionary to another, but at least you will have a guide to consistency.

One reader of the previous edition sent me the following email:

> Aoccdrnig to a rscheearch at Cmabrigde Uinervtisy, it deosn't mttaer in what oredr the ltteers in a wrod are, the olny iprmoetnt tihng is taht the frist and lsat ltteer be at the rghit pclae. The rset can be a total mses and you can sitll raed it wouthit porbelm. Tihs is bcuseae the huamn mnid deos not raed ervey lteter by istlef, but the wrod as a wlohe.

How right she (and CU) are. Did you notcie that you raed that paragarph at vritullay normal spede? But 'shirt' and 'short' commece and finsh with the same letter. Drop the vowel and you are in the s..t.

No, I do tink speling maters.

Terminology

When proofreading I do encounter some strange terms. Of course, every subject has its own jargon, but my rule of thumb is that if it is not found in the *Oxford English Dictionary* or *Encarta*, it probably does not exist! At least, not at that point in time nor in normal usage.

But language is a living science and new words are being born by the day and by the hour. We may all find ourselves playing the role of *neologist*. Recently I encountered a phrase expounding the *attractivity* of something or other. Naturally, I thought the author meant *attraction*, or even *attractiveness*. Could the sentence be turned around to make the subject *an attraction*? There was something or other which appealed in the term, and I realised that as soon as the author had defined or justified the use of the word, it was very appropriate *in that context*. (After all, we do have *perceptivity* in the language!) A similar situation arose when one of my clients referred to *multiculturality*! Somehow this was more appropriate in the given context than *multiculturalism*! The suffix *–ity*, means 'a state of', whereas *–ism* relates to a doctrine or practice.

Recently I had a few more: 'undogmatic', 'solidaristic, 'ghettoisation', 'internationalism'. Oh, the 'isms' – how they rescue us when we begin to flag from lack of ideas. We can always revert to verbalism as did the US Secretary of State: 'We must not icentify these terrorists!'

New words may be invented; others may be given new, flexible definitions. Flexibility is indeed an element of style. You may be surprised at what has already found its way into print. Take a glance at *The Oxford Dictionary of New Words* (1998). Nevertheless it is your responsibility to ensure the reader understands your definition of a word. At the end of the day you are the author, and you take the final responsibility for your product. The proofreader will assist you in the general presentation, grammar, punctuation and style, even layout, typefaces, fonts and compilation of a table of contents and an index – the latter often being a matter of familiarity with the word-processing program. The aim of the following is to assist you in presenting your material in a lucid and logical manner such that your audience readily appreciates and understands your message and, however 'heavy' the subject matter, enjoys your approach. Remember that you know the subject matter of what you are writing or talking about. Your readers or listeners may not. You have to convey it to them.

In assembling material for this book I have also looked at what others have assembled. The list of references contains many of these (See Chapter 24). Somewhere along the way I realised that the books which were most enlightening were those written by practising authors, possibly more so than those by practising teachers. But, to be fair, the latter were catering for a different market. I have previously mentioned *The King's English* by Kingsley Amis. Amis wrote a couple of dozen best-seller novels and a dozen or so non-fiction works. While *The King's English* is neither a grammar book nor a guide to punctuation, there is so much to learn from the sheer joy of reading this text.

Possibly the ultimate guide to punctuation is Eric Partridge's *You have a point there*. As it was first published in 1953, we can note that customs and habits have changed. But the twenty-eight pages (no less) devoted to the comma alone, and thirteen to the semicolon contain many words of wisdom and not a few words of caution.

These texts are at the top end of the scale – even for the doctoral candidate in the history of the English language. But all of the books mentioned have pointed to one thing: punctuation is not fixed, rigid and inflexible. Punctuation is what makes the text clear, lucid, intelligible – and stimulating. Nobody should insist absolutely that a comma and nothing else is correct. *You* are the writer – it is *your* book – you know what you want to say. Well say it, and make sure you say what you mean. If someone comes back to you and says 'well, I was sure that what you meant was', and it wasn't, then you had better look at your punctuation too. If you are in doubt about the punctuation, then hopefully this book will help.

A final comment might be to cite the immortal words of Lewis Carroll, expressed through Humpty Dumpty: 'When *I* use a word, it means just what I choose it to mean – neither more nor less.'

Style

As to the adjective: when in doubt, strike it out. – Mark Twain (1835– 1910)

Clearly, much can be – and has been – written on 'style'. Mark Twain's comment might well be applied even more broadly. Style is something that we should be aware of whenever we apply pen to paper, likewise finger to keyboard, but are we sure what style is? We may think we have got it but it is probably not until we read through the finished work that we realise that our grammatically-correct article with its politically-correct content lacks something so that it is not quite so *pièce bien fait* as we had imagined.

The original draft of this chapter contained a few paragraphs at this point on style. But when these were refined and polished, a 'few' became 'not so few', to the extent that these became the material of a separate chapter (Chapter 22, Style). Here I focus more on what to avoid rather than what to do. However bad our own style, we instantly recognise the failings of others. Hopefully, a discussion of these elements will provide guidelines for recognising our own.

3
Punctuation and Common Usage

'If you want a silver medal, you should not write to the head of the country on such a piece of paper and with mistakes.' Nicolai Sych, head of education in the region of Vologda, reacting to a Russian schoolgirl's letter to President Putin in which she failed to capitalise one letter and missed an exclamation mark. [Quoted in *Newsweek,* 3.7.2000.]

(The major mistake, apparently – reported elsewhere – was to omit the exclamation mark: 'Dear President Putin!')

Introduction

Punctuation is quite explicitly defined in most dictionaries, as for example:

> ***marks used to organize writing:*** *the standardized non-alphabetical symbols or marks that are used to organize writing into clauses, phrases, and sentences, and in this way make its meaning clear (Encarta Dictionary).*

Hardly to be disputed. But there are many more conventions – usage – which, when incorrectly applied, may fail to make the meaning clear at best, or result in ambiguity or obscurity at worst. It is with this thought in mind

---

KEY

▶ A new point! I have found that this symbol is preferable to numbering each point a), b), or i), ii)... etc.

In the examples, the **preferred** use is indicated as follows:

✓ The dash – although infrequently used – is a useful substitute for parentheses.

Examples of the **misuse** of punctuation symbols are indicated:

✗ The dash should not follow:- a colon before a list, after 'e.g.', a comma or full point.

Other illustrative examples are given in Arial typeface.

---

that I have included *usage* in this section with the aim of including all those points which the writer may encounter in presenting his book, thesis, article or paper. All the examples shown as correct usage are based on actual extracts (although the editor of this series pointed out that several were, in fact, incorrect. They have either been removed or pointed out as erroneous). Reference has been made to a number of dictionaries: *Cambridge International, Cassells, Collins, Chambers, Longmans, Macmillan, Penguin, The Oxford Dictionary of English (OED), The Concise Oxford English Dictionary (COD), The New Oxford Dictionary of English (NODE)*, and others. Several US dictionaries were also consulted including *Merriam Webster, Websters, Random House*, and *Encarta*.

Abbreviations

A summary of the most frequently encountered abbreviations is given in Chapter 12.

Abbreviations are an aid to quick reading. It is tiresome to repeatedly encounter The North Atlantic Treaty Organisation when NATO is more than adequate (although possibly less so in a military sense!). But we become lazy and use *e.g.* when *for example* is m.p. (more proper). Worse, we assume everyone is familiar with *i.r.o.*, even to the extent that we make it into an acronym, *iro*. We are able to offer you a salary iro 20K with a rda of 25p. By now we have realised that *iro* is an abbreviation for 'in the region of', and we all know that *rda* means *recommended daily allowance*. Pathetic to put these in a glossary along with KWOC (Keyword out of context), MOC (mother of the chapel), and QAB (Queen Anne's Bounty), all of which I found in *The Oxford Dictionary for Writers & Editors*.

The above illustrated examples with and without the full point. In many instances the full point is superfluous or even incorrect. In general, the full point is used far less frequently today than previously in abbreviations. The *Concise Oxford Dictionary* (4th edn, 1954) gives T.T. for teetotaller and tuberculin tested. In the 7th edition (1982), TT (no full points) is given for both as is also the case in the *Oxford Dictionary for Writers and Editors* (2000). *Collins Abbreviations* does not use the full point at all. I do not think that many editors would accept this. While the context will normally clear any confusion, it is important to retain the full point to distinguish between certain abbreviations such as I.B.M. (Intercontinental Ballistic Missile) and IBM (the computer company, International Business Machines Corporation).

Important components of the I.B.M. were manufactured by IBM.

IBM is also an abbreviation for 'The International Brotherhood of Magicians', who are not particularly known for their involvement in missile production.

▶ A common error with abbreviations is to use a full point where it is not required, or to omit one. As a general rule a full point is used where the final letter of the abbreviation differs from that of the whole word, for example Rd (Road), Ave (Avenue), Sq. (Square), Str. (Street). But this is an area where there is an increasing tendency to omit the full point altogether. US English does, however, retain the full point in all of these (Ave., Rd., etc.)

Abbreviations, acronyms and titles

▶ Abbreviations for institutions, organisations and other bodies do not normally use full points: UN, EFTA, EEC, IBM. An acronym is a word derived from the initial letters of the words incorporated, and pronounced as spelt! Example: NATO, BAMMO (Battered and Maltreated Mistresses Organisation).

▶ Titles no longer employ full points although this was common previously: Mr., Mrs., etc. This actually broke with the 'rule' that abbreviations concluding with the final letter of the unabbreviated form do not need a full point. These have nevertheless gone today and it appears logical when we encounter Revd (for Reverend), and also Rev. But we will also encounter Rev (without a full point), likewise Rt Rev and Rt. Rev. (with full points). Interesting to note that here also US English retains the full point, even with Messrs. (plural of Mr.).

It is now quite common for honours such as OBE, DSO, etc. not to use full points.

The full point may be found on more formal documents: Ph.D., M.Sc.(Econ.) etc., but PhD, MSc etc. are widely used. The full point is normally retained in names: J. G. Taylor. But even here the practice is less widespread than previously (J G Taylor).

French used to require M. (for monsieur) but here also we encounter M, Mme and so forth, again without the full point.

▶ Organisations and bodies such as the EU, NATO (also Nato) do not use full points.

▶ All correct.

✓ O.K., o.k., or OK
✗ Neither 'Ok' nor 'ok' are o.k.

'okay' is not accepted by *The Authors' and Printers' Dictionary* (OUP), but is okay by *NODE*, *The Cambridge International Dictionary* and US dictionaries.

Abbreviated words

▶ A full point is not used for:
- cardinal points (S, NE)
- elements (Al, Mg)
- metric measurements (km, m) (See Measures below.)
- mass in scientific use (oz, lb)
- currencies (USD, Kr, p)
- plurals do not normally use a full point: hrs, mins and so forth. The journey takes 2 hrs 3 mins, arriving at 4.30 p.m.

▶ Upper case M is sometimes preferred for million to distinguish from m (metres). However, note that M is also the Roman figure for 1000.

▶ References to nationality, when abbreviated, do not require to use a full point:

The participants included M. LeClerc (Fra), Herr Staffenbaum (Ger) and Sir Snoddley-Scratchit (Eng).

▶ Latin words tend to retain the full point: et al., et seq., etc. Note that cf. is derived from the Latin 'to confer'; cf (without a full point) means 'cost and freight', while c/f is an auditing term meaning 'carried forward'. However, eg is now also encountered as well as e.g., although your spellchecker may still react. The same applies to ie (and i.e.). I prefer to stick to the points.

We may note here that Latin terms and abbreviations do not require italics where they are in everyday use: ibid., op. cit., but *ipso facto* (by virtue of the fact), *loc. cit.* (at the place cited) and *sic*[5] are less frequently encountered, and therefore normally italicised.

▶ Abbreviated phrases tend to use the full point, c.i.f. (cost, insurance, freight), but this is also less common than previously and cif will be encountered. Similarly, we find both f.o.b. and fob (free on board), plc (public limited company), etc. R.S.V.P. is frequently encountered as RSVP (*répondez s'il vous plait*). aka (also known as) was previously written as an abbreviation [a.k.a.], but now appears to be an accepted word as in 'Jones aka Jones the Bones was found guilty', and is pronounced as spelt. The

5 Nearly always in square brackets [*sic*].

upper case version may be found, but is largely historic e.g.: Reg Green, AKA 'veg'.

▶ Words reduced to a single letter, other than those relating to measurement, normally use a full point: b. (born), d. (died), f. (female), m. (male, married, month). (See Chapter 12, Abbreviations – measures.)

▶ Generally, the plural of an abbreviated word does not require the full point: (ed., eds), but eds. with a full point is certainly not uncommon. Note that ch. (chapter) has chs as the plural form. The abbreviation for typescript is TS, plural TSS (no full point).

Common mistakes

▶ Some abbreviated words have become everyday expressions and do not use a full point when used colloquially:

✓ We will put an advert (ad) in the paper. She is having her op on Thursday.

▶ e.g. (*exempli gratia*) should be interpreted as 'including' or 'such as' or 'for example'. The correct use is before a list:

✓ Serif typefaces are required, e.g. Times Roman, Century Schoolbook, Garamond.

Do not use 'e.g.' as in the following:

✗ It was claimed for e.g. that the bank statement had been falsified!

I do not like the following, but encounter it quite often:

The theory was questionable (see e.g. Jones (1998)).

Preferably write in full: 'See, for example, Jones ...'

▶ E.g. should not be followed by a colon, dash, etc.

✗ There are at least a hundred group names, e.g.: herd, flock, flight, pack.

▶ Etc. (et cetera). While meaning 'and so forth', it is preferably used following a list:

✓ The consignment consisted of pistols, howitzers, V2s, frisbees, etc.

'And' is not normally required in a list concluding with 'etc.'.

The consignment comprised naughty nighties, men's mags., fig leaves and figs, etc.

Measures

▶ Metric measurements do not use the full point; Imperial measurements, with few exceptions, normally do. (See Chapter 12.) However, a number of scientific journals tend not to use the full point. Incidentally, a comprehensive conversion table is given in Chapter 8.

Other

Do we use U.K. or UK, similarly U.S.A. or USA? Older dictionaries give only the former versions. Indeed, the full points have been generally dropped and the forms UK and USA are now given in *Oxford Dictionary for Writers & Editors*. Interesting to note that the *Oxford Dictionary of Abbreviations* (1998) also gives USA for United States Army.

American dictionaries vary. *Random House* prefers U.K. to UK but USA to U.S.A. – the latter given as the abbreviation for United States Army. The Princeton Language Institute gives only U.S.A. for United States of America (the army isn't mentioned). Cambridge University Press advises against the use of the period in these abbreviations. Conclusion: consistency!

▶ Do not abbreviate references in the text other than 'page' (e.g. see p. 27).

✗ It was mentioned in Ch.3 ... Para. 4 covers ...

Affixes

See also Prefixes and Suffixes: Chapter 13, Prefixes Chapter 14, Suffixes.

An affix is attached to the beginning (e.g. in–, mis–, non–), or the end of a word (e.g. –al, –ly) in order to modify or change the meaning. An affix may also comprise a word which is either prefixed (e.g. over-), or suffixed (e.g. –out). Affixed words may be conjoined (overjoyed, lockout), or hyphenated (over-excite, line-out). Where neither conjoined nor hyphenated, they may form an adjectival phrase or phrasal verb, for example. We encounter differences in meaning for hyphenated, conjoined and separate word forms (a backup or substitute, a back-up file, to back up the hard-disk). These are discussed in more detail in the references above.

Ampersand [&]

Normally only used in firms' names: Smith, Brown & Brown (Solicitors) or concise terms such as Lost & Found. We also find it in R&D (research and development).

The ampersand should be used in literature lists where it is included in the publisher's trade name A&C Black, Oliver & Boyd. Do not replace the 'and' with the ampersand if it is not part of the publisher's trade name: Thames and Hudson Ltd. There is a tendency to use the ampersand in references in the text: but this is not recommended.

✗ (Johnson & Wright, 1996:85),

See Chapter 4, Bibliographies, Literature Lists, References.

Apostrophe [']

The apostrophe is mainly used to indicate possession – the so-called genitive *s*. But it is also used in omission of letters. However, the first-mentioned will occupy much of the following discussion. The apostrophe is one of the most discussed and commented points of punctuation in virtually every book on the subject. Many attempt to determine rules but end up with so many exceptions that the mind boggles (or should that be *boggle's*?). Actually, no. But let us take a breath, relax and ...

Possession

▶ An apostrophe is used to indicate ownership, possession, or as a connection between a subject and an object. For example: The girl's friend; the girl's friends; the girls' friend; the girls' friends. It is immaterial whether the object is singular or plural. But there are some considerations which have to be made for a) single- and multiple-syllable words, b) singular or plural subjects, c) whether the noun ends in a single *s* or a double-*s*. Pronunciation often provides a good guide as we often find that –*s* is preceded by a long vowel, and –*ss* by a short vowel. We will see the significance of this further in this section.

Common nouns

Generally, *'s* is added to singular nouns; *s'* to plural nouns.[6]

✓ The bus's seats had to be replaced.
✓ The buses' colours were changed from red and white to blue and cream.

This also applies to nouns ending in double *s*:

6 I should refer to these as the genitive *s*. However, it has proved more convenient to refer to the apostrophe throughout.

✓ The boss's daughter had two advantages, both of which led to her downfall.
✓ The bosses' convention was unconventional: no weapons allowed.

Some caution is required with polysyllabic nouns ending in double *s*. It may be thought that an apostrophe is sufficient in the singular in order to avoid confusion with the plural noun. This is not so.

✓ The actress's contract; the princess's dowry
✗ Actress' body found in lagoon. (Newspaper headline)

The apostrophe is, of course, added to the plural form:

✓ The princesses' charms were more charming than Prince Charming's.

There is a reservation about the final genitive *s*. I return to this below.

Some polysyllabic nouns ending in *s* may take just the apostrophe. This applies to words ending in *–is*: the oasis' water-purifier did not remove the saline taste; myxomatosis' symptoms were manifest and *–ies*: the series' covers, the species' sub-groups. Others, particularly those ending *–us*, employ the apostrophe *s*: the walrus's whiskers. The circus's managing director.

▶ When a noun changes form in the plural [e.g. man/men] we treat this similarly to the single noun, just adding 's.

✓ The men's clothes department had certainly never been visited by Brown (and neither had the women's). The children's department might have been an inspiration.
✗ Neither mens' nor womens' fashions seemed to appeal to him. Possibly the childrens' did.

Polysyllabic nouns changing form only require the apostrophe: The Ladies' Gala Night; babies' bonnets.

Some books offer the general guidance that if a singular noun has one syllable, add 's; if it has two (or more) syllables, add just the apostrophe. Thus, we have the ass's tail and the compass' error. Consequently we also have for goodness' sake. However, most polysyllabic words seem to follow the rule for single syllable words: The congress's venue will be changed. The congresses' venues will be switched. We can also write the headmistress's headache was a boy called [enter your own name here]. We have also mentioned pronunciation as a guide and while writing His Highness's pleasure, I think I would be inclined to address him personally and ask: And what might His Highness' pleasure be? But as I am not likely to get the chance, I will not draw any conclusions from that.

While we are on the subject there are some interesting variations to be found: for pete's sake (less commonly Pete's sake); for heaven's sake (or for heavens' sake); old time's sake (or old times' sake). Whether we use the singular or plural seems to be a whim of the moment.

Proper nouns

With the exception of some commercial names, the apostrophe *s* is added to proper names: Bush's poodle – Blair's master. This is where it gets a bit complicated. Single syllable proper nouns ending in *s* normally add the apostrophe: Mars' red spot. This is because the pronunciation of these words employs a long vowel. Where the name ends in double *s* (often preceded by the short vowel) then *'s* is added: Bess's mother was a bit of a bother. But polysyllabic words often add just the apostrophe: Jesus' disciples, Pythagoras' theorem. But this does not exclude the pronunciation rule. Thomas's solutions for solving Frances' problems reflected Phyllis's suggestions – they were neat, expensive and illegal.

When do we use Jones', Jones's or Joneses'. The general rule is just to add the apostrophe: Jones' dog has a bite worse than his bark. If we are talking in the plural, so to speak, then we are referring to the Jones family, commonly referred to as the Joneses. As such we may refer to the Joneses' house. My impression is that this form is more common in US English; in UK English we would save our breath and refer to the Jones' house. The context implies that we are referring to family (a collective noun).

And just to take a two-syllable example: Harris. The singular form is Harris's dog; and plural The Harrises' house.

Kingsley Amis points out that foreign words ending with a *silent* 's' use the genitive *s*:

✓ Louis's book

▶ Words ending in x

Proper names ending in *x* may not always use the genitive *s* as the following headline illustrates:

Blix' statement to the Security Council ...

Do not make the mistake of using the plural when a possessive is required:

The foxes jumped over the dog; they ran to the foxes' lair. The fox's fur is no longer in demand.

Compound terms

The apostrophe is only required for the last subject in a list or sequence, i.e. the final subject before the object:

- ✗ None of the men's club's accounts had been correctly kept. (*Use* mens club's accounts.)
- ✓ The womens unions' joint opinion was to oppose the policy.
- ✗ Leaders' and citizens trust in government
- ✓ Leaders and citizens' trust in government

Compound terms require caution, particularly in the plural: The attorneys at law's briefs were far from brief. Similarly, the plural of sergeant major is sergeants major. A bit of a mouthful but it is correct to say the sergeants majors passing out ceremony.

Possession or affiliation?

A distinction should be made between *ownership* (possession), and *affiliation*. Does it belong to somebody or something, i.e. is it an association or federation *of* persons, or is it a body or organisation *for* somebody or something? Another way of looking at this is to ask whether the title is descriptive of its functions, or is it indicative of affiliation through membership?

An apostrophe is not required when the term is descriptive rather than possessive. This is particularly found in organisations: Trades Union Congress; The Boy Scouts Association of Zimbabwe. The latter is more an association *for* scouts rather than one where membership is suggested. We also find this with The Airline Pilots Association. On the other hand, where personal engagement is involved we often find the apostrophe: Bradford Working Men's Club – that is a club owned and run by working men (in theory). We also have The Ladies' Golf Union and The National Cyclists' Union. I did encounter The Women Priests Movement (in a text I hasten to add). Instinct suggests *Priests'*. However, this was not an organisation to which women priests belonged. In fact, it was a body supporting the ordination of women as priests. In this case s' could have been misleading.

To clarify this point, consider the following:

- ✗ The teachers' training college and the Refugees and Immigrants' Office have both been relocated.
- ✓ The teachers training college and the Refugees and Immigrants Office have both been relocated.

Here, we are referring to the college *for* teachers, and the office *for* refugees and immigrants, neither being an institution based on membership. Strangely, though, we have The Ramblers' Association but The European Ramblers Association suggesting, possibly, that the former is one based on membership, the latter more as an interest organisation. In fact, looking at the respective web pages, this could be the case.

I won't say that exceptions do not exist, but hopefully they do not outnumber the general terms. Are there any other clues to omitting or including an apostrophe? I return to the original suggestion that *ownership* and *of* indicate possession and personal participation; *affiliation* is *for* general interests. Let's apply that: The Workers' Educational Association, YMCA – Young Men's Christian Association. How would I distinguish these from the American Pilots Association, for example? Try reversing the order: the Association for American Pilots. The Association for Young Christian Men! Get the point?

Actually, one of the readers of this draft did not get the point and suggested that where an organisation is an association *of* individuals rather than *for* individuals, the apostrophe is required. I'll buy that.

Finally, the apostrophe is dropped in titles of reference books ending in -s: *Chambers Dictionary*, *Collins Cobuild*, *Longmans Word Activator* (but *Longmans Dictionary of Contemporary English*). It is also dropped in company names ending in -s: Watneys Best Pale Ale, Charringtons brewery. There is an increasing tendency to drop the 's even where the name does not end in –s: Woolworths sale, McDonalds restaurants (the family names being Woolworth, McDonald).

But in more personal or individual works, institutions and organisations will use the apostrophe: Shakespeare's Sonnets; Valentine's Day, Madame Tussaud's, Sadler's Wells, Ali Baba's bazaar.

Joint possession

Joint possession requires only that the last item is given an apostrophe or the genitive form:

> Laurel and Hardy's last films anticipated their demise. Tom and Jerry's antics appeal to all ages.

We do need apostrophe 's' for all three possessives in: Bill's daughter's friend's house.

Where the subject is not joint, i.e. we wish to make a distinction between them, then we would write: Laurel's and Hardy's approaches to a situation determined the level of comedy. Implicit in this is that both Laurel and Hardy had a number of approaches to a situation; they might only have had a single standard approach: Laurel's and Hardy's interpretation of a situation was often foreseeable.

Another example: Soldiers', Sailors' and Airmen's Families Association (S.S.A.F.A.). Observe also that 'families' is the object of the three armed forces rather than the subject 'association'.

Not least does the apostrophe serve to avoid confusion:

- ✗ Immigrants and refugees' clothes requiring to be bleached, must be soaked properly afterwards.
- ✓ Immigrants' and refugees' clothes requiring to be bleached, must be soaked properly afterwards.

The spellchecker may well react to these.

An exception is with personal names, and 'Saint' (St.). St. Peter's children's home. This is more an option than a rule as we shall see.

Possessive pronouns

It is quite surprising how habit breeds contempt. Possessive pronouns ending in 's' (yours, his, hers, its) do *not* use an apostrophe. Of course, it's is an abbreviation (strictly speaking a contraction) for it is.

- ✗ I am a friend of Jane's. It is not her's. But it is not their's either.
- ✓ I am a friend of Jane (= I am Jane's friend). It is Jane's, I know it is hers and not theirs.

▶ Some texts advise against concluding a sentence with a possessive:

- ✗ The parent's views were the same as the boy's.

and advise rewriting:

- ✓ The parent's views were the same as those of the boy.

We probably observed that this was a single parent who had views on the matter. Of course, both parents might have shared these: The parents' views ... But both parents might even have held one and the same view: The parents' view was that ...

It is permissible not to repeat the object (here, birthday) in sentences such as: Brian's birthday is on the 27th, and Bob's is a couple of days later.

The following from *Sky News* illustrates the point that care is required with pronouns:

- ✓ When pressed she said that her and Huntley's views were the same.

It is very tempting to write that hers and Huntley's views were the same. But it is 'her views' which are the same as those of Huntley. It is also tempting to write:

Her views were the same as Huntley's.

Many texts will advise against concluding a sentence with an apostrophe *s*. So we can try to 'correct' this by writing:

✗ Hers were the same as Huntley's views.

But now we are really into the mire. 'Hers' is a pronoun (as in 'the views were hers'). In fact, the analysis begins to get pretty heavy when I look at *Chambers Dictionary* – and did you notice no apostrophe in '*Chambers*'? This gives: pronoun, genitive (or possessive adjective), dative and accusative of the pronoun she; herself (reflexive; poetic or dialect); she (colloquial nominative). I return to common sense and ask myself 'hers?'. Well, it can't be 'hers views'. And there we have it. Pronouns are often misused or assumed and not infrequently used to refer to the wrong subject or verb. But we do not have to be grammatical experts to break down the sentence in our minds just to make sure that the pronoun 'her' is not confused with the possessive pronoun 'hers'.

Rewriting sentences to avoid a final possessive is not always easy, and neither is it desirable: I'll meet you outside Anne's. Implicit in this is Anne's house. But if the arrangement was to meet outside a shop or building, an apostrophe is not used. Let's meet at Paddy's Pub – Let's meet at Paddys.

I did read in an article: Life as a student's can be stimulating to study. Now, I would not want to go into an discourse on the grammatical structure of this sentence (either), but this example serves to show that the possessive does not necessarily have to be followed by an object. It is perfectly clear what we are discussing (the student's life), and the purist's argument of avoiding a closing apostrophe *s* is complied with. Another example: I'll see you at Anne's in the morning. It's all a matter of style.

Complex possessives

Occasionally we meet a complex possessive (for want of a better word). Mens clothes' styles, the managers wife's speech. The 's is only required for the last possessive. Strangely, but in accordance with this, we have: the mens team's potential, or the mens teams' changing rooms. It is necessary, of course, to indicate whether we are referring to one or several teams as these examples indicate.

The general rule is a single apostrophe *s* placed before the last item. But where a distinction is required then, of course, both possessives will need an apostrophe:

The girl's parent's views
The girl's parents' views
The girls' parent's views
The girls' parents' views

Numbers, quantities

The apostrophe is not used when referring to numbers generally:

✗ They came in two's and three's, except those who came on all four's.
✓ They were, in fact, all fives and sixes.

An apostrophe is generally not used for *age* groups:

✗ the under two's; the over 5's.

Note the plural form in the text (not the singular form).

✓ the over-thirties.
✗ the under-twentys; the over-fifty's.

Hyphenate words, but not numbers:

✓ the under-twos; the over 5s

Incidentally, make sure that you do not confuse ones and one's: one's own accord and they came in ones and twos; also the apostrophe to indicate a missing letter or word: One's responsible for payment [one is responsible].

If single alpha-numeric characters are used, the apostrophe is correct:

✓ They were grouped in 2's and 3's. Don't forget to dot your *i*'s and cross your *t*'s.

Time and dates

The quantity of the unit will determine where the apostrophe is placed: one day's time; two days' time; next week's rent; three months' rent; New Year's Day.

An apostrophe is used with omitted numbers in dates:

✓ The '68 revolution that wasn't. Its main effects were felt in the '70s.
✗ Rationing still applied in the early 50s as it had done from '40–'45. [Use 1940–45.]
✗ Petrol prices peaked in the 70's. [But OK in US English]

When the full date is used only US English applies the apostrophe:

The 1950s were ten years of foreplay. – Germaine Greer. [UK]

If you can remember the 1960's you weren't really there. – Anon. [US]

But: Elizabeth II's accession.

(See Dates).

Place names, institutions

Place names

Place names involving possession normally use 's: Land's End, Shepherd's Bush. However, there are many irregularities and inconsistencies. For example, many visitors to London have walked in St. James's Park. You might even live in St. James Grove in SW11, or St. James' Court in SW1. But other saints seem equally confused. Even the patron saint has his moments and is not sure if it should be St Georges Square in E7, or St George's Square in E14. Again we have St. Giles Circus, Blackfriars church (the church in the district of Blackfriars in east London and which happens to be in Black Friars Lane).

Similarly, we also find St. Bees Head (in Cumbria) with no apostrophe, but the town of St. Mary's (in the Scilly Isles) apparently possessing nothing. (Those who have been there might differ in their views on this.) Finally, the capital of Guernsey, one of the Channel Islands, avoids all possible confusion by dropping both an apostrophe and the genitive s – St. Peter Port (rather giving the impression that Port was his surname).

These irregularities appear to be at the whim of the local town planning office. My advice is to check in an atlas or gazetteer. The above examples were from the *Greater London Street Atlas* (Nicholson) and *Philips Atlas*.

Buildings, institutions

Generally, 's is omitted today for many buildings and monuments. Barnes Bridge, Wells Cathedral. The saints generally retain theirs: St Paul's Cathedral, even in abbreviations: St. Bart's Hospital. St. Mark's Road in London W7 does, but not St. Marks Road in W5.

A colleague pointed out the following college names; Kings College, London; King's College, Cambridge; Queens' College, Cambridge; The Queen's College, Oxford; All Souls College, Oxford. (These are the institutions what sets the standards for English!)

National and international bodies

Countries and international and national organisations ending in *s* do not use the apostrophe:

✓ United Nations Organisation. United States intervention. Nine Elms goods yard. The Trades Union Congress resolutions. The Six Nations Cup.

Nevertheless, where there is clear possession the apostrophe seems appropriate: Wales' heritage is in the valleys.

Omissions (contractions)

The apostrophe is used to show omissions in contractions, particularly in colloquial language: George, don't do that. That's not nice. Why d'you do it?. – 'cos it's almost five 'clock. – I've no answer to that.

Many words have become abbreviated where part of the original word has been dropped. These are sometimes referred to as clipped forms. In many instances the clipped form used an apostrophe: omnibus – 'bus, helicopter – 'copter. This would be extremely unusual today.

Abbreviations

▶ Plurals of abbreviations, single letters and numbers *may* use the apostrophe:

More BA's were granted in 2003 than hitherto. This reflected the large number of grade 1's in 1999.

Names in references

Where a reference is made in the text in the following manner, it is a matter of preference whether the date should divide the subject and the object:

Smith's (1995) study was strongly criticised.

Personally, I prefer: Smith's study (1995) was ...

Other

Some texts inform that an apostrophe is occasionally used to indicate a plural: PC's and TV's have become much cheaper. This is encountered infrequently today, most preferring: TVs and PCs are inexpensive today.

My word speller reacts to the accused's excuse was ... I am not sure why. But on the other hand it did not react to The Fed.'s officers bungled the evidence.

Errors to avoid

Some people have got it into their heads that a noun ending with a vowel needs an apostrophe in the plural form: PC's, video's, potato's. These are the possessive versions: plurals need no apostrophe. In any case the plural of potato is potatoes

✓ The PCs of today are more powerful than many mainframes of the '70s. The PC's power is more than a byte.

▶ We may encounter: 'I went to the doctor's the other day.' Clearly what is meant is 'doctor's surgery'. This is acceptable in colloquial form but it is more correct to say 'I went to the doctor the other day.' One publisher rejected my use of the apostrophe in one week's salary, and two months' vacation. I would argue that the link between the adjective and the noun suggests that the apostrophe is (strictly) correct as, for example 'Today's train is cancelled'. But there again styles are changing and the modern argument seems to be 'if it's in doubt, it's probably superfluous – and if it's superfluous, drop it'.

▶ A common error is to use an apostrophe where it is not needed and has no significance:

✗ I found this. Is it your's?

This mistake is particularly rife with the personal pronouns, yours, hers, theirs, its. We include the apostrophe to mean 'it is'.

I also read: Your's and others' knowledge of the affair...

But again, it is your knowledge and others' knowledge which is being referred to.

To conclude this section with a gem: The Trust wishes to place on record its' sincere appreciation. (Quoted in *The Daily Telegraph*, 29.5.01.)

Typographical note

Sometimes the single and double apostrophe may appear as ['...', "..."] instead of ['... '] and ["... "]. Under 'Tools' and 'AutoCorrect' in Word, select 'AutoFormat' and tick 'Replace straight quotes with smart quotes'.

Asterisks [*]

▶ These may be used to avoid publishing an offensive word:

✓ He told him to go to ****!

A more usual form in today's permissive society is:

✓ He told him to go to h ...!

Typographical note:

Typing three asterisks and then ‹Enter› places a stippled line (small solid squares) across the page. I am not sure of the purpose of this. Much more useful is the solid line produced by typing three minus signs and ‹Enter›.

Braces

In mathematics parentheses the curly brace may be encountered { }. These form the highest order of parentheses. Square brackets are the secondary level and normal parentheses are the primary form {...[...()...]...} and should be used accordingly:

a. $(2/3)(6-2) = 2.667$
b. $[2+(6\times3)-5] = 15$
c. $2+\{\sqrt{[(6\times3)-(2\times4.5)]}+3\}^2 = 38$

Brackets [ ]

See also Parentheses (page 114).

These are normally referred to as 'square brackets', and are used as follows.

Editorial notes

▶ The square bracket is used to indicate editorial notes within a text or a quoted passage:

✓ Jones maintained that Smith had confirmed that he [Jones] had not signed the cheque.

✓ Smith maintains that 'the commune [i.e. municipality], and not the state, is the true representative of the people' (ibid.).

Secondary level parentheses

See 'Parentheses'.

▶ Square brackets are used as parentheses within parentheses (except bibliographic dates). They are occasionally used to house an explanatory note in the text.

✓ A hypothesis has no validity until tested (see, for example, Smith, A. R. (1958)). [Smith discusses the relationship between a theory, a hypothesis and a model.]

Bullets and Lists

(See also Lists, page 92)
▶ Bullets are typographical symbols and a useful tool for clarification in lists. They serve to improve layout and make the text clear. However, they do have a tendency to give a text something of a 'schoolbook' character, i.e. lists of terms to be memorised, when used without discretion. An example:

A full point is not used for:
- cardinal points (S, NE)
- elements (Al, Mg)
- metric measures (km, m)
- mass (kg, lb)
- US Postal abbreviations (NY, CA)
- currencies (SEK, p).

Note that the full point occurs *only* at the end of the list. An exception is where each item comprises a longer phrase, a sentence (or even several sentences). In this case each item may then conclude with a semicolon or a full point. Secondary level (sub-lists) may use a dash. Again, check the publisher's preferences for primary and secondary level bullets.

The following issues will be taken up at the meeting:
- Salaries. A bonus scheme will be presented.
- Holidays:
    - Longer working hours in exchange for an extra week's holiday?
    - Extension of Easter holiday.
- New safety regulations; compulsory helmets.

Capitals or not? Shorter items do not require capitals, but where information concluding with a period is used (as in the last example), each item should begin with a capital letter.

A variety of symbols may be used; in this text I have found the following to be useful [✓] and [✗]. Many others such as ¶ ◆ ☞ are to be found under

Symbols, Webdings and Wingdings, although you should avoid those which are obviously psychedelic. Chosen bullets may be set as a standard symbol under Format – Bullets and Numbering – Bulleted. Then select Customize – Bullet. Select from the font types (Symbols, Webdings, Wingdings etc.).

Numbered lists

Numbered lists are an alternative. These may be Arabic [1, 2, 3...] or Roman (usually lower case): [i, ii, iii...]. However, numbered lists give the impression of ranking when used 'list-wise' as above. They are preferably used where items are listed in a text as in this example from a Penguin publication: The curling pins were observed by three independent witnesses: (1) By the landlady (2) by a barmaid (3) by the bookseller. It is not necessary for each item to commence with a capital letter. Even though double parentheses [( )] are used, I still feel the need for a comma: ... landlady, (2) by a ... This would definitely be required if a single (right hand) parenthesis was used: ... landlady, 2) by a ...

▶ Numbered bullets are best avoided where listed items also contain brackets. Even italics do not serve to clarify a list:

The following were stolen: *1)* Radios (3); *2)* TVs (3); *3)* videos (2); *4)* cameras (5).

Compare this with the visual impression of the following:

✓ The following were stolen: i) Radios (3); ii) TVs (3); iii) videos (2); iv) cameras (5).

– or possibly better:

✓ The following were stolen: a. Radios (3); b. TVs (3); c. videos (2); d. cameras (5).

Parentheses also provide a visual aid to locating the individual items which are to be emphasised:

The points to be noted concerning Lösch's equilibrium assumption are that (a) the theory is normative as opposed to positive, (b) it is descriptive rather than analytical, and (c) it lacks any element of teleology.

If the items are to be listed in the text and are introduced by a colon, then semicolons may be used to separate the items. Semicolons should also be considered as separators where the items themselves contain commas.

It was unclear whether the United States was trying to establish: (a) a *monopoly* by encouraging foreign investment, that is a solely US-financed development of the Iraq oil industry; (b) a *monopsony*, that is control over prices by becoming the sole purchaser; (c) a combination of both, a form of commercial *monogamy*.

▶ It will have been understood that a variety of bulleted and numbered lists may be used. But select one for each of these categories and stick to it. If you really need to include sub-categories select a numbered list [1, 2, 3...] and alphabetical subgroups [a, b, c...].

The following issues will be taken up at the meeting:
1. Salaries. A bonus scheme will be presented.
2. Holidays:
     a. Longer working hours in exchange for an extra week's holiday?
     b. Extension of Easter holiday.
3. New safety regulations; compulsory helmets.

It is matter of taste whether the subsections a and b are indented. The alternative could be a change in font size:

2. Holidays:
     a. Longer working hours in exchange for an extra week's holiday?
     b. Extension of Easter holiday.

It is easy to become 'too busy' with fonts and bullets. A simple layout is often the best.

Numbers should be used if the list is headed: 'The following five points should be noted', for example. But otherwise ask yourself 'do I really need numbered bullets at all?'.

Capital Letters

These are used more frequently in English than in some languages. However, times are changing. A useful guideline is 'capitalise the specific, but not the general'.

✓ The Board will meet on Tuesday.
✓ A new board of directors will be elected on Wednesday.

But either The Board of Directors disagreed or The board of directors resigned is acceptable. My inclination is that a specific action requires the specific rule:

The Board of Directors has proposed a dividend of 28p.

Days, months, periods

▶ These employ capitals in English. Many languages use lower case.

✓ It was a Monday in late June that I first met her.

▶ Lower case is used for the seasons in English:

✓ It is said that the worst gales of winter usually come in the autumn. The May Bank Holiday is often called the Spring Holiday. It would be nice if Christmas came in the spring.

▶ Periods in history are capitalised:

✓ Iron Age men were of iron, but men from the Middle Ages were fairly 'middling'. As for those from the Dark Ages, we can only guess!

Nationality, language, religion

Capitals are required in English when referring to nationality:

✓ The manuscript was written in French, but the author was a German with a taste for Italian wine!

Note the following:

✓ He was Russian, but his wife came from Byelorussia.

(This may be encountered as Byelo-russia, but is incorrect. The modern form is now *Belarus*.)

▶ Prefixes are not capitalised.

✓ She was a non-believer, a non-Catholic. He was a Nonconformist.
✗ She was a Non-Catholic.

▶ A capital is used for Anglo-Irish, Franco-Russian, Afro-Asian, etc. It is also required for Franconian (a group of dialects), and Francophile (person admiring the French and French culture).

▶ Derived words should retain the capital such as in: Germanic, Liverpudlian, Brummie (from Birmingham).

Many foreign languages are less demanding as, for example, the French *quartier latin* – the Latin Quarter of Paris.

▶ If the product is related to a specific town or city, the capital is retained: Edam (cheese), plaster of Paris. This also applies to products from a *specific* region: Cornish cream, Yorkshire pudding, Jersey cow, Cheddar cheese, Scotch whisky (and incidentally, Irish and US whiskey), Welsh dresser, Russian roulette, etc. Where the product is widely produced the capital is often retained as in Brussels sprouts, French fries, Swiss roll, Indian ink, Roman numerals, (but roman typeface), Pekinese dog, Siamese cat, but surprisingly, gum arabic. We also encounter both béarnaise and Béarnaise sauce, but in general the adjectival form should retain the capital. Thus, even though we may encounter swiss cheese and french dressing, these are incorrect.

As terms are increasingly drawn into the language we find that the capital is less frequently employed for nouns: champagne, china, swede (vegetable), jersey and guernsey (sweaters) an oxford (low-heeled laced shoe), a berlin (or berline) (chauffeur-driven car of particular design originally from Berlin), mongol (now a taboo expression for a person with Down's syndrome), guinea-pig (but Guinea fowl).

You may find that your spellchecker capitalises most of these (if 'AutoCorrect' is on) even where the capital is not required.

▶ Religions are capitalised:

✓ The assembly attracted Roman Catholics, Protestants and followers of the Islamic religion – Muslims. Members of the Jewry were also present.

The *abstract* noun is not capitalised, nor is the verb:

✓ The papal brief was discussed as was christianisation in Africa. In general their views were fairly catholic.

Note: Christendom, Christian name, but christening.

▶ Ethnic groups are always capitalised:

✓ The Red Indians (now referred to as Native Americans) and the Aborigines have survived as indigenous peoples.

▶ Specific references to groups of countries, movements, etc., use capitals:

✓ While the former Communist bloc is now considered capitalist, the Third World has yet to benefit from the New Order.

But where referred to in general terms these do not require capitals:

✓ Members of the white race in third world countries are no longer regarded as colonialists. Indeed, communism here has taken on another meaning. It's all part of the new order of things.

Personal titles

▶ If the title refers to a specific person, capitals are used.

✓ Crown Prince Charles. The Minister of Finance. It was stated by Professor Smart ...

They are not used when talking in general terms.

✓ The doctor, minister and the professor all agreed.

▶ Capitals are used for both words in a title, and also in a hyphenated title:

✓ The Deputy Director, The Vice-Chairman.

▶ Surnames of persons such as Walter de la Mare are capitalised when they commence a sentence:

✓ famous authors. De la Mare has long been a favourite poet of children of all ages.

Views seem to be divided on capitalising names such as d'Almeida:

... famous authors. d'Almeida was one of these.

▶ Curiously, some continental languages do not use capitals where English does.

✓ The Marshallian experience, The Marxist–Leninist doctrine, The Churchillian temperament ...

Having said that, we do find caesarean operation although many dictionaries do capitalise this, especially if the correct spelling, Cæsarian, is used. (Also encountered as 'cesarean' or 'cesarian'.) Lower case is used for fictional characters: He had a quixotic temperament.

Note also, Smith Junior, but Smith jr. You may also encounter Smith Jr.

Geography and space

▶ Cardinal points use capitals: N, SW, SSE.

Originally, compass points as *general* terms were not hyphenated: The industrial area lies to the north west of the town. The adjectival term was hyphenated, however: The property has a south-west orientation. Today these are all hyphenated: north-east, north-western, south-westerly. Incidentally, a single word for the wind known as a northeaster.

US English does not hyphenate: northwest, northwesterly, northwestern. We should use this form when referring to geographical regions in the USA:

The opening up of the Northwest was to await the arrival of the railroad.

Similarly, US English refers to the Northwest Passage. Considered as an international seaway, the UK English form is The North-west Passage

▶ Compass directions (names) use lower case unless incorporated in a place-name:

✓ His cottage was situated to the south of London, on the South Downs near a station on the (pre-British Railways) Southern Railway, approached from an easterly direction coming from west Brighton.

There is no place called West Brighton. Therefore, west Brighton refers to the western end of the town of Brighton. The Southern Railway served the south of England prior to nationalisation in 1948. The inversion Brighton West is a form used for administrative and electoral districts. We also find this in New York Central (station).

Only capitalise words that are part of the official name.

✓ The City of London, but the city of New York. Also the North Star, the South Pole., Similarly we have the West Country, the South Downs, the Western Isles, etc.

It is also interesting to note that the correct names are the Netherlands and the Kingdom of Norway (both lower case definite article), but The Yemen and The People's Republic of China.

▶ Scientific articles on the planets and space will capitalise earth, sun and moon; general texts will not.

Some planets have several moons; Earth has just one – The Moon.

When speaking generally we may say: 'We can see the moon from the earth. In fact, when it's full moon you can see the man in the moon.'

▶ Where referring to specific geographical regions, cultures, etc., we capitalise Western, Oriental. But in general terms the lower case is used:

✓ The modern jazz style known as West Coast jazz was essentially related to a number of musicians playing in the western states. On the other hand East Coast jazz seemed to apply to the music of any state east of California. The eastern and western styles are quite distinctive, but both are played by both black and white musicians. This contrasts with the broad categories of Traditional and Modern where traditional jazz had its roots in the Negro culture of the time. Strangely, modern jazz has many of its roots in the music of leading coloured musicians, particularly the bebop era of the 40s and 50s.

✓ The gemstone known as Oriental emerald is neither a gemstone nor oriental.

Some dictionaries use oriental ruby (no capital), etc.

✓ The film on TV tonight is a western.

Interestingly, CUP advises western Europe rather than Western Europe. This may reflect the fact that since the end of the cold war we no longer regard Europe as being divided into two politico-geographical camps. Further, the 'cold war' was not a defined historical event and hence not capitalised.

Institutions and academia

▶ It is the practice in many languages to capitalise only the initial letter of an institution name: The Norwegian school of librarianship, The Institute of political science. These are capitalised in English: London School of Economics, The Institute of Sociology. Translations should also be capitalised: The Norwegian School of Librarianship.

Only those words forming part of the title are capitalised: the city of Vilnius; the Andes mountains; the UNO, but The International Court of Justice; City of London; Luton Town F.C.

▶ Academic subjects used to be capitalised: Among the new studies were Sociology, Maritime Law and Phrenology. This is generally not practised today:

✓ She was the first professor of physics at Oxford. (*But her title would be Professor of Physics.*)
✓ Students had a choice of anthropology or primeval history as a subsidiary subject.

('Primeval' may also be spelt 'primaeval'.)

An academic title is normally capitalised:

✓ The Director of Education was dismissed. He was subsequently appointed Emeritus Professor of Sociology.

▶ Institutions are often abbreviated and capitalised, e.g. FAO, UNO, WFP. These should be referred to as the FAO ..., the UNO ..., etc. The *pronunciation* will determine the nature of the definite article.

✓ A United Nations official was expedited to the region.
✓ An FAO grant ensured that the risk of famine was reduced.

Note that we use capitals for the Soviet Union, but the soviet was re-elected. (A soviet is a council and thus we have the verb *to sovietise*).

▶ Capitals should apply to all names in an institution or body.

✓ Rutland County Council, The Trades Union Congress, Arsenal Football Club.

These may be dropped for council bodies when referring to them generally:

✓ Islington social services were praised by the minister. The borough council voted to increase the transport subsidy.

Capitals should be retained in a formal document:

✓ The Court sentenced him to thirty days.

But again times are changing and many would not capitalise 'court'. In a newspaper report, lower case would be normal.

Political parties

Capitalise. Christian Democratic Party, the Social Democrats. But: a fascist régime; a communist government.

Publications

▶ The title of a manuscript may use capitals or be entirely upper case:

Regional Economic Growth or REGIONAL ECONOMIC GROWTH.

▶ Upper case is sometimes preferred with lower case capitalised for subtitle:

REGIONAL ECONOMICS: An Introduction.

▶ Capitals are optional for chapter titles:

✓ Chapter 1. Regional economic growth in perspective.

or –

✓ Chapter 1. Regional Economic Growth in Perspective.

Note that a capital normally follows the colon in titles:

✓ Chapter 2. Regional government: An institution in decline?

▶ If quoting a title, this should be set in italics: do not use capitals.

✓ In his treatise *Regional growth in perspective,* the author argues for local income tax.

▶ References to *numbered* volumes, chapters, divisions or sections, tables, diagrams and figures should be in capitals:

✓ Further information is given in Chapter 6. See also Table 3.1 and Figure 5a. In the previous section, we saw that ...

▶ References to paragraphs, lines, sections, items, formulae, do not use capitals.

Avoid abbreviations for chapter etc. in the text:

✗ See Chap. 6. As shown in Fig. 3 ... This was mentioned in para. 2. Art. 3 of the Convention ...

▶ References to plays: In Act II, Scene i but: In the first scene of the second act ... Note the use of upper and lower case roman.

History

A capital letter is normally used for the Mediaeval period, the Middle Ages. CUP is one of those preferring lower case for general uses: It was felt that mediaeval architecture owed much to the inventiveness of the middle ages.

General references use lower case: During the war, civilian losses were high. Major events and specific periods should retain the capital letter. Nevertheless we encounter both ... during the Second World War and ... during the second World War. Really a matter of taste. If we are referring specifically to an event or period, then capitalise. But there is an increasing trend towards lower case throughout: Rationing continued for many years after the second world war.

Other

▶ In advertisements a 'telegraphic' form may be used where two contrasting statements, or similar, are employed. Each statement may begin with a capital letter:

✓ Change of Government – Change of Policy.

Nevertheless, it is still possible to regard government and policy as general rather than specific issues such that the following perfectly acceptable:

✓ Change of government – change of policy.

▶ Brand names use capitals such as Hoover Inc. Many products now in general use have taken the name of the original manufacturer. These use lower case. The hoover was a revolution for the housewife. Xerox® is a brand name, but the verb 'to *xerox*' is derived from the term xerographic reproduction. The spellchecker may react to some (e.g. the lower case 'hoover'). I was surprised to learn that some companies actually legally oppose names of their products from becoming generic terms. But that is rather like the EU commissioners who tried to have name 'ice cream' changed because it was neither ice nor cream. But I can understand Rolls-Royce® objecting to the colloquialism 'a roller'.

▶ Acts of Parliament, laws, statutes and so forth, are capitalised:

✓ The Transport Act; The Green Paper on Recirculation; The Bill of Rights; The Parking Bye-Law; The Rio Convention, and indeed an Act of Parliament.

Note that bye-law *or* by-law is acceptable. The latter appears to have become more popular in recent years.

Capitalisation is not required when referring to acts in general terms: A number of acts were passed in the period; the bye-law relating to parking. Neither should 'act' be capitalised when it is not part of the title: The act relating to Child Chastisement; the Banking, Monetary Exchange, and Foreign Trade acts (three separate acts). *Collins Cobuild* provides a number of examples suggesting that where the reference is general, then lower case is acceptable: Critics say such flaws in the way e-mail is handled are incompatible with accountability – and make a mockery of the government's plans for a freedom of information act. Surprisingly, the following example is also given: Hopes were high that 1999 would – after 20 years of trying – at long last see the demise of the unpopular Glass-Steagall act, enacted in 1933 to enforce a separation of commercial banking, investment banking and insurance.

The above also illustrate the tendency towards lower case 'g' in government. 'Government' may refer to a) the Cabinet, b) the majority party (or coalition parties) in parliament, c) The House of Commons, d) the Commons *and* The House of Lords (the executive), e) the civil service including local government (the administration). Clearly, this does not have to be capitalised when referring to government in general: Plans have been outlined for government reform. Blair's government has clearly lost support. Even as the subject, a capital is not required as another example from Collins *Cobuild* illustrates: The government has had to cut back on public expenditure. When specific reference is being made to the Cabinet or the majority in the Commons, this should be capitalised: The Government's proposal for the reform was not popular.

I am sure that more conservative readers will disagree, although I hasten to add that these examples have been fetched from various sources. Indeed, in the very first example I would also question use of lower case, ... the government's plans ... The interpretation thus has to be that this is an intention of the Commons rather than a specific Cabinet proposal.

'Parliament' is not capitalised when referring to governments (parliaments) in general: The British parliament comprises the two Houses of Parliament. Many European parliaments comprise just a single chamber. The issue has been raised in several parliamentary debates. Specific reference is always capitalised: It is expected that Parliament will re-introduce the act.

▶ Both words should be capitalised in compound terms:

✗ The Cold war
✓ The Cold War.

▶ The definite article is capitalised only when part of the title:

✓ It was mentioned in the *Local Government Chronicle*, but not in *The Illustrated London News*.

▶ I encountered a rather special use of the capital letter in a crime book where 'the perpetrator went into his Other state of mind prior to executing the dastardly deed!' This reminds me that members of the House of Commons refer to the House of Lords as 'The Other Place'. *COD* does not capitalise this, but I feel this to be wrong.

▶ Capitals are often used for many abbreviations even though the full text is not capitalised; e.g. the PC, the WC.

▶ Capitalise hyphenated words in a title: History of The Fifty-First Regiment (or History of the Fifty-First regiment).

▶ Strangely, perhaps, 'roman' is not capitalised when referring to fonts: Please use roman numbers for plays – Act IV, Scene iii.

▶ Finally, TV addicts will have noted the title of the world's most famous soap: *EastEnders*.

Colon [:]

See also semicolon p. 136.

▶ The colon appears to be used relatively infrequently. Glancing through five or six academic texts I found several chapters without a single colon. But like the semicolon, it can be used to improve the structure, and thereby the clarity of a sentence. It may introduce an explanation or elaboration of that which has preceded the colon.

The Rio treaty was soon forgotten by the delegates: Rio was remembered only for its beaches.

It may also be a contrasting or contradictory statement (sometimes called an appositive. Note that a colon does not have to be followed by a complete sentence. (See Comma, omissions, p. 54.)

✓ Two's company: three, an orgy.

Lists and examples

▶ The colon is used prior to a list. The list is normally contained within the sentence.

✓ The following issues have been included for discussion: the economy, employment, exports and party membership.

▶ If the subject matter is discussed issue by issue in subsequent paragraph(s), the colon is best replaced by a full point.

✓ There were three points in his argument. The first was the validity of the evidence; in his view the true rate of inflation was much lower than originally projected. Secondly, unemployment was expected to continue to fall; substantial new investments had been made by foreign investors: national investment was non-existent. Thirdly, the rate of interest had remained stable; the reason believed to be the low rate of inflation as mentioned above.

Note the use of the semicolon, here used to separate the subsidiary information on each issue (see Semicolon).

▶ A colon should not normally be used following 'such as' or 'including'.

✗ The menu included a variety of exotic foods such as: quail, snail, donkey-tail soup, poached zebra kidneys and more.

▶ The colon should not be used following 'e.g.' in lists:

✗ Many clues were found, e.g.: footprints, fingerprints, and a questionable lady's item.

Rewrite using 'for example' or 'including' and exclude the colon. Yes, I have deliberately left it to the reader to determine whether it was the lady of the item that was questionable.

▶ A colon is not required following a question mark:

✗ How many variables are included?: five, six, ten?
✓ How many are included: five, ten?

▶ A colon should precede a formula.

The orbit of Beagle 2 could be expressed as:

$$\eta = \theta^2 \, [\xi/\Omega] \tag{16}$$

Formulae are usually numbered sequentially on the right hand side of the page.

▶ Items in a list can be separated by commas unless commas are also used in qualifying the item. In that case use semicolons.

✓ The following were called as witnesses: the shopkeeper, now retired; the bank manager, currently suspended; his mother-in-law, the chief suspect.

Speech

▶ A colon is used before a quotation or a question contained in inverted commas:

✓ As Cindy Adams once said: 'Success has made failures of many men.'
✓ The trade union leader wanted an explanation: 'If Rome was built in a day, who was in charge of that job?'

A colon is incorrect in the following:

✗ His answer was that: 'the price has already been adjusted.'

In fact, we do not even need the inverted commas here at all as this is indirect speech. But we could write:

✓ His answer was: 'The price has already been adjusted.'

Dividing a sentence

▶ A colon may be used to divide a sentence where the second part is a dividing clause, for example, where this is contrary to or negates the main clause:

✓ The Labour Party voted for reduced state control: this was, however, a contradiction of their election manifesto.

▶ The colon is used relatively infrequently in many European languages. Where used, it is often the norm to follow the colon with a capital letter. This *not* the case in UK English where a capital will only apply to speech and proper nouns.

✗ He repeated the question: She still refused to answer.
✓ She was stubborn: he was belittled.

A question (direct speech) preceded by a colon commences with a capital.

✓ She asked the inevitable question: 'Where on earth were you last night?'

A capital may also be used for indirect speech.

✓ One repeats the inevitable question: Why were the annual accounts 'fixed'?

▶ Avoid more than one colon in a sentence:

✗ Note: Committee meetings will be held as follows: Monday and Thursday mornings.

The first colon (following 'Note') should be replaced with a full point or exclamation mark.

✓ Note. Committee meetings will be held as follows: Monday and Thursday mornings.

Several *semicolons* may, of course, be used in a sentence.

✓ Note. Committee meetings will be held as follows: Monday and Thursday mornings; Friday evenings; alternate Sundays.

Introducing quotations

Longer quotations usually four or more lines are introduced by a colon and indented.

He handed over the book, and I read:

Moran, Sebastian, Colonel. Unemployed. Formerly 1ˢᵗ Bangalore Pioneers...(Address), the Tankerville, the Bagatelle Card Club.

The above, from *The Penguin Complete Sherlock Holmes,* is a part-extract, the original and full quotation being about seven lines. Shorter extracts, as mentioned above, may be included in the sentence and not indented.

Among others, his addresses were given as: 'the Tankerville [and] the Bagatelle Card Club.'

Date and time

▶ The colon is occasionally used in dates and times, especially where resulting from a computer output, e.g.: 02:10:94; 01:30

It is preferable to reserve the colon for hours, minutes, and seconds:

✓ 12.10.98; 10:23:07.

When using text, remember the hyphen: Let's meet at two-thirty.

See Dates.

Business salutations

▶ The colon was previously used in business letters but is not used today:

✗ Dear Sir or Madam:

References

See References. References in the text use the form Jones (1994: 15) – space after the colon. This does not apply to biblical references: Galatians 11:6.

Other

▶ Where lower case is used for chapter titles, lower case *normally* follows the colon although exceptions will be found.

The immediate post-war years: a new era dawns

(No full point at the end of a title.)

▶ If the word following a break is *however, indeed* or *nevertheless*, a semicolon is preferable to a colon. (See Semicolon, p. 136.)

✓ The pre-war period was one of prolonged scepticism: it was one of growing fear. The post-war period was eventful; however, it scarcely constituted a new era.

▶ A complete sentence is normally required following a semicolon. This does not apply to the colon.

✓ The election was democratic: the voters, Republican! The results were proclaimed; they were also disclaimed.

▶ A colon is used in ratios such as 1:3, meaning one out of every *four*. (See Numbers, Proportions and ratios, p. 104.)

Comma [,]

I was working on the proof of one of my poems all the morning, and I took out a comma. In the afternoon I put it back again. – Oscar Wilde (Attrib.)

The comma is probably the most used – and misused – punctuation character in English. An important point to be remembered with the comma is that 'quick reading' is becoming common practice (quick reading courses are widely offered – and not only in academic institutions). Used properly, it is the key to clarification: used improperly it is the key to confusion. Neither is a comma a substitute for 'and'. 'In addition to the regulars Charles, Smokey, Harry, Billy, Bob and Ann were at the meeting.' A comma after 'regulars' would indicate that Charles and the rest were occasional participants. Comma or not, the placement of 'and' between Charles and Smokey, would then indicate that the these were the regulars.

Some general observations

The golden rule about commas is that a comma is *only* used where it serves to clarify the meaning.

The comma is the natural break in speech and in the written text. However, we read more quickly than we can speak aloud and fewer commas *may* be needed in the written text. English tolerates longer sentences than is the case in several European languages requiring more commas. Indeed, one important use of the comma (or indeed, its omission) is to introduce clarity into a text. But excessive use of commas is a common disease. Even a single innocent comma may confuse rather than clarify, as I once read:

> ✗ By voluntarily relinquishing some personal freedom, when they unite in a labour union, workers may be able to overpower the social forces that are allied against them.

My guess is that the author was not really sure about the point he was making, and so included a comma as if to ensure the reader that this was all good solid stuff. It is not immaterial which of the commas is dropped.

▶ Do not use the comma to join two sentences which are clearly not connected. For example, the following mistake is not uncommon:

> ✗ Bush was elected, he had been sure of his father's influence.

In this case the comma may be replaced by a semicolon.

On the other hand, much is made of coordinating conjunctions (and, but, or, nor, etc.) in many texts. Previously, there was not much doubt that these had to be separated by a comma:

> She knew it, and he knew it.
> He knew it, but he didn't know that she knew it.
> He knew that she knew it, or did she?

But it is a mistake to think that every time one of these conjunctions is used that a comma is obligatory. Where the context does not necessarily imply apposition, the comma is optional – in fact it is frequently dropped today. Why? My impression is that this has more to do with quick reading than grammatical tradition.

> She knew it and he knew it.
> He knew it but she didn't.
> He didn't nor did she.

Nevertheless, there are still a number of traditions regarding use of the comma, some of which are fading. A good example is the comma after salutations in letters (see Salutations, p. 54). This is not used in modern English, although old traditions die hard. Generally, we do not seem to be bound by many of the 'rules' of yesteryear. A comma in addresses is now almost taboo:

✗ 16, London Road
✗ Dear Mr. Smith,

Lists

▶ Commas are required in lists of adjectives or nouns:

✓ Rarely had there been voiced such vociferous, compelling, overbearing and clear, yet unsubstantiated evidence against a minister.

▶ US English tends to place a comma before the 'and', more so than in English although this is also the norm for some UK publishers. It is certainly required where the last item is qualified or where clarification is necessary. The uninitiated might just believe that there was a single football club called Fulham and Chelsea. Careful punctuation will eliminate any doubt.

Arsenal, Bolton, Fulham and Chelsea, the leader just a month ago, all face relegation.
✓ Arsenal, Bolton, Fulham, and Chelsea (the leader just a month ago), all face relegation.

Speech

▶ As seen above (Colon, speech), particularly the shorter comment should be introduced by a colon. Tom emphasised the point: 'The offer is refused.'

The comma is occasionally a better choice than the colon with regard to the flow of the text:

Tom thought carefully before saying, 'No, the offer is too low.'

In a divided sentence, the comma should be used.

✓ 'Yes,' he answered, 'but only with a discount.'

▶ Note the comma *inside* the inverted commas: 'Yes,'...

General points of clarity

▶ A comma is clearly required in the following:

Dickins and Jones and Barkers are popular London stores for tourists.

Do we mean Dickins and Jones, and Barkers, or Dickens, and Jones and Barkers? (Actually, we mean the former.)

▶ Commas should not be used to separate adverbs where they serve no purpose. Even so, the comma may serve to emphasise the suspense of a situation:

✓ Anxiously, they awaited the return of the jury.

One author 'corrected' my translation of his article to read: 'They anxiously awaited the return of the jury.' To my mind, this was a change of style and lacked the 'drama' of my original.

▶ It is frequently the case that a comma is thought to be necessary but the author is not sure why. If you are unsure, then it is probably not necessary.

The new public transport act was controversial, (Stepinoffabus, 1999:23).

Do we really need the comma before the opening parenthesis?

Separating phrases and clauses

▶ There is a rule which states that a comma is used following an adverbial clause when this precedes the main clause.

The transfer had been made, even though it had clearly been delayed.

This is surely another rule in decay. The following seems absolutely o.k. to me.

The transfer had been made even though it had clearly been delayed.

We will not concern ourselves too much with grammatical rules but should, perhaps, emphasise the importance of style. Inverting a sentence is one way of introducing style into a text: as well as removing superfluous commas:

✓ When the letter arrives, please post it on.

as an alternative to:

Please post the letter on when it arrives.

▶ A useful rule (principle) is to avoid unnecessary commas.

✓ It was stated, on the other hand, that the rules could be bent.

Re-ordering gives a better flow:

On the other hand, it was stated that the rules could be bent.

As the above suggests, rewriting such as to reduce the number of commas often improves the 'readability'.

▶ Subsidiary clauses formerly needed to be separated by commas:

The committee, which had just been re-elected, now included three women.

Some writers consider that this interrupts the flow for the quick reader, especially where the clause is concise and the sentence not unreasonably long, and prefer:

The committee which had just been re-elected now included three women.

While some may disapprove, if you do select to drop the commas, drop both. This does point to the subtlety of punctuating the written word and that which has to be spoken.

▶ A comma is not used in conjunction with 'and' where the same subject applies or the two clauses are clearly related.

✗ The proposal was made, and the resolution was formally adopted.
✓ The proposal was made and the resolution was formally adopted.

▶ A common mistake is to place the comma before *and* instead of after when isolating a clause or phrase:

✗ The proposal was re-drafted, and in spite of some further objections, was then approved.
✓ The proposal was re-drafted and, in spite of some further objections, was then approved.

This error can occur with several prepositions and conjunctions:

✗ The regional plan was debated, but in spite of several attempts, was not put to the vote.

✓ The regional plan was debated but, in spite of several attempts, was not put to the vote.

Hint: Read the sentence without the intervening phrase or clause.

Interjections

▶ An interjection may be a single word, address (salutation), or a phrase. A pair of commas is required:

✓ The leader, Wacky Jacky, was ousted by his opponent, Silly Willy.
✓ At the present time, no, although we are expecting new supplies.

Phrases (often adverbial), or even clauses, are interjections in so far as they interrupt the argument, although frequently explaining or embellishing what has gone before, and require setting off with a comma:

Having accepted that the photos were fabricated, those responsible were court-martialled.

This is frequently the case when the phrase or clause commences with a proper noun or pronoun. Otherwise it may be that a comma is superfluous:

Having accepted that the photos were not fabricated it was not necessary to press charges.

▶ Commas, in pairs, are required when addressing a person or a group:

✓ Believe me, Sir, you have not heard the last of this.
✓ As I informed you, Minister, the workers are revolting.

▶ Formerly, it was a rule that commas were required in pairs where a phrase or clause is placed in the middle of sentence.

The court rose early, about three-thirty, with instructions to convene at nine the next day.

As the intervening phrase qualifies 'early', the logic of the punctuation is clear, but not in the following:

✗ The secretary, who had recorded the statement, was asked for a verbatim report.

The following is correct:

✓ The secretary who had recorded the statement was asked for a verbatim report.

The following provide examples of the use the comma which fails to clarify a situation. Who actually recorded the statement? And who wants the transcript?

The secretary to the Director who had recorded the statement asked for the transcript.

The secretary to the Director, who had recorded the statement, asked for the transcript.

Indeed, this illustrates the point that, rather than rules, commas should be placed where appropriate in order to facilitate understanding, and to 'lubricate' the flow of the written word. If it doesn't, ask yourself if re-writing the sentence or using alternative punctuation is better? The Director's secretary, who had recorded the statement, asked for the transcript. In fact, we could even drop the commas entirely.

Dates

▶ Originally, the comma was used to separate dates (the adverbial phrase):

By 1992, the government had been in power for thirteen years. In 1993, new electoral boundary reforms were proposed.

Many appear not to consider this necessary today. By 1992 the government had been in power for thirteen years. It should nevertheless be retained to separate a subordinate clause:

✓ In 1993, by which time the government had been in power for thirteen years, there was considerable need for new legislation on the homeless.

▶ A comma should also be retained to separate dates and numbers:

✓ In the debate held in March 1993, 256 members voted against the proposal.

This would also be used where the written form is given as this is, in effect, a reversal of the sentence structure:

✓ In the debate of March 1994, six members abstained.

See Dates for a further discussion of the comma in months and dates p.71.

Numbers

(See also Numbers, Roman numbers)

▶ Figures exceeding 4 digits.

✓ 9999; 10,000; 100,000.

Continental convention is to employ a full point here (and a comma in place of a decimal point):

There were 100.000 at the match. The temperature was 15,5º centigrade.

Omissions

The comma can indicate an omission as in the following:

✓ The manager wanted the issue postponed; the delegation, an immediate debate.

derived from:

The manager wanted the issue postponed: the delegation [wanted] an immediate debate.

Salutations, etc.

▶ Previously, salutations in letters employed the comma:

✗ Dear Sir, ... Yours faithfully,
✗ Dear Mr. Jones,

▶ Modern business practice is not to use the comma although a few text books still suggest it. The full point after Mr is gone – and was never really necessary.

✓ Dear Mr Jones ... Yours faithfully

See under Colon for formal business letters p.43.

I have read that a comma is required in addresses: Bob Scratchit, Ph.D. But my impression is that this is disappearing as is the comma in Dear Scratchit, I find it acceptable to write: Bob Scratchit PhD was awarded the degree on the basis of his research on fleas. It is another of those cumbersome punctuation habits which destroys the reader's concentration. But your editor may be a bit old-fashioned.

Other

▶ As indicated above, there used to be a number of rules (and possibly still are) about commas and phrases, but the modern trend seems to be *logic*! Is that comma really necessary? For example, the use of a comma with 'that':

It was decided that, if the motion was defeated, the committee would resign.

This conditional clause, '*if ...*', does not strictly need to be distinguished by the presence of commas. On the other hand, we might want to draw attention to an exceptional state of affairs:

✓ It was thought that, in spite of the vote, the Chairman would continue.

Some would argue that the structure of the sentence leaves something to be desired, but it is those occasional quirks of style which draw attention to the subject matter.

▶ A comma may serve to emphasise a point. Consider the following:

The question was: 'Did he or didn't he?'
Was the painting genuine or was it a clever fake?

The inclusion of a comma can draw particular attention to a phrase:

The question was: 'Did he, or didn't he?'
Was the painting genuine, or was it a clever fake?

The dash (–) may be even more appropriate:

The question was: 'Did he – or didn't he?'

▶ The dash is occasionally preferable to the comma, especially where a sentence can contain many commas:

✗ It was stated on the other hand, that in spite of objections by the board of management, itself comprising minority shareholders, the rejection of the proposal would have several short-term consequences, some of which, in spite of government support, would have long-term, if not permanent consequences for the company, and quite probably, the board.

The above sentence, while grammatically correct, contains no less than nine commas. We can isolate a particular phrase with the use of a dash, and thereby facilitate reading. We might also examine the possibility of reducing the use of commas:

✓ It was stated on the other hand, that in spite of objections by the board of management – itself comprising minority shareholders – the rejection of the proposal would have several short-term consequences, some of which (in spite of government support) would have long-term, if not permanent consequences for the company – and quite probably, the board.

▶ Avoid using the dash as an alternative to the comma. Whereas the comma is essentially for clarification, the dash is more akin to a semicolon or colon and introduces a change in the line of thought or an emphasis. Implicit in this is that the use of a comma *and* a dash is taboo:

✗ The judgement was wrong, – in fact it was ludicrous.
✓ The judgement was wrong – in fact it was ludicrous.
✓ The judgement was wrong: in fact it was ludicrous.

▶ Tag questions are questions attached to statements. These need to be separated by a comma.

✓ It was beyond belief, wasn't it?

Of course, omitting the question mark places quite a different emphasis on the expression.

▶ Finally, we could remind ourselves of the two quick fixes for removing commas:

1. Invert the sentence (with the possible loss of style):

   Nevertheless, it was decided ... → It was nevertheless decided ...

2. Replace the comma with 'and' or another conjunction – or even divide the sentence.

When dividing the sentence, use a colon or semicolon as appropriate:

✗ The Socialists opposed the motion, the Centre abstained, the right wing was unanimous in its vote, the others were just confused!

✓ The Socialists opposed the motion and the Centre abstained; the right wing was unanimous in its vote. The others were just confused!

▶ Excessive use of commas is a disease. The writer loses his train of thought and inserts a comma, if not a semicolon, believing that this will clarify the situation. Interestingly, he/she will often start using 'we' instead of 'I' – a further indication that he or she, as author, can blame 'us' or 'them' for any confusion.

Whereas the use of commas for this purpose is common, we can nevertheless cut out many commas using other means:

In the model each member, i, represents a client.

Far better to use italics:

In the model each member *i* represents a client.

This is really a question of *readability* rather than any formal adoption of a rule.

Compound and Conjoined Words

(See Hyphenation (soft); Affixes; Prefixes and suffixes)

Compound words

When I started to gather material for this section I soon realised that there were more exceptions to the rule than there were rules to which exceptions could be made. I could have reduced this entry to a couple of paragraphs, but spurred on by the hunt for reason and logic I decided to retain my collection and present it as it is. Don't sweat on trying to reason with hyphens and the vagaries of compounds: just use common sense, or your dictionary. (The latter might not show much common sense either.)

A compound word or term is two words (occasionally more) which when used in conjunction form another word. Sometimes these may take on quite a different meaning, for example a chicken run, or we might say 'she's very high class'. Some compound words are hyphenated; others are what I term 'conjoined'. It is interesting to note that many compound words develop in stages, the modern version frequently being the conjoined word. Thus, we may encounter *oil field, oil-field,* or *oilfield,* and similarly *data base, data-base, database* (the latter is now normal). Indeed, we find both *word processor and word processor.*

Sometimes the three versions may all exist but with a nuance in their respective use. For example, *under ground, under-ground,* or *underground.* This example enables us to observe the generalisation whereby separate words often form an adverbial phrase (they live under ground); the hyphenated version forms an adjective (they have an under-ground lair); the conjoined form is a noun (the gang was part of an underground movement). The conjoined version is increasingly used as an adjective. Most would probably have written 'underground lair' to which few would react.

There are no rules or even guidelines as to whether separate, hyphenated or conjoined words apply to nouns, adjectives or adverbs. We find that separate words may comprise a compound noun, (*cross action, through ticket*). But again, we might find both of these hyphenated. Then again we have prefixed nouns (*non-smoker,* also found as *nonsmoker* (*Collins Cobuild*)).

Where a compound or conjoined word forms an adjective or occasionally an adverb, it is called a compound modifier (e.g. *double-glazed [window], undercover [agent]*).

▶ US English tends to favour a compound word without a hyphen. This applies particularly to nouns (US *crankshaft,* UK *crank-shaft*), although verbs generally remain as separate words in both languages. Previously, the distinction between the US and UK English in this respect seemed to relate to single syllable words. US English more readily adopted polysyllabic conjoined terms than did UK English (US *underprivileged,* UK *under-privileged*) although there is an increasing tendency to conjoin polysyllabic words in UK English as well: *over development* may now be encountered as *overdevelopment* and *weight-lifting* as *weightlifting*. As might be expected the *Encarta Dictionary* uses the conjoined form, but retains separate words for *body building*. Now I would have thought that to be very English, but that *COD* gives *bodybuilding* while retaining the hyphen in *weight-lifting*. *Chambers Dictionary* retains the hyphen for both terms. All of which proves nothing but arouses my curiosity. If yours is also aroused, then read on. You won't learn much but your curiosity may be satisfied.

Compound modifiers

▶ Where compound words preface a noun or a verb, they are called compound modifiers. Examples are: an *upper-class* family, a *newly-decorated* room, *ground-to-air* missile.

Compound nouns may comprise an adjective + noun (long-line, shortfall); two nouns (picture-postcard, tablecloth); adverb + noun (up-train, upkeep), and which may be hyphenated or conjoined. There are also many terms which are not hyphenated e.g. coffee table. There may be a distinction between separate and conjoined forms as with wood pulp (pulp made from wood), but woodscrew (a screw to be used on or with wood). Compounds commencing with a prefix may be hyphenated (a mini-skirt), but there is a growing trend towards conjoined nouns (minicab, minicruise).

Compound verbs comprising an adverb plus a verb are normally either hyphenated (to over-excite) or conjoined (to undercut). Where a verb has a noun form, the latter is often hyphenated (to pay off – a pay-off: to hand out – a hand-out).

Compound adjectives often do need a hyphen. But notice that when these terms follow the subject, the hyphen is dropped: She had a full-time job. The job was full time. This is interesting in so far as if this is an *adverbial phrase*, we probably would hyphenate it: She worked full-time.

There is an exception (of course); that is when a modifier immediately follows was/is/be. Then the hyphen is always retained. The much-loved Queen Mother...; The Queen Mother was much-loved. Another example. The over-weight parcel will have to be repacked. The parcel is over-weight. It was clearly over weight.

When an adjective is formed from a noun phrase, a hyphen is normally used:

✓ In the long term shares will recover. Some must be regarded as a long-term investment.

▶ Where the present continuous '-ing' form is used to form an adjective, the term is nearly always hyphenated, fast-talking salesman, the measures were far-reaching. (This does not apply to nouns, e.g. a shortcoming).

▶ There is a 'double-consonant rule' which states that when two words are conjoined resulting in a double consonant, a hyphen should be used. But the trend even here is to drop the hyphen. Thus we find book-keeper and bookkeeper, also under-run and underrun. We will encounter over-regulate (conforming to the rule), but overrule, override, underrate (apparently contradicting it).

The 'double-consonant rule' does not apply to prefixes (to misspell). However, it will normally apply where the prefix ends in a vowel (to re-elect), but we find both to re-enter and to reenter (mainly US). It has been brought to my attention that one publisher preferred the diaereses for words such as this where there is a change in the pronunciation of a second adjacent vowel: reënter. Seems a bit snobbish to me.

The spellchecker may or may not react to these. As indicated above, it will not show that baby sitter (two words) or over-ride are incorrect! Worse, it will not detect pre-amble (preamble); in-sufficient (insufficient) or any other mis-hyphenated term, regarding these as 'soft' hyphens as encountered at the end of a line.

What we can determine from the above is that common sense is the order of the day. If a hyphen makes sense, then use it. Clue: the adjective immediately preceding the noun is determinant. As such we can differentiate between a high heeled shoe and a high-heeled shoe. When a compound word is formed with a noun or adjective commencing with a capital, the term is not hyphenated as with High Commissioner and west Europe. Surprisingly, perhaps, High Church is a compound adjective and thus we have a High Church Priest. But no-one would take this as suggesting he is more than 6 feet (183 cm) tall.

Oh yes, there's always something which upsets the apple-cart. In computing we have a high-level language, but in nuclear physics we have high level waste, which rather contradicts our comment about the importance of the adjective.

▶ You may read (elsewhere) that adverbs ending in –ly are hyphenated: fully-fashioned, fully-fledged. But we would not hyphenate a beautifully dressed woman. Recalling that the adjective preceding the noun is the vital one, the same might seem to apply here. But then again, the fact that we have not hyphenated beautifully dressed woman does not divert our attention to the fact that the woman was dressed rather than undressed. Yes, we are back to our common-sense rule.

Sometimes the hyphenation can make all the difference. Her husband was a good-for-nothing. Not only that he was good for nothing. The first term suggests he was a lazy bum; the second, that he had no wealth or assets.

A final comment about conjoined words are constructed terms such as *smog* = *smoke* + *fog*, and one I like, *guess* + *estimate* = *guestimate* (*COD*).

Conclusion: if it looks right, then it probably is. If your spellchecker reacts (e.g. to *nonsmoker*) it may be out-of-date. But different publishing houses also have their own choices. Some, like the *Concise Oxford Dictionary* and *Chambers Dictionary* are quite conservative; others such as *Collins* have a modern approach favouring conjoined words.

Are we going to remember all this? Probably not – that's why I wrote this book.

Hyphenated words and the spellchecker

There are at least 18,000 hyphenated terms and conjoined words in the major dictionaries, and probably about 2000 or so in daily use, essentially nouns and adjectives. There are no concrete rules about hyphenation, or even when words should be conjoined. For example, we may encounter *oak leaf* and *oakleaf* in different dictionaries. A problem arises when we hyphenate a word that should not be hyphenated, i.e. it should either comprise two separate words or a conjoined word. Thus, *post-master* will not be recognised as an error for *postmaster* by the spellchecker. Of course, conjoined words will be recognised when they are incorrect, e.g. *bridgebuilder*. The word processor will probably suggest *bridge builder*, but will not react to *bridge-builder*. Indeed, the hyphenated version may be given in another dictionary!

It is clear that differences may be discerned between, for example, *down town* and *down-town* or *downtown*. The former is an adverbial phrase (*I thought that we could go down town this evening*). The hyphenated form is frequently used as an adjective (*There's a down-town café which has excellent kebab*). The conjoined term is also encountered as an adjective or noun (*The café is located in the downtown. After she became a punk, I feel that she has become very downtown!*). For some terms, the hyphen may indicate quite a different meaning, e.g. *air force* and *air-force* (both nouns).

This problem may be further expounded using 'air'. We have an *air bag*, an *airport*, and an *air-brake*. We also have an *air lieutenant*, an *airman* and an *air-hostess*. We may travel by *air taxi*, an *airship* or an *air-bus*. (*Airbus* is a trade name. Verbs, however, are frequently conjoined: *to crosscheck, to overthrow, to undertake*, etc.

So where and what are the rules? Answer: There aren't any; better to call these generalisations!

There are no rules concerning hyphenation but the following may be noted:

▶ Occasionally three words or more words may be hyphenated into a compound word:

The natural-gas-based industries. She used a carmine-rose-colour-base make-up!

I think that I can just about accept the last example, not knowing which hyphen to drop!

Clearly, there is no general rule. We may find *farm-hand* and *fish-farm-hand* but also *oyster-farm* and *pearl-oyster farm*. Rather, consideration should be given to the meaning. Technical articles in particular will require careful use of the hyphen. The placement of the hyphens in terms such as *cast iron wheel flange machine tools* may need some thought.

Place names, routes

A distinction should be made between names which are hyphened:

✓ Take the tube to London-Heathrow.

and routes where a spaced dash means 'to':

✓ The flight route is London-Heathrow – Paris-Orly.

You may find The London–Paris flight.

Numbers

Written numbers between twenty-one and ninety-nine.

Values of 100 and above normally use numerals, but text will be more appropriate in a title. Hyphenation might also be appropriate:

✓ Six-hundred freqwently misspellt words.
✓ One-hundred-and-two Dalmatians.

Special measurements use numbers and are hyphenated:

✓ It was made of 18-carat gold. It filled a 2-gallon barrel.

Time

When text is used, time is hyphenated:

✓ The train departs at seven-thirty; the connecting bus leaves at four-fifteen.

Compass points

Most compass points are hyphenated:

✓ north-west, east-north-east, south-west-by-south.

Note the following, (but don't ask the logic of this):

east-by-north, east-by-south, west-by-north, west-by-south, BUT north by east, north by west, south by east, south by west.

Colloquial and other phrases

Many of these comprise three or more words and are largely, but not exclusively, hyphenated.

Once upon a time there was a man, a real man-about-town, although he lived in no-man's-land. He had a get-rich-quick attitude and was a right so-and-so. Life had its ups-and-downs for his mother-in-law, largely on account of his devil-may-care attitude. His attitude was hard-and-fast but his head was soft-centred.

We may encounter some phrases which certain dictionaries choose not to hyphenate, for example, over-and-out and over and out. Generally, if the term has an adjectival function it is hyphenated, e.g. down-and-out, a step-by-step approach.

▶ The adverbial form is not generally hyphenated: We will go through this step by step.

Titles, occupations, nationalities

Titles are mostly hyphenated such as air-vice-marshal, Attorney-General, as are many occupations: ballet-dancer, office-boy, delivery-man, lady-in-waiting. But there are also not a few exceptions: car mechanic, steel worker, bank manager, office cleaner. Occupations ending in 'man', 'lady', 'master' are frequently conjoined: milkman, charlady, postmaster (exception station-master). Curiously, we have the music mistress, but the postmistress.

Nationalities are hyphenated as in Anglo-Chinese, Italian-French, but not Latin American, French Canadian, High Dutch, or Low German.

Clarification

▶ A hyphen is clearly required when used to distinguish between two different meanings. Observe the difference between the following:

The jacket was made of a light brown material ... It was a lightweight, brown material
The jacket was made of a light-brown material ... It was light-brown in colour

▶ A hyphen is used to separate a prefix where necessary to distinguish between two forms of a word. The following are examples where the hyphenated prefix changes the meaning of the word, e.g. recount (re-count), recollect (re-collect), recover (re-cover), recreation (re-creation), reform (re-form), refund (re-fund), resign (re-sign), pretension (pre-tension).

Other

Many other words are used in compound form where hyphenation may also clarify the text as in:

The project was now regarded as being less important in the revised budget.

– as opposed to:

There were more less-important projects for which money was then available. (I actually read this in a report. I found it acceptable in the context.)

▶ A 'suspended hyphen' is used to avoid repetition. (See Dash, p. 64.)

✓ Two-, three-, and four-room apartments were available.

A hyphen may be used to create a compound word where this serves to clarify a point:

✓ There were only two kilo packets available. (Just two packets of one kilo each.)
✓ There were only two-kilo packets available. (Only packets weighing two kilos were available.)

A common mistake is can-not for cannot. It may nevertheless be noted that a point may be emphasised by keeping the two words separate: 'I told you,' John said emphatically, 'I can not do that – so don't ask me again. Well, not before Saturday!'

Book titles: both words in a hyphenated term retain the upper case where the upper case is used throughout the title.

✓ *Counter-Revolution: Inter-Regional and Urban–Rural Conflict in Indonesia.*

▶ A hyphenated prefix before a proper noun is not capitalised.

✓ This sub-Saharan region is now ruled by an ex-Congo war lord.

▶ Note the hyphens in: a 24-page document; a 12-page-long note. (But then I ask myself why the author used 'long'? 12 pages seems short to me!)

▶ Single letter prefixes. You wouldn't use the B-word, would you?

▶ Some writers have developed the habit of hyphenating abbreviations as in UN-delegate, IBM-patent, LEA-Director. Dropping the hyphen won't save a lot of ink in the printer, but it really isn't necessary.

Dash [–]

Typographically, there are a number of different forms of dash. The restrictions of the typewriter led us into bad habits where many use the 'minus' sign [-] both as a hyphen and a dash [–]. Indeed, negative values should be preceded by the dash. (Example –32, not -32). In consequence we now understand that the key we refer to as the minus key is not a minus at all: it is a hyphen and should only be used as such. How to achieve the dash on your word processor is discussed below.

Before proceeding, it must be noted that a number of punctuation books are not only quite confusing on the different types of dash, they are completely in error. One text even confuses typographically the hyphen and the dash and then proceeds to refer to the en dash (typographically correct) as the em dash.

The *hyphen* is used in compound words and is not discussed here. (See Hyphenated, conjoined and compound words, Chapter 15). We include it, however, within the discussion of the typography in order to distinguish it from the normal dash, the en rule and the em rule. (The term 'rule' here means 'dash'. Many US text books use the term dash instead.)

Dashes – a typographical note

The typographer will tell us that there are several forms of dash other than the hyphen [-]: the normal dash [–], the en dash (spaced) [–], the em rule [—], the two-em rule [——] and the three-em rule [———].

The typewriter gave little choice in distinguishing between a hyphen, a dash and an en or em rule. The minus sign frequently sufficed for the dash and the en dash: the longer em rule employed a double hyphen [- -]. Curiously, I encountered this in a fairly recent publication but this really was an exception. The basic dashes/rules, distinguished by their length, may be obtained with the use of short-cut keys. The normal dash and the en rule are identical in length. The important distinction between the dash and the en rule is that the latter is 'spaced', i.e. has spaces on either side. The en rule and em rule are sometimes referred to as the N-rule and M-rule, respectively and are longer.

The dash

A dash is typed using the Ctrl + '*numerical keypad minus*'

The en rule

Word contains an 'automatic' en rule. Where a hyphen is typed with a space on either side. For example, typing 'Democrats - Republicans' becomes 'Democrats – Republicans'. Alternatively, hold down the Ctrl key while hitting the numerical 'minus' (hyphen) key once. If you are getting two dashes rather than a symbol, got to Tools – AutoCorrect – AutoFormat as you type and click the appropriate box.

The em rule

Word also contains an automatic em rule. If two consecutive hyphens are typed *without a space between two letters or a punctuation sign*, this automatically converts to an em rule [—]. Alternatively, hold down the Ctrl key while hitting the *numerical* keypad 'minus' (hyphen) key twice. You would have to use this to write 'Go to h——.'

Two- and three em rules

Two- and three em dashes may be typed using the Ctrl key and hitting the numerical minus key three and four times respectively to give —— and ————.

Uses for all the above are given below.

The dash

See also Hyphen

The dash is distinguished from the en rule in that it is not bounded by spaces. In fact, many books discuss these two dashes under the same heading. The dash is used as a 'joiner' as in the following, occasionally implying 'and', 'to'. (Do not use the 'minus' sign, i.e. a hyphen.)

✓ The Baltic states: Estonia–Latvia–Lithuania.

Thus, the following would be incorrect:

✗ Radio – television communication channels; the staff – student ratio.

▶ The dash is used as follows for events, treaties, etc.:

✓ The G7–Soviet Agreement. The Lib.–Lab. Alliance, The Sino–Japanese war.

▶ Routes: Euston–Glasgow express. But a spaced dash is preferable in compound terms: New York-Kennedy – Stockholm-Arlanda; Birmingham (New Street) – York (Central).

▶ The dash is also the correct sign for negative values. [A typesetter will normally use a sign which is longer than a hyphen but shorter than an en rule.]

✓ Absolute zero is –273.15° c.
✓ 3 + (–4) = –1. Another example from higher mathematics: –8 – (–12) = +4

The spaced dash should be used where this symbol means 'subtract':

✓ –2 – 4 = +2

▶ A dash is used to repeat a suffix which is not normally hyphenated.

✓ Courses in both macro– and microeconomics were introduced for the sixth form.

But where terms are hyphenated then the hyphen (sometimes referred to as a floating hyphen) should be retained.

✓ Two- and three-room apartments were available on short- and long-term lease.

▶ The dash is also useful in clarifying compound nouns. Neither a hyphen nor a dash may be necessary in: Both ownership and management structure need to be looked at. However, if it is the ownership structure as well as the management structure which has to be examined, then a dash may be used for clarity: Both ownership– and management structure need to be looked at.

You get an unexpected bill from a cowboy handyman who used the opportunity to paint a little more than you had intended:

'Well, you told me to paint the window and door frames.'
'No I asked you to paint the window – and door frames.'
'Yes, that's what I understood.'
'Forget it! Next time I'll specify it in detail.'

Probably best to rephrase.

▶ The dash is normally used for time periods involving hours: Closed 12.30–13.30.

The dash does not mean 'to' when used with a preposition such as 'from':

✗ He was minister from May–October. Open between 9–5.

The dash may be used in dates and bibliographic references, although many publishers prefer the spaced dash. (See below).

Dates

The dash is used in dates meaning 'to':

Mozart 1756–1791. The 1939–45 War

– but not where it signifies 'between':

✗ She was managing director 1995–1998.
✓ She was managing director between 1995 and 1998, or... from 1995 to 1998.

▶ Where names are involved, the hyphen rather than the dash is used: Rolls-Royce Ltd., The Durbin-Watson test (a statistical test developed by Durbin and Watson).

The spaced dash

In the preceding section, the dash was described as a 'joiner'. Where the dash, by implication, means 'to', some publishers (but not all) prefer the spaced dash (similar to the en rule). The spaced dash is used in the following.

Ranges

Technical documents, reports may use:

✓ In the range £2000 – £3000. Salary $60,000 – $75,000.

The currency sign should not be omitted on the second element: Salary $60,000 – 75,000. In any case, avoid the salary is 2–3,000 pounds. More general texts should spell out round hundreds, and thousands less than ten. The price range is expected to be two- to three-thousand pounds.

Dates

✓ Some publishers use a spaced dash: J. S. Bach (1685 – 1850). However the majority do not appear to do so: Mozart (1756–91). Note dash [–] not hyphen [-].

A spaced dash will be required in any case in the following:

✓ Augustus 63 BC – AD 14; Inhabited AD 763 – ca. 831.

Bibliographic references

✓ See pp. 40 – 54.
✓ Vols II – IV cover the post-war period.

As mentioned, you may encounter 1939–45; $10–$20; pp. 4–7. The hyphen *is* encountered but most publishers would regard it as incorrect: pp. 47-53.

The en rule

Typographically, the en rule and the dash are identical, except that the en rule is *always spaced*. The en rule differs from the *spaced* dash in usage. Whereas the latter is used in connection with numbers (ranges, dates, etc.), the en rule is used in text.

The en rule is a useful substitute for other punctuation symbols and may replace the comma, semicolon, colon or, when used in pairs, parentheses.

✓ The major powers were present – England, France, Germany and the USA.
✓ The motion was passed – in spite of the intense opposition – and enacted the following day.

It is observed that the en rule is stronger than the comma and, as the latter example shows, draws attention to a particular point to be emphasised. The use of the en rule should not be overdone but will bring clarity to a long sentence already containing many commas.

▶ The en rule may also be used to indicate a break in the train of thought or continuity:

✓ The governor declared that he had been elected – but this was a little premature it seemed.

– or an afterthought:

✓ The Chairman stated that he had resigned – he was, in fact, dismissed.

▶ One useful application is as an alternative to parentheses:

✓ The TV – not the PC – will probably be the two-way communication means of the future.

▶ Sometimes, a comma would appear more natural than a colon, but for reasons of clarity the en rule is the most appropriate punctuation. In one manuscript I encountered the following:

> Caffeine binds to the adenosine receptors, but creates effects which are quite the opposite – energising, stimulating and anxiogenic.

Clearly, neither a comma nor a colon would be appropriate here. Why? The reason is that we do not have a list of objects; rather, these are adjectives describing the various qualities. This example goes to show that common sense rather than hard-and-fast rules should be the essential guideline for punctuation.

▶ The en rule may be used in lists in place of a colon:

✓ The economy is expanding in several directions – employment, trade, exports, and not least in business confidence.

– or at the end of a list:

✓ Employment, trade, exports, consumer sales, tourism – all confirmed the success of the budget.

Formerly, it was not uncommon to find the colon and the dash used before a list:

✗ The attic was full to the rafters:– shoes, picture frames, chests, books, and even – of all things – a harp!

This is not used today – and neither should the dash be preceded by a semicolon.

✓ The attic was full to the rafters – shoes, picture frames, chests, books, and even – of all things – a harp!

Do not make the mistake of placing the en rule in the wrong place when used in pairs. Is the sentence grammatically correct if the 'interjection' (of all things) is removed?

A note on syntax

Writers seem to either to use the en rule too frequently, or virtually not at all. The 'paired en rule' – sometime called the 'parenthetical dash – is useful for inserting explanatory points or for clarification, but when removed should still leave the syntax complete:

✗ The need for a re-evaluation of GM products – of which few alternatives are found outside health stores – suggesting that supermarkets have restricted suppliers.

This would read: 'The need for a re-evaluation of GM products suggesting that supermarkets have restricted suppliers.' But it is not only the absence of the finite verb which can result in these errors. The problem often arises when we try to pack too much information between the rules. Neither does more than one set of en rules help:

✗ The need for a re-evaluation of GM products – of which few alternatives are found outside health stores – is all the more urgent and – as emphasised in several articles in several bio-technology journals – where GM plants are 'polluting' agricultural products far from the sites where they are being grown.

The em rule

▶ The em rule is longer than the en rule, and not spaced.

Although an en rule may be found, the em rule is normally used to indicate an interruption.

✓ 'I was just going to t——'. At this point he was clubbed down.

▶ The em rule is also used to show omission.

✓ He told her to go to d——, but her knowledge of such words was restricted to those beginning with 'b' such as bl—— and she failed to get the message.

▶ The em rule is frequently used in novels in place of the en rule, especially in US English.

Smithers—now desperate—made a final bid to escape her clutches.

▶ The em dash is found preceding an author in quotations:

'Woman was God's second mistake.' —Nietzsche (1844–1900).

▶ The em rule may also be used to indicate a change of speaker and where inverted commas are not used. This seems to be popular with some crime writers in accounting trials:

—But I put it to you, Smith, the proof is there.
—I still say that the evidence was planted.
—I am talking about hard proof, not figments of the imagination.

or even separating question and answer with the em rule:

Well, did you agree to that?—Not in so many words.
How many words then?—I am not given to verbosity.

This style was popular in a series *Notable British Trials* published in the 1930s by Hodge & Co. Ltd., London, and is still occasionally encountered.

▶ The em rule may be attached to a word (or syllable, etc.) to indicate omission of text, particularly an interrupted word.

I was saying that the Enron hearing was a scand—

The double em rule

You may find this referred to as the double-em dash or the two-em dash.

▶ The double em rule is frequently encountered as an affix, following a letter or preceding a punctuation symbol.

She told him to p—— off. He did, and ended up in ——.

▶ Some publishing houses use a double em rule in references lists to indicate the same author. Sometimes two double ems may be encountered, especially where two levels of institution are given:

Swan, Michael (1991). *Practical English Usage*. OUP. 639 pp.
— (1992). *Oxford Pocket Basic English Usage*. OUP. 288 pp.
Norway. Ministry of Local Government (1990). Local elections. Oslo. 67 pp.
— — (1992). Local Government Finances. Oslo. 13 pp.
— Ministry of Transport (1991). Transport subsidies. Oslo. 122 pp.

The triple em rule

This one seems a bit excessive but is occasionally used where an entire word is omitted.

He told the court that ——— did it.

Dates

See also **Time**

A common format for dates is 8th May 1995, alternatively 08.05.1995 (DD.MM.CCYY), or 08.05.95 (DD.MM.YY). This is the ISO standard as used in the EU and EEA. However, national customs do not always adhere to these conventions.

Current date

▶ The UK norm for dates is day-month-year (d-m-y) whereas the US norm is m-d-y. Thus, 08.05.1995 indicates the 8th of May 1995 in UK English, but August 5th 1995 in US English. Some European countries follow the UK standard, others the US standard. Your word processor should allow you to select the appropriate style as default.

The international system for all-numeric dates uses y-m-d. This is also convenient for sorting, encountered as *2000:04:20* (reflecting the sort keys), but colons are best left to hours and minutes, for example *2000-04-20 19:25*.

▶ A tip here is that it is preferable to use the full date, *2000-04-20* rather than *00-04-20*. Curious things can happen when a zero occurs at the beginning of a number which is to be subjected to a PC sorting routine.

References to dates

As indicated above, the full version is normally required.

✓ He was born on 8 May 1910.

▶ A full point after the date is not normally used (8. May 1910), but a comma may be used following the month, 8th May, 1910. A full point is used, however, in many foreign languages – (which may not capitalise the month): 8. juni 1910.

A full point should not follow '5th' as in the following.

✗ May 5th. was finally determined as the date for the election.

▶ Most modern word processors automatically superscript ordinals such as 1st, 2nd, 3rd and 4th. This feature may be turned off. He died on May 5th is preferred by many to He died on May 5th. In literary works, text is appropriate: He was married on June the third – and repented on the fourth. (See Digits or text? p. 107.)

Some of us may have learnt to place a comma following the date when occurring at the beginning of a sentence: In June 1946, the climate of post-war optimism was cooling. This is not practised today, although would be appropriate where a complementary phrase or clause is used: In June 1946, just as summer was revealing its true colours, so was the government. It is also generally required when the date occurs in the middle of a sentence: After a trial which had commenced soon after the New Year, the sentence was pronounced on 13 January 1950, and the date for execution was then set.

Years

Originally, A.D. (*Anno Domini*) and B.C. (Before Christ) were used, with full points. Many dictionaries have dropped these and now use AD and BC. Note SMALL CAPS. Incidentally, a.d. (*ante diem*) means 'before the day'. BC follows the date; AD precedes it:

✓ 600 BC and AD 2000

We may nevertheless encounter the following, which is incorrect:

✗ We all know what happened in 79 AD.

There is something called CE (Common Era, or the Christian Era). Likewise BCE (before Christian Era). The Muslim era, AH (*anno Hegirae*), commenced 16th July 622; AM (*anno mundi*) is the Jewish era dating from 7th October 3761 BC; and BP (Before Present, i.e. before 1950) used by geologists. Treat all these as AD.

▶ A number of versions of reference to decades exist. Some are no longer recommended, others are taboo.

The present norm is a single *s* following the date: In the 1990s ... In the '90s ... (occasionally without the apostrophe, the 90s).

✓ In the 1890s, the music hall reached its prime: by the 1990s, barely a half-dozen theatres remained. Oh for the good old '20s.

The plural form –ies must be used in the following:

✓ In the Nineties, the music hall reached its prime.
✗ In the forty's and fifty's ...

▶ If the number is shortened then the apostrophe should be used:

✓ The gold rush of the '80s became a stampede in the '90s.

The following use of the apostrophe may be encountered more often in US than UK English, but is not recommended.

In the 90's, the music hall reached its prime.

The apostrophe is encountered, however, in the adjectival form:

The 1950's style was not to my taste.

Nevertheless, the preferred adjectival form is s' – both for singular and plural.

✓ The 1980s' music style was dominated by heavy metal.
✓ The 1990s' styles were considered tasteless by many.

But do not use:

✗ In the 90ies, the music hall reached its prime.
✗ The '90's styles were cheap – and nasty.

You may encounter The 90's styles in US English.

Periods

▶ Avoid the hyphen (minus sign) for periods:

✗ 1914-1918.

The dash should be used. Many publishers use a spaced dash, particularly where the full year is used.

✓ 1914–1918; 1939 – 1945; AD 763 – ca. 831.

The second date in a period may be abbreviated: 1939–45. The spaced dash should not be used here:

✗ 1939 – 45

▶ Practically every punctuation book points out the error of (mis)using the hyphenated date, indicating how frequently this error is encountered:

✗ The war lasted from 1939–1945 (instead of from 1939 to 1945).

Many European languages use a text form which when translated directly becomes 'in recent decades'. The nearest translation would be: 'in the last twenty to thirty years ... (thirty to forty years)', etc. It is possible to write 'during the last decade' but this may be misunderstood. Webster's *New World Dictionary* gives the following definition:

Decade: a period of ten years; esp., in the Gregorian calendar

a) officially, a ten-year period beginning with the year 1, as 1921–1930, 1931–1940, etc.
b) in common usage, a ten-year period beginning with a year 0, as 1920–1929, 1930–1939, etc.

The adjective (rarely encountered) is *decadal*.

Century. Most publishers seem to prefer text:

In the nineteenth century the typewriter encouraged would-be writers

rather than:

In the 20th century the PC confirmed that neither mechanics nor electronics could produce a Shakespeare.

Other

It is immaterial whether you write 'It was announced in 1990 that the law would be changed', or 'In 1990 it was announced that the law would be changed.' A comma after the date is only necessary where a qualifying phrase, interjection or similar, is used: In 1990, seven years before being elected as PM, Blair already had his sights on the top job.

Some publishers drop the apostrophe in the following, but strictly speaking it should be retained: I will arrive in 3 days' time. My wife is taking 2 weeks' holiday in Brazil. Note nevertheless: It is a two-hour journey, and not It is a two hours' journey.

Definite Article, (The)

This is used more frequently in certain continental languages than in English. A common mistake made by foreigners writing in English is to use the definite form where this is not required.

▶ Avoid repetitive use of the definite article. The following is heavy reading:

Check the use of the capital letter in the titles.

At the other extreme is the command:

Check use of capital letters in titles!

It is recommended that the definite article is used to stress the main subject(s) of the sentence.

Check the use of capital letters in titles.

▶ The definite article is italicised when part of the name of a publication:

✗ The report appeared in both *The Times* and the *Daily Mail*.

The correct titles of the newspapers are: *The Times* and *Daily Mail*.

Singular or plural?

'The family is coming to dinner on Sunday' or 'The family are coming to dinner on Sunday'?

This problem is commonly encountered. Another example might be 'The Committee was in agreement...' or 'The Committee were in agreement ...'. The norm here is whether the family or committee, or whatever, is regarded as an entity or as a group of individuals. If you consider the family to comprise Aunt Jane, Cousin Bill, Grandma and your sister's children, they could be considered as a group of individuals. Individuals are plural! So, they *are coming to dinner.*

If, on the other hand, your visitors are your parents, brother and sister and their respective partners and children, you will probably consider them as an entity. An entity is singular: the family *is* coming to dinner.

The same applies to the committee. If the committee members voted differently, you could write: The committee were divided in their opinion. Alternatively: The committee was unanimous in its decision. But it would not be wrong if you wrote: The committee was divided... the committee were unanimous in their decision. It really depends upon where you wish to place the emphasis.

Incidentally, I am informed that US English is far more focused on the collective noun in the singular.

Some words are slightly ambiguous: The minutes of the meeting are available in the library. But we could say: The minutes of the board is one of several sources of information; the annual reports are another. Strictly speaking 'minutes' is plural, but again we are thinking of these as a document or a record of the proceedings. Similarly: Improved communications was the reason for the development. I encountered 'Politics stagnates' in one article which left me wondering. This is different from 'a means of tackling the problem ...'. We do not say 'a politics'. The *NODE* states this to be a 'plural noun usually treated in the singular'. Then I'll accept that politics stagnates. Blair beware!

Other

It is very tempting to be patriotic, even a trifle condescending with the definite article: As noted by the English philosopher, Roland Butter, the sandwich can be eaten upside down without the contents falling out. Who, exactly, is *the* philosopher R.B.? I encounter this not infrequently in articles where a relatively unknown academic is credited with a seminal work. A different kettle of fish if we had written: As the German philosopher, Kant (author of *Critique of Pure Reason*), would probably have noted, the sandwich theory does not apply to *apfelstrudel*.

The borderline between a plain 'mister' and those endowed with the title 'the' (albeit in lower case) is, I would have thought, quite clear. Nothing at all wrong with the indefinite form: As noted by a Greek economist, Georg Stepinoffabus, privatisation of public transport is a hit-and-myth policy.

Direct and Indirect Speech

A mistake commonly encountered is the difference between direct and indirect speech. Of course, direct speech should be given in inverted commas:

Politely said, his comment was 'rubbish'. Indirectly, this could be stated: His comment was that it was rubbish.

A problem often arises with quotations from books. Consider the following:

According to Fowler, one function of the hyphen is to announce that a compound expression consisting of a noun qualified adjectivally by the other element means something different from what its elements left separate would or might mean, he says.

The problem is the final remark 'he says'. But even if we cut this out we are still left with the impression that Fowler specifically said 'One function ...' Further consideration might prompt us to remove the first comma. We can then choose between: According to Fowler one function of ... and According to Fowler, 'One function ...'

In any case, be aware to include *only* the spoken word in inverted commas:

✗ He claimed in court 'that the records were misleading'.
✓ He claimed in court that 'the records were misleading'.

Ellipsis [...]

The symbol [...] is known as an ellipsis. This may be used to indicate missing text, especially where the text is familiar:

✓ The story commenced as normal: 'Once upon a time ...'
✓ The chart showed each planet in detail: Mars, Jupiter ... Pluto, and the new discoveries.

Similarly, the ellipsis may indicate food for thought:

✓ Like another previous tyrant, the PM thought she would last a thousand years ...

There are no fixed rules about the number of full points in an ellipsis but is normally three and I suggest that you stick to this, especially as you can insert the symbol with Ctrl + Alt,. [period].

Exclamation Mark [!]

The exclamation mark takes the place of a full point unless included in quoted speech.

Following exclamations

Short exclamations of shock or surprise are followed by an exclamation mark.

✓ 'Stop that!'

Strictly speaking, the exclamation mark serves as a terminator and a final full point is not required.

✗ She shouted, he stopped, and she availed herself of the situation!.

The exclamation mark may be included in the sentence:

✓ He shouted 'Stop!' at the top of his voice, but to no avail.

Emphasis

Where it is intended to draw attention to a remark or a deliberate misquote, the exclamation mark is appropriate:

✓ His high-jump record was considered quite a feet!

It may occasionally appear in the middle of the sentence:

✓ Having hopped the whole twelve inches was considered quite a feet(!) for a flea.

A double exclamation mark is rarely encountered, but makes a point:

✓ He married on the fifth – and repented on the sixth! So did she!!

Placement of the exclamation mark

If an entire sentence is in parentheses, the final exclamation mark is placed before the closing parenthesis.

✓ (The room was painted blue – the political colour of those who used it!)

If an exclamatory comment is in parentheses, the exclamation mark will also be inside the parentheses, but a closing period is required.

✓ The room was painted red (bright socialist red!).

Very occasionally the whole sentence may require an exclamation mark where a final term is in parentheses. In this case the exclamation mark falls at the end:

✓ The result was a *fait accompli* (disaster)!

▶ It is not essential that the exclamation mark indicates the end of a sentence, to be followed by a capital letter. The following is permissible:

'Gee! you have got a hoo-doo here. Green paper! you'll have bad luck as sure as fate.' (Mrs Crippen, cited in *Famous Trials).*

Extracts

(See Parentheses, Quotations, References)

Extracts, quotations and citations are all terms used with reference to material quoted from other sources. The term 'citation' was previously used to denote a quotation from or reference to a book, paper, or author, especially in a scholarly work (*New Oxford English Dictionary*); a passage quoted from a book or other work: 'the quoting of a book or author in support of a fact' (*Collins Dictionary*), normally about 50 words in length. This will be retained within the text and placed in inverted commas. The term 'quotation' rather than 'citation' seems to be preferred today.

An 'extract' usually refers to a longer passage, sometimes as much as a page or more. These are often presented as an indented paragraph, sometimes using a smaller typeface and single line spacing, even if the main text employs broader line spacing. These do not use quotation marks.

The student of the behavioural sciences soon grows accustomed to using familiar words in initially unfamiliar ways ... He knows that the scientific denotation of the term 'personality' has little or nothing to do with the teenager's meaning. (Siegel 1956: 1)

▶ A final full point after the reference to the extract (as in the above example) is not normally employed. Some publishers place it following the final closing parentheses, but omitting the full point at the end of the quoted text: ... teenager's meaning (Siegel 1956: 1).

▶ The author's name at the end of the extract may be omitted if this *immediately* precedes the citation.

✓ This apparent anomaly is explained by Siegel (1956: 1):

The student of the behavioural sciences soon grows accustomed to using familiar words in initially unfamiliar ways ... He knows that the scientific denotation of the term 'personality' has little or nothing to do with the teenager's meaning.

Footnotes and Endnotes

Somewhere, with reference to footnotes, I read 'avoid them!'. Indeed, even where more convenient than endnotes they may nevertheless be tiresome interruptions. Their main function is to provide useful *supplementary* information. The golden rule has to be: 'if it is important, retain it in the text.' A ten-line footnote seems to indicate something important that you forgot to put in the main body of the text. Keep 'em short – to the point. But neither make the point so short that it is meaningless.

▶ Placement of the footnote reference is important. If possible, and where there is no ambiguity, placement at the end of the sentence is preferable (readability).

✓ It was suggested that a logit analysis would reveal the relationship.[6]

Otherwise, the footnote references should be unambiguous. Note that they are placed after the punctuation sign. (Some older texts place the number before the *comma*, but this practice has changed.)

✓ The methods used included ANOVA,[5] multiple regression and guestimates.[6]

▶ Do not use footnotes in a title or sub-title. This may be tempting when adding an acknowledgement (This book was inspired by ... Thanks to ... .)

✗ Foot-and-mouth: Better to cull the minister.[1]

Even though this footnote is 'Thanks to John Brown for comments', the footnote reference number gives the immediate impression that you are having to explain what the title means. This and other information, for example reference to the sponsor of the project, should be given separately in the introduction or even under 'Acknowledgements'.

Endnotes are an alternative to footnotes; they get everything 'out of the way'. But if we are honest, few can be bothered to flick to the end of the book. But whatever you do, do *not* use footnotes *and* endnotes. Only once did I encounter both in a scientific article where formulae were found in footnotes; all other supplementary information in endnotes. Naturally, these employed different numbering styles for the references in the text.

▶ Where a footnote refers *only* to the last item in a sentence it is very tempting to place the footnote reference number *before* the period. But convention is after the period or comma.

✓ There were two issues to be discussed, NPM and MBO.[1]

✗ There were two issues to be discussed, NPM and MBO[1].

Full Point (Full Stop, Period)

The term 'full point' is used in many books on copy-editing, while 'full stop' seems to prevail in a number of punctuation handbooks. The American term is 'period' (also used by Shakespeare). Generally, I have preferred to use 'full point'.

Sentence

The full point concludes a sentence. This means that a full point cannot appear at the beginning of a line. Those of you who remember that excellent 7-bits word processor, *Perfect Writer*, may recall that a new line commencing with a period followed by a couple of alphabetic characters served as command codes to the printer. Ingenious!

Abbreviations

See also Abbreviations, Chapter 12.

The general rule is that if the abbreviation concludes with the same letter as the full word, then it does not require a full point. (This does not apply to measurements.)

Originally the rule was that if the singular version employed a full point, then one was applied after the plural 's'. Thus we had *ed.* (editor) and *eds.* (editors). But there were some anomalies, as for example *ch.* (chapter) and *chs* (chapters). Generally, the plural does not employ a full point after the plural *s* in modern writing.

Full points were previously used in degrees – and still are:

✓ Ph.D., M.Sc.,(Econ.), B.Sc.

– but times change and it is now common to find:

✓ BA, DLitt, PhD

In forms of address the norm has definitely changed:

✗ Dear Mr. and Mrs. Jones. This style is now considered out-of-date. The modern usage is:

✓ Mr, Mrs, Ms, Dr, etc.

You may find Rev or Rev. (largely US), and also Revd – no full point.

▶ Time should be given in lower case with full points. 4 a.m., 6 p.m. (not am, pm. See Time, also Abbreviations).

▶ More common, perhaps, OK or even O.K. Note that o.k. is OK, but *not* ok! Forgotten already? Then use 'okay'.

Numbers

The decimal point is used in British and American English. The continental norm is the reverse use of points and commas in figures.

US, UK: $135,725.50   e.g. Norwegian: NOK 135.725,50

The decimal character required may be selected on the modern spreadsheet, if required.

Parentheses

▶ The full point is placed inside the parentheses if the entire sentence is contained within them:

✓ (His innocence was proved at a later date.)

Otherwise, outside:

✓ He had served his time (his innocence was proved at a later date).

This principle also applies where the text concludes with an abbreviation:

✓ (This has been referred to by Isaksen et al.)
✓ He was re-elected for a new term. (He was eighty years old at the time.)

▶ A closing full point is not required for references such as:

✓ 'Thank you for your e-mail. This Internet of yours is a wonderful invention.'
(George Bush, quoted in *Newsweek*)

Quotations

▶ The full point remains inside the quotation marks where it concludes a sentence:

✓ On being asked which language he preferred, Abdul commented: 'English is Greek to me! I prefer French.'

▶ The full point will lie outside a quotation which is a phrase or term forming part of a sentence:

✓ I may have been mistaken but I didn't hear Prescott say 'sorry'.

If the entire sentence above is speech, it will be punctuated as follows:

✓ He retorted angrily: 'I may have been mistaken but *I* didn't hear Prescott say "sorry".'

▶ In the *Instructions to Authors* issued by one publisher I read the following:

Punctuation should follow the British style, e.g. 'quotes precede punctuation'.

I also noticed that this publisher did not include a final full point as in the example below:

... much comment (particularly by Isaksen et al.)

Times may be changing!

Where to put the final point

The placement of the final point is sometimes a cause of confusion. Is it placed before a closing parenthesis, or after. What about question marks? And what about inverted commas?

There is a general rule here – if ever one is to be found for punctuation. Consider the entire sentence. If the entire sentence is speech contained within inverted commas (single or double), *or* if the text following the colon comprises an entire sentence, then the full point (period, exclamation mark or question mark) is contained within the final inverted comma or parenthesis. This is one of the most common errors and a number of examples may serve to illustrate.

Examples:

He exclaimed: 'Tom did it.'
'Was it correct that Tom did it?'
He asked: 'Was it correct that Tom did it?'
His comment was that 'Tim did it'.
'Tom done it!' he stammered.
He stammered: 'No, Tim done it!'
Tim suggested that Tom had done it. (Tim and Tom were twins.)
(Tim and Tom were known as 'the terrible twins'.)
Tim and Tom blamed Terry (the dog).
'Tim and Terry did it!'

Where the punctuation refers to the text within inverted commas, or an explanatory note in parentheses concludes the sentence, a final full point is required.

Terry, the dog, was known as 'Terry the terror'.
Tim and Tom were twins (the terrible twins!).
When confronted with the question as to who did it, he commented tersely that it was 'Tom, the old dog!'.
Terry was asking himself if 'this is what they call a dog's life?'.

Other

▶ Full points are not used in titles, chapter headings, sub-headings, etc. They may (rarely) be omitted at the end of a sentence if it creates confusion. The full point is a vital element of the email address and entering *www.hotmail.uk.* (with a final full point) would result in an error message.

My former e-mail address was jgtaylor@online.no It is now jgtaylor@c2i.net

Better to use square brackets:

... address is [jgtaylor@online.no]. It is now jgtaylor@c2i.net].

It is important to use the full point when referring to types of computer programs:

His .exe files malfunctioned but the .com files were fine, so he established a 'dot.com' company.

▶ Full points are not use in bulleted and similar lists of short items, with the exception of the final item. Neither are commas required at the end of each line.

✓ The following comprised the main elements of the party's new policy:
  – lower taxes
  – a minimum wage
  – smaller class sizes
  – cheaper whisky.

▶ A full point is not used for cardinal points (S, NE), elements (Al, Mg), metric measurements (i, km, m), mass (kg, lb), currencies (SEK, p).

Plurals do not use a full point: hrs, mins, and so forth. (See Chapter 11)

Geographical Location

See also Geography and space, p. 37.

It is possibly worth repeating some of the main points given under 'Capitals', especially as some confusion seems to arise with terms such as 'the West', 'western Europe', 'Eastern Europe'.

Generally, specific regions will use a capital such as 'The West of England'. We consider this as a (non-administrative) region comprising Cornwall, Devon, Somerset, and possibly even a part of Wiltshire. But West Yorkshire is for some purposes an administrative region. If my memory serves me rightly, there was something once called the West Yorkshire Traction Company. But possibly my memory serves me wrongly. (Don't even bother to use my email address.) Certainly West Sussex was an administrative district, but if I am referring in general to that district, then I would write: 'The spiders of west Sussex are more long-legged than those of east Yorkshire.'

There is no such region as 'Western Europe'. Rather, western Europe is a geographical area. We might speak of Western Europe as a political entity in the same vein as we speak of Eastern Europe. But publishers such as Cambridge University Press explicitly prefer lower case for regions whose names are recognised as *official* titles.

Where a geographical term is used as part of a title for a recognised region, capitals are employed. So just to remind ourselves:

The Midlands	West Yorkshire
The Southern Railway	west London
southern England	The West
The Far East	Southern America (or South America)
western Europe (general term);	the northern limits
Western Europe (as a political entity)	The North (indicating the polar
the central states	regions, for example).
Central America	the north (he lives in the north).
the southern states	

Headings and Titles

See also Typefaces and Fonts, p. 151.

Headings provide a structure to the text. There may be several levels of headings to consider and these may be distinguished by the font size and typeface. Chapter headings may be in upper case, capitalised (know as 'title case') or lower case:

1. GOVERNMENT EXPENDITURE AND THE RATE OF INFLATION
2. Government Expenditure and the Rate of Inflation
3. Government expenditure and the rate of inflation

Previously, US publishers largely preferred the second example, UK publishers the third. Today, both of these forms are widely used in both the US and the UK.

▶ Headings and titles do not end with a full point. Neither should they contain abbreviations:

✗　Govt. Income and Expenditure Following Devaluation.

This also applies to tables which may employ a period to separate parts of the title:

✓ United Kingdom: Imports and Exports. Main trading partners. 1998 and 1999

▶ Avoid floating hyphens in titles:

✗ Short- and long-term investment strategy – an analyst's approach
✓ Short-term and long-term investment strategy – an analyst's approach

The title may comprise two fragments. These should normally be separated by a colon:

✓ The Multinationals: IBM, GEC and Ford

As indicated, abbreviations and acronyms (IBM etc.) are permitted in titles where familiar.

A full point may be necessary where a colon is already in use:

The Multinationals: IBM, GEC and Ford. A critique

Normally the text following the full point is the sub-title unless a dash is used. Handbook for writers – a guide to punctuation, common practice and usage or Handbook for writers: a guide to punctuation, common practice and usage.

A capital letter *may* follow a colon in a title. The article following a colon in a title is normally lower case.

Levels of headings

It is advantageous to consider the number of levels of headings before commencing writing. At the same time the typeface and font for each level should be determined. These can be changed later and extra levels added if necessary.

One consideration is whether numbered levels are required. These are useful in technical and legal texts, and also in certain academic texts where clarity in the structure is helpful to the student. This structure can become somewhat diffuse if too many levels are used. A maximum of four is normally sufficient. Remember also that the font size will assist in clarification. It is not necessary to include all levels in the table of contents (TOC), and indeed, the layout of the TOC will be helpful in portraying the contents of the book. Even a TOC containing the chapter subheadings is often preferable to the practice of using a page or so of the introduction of each chapter to state the aim of the ensuing discussion.

▶ Even though your text may use 1.5 line spacing, keep long titles to single line spacing. The TOC should be single line spacing. I prefer to give an extra half line above and below the chapter heading, but the publisher may have a preference.

▶ As far as possible, determine the number of levels required and the typeface and font for each level *before* you begin. It might not be necessary to number the lowest level. The following example contains six levels (five numbered), and is excessive, not least visually. Four levels (three numbered) is often sufficient.

Chapter 1. LOCAL GOVERNMENT
1.1   The County Council
...
...
1.2   The Town Council
1.2.1   THE MAYOR
1.2.2   COUNCIL MEMBERS
1.2.3   THE COUNCIL'S FUNCTIONS
1.2.3.1   Budget and finance
1.2.3.1.1   Local financial income
1.2.3.1.2   Government grants
            Block grants
            Ear-marked grants
1.2.4   TOWN PLANNING
1.2.5   COUNCIL ELECTIONS
...

In any case, three levels will be sufficient for the Table of Contents and which, for the above, can appear:

Chapter 1.   Levels of government
1.1   Central Government
1.2   The County Council
1.3   The Town Council

You may well consider that section numbering is not necessary throughout the text at all. Congress and seminar reports which will be taken up in group discussions may nevertheless also benefit from section or even paragraph numbering. It is probably advantageous to remove these when preparing for publication in the *Congress Papers*, for example.

Users of judicial documents in particular benefit from comprehensive numbering as I know from my experience as a court interpreter. As the prosecution may well express in nasal tones: 'M'lud, I refer to Section 3, Paragraph 2, Subsection 5, the third clause, second sentence ...' How convenient when this is numbered 3.2.5.3.2. I am immediately able to jot down the reference, look it up, and instantly observe that the poor sod has been declared guilty on all counts. But not all of us have this cross to bear.

Hyperlinks

In this technological age your manuscript may well refer to email addresses, web pages, etc. When you type these, the default may be that your word processor sets this as a hyperlink. The address will change colour, normally blue, and be underlined.

http://www.askjeeves.com or john@jgtaylor.com

If you are connected to the web, just clicking either of these in your text will connect you to that site.

▶ A hyperlink may be removed while retaining the text of the e-mail address or web site. Use the help menu on your word processor to look up *Hyperlink, Remove*. In Word the hyperlink is removed by placing the cursor on the address and clicking the RIGHT-hand mouse. Select *Remove Hyperlink* or uncheck the *Activate Hyperlink* box. The colour of the address should now be the default (black), and the cursor is normal. At least you will no longer risk activating the link while editing your manuscript. You can, however, disable this feature entirely. Use Tools – AutoFormat – AutoCorrect As You Type. Uncheck the box Internet and network paths with hyperlinks.

Hyphenation (Hard)

Hard hyphenation is usually associated with compound words, i.e. two words linked so as to make a new noun, adjective (or adjectival phrase), adverb (or adverbial phrase) or a verb. Example. We write a word in *lower case*, but we may have a *lower-case* sub-title. But there are no rules here. We may own a CD player. but we use a CD-ROM. There seems to be a tendency to drop the hyphen in favour of a conjoined term as is particularly US practice. For example, *proof-reader* is now frequently spelt *proofreader*. Occasionally, where we might expect a hyphen, we may be disappointed, or even confused: *COD time frame, Collins timeframe*. The problem is that the spellchecker will not pick up out hyphenated preference *time-frame*.

Hyphenated works are comprehensively covered under Compound and conjoined words.

Hyphenation (Soft)

By soft hyphenation we mean the division of words, usually into syllables, at the end of a line – a process sometimes referred to as *syllabification*. The word processor has a hyphenation function which may be turned off enabling manual hyphenation to be undertaken if desired.

A useful definition of a syllable is given in *Collins English Dictionary*:

syllable:
– a combination or set of one or more units of sound in a language that must consist of a sonorous element (a sonant or a vowel) and may or may not contain less sonorous elements (consonants or semivowels) flanking it on either side or both sides: for example 'paper' has two syllables.
– or in brief 'a word, or component of a word, perceived as a single sound unit.'

Most publishing houses include several options for hyphenation and most word processors contain a hyphenation option although this may not necessarily comply with the requirements of the publishing house. There are a number of basic phonetic rules:

1 Short words. Words of five letters or fewer should not be divided. Exceptions are prefixed words. Division may take place after the second or third letters where this does not create confusion. For example, re-creation (to make new) and recreation (leisure activity) are two different words. These may be hyphenated respectively: re-cre-ation, recre-ation.

2   Where possible, avoid hyphenating already-hyphenated terms, although long words commencing with a hyphenated prefix may use a soft hyphen, e.g. re-embellish-ment.

3   Initial letter. Somewhere I read 'Do not divide after the first letter of a word. An exception may be permitted where the remainder of the word forms a variant of the whole'. Example: evaluation, e-valuation. But why would you want to do that anyway?

4   Avoid hyphenation where this may result in two separate words: carpet > car-pet; therapist > the-rapist; anaesthetic > an aesthetic. Not always easy – ontogenesis > onto-genesis(?) or even intonation > into-nation. In fact, the ideal fun-game for the kids on a wet Saturday afternoon: Find as many words as possible which when hyphenated mean something else. (I am sure that there is a name for such words.)

The word *station* should be hyphenated sta-tion (and not stat-ion). Generally, the final syllable following the hyphen will commence with a consonant, e.g. industrious-ly. However, it is quite permissible to hyphenate the word between two vowels where these belong to two separate syllables: industri-ous; (as well as in-dustrious). Another possibility: indus-trious (but not indust-rious). By way of further example we have nec·es·sary and un·nec·es·sary (where · illustrates the optional hyphenation points). A colleague tried this and suggested separate words into conjoined words, e.g. under growth (developing) > undergrowth (shrubs on a forest floor).

When in doubt, follow the phonetics of a word. If the first syllable is not accentuated, then divide before the accented syllable: manipu-*la*tion rather than mani-pulation or manip-ulation!

Collins English Spelling Dictionary provides all options for 150,000 UK and US words. This handy reference shows, for example, evalu-ation. However, when a prefix ending in a vowel is affixed to a word commencing with a vowel, hyphenation (other than after the affix) is not recommended: re-evaluation and not re-evalu-ation. But there are considerable differences between publishing houses as well as word processors.

Indefinite Article ('A', 'An')

As soon as the Jubilee [of 1897] was over we went to what is called in England 'an hotel'. If we could have afforded an horse and an hackney cab we could have had an heavenly time flitting around.
–Mark Twain. American writer (1835–1910).

▶   Generally, 'a' is used before consonants and 'an' before vowels. But it is the pronunciation which determines the nature of the article. Thus, we have a hair, a hierarchy, etc., but an honest man, an heir to the throne, an HIV-induced illness, and so forth. A historic event, an historical meeting are both acceptable, but I have had second thoughts about asking my lady if she would like to spend the night at 'an hotel'.

Words beginning with 'u' may also take on 'a' or 'an' – dependent upon pronunciation: He was a unique musician with an understanding for an umbilical chord. And while we are looking at vowels, you may read 'an European', but it should be 'a European'. On the other hand Sky News stated that 'they staged a exercise' (but probably not in linguistics).

▶ The indefinite article preceding an abbreviation is dependent upon the pronunciation of the initial letter: a PhD, an MA.

▶ The indefinite article may be dropped in 'telegram style' as used in advertisements. This can be an effective style for chapter headings:

✓ Change of government – change of direction.

Italics

Emphasis

Italics are used to emphasise a word. '*Don't* do that, George,' (and two minutes later), 'Don't do *that*, George.'

Titles

Book and journal titles should be italicised in the text.

✓ More information is found in Partridge's book *Usage and Abusage*.

▶ There are particular rules to follow for references in the literature list. (See Chapter 4, Bibliographies, Literature lists, References)

Names

Ships, trains etc. should be italicised, but not buildings.

✓ The most famous train in those days was *The Orient Express*. It was as popular as the Tower of London among tourists.

Latin and foreign terms

✓ As a politician his speeches could continue *ad infinitum*, some would say *ad nauseam.*

▶ Latin abbreviations in common use do not employ italics: op. cit., ibid., et al. Others, less familiar, will do so, *ipso facto.*

✓ He maintained that it was his rite [*sic*] to get drunk on a Saturday night.

▶ Many foreign words such as café and bistro (French slang), even force majeure, have become anglicised and do not employ italics. But, again, check with the publisher.

Where a foreign title is in italics the translation should use the normal typeface:

✓ His best seller was *La femme fatale* (The fatal sex).

Other

In statistics we would write: The ith term; to the nth degree. The 'th' does not automatically become a superscript after a letter and will have to be done manually. The easiest way is to type 4th and then substitute the numeral.

Lists

See also Bullets, p. 32.

Consider the following:

The increase in the total number of asylum seekers between 2000 and 2002 amounted to nearly 40 percent. However, those originating from Eastern Europe increased by 70%. There were considerable differences between countries where Polish applicants increased by 37%, Slovakia by 22%. Those from Hungary actually declined by 15%.

Clearly, some sort of a table or diagram would clarify the situation. All too frequently an author overlooks these, or chooses to 'forget' simply because he has no knowledge of the basics of Excel. See Chapter 19.

But we might also list this information, possibly using bullets (See Bullets). Normal practice is to use neither a comma nor a semicolon at the end of each line. A final period should be placed at the end of the *final* item.

The following changes in asylum applicants can be noted:
i.   Overall increase 2000–2002, + 40%

ii.   Eastern Europe, 15% (aggregate)
iii. of which:
> Poland, 37%
> Slovakia 22%
> Hungary, −15%.

If each item in a list comprises a sentence, a comma or colon may be used:

i.   The overall increase in asylum seekers 2000–2002 was 40%;
ii.   Applicants from Eastern Europe increased by 15%;
iii. Polish applicants increased by 37%;
iv.   Applicants from Slovakia increased by 22%;
v.   A decline of 15% was registered in applicants from Hungary.

Where each item comprises sentences with a different structure, or where some items contain more than one sentence, each item should be concluded with a period:

i.   The overall increase in asylum seekers 2000–2002 was 40%, in total 34,617 applicants.
ii.   Applicants from Eastern Europe increased by 15%. This was less than expected.
iii. Polish applicants increased by 37%. The Ministry regarded this as 'surprising'.

I have not found the above specified in any text, but my remarks are based on observation. If you feel that a numbered list is necessary, look at the result and ask yourself whether numbering or bullets really were necessary.

Manuscript: Structure and Layout

Journal articles

An article in a journal will normally require an abstract followed by the main text and references.

Abstract

The abstract should not exceed more than twenty lines, preferably ten or twelve. Remember who the target group (the potential readers) are. Are they specialists who are already very familiar with the field? Are they students or persons interested in the field without specialist background knowledge?

The abstract may well be the first contact that the (potential) reader has with the subject. It should present the subject matter and argument in a straightforward manner, but should also contain sufficient information to indicate the required level of background knowledge required in order that the content may be comprehended and will be informative, either for the general public or the specialist.

Article: main text

Although an article will not contain a table of contents, subheadings add clarity to the structure. One level of subheadings, occasionally two, should be sufficient. The first section, *Introduction*, should contain a comprehensive account of the content, the hypothesis to be tested and the methods used in the analysis. The nature and source of the data should be sufficiently described. Naturally, the content of this section will depend on the nature of the subject to be treated, but all too often I read articles which assume that the reader is already familiar with the content and where the introduction offers little enlightenment on the subject to be discussed.

The *Summary and conclusions* are the vital ingredient. Even if the argument in the main text has been difficult to follow, the summary and conclusions should clarify the results of the discussion. It may be that the argument has been difficult to follow, but this final section should serve to clarify the preceding discussion enabling the article to be re-read, if necessary, with a better understanding.

Books

If your book is to be printed by a publishing house, then the publisher will take care of most of the layout. But even if this is a research report to be photocopied and distributed in just a few dozen copies, a professional approach to layout and structure will be appreciated by the reader. The following summarises the main elements of the layout although many are not necessarily obligatory. You may find more detailed information in a number of publications in the *How To* series on writing a dissertation, an assignment, a textbook, a report, and more.

Pagination

Pagination commences with the first right-hand page of the book (often the title page): all right-hand pages are therefore odd numbers. Each new section in the introductory section, known as the *prelims* normally begins on the next right-hand page.

The introductory sections – the *prelims* – are normally numbered in lower case Roman. (i, ii etc.). However, I notice that several publishers now use normal (Arabic) numerals throughout. As the page number is not given on the first page of each section in the prelims (nor on blank pages) – plus the fact that some sections may comprise only a single page – the first page on which the number actually appears might be viii or ix, or even higher (8 or 9 if Arabic numerals are used).

Page numbers of the main section may be placed top- or bottom-outside (i.e. towards the page edge), occasionally middle-bottom. Technical journals may commence numbering with each chapter: 1-1, 1-2 ... 2-1, 2-2 ... etc. Check with the publisher.

New chapters normally, but not necessarily, begin on the next right hand page. Where the publisher chooses to commence each new chapter on the next right-hand (odd-numbered) page, this will mean that the page number is not given on either the preceding page which is blank, nor on the first page of the ensuing chapter. Some publishers therefore number the first page of each chapter where this commences on a right-hand page.

The Prelims
The *prelims* contain general information about the book.

- First page of each section not numbered.
- Each section commences on next right-hand page (except where stated).

Dedication
- Often first right-hand page of the book. Text frequently italics: *To my wife ...*

Title page
- Title, author, position or title.
- Next right-hand page.

Table of Contents (TOC)
- Next right-hand page.

The TOC can be generated automatically by most word processors, and incorporate several levels of headings.

The following lists may appear on consecutive pages. They do not have to commence on a new right-hand page.

List of illustrations

List of tables

List of contributors
- Used where several authors are involved. May follow Preface (see below) or be included in the final section 'About the Authors'.

Preface (occasionally called Foreword)

Acknowledgements
- Advisors, consultants, typists, etc. Usually included at the end of the Preface but may comprise a separate section.
- Commences on right-hand page.

Abbreviations
- Abbreviations. The full text of a term should be given the first time an abbreviation is used in the main text. These include institutions, organisations, treaties and so forth. But we don't always store these in our head and a list is often useful. This list may also appear at the end of the book.

Glossary
- A glossary may be included here or at the end of the book. It contains a list of specialist terms which may need to be explained.

Notation
- Notation (mathematical symbols) may also be listed. Technical texts may employ many symbols, not necessarily used traditionally (there is only a limited number of Greek symbols). ζ and ψ may have very specific meanings in a specialised article.

MAIN BODY OF THE TEXT

Chapters
Each chapter should begin on the first available right-hand page, but may begin on the next new page even if this is a left-hand page. If the book is an anthology with different authors for each chapter, then a new chapter should begin on the next right-hand page. Chapter title pages are normally not numbered. A blank (left-hand) page at the end of a chapter is not numbered.

Bibliography
Usually commences on next page after final chapter. Where literature lists are included in each chapter these may follow on after the text or preferably commence on the next page.

Appendixes
Often numbered I, II, III etc, alternatively A, B, C...
The term 'annex' rather than 'appendix' is now used by some publishers.

Index
The index may be generated by the word processor (see Chapter 18), or manually using the Sort procedure when completed. This will necessitate (re)typing the keyword (first level entry) in front of second level entries where the latter are to be on a separate line and indented. These superfluous keywords are then deleted after sorting.

Entries in the Index, other than proper nounds, should not be capitalised.

About the author(s)
A short autobiographical note. Commences on next available page. The *List of Contributors* may also be included here. This section may also be located at the beginning of the prelims.

General

Article or book, presentation matters. But don't think that right-justifying your article will upgrade its quality. Most publishers want ordinary unjustified text and no hyphenation, except possibly in tables.

Check the spacing and indentation between paragraphs. A half or single-line space will not normally require indentation. You may set the paragraph structure using Format – Paragraph.

I prefer to format the bibliography or literature list. In MS Word I use Format – Paragraph; single line spacing with 6 pt spacing after; Special, Hanging, By 0.5. This provides:

McIntyre, A. (1993) 'Indonesia, Thailand and the Northeast Asian Connection', in R. Higgott, R. Leaver and J. Ravenhill (eds). *Pacific Economic Relations in the 1990s.* St. Leonards: Allen and Unwin. pp. 120–35.

Tuma, Nancy Brandon (1985) 'Effects of labor market structure on job-shift patterns', in James J. Heckman and Burton Singer (eds), *Longitudinal Analysis of Labor Market Data.* Cambridge: Cambridge University Press. pp. 327–63.

Numbers

Numbers generally

Originally there was a clear distinction between UK and US values of a billion and more.

The *original* UK scale relates to powers of a million:

A million = 10^6 = 1000^2 = 1 million.
A billion = 10^{12} = 1 million^3 = 1,000,000,000,000 = a million million.
A trillion = 10^{18} = 1 million^3 = a million billion (or a million million million).
A quadrillion is 10^{24} (UK).

France and Germany previously used the same scales as the UK, but these countries later adopted the US system. This is also gaining popularity in the UK, particularly in scientific journals. Confusion may be avoided by ignoring the terms million, billion and trillion by referring to powers of 10. (The power indicates the number of zeros following the 1.) The most commonly encountered term where confusion arises is 'billion' – also called a milliard – (a million million UK; a thousand million US). As stated, times are changing, but add a footnote if you think that there is any doubt.

Value	UK		US
million	10^6		10^6
billion	10^{12}		10^9 (UK = 1,000,000,000,000; US = 1,000,000,000)
trillion	10^{18}		10^{12}
quadrillion	10^{24}		10^{15}
quintillion	10^{30}		10^{18}
sextillion	10^{36}		10^{21}
septillion	10^{42}		10^{24}
octillion	10^{48}		10^{27}
nonillion	10^{54}		10^{30}
decillion	10^{60}		10^{33} (Originally, a billion billion UK)
milliard	10^9		(now obsolete) = (US) 1 billion
zillion	10^{00}	10^{00}	(an infinitely large number). *There are a zillion stars in the universe.*
squillion	$(10^{00})^{00}$		I am guessing at this formula, but it was the amount earned by David and Posh in a year (possibly two). Anyway, this was quoted in a leading UK Sunday newspaper. (My earnings were a squillionth of this.)

A 'nano' is a prefix denoting a billionth part or 10^{-9}, e.g. a nanogram

By the way, a google is 1 followed by 100 zeros:

1,000,000,000,000,000,000,000,000,000,000,000,000,000,000,000,000,000,
000,000,000,000,000,000,000,000,000,000,000,000,000,000,000.
(Actually, that was 99 zeros. Just multiply by ten.)

The abbreviation for a million can be confusing. Personally, I previously used mill. (which only seems to appear in the *Random House (US) Dictionary*. This is interesting as *mill* (no full point) signifies one-tenth of a US cent. The following is a summary of several dictionaries:

Dictionary

Cambridge International Dictionary of English	m or M
Chamber's Dictionary	m, m., M, M.
Collins Authors' and Printers' Dictionary	m.
Collins Dictionary	M or M.
New Oxford English Dictionary	m
Oxford Concise Dictionary	m.
Oxford Dictionary for Writers & Editors	m.
Oxford Dictionary of Abbreviations	m
The Longman Dictionary	m
The Penguin Dictionary	m
The American Heritage Dictionary	-
Encarta Dictionary	m
Random House Dictionary	mill.
Merriam Webster	-

The above table is based on material consulted for the first edition of this book, but I doubt whether many changes have been made since. The most common symbol appears to be m (for mille = 1000). Once again, the publishing house might have views on this, but as long as you are consistent your preference will probably be accepted. Note also that M is the Roman symbol for 1000.

For astronomical (lit.) values, light years or parsecs may be used. A parsec is the distance at which the mean radius of the earth's orbit subtends an angle of one second of arc, about 3.26 light-years. One light-year is the equivalent of 6,000,000,000,000 miles. Impressed? Well, try this. If the earth's orbit (the distance from the earth to the sun, some 93 million miles) was represented by a scale of one inch, the nearest star would be more than three miles distant. If the spaceship was steaming along the M1 it would never get there.

▶ Punctuating numbers. Commas are used to separate thousands, millions, etc.

✓ The population of the USA is 285,538,566.

Some publishers require a comma for all values above 999; others permit 9999 rather than 9,999. However, if the value is a round 100, the comma may be dropped: 2500 instead of 2,500. Numbers 10,000 and higher always use a comma: 10,643; 123,321.

Having said that, it appears to be increasingly the practice to omit commas, replacing these by a space: 3 456; 10 121; 103 666 000. This certainly provides a clearer picture in tables. But beware that your word processor may automatically break line at a space thereby splitting the number.[7] Further, spacing may appear excessive where right-margin justification is used. This can be fixed in Word (for example), by highlighting the numbers and then using Format – Font – Character spacing – Condensed – By ... and then setting to 0.7 or other appropriate value. If you have a lot of numbers to be condensed, make a macro. (See Chapter 18 MS Word. Some practical tips.)

One exception to the above 'rule' for commas or spacing is where a number is assigned to a product or commodity. For example:

✓ It is stated in Act no. 25466 that the fishing rights are protected according to international convention.

✓ The relevant stock part no. 423959 had been replaced by no. 2444324.

▶ Ordinal numbers. Text is normally used such as 'the eighth grade', 'the Fifth Regiment'. In technical texts numbers may be used: 'the 3rd quartile'. Do not use a period for ordinal numbers:

✗ The 2nd. level

▶ US English uses the symbol # to mean 'number', for example, Apartment #34.

▶ Continental countries generally indicate a negative value using what the English refer to as the division sign: $\div 2$ rather than -2. Whereas the English would write $8 \div 4 = 2$, the continental (and scientific) method would be $8/4 = 2$.

Decimals

▶ Strictly speaking the decimal point is typed as $1 \cdot 2$ as opposed to a full point: 1.2. But most publishers will accept the latter, even in technical articles.

For four-digit amounts the comma is usually omitted: $1,234.50 > $1234.50

▶ Whereas the UK and US custom is to use the full point as the decimal point, and the comma to separate thousands, the continental usage is the opposite:

US/UK: $12,345,678.90
Continental: NOK 12.345.678,90

At least one scientific journal has adopted the continental system. Check with the publisher.

---

7 Janet Calderbank has brought to my attention the 'non-breaking space'. Use Ctrl + Shift + Spacebar. This prevents a particular space from becoming a line break.

▶ Generally, do not commence a sentence with a decimal point:

✗ .37 kilograms of sodium was added to the mixture.

Rewrite commencing with a zero: 0.37 kg ..., or preferably rewrite the sentence:

✓ The amount of 0.37 kilograms was added to the mixture.

A leading zero should be used in the middle of a sentence, 0.37 rather than .37, as this gives clarity.

Some publishers will frown upon sentences commencing with a number, including a decimal number. However, it is my impression that this may be permissible in technical and medical journals particularly where a decimal figure relates to millions, billions, etc.:

2.6 million refugees arrived in just three weeks.

▶ Long decimals values are normally written without punctuation:

✓ Napier's constant, $e = (1 + 1/n)^n = 2.71821828459045$ ...

but grouping into fours or fives increases legibility:

✓ pi = 3.14159 26535 89793 23846 26433 83279 50288 41971 69399 37510 ...

Percentages

As a percentage is a specific amount, numbers are often preferred:

✓ Vacancies rose by 23%, unemployment fell by 7% in the period.

▶ Avoid commencing a sentence with a percentage given in numbers. It is preferable to rewrite it.

✗ 26% of total production was lost.
✓ Of the total amount produced, 26% was lost.

▶ The verb should correspond with the subject. In the above we were concerned with *an* amount. In the example below, the amount is considered as a plural.

Of all units imported, 26 per cent were damaged in transport.

▶ (Note US percent, UK per cent, but percentage.) Incidentally, use 'percentage' (and not 'per cent') in sentences such as The percentage increase in exports exceeded expectations. A recent trend noted in the UK press is to use the abbreviation pc. Example: Demand fell by 40 pc in October.

▶ The percentage symbol [%] is preferable with decimals: 2.1%, 6.785%, rather than 2.1 per cent, etc.

The European continental style normally places a space before the % character (e.g. 2.6 %). The sign comes immediately after the final number in UK and US texts.

Further, avoid the following:

✗ Six % were rejected. The %-age declined steadily in the period.

▶ Percentages can be confusing when used relatively as:

✗ Whereas unemployment was 6% in 1987, it had increased to 10% in 1990, a 60% increase in four years.

Not only are we referring to absolute and relative amounts in the same sentence, such statements also require to be qualified with a reference to the absolute numbers.

▶ For very small amounts it is convenient to use per mill (or per mil), or ‰ (= per thousand) rather than using a percentage, e.g.: The level was determined to be less than 2‰. If decimals are involved, it may be better to use text: The level was under 1.5 parts per thousand.

▶ 'Per mill' (per mil) – from the Latin 'per mille' – does not use a full point. Observe that 'per mill.' (with a full point) means per million.

▶ Consideration should be given to using proportions rather than percentages in certain circumstances. 'Almost 63% of customers lived within a mile of the shop.' Surely more informative to write 'About 5 of every 8 customers ...'

Fractions

▶ Generally, use the text form for fractions less than 1 unless a very precise amount is to be stated. Use numbers for values incorporating fractions which exceed 1 (e.g. 1½).

✓ The test tube was half full; the normal amount was at least five-eighths. Wastage was five-sixteenths.
✓ There were between 2¼ and 2½ lbs in each box. Normally there were approximately 3 lbs.

Abbreviations for mass etc. may be used when numbers are employed.

▶ That doyen of the English language, Alistair Cooke, said in one of his 'Letters from America' in the autumn of 2003 words to the effect that: 'The British Empire had between one third and one quarter of the world population at that time.' Sorry, Alistair, the general rule is from small to large – a quarter to a third; two-thirds to three-quarters; between 5 and 6.

Most word processors will automatically convert the quarters and halves: 1/2 becomes $^1/_2$, 3/4 becomes $^3/_4$, for example. Fractions in thirds eighths ($^2/_3$, $^5/_8$ etc.) will have to be inserted from the 'Symbols' table (using 'Insert'). To type 1½ (for example), a space has to follow the initial '1' before typing 1/2 to give 1 ½. If this is not done the result will be 11/2. The space must then be removed, giving 1½. For other fractions, rather than 3/5 for example, another method is to superscript the numerator and subscript the denominator giving $^3/_5$, $1^5/_9$ and so forth.

The automatic fraction feature may be disabled (or enabled) using Tools – AutoCorrect – AutoFormat as you type, and by clicking the appropriate box.

Converting fractions to decimal equivalents

To convert fractions to decimals, simply divide the numerator by the denominator: $^7/_{16}$ = 0.4375.

Converting decimals to fractions (proportions)

This conversion is more problematic than the other way round, but the occasion might arise where such a conversion serves a purpose. Occasionally it is more convenient to state a proportion (or fraction) rather than a decimal or a percentage. For example: 'About 2 in every 7 of those released were apprehended again within twelve months.' Much better than 'about 28 per cent'.

The table shows the corresponding numerator (N) and denominator (D) for all decimal values greater than or equal to 1/20 and less than or equal to 19/20. These are approximate in that certain inconvenient denominators are excluded (thirteenths, seventeenths, etc.).

Dec. N/D					
.04 1/20	.19 3/16	.35 7/20	.51 1/2	.67 2/3	.83 5/6
.05 1/20	.20 1/5	.36 4/11	.52 8/15	.68 11/16	.84 5/6
.06 1/16	.21 1/5	.37 3/8	.53 8/15	.69 11/16	.85 17/20
.07 1/15	.22 2/9	.38 3/8	.54 6/11	.70 7/10	.86 6/7
.08 1/12	.23 2/9	.39 2/5	.55 11/20	.71 5/7	.87 13/15
.09 1/11	.24 1/4	.40 2/5	.56 9/16	.72 5 /7	.88 7/8
.10 1/10	.25 1/4	.41 5/12	.57 4/7	.73 8/11	.89 8/9
.11 1/9	.26 4/15	.42 5/12	.58 7/12	.74 11/15	.90 9/10
.12 1/8	.27 3/11	.43 3/7	.59 7/12	.75 3/4	.91 10/11
.13 2/15	.28 2/7	.44 7/16	.60 4/5	.76 3/4	.92 11/12
.14 1/7	.29 2/7	.45 9/20	.61 4/5	.77 7/9	.93 14/15
.15 3/20	.30 3/10	.46 5/11	.62 5/8	.78 7/9	.94 15/16
.16 1/6	.31 5/16	.47 7/15	.63 5/8	.79 4/5	.95 19/20
.17 1/6	.32 5/16	.48 7/15	.64 7/11	.80 4/5	.96 19/20
.18 2/11	.33 1/3	.49 1/2	.65 13/20	.81 13/16	.97 19/20
	.34 1/3	.50 1/2	.66 2/3	.82 9/11	.98 19/20

Formulae, E-notation

Very often formulae in technical articles are difficult to read because of poor spacing. There are no rules here, but compare:

$e = 1 + 1 + (1/2!) + (1/3!) + (1/4!) + (1/5!) \ldots (1/n!)$

$Logit(p) = \beta_0 + \beta_1 PA + \beta_2 R + \beta_3 L + \beta_4 T$

with:

✓ $e = 1 + 1 + (1/2!) + (1/3!) + (1/4!) + (1/5!) \ldots (1/n!)$

✓ $Logit(p) = \beta_0 + \beta_1 PA + \beta_2 R + \beta_3 L + \beta_4 T$

▶ Another problem of clarity arises with exponentials – largely because writers either do not know what they represent, or assume everyone else does! The difficulty arises with output from statistical programs giving, for example:

The results of the analysis showed $a = 2E4$, while $b = 1.7E\text{-}3$

This E-notation should be converted to normal notation. $E2 = 10^2$; $E\text{-}3 = 1/10^3$ etc.

In the above: $a = 2E4 = 2 \times 10^4 = 20000$ (or 2 followed by 4 zeros). (The '2' has been moved 4 places to the *left*). By the same argument, we move the decimal point the other way for $b = 1.7E\text{-}3$. That is, $b = 1.7 \times 10^{-3}$ or $1.7 \times 1/(10^3) = 0.0017$. (The '1' has been moved 3 places to the *right*.)

I recently read in a book about the Universe by Azimov: 'An ordinary galaxy will emit about ten thousand trillion trillion (10,000,000,000,000,000,000, 000,000,000) kilowatts of energy in the form of microwaves.' I would have been just as vague if he had said 10E27, but a little more impressed if he had written 10^{27}.

Proportions and ratios

Proportions are normally easily comprehended.

✓ One in five objected: one in ten abstained.

You may encounter '8 out of 10 voted'. Isn't it easier to say '4 out of 5'? There is no rule for using the lowest common denominator or even for using percentages. The context may be indicative of the best term to use.

The term 'share' is occasionally and mistakenly used for 'proportion'. The former is a portion or part and is a general term: Her share of the profits reflected her talent. *Random House* defines a proportion as 'a *comparative relation* between things or magnitudes as to size, quantity, number, etc.; ratio', (my italics). As this definition implies, a proportion may be expressed as a ratio (see below).

Do not mix proportions and percentages:

✗ Whereas two-fifths agreed, 27 per cent abstained.

Even worse is:

✗ Two-fifths were in favour, three elevenths abstained: the remainder opposed the resolution.

We are none the wiser about the majority who opposed, and don't think that I am joking. I have actually seen this. Even proportions more readily assimilated do not necessarily provide the whole picture:

Almost a half were opposed while more than two-fifths abstained.

The mind boggles at calculating the proportion who actually agreed in the latter example! In fact, it was probably about one ninth. Try converting these to proportions based on the same unit (here, ninths would probably suffice). Remember that some readers have difficulty with numbers above 100, proportions other than quarters, and percentages of any amount! Try explaining to someone the logic of the following: Output more than doubled, from 400 to 900 units – an increase of 125 per cent.

▶ It is sometimes a mistake to convert absolute numbers to a percentage unreservedly. Absolute values keep the volume in perspective:

Of the 355,000 tons produced, 49% were exported.

✓ Of the 355,000 tons produced, 175,000 (49%) were exported.

▶ Ratios are sometimes misunderstood. A ratio of one to three is given as 1:3. Note that this implies 'one in four'. ('The ratio of men to women was 1:3' meaning that of every four persons, three were women). Ratios should be expressed in numerals, not words. In consequence it is incorrect to say: There was a higher ratio of Africans on the committee. Here, 'proportion' should be used.

A scale is normally given in numbers, e.g. 1 to 10 or 1:10. Gradients are given as inclines such as 1 in 10 or, again 1:10, defined as the change in height divided by the distance travelled. Continental road signs often express this as a percentage. Confusing, as I know my car can manage a gradient of 1 in 5, but a 20% incline?

Monetary and financial units

It is immaterial whether one writes The budget exceeded 13 million USD, or The budget exceeded $13 million. However, with amounts under 10 units either: The budget was under $3 million, or The budget was under three million USD.

That brings us to the question: $3 million was budgeted, or $3 million were budgeted.

Instinctively, if the whole amount was budgeted for one purpose, then '$3 million was budgeted for defence'. If this amount was to be apportioned to several purposes, then '$3 million were budgeted for schools, hospitals and the police'. This is one of those grey areas where the more conservative would maintain that $3 million is a plural amount. See note under Plurals.

▶ The Euro symbol [€] is found on all modern keyboards and is available with Windows 98 and later. It is achieved using AltGr + E.

▶ In finance, the expression 'the market rose by 25 points' refers to decimal points, here, a quarter of one per cent.

Abbreviations for the main monetary units are given in Chapter 10.

Roman numerals

(See also section on Roman numerals)

Roman numerals are used for volumes (occasionally chapters):

✓ This is discussed in Paine, R., *Coast Lapp Society* vol. II.
✓ Described in Chapter III.

While Henry V is acceptable, the following is not. in the Vth chapter!

✗ A full description is given in the Vth chapter!

▶ Lower case Roman numbers are used for the introductory pages (prelims) in a book.

▶ Copyright date uses Roman numbers.

✓ © MCMLXXXIX

Page numbers

References are given as p. 5.

▶ The dash (–) and not the minus sign (-) is used to mean 'up to and including'. Most publishers use an unspaced dash. There should be a space after 'p.' or 'pp.'.

✗ pp. 26-28; pp.105–8.
✓ pp. 10–15.

▶ pp. 126–28 is an alternative to pp. 126–128. Most publishers prefer the full number, in any case for numbers less than 100; pp. 95–98 and not pp. 95–8.

Some publishers prefer the spaced dash: pp. 95 – 98.

Periods

It is a matter of choice as to whether one uses 1756–91 or 1756–1791. The latter is often easier to read and will result in consistency insofar as it is necessary to write 1788–1823, for example. The dashed date is suitable for dates of birth and death, but in other cases the preposition is correct.

✓ Mozart (1756–1791) wrote 41 symphonies.
✓ The dispute lasted from 1932 until 1939.
✓ Rationing lasted from 1945 to 1952.

A common mistake when referring to a period is to treat the dash as meaning 'until' or 'and':

✗ Rationing lasted from 1945–1952: Cheese was rationed between 1942 – 1950.

▶ A hyphen is used for numbers in periods: a twelve-day search was concluded; a three-day trial followed.

Digits or text?

▶ This is an area where each publishing company has its own rules, but as there are many exceptions these are no more than guidelines. We may also distinguish between general texts and scientific/technical texts. Numerical information in the latter is often more specific and precise and where numbers may be preferable to text. Another point to be considered is readability.

General texts

Numbers in the range 1 to 10 normally use text. Many publishers extend this 'rule' through to 99.

✓ The number of applications for the course was twenty-two: thirteen withdrew, five men and four women graduated.

Exceptions to the 'text rule' are dates, time, references to pages or chapters, etc., ages:

the 8-year old boy, *etc.*, but eight years old

A digit may precede 'million'. There is no rule here, but 5 is normally the lower limit.

✓ The city had almost one million inhabitants in 1980; twenty years later the population exceeded 5 million.

Also units of measurement and percentages:

✓ Two 6-inch planks. There was a 4% increase in turnover.

▶ Avoid commencing a sentence with decimals in general texts. This may be permitted in scientific texts:

✗ 3.15 grams were extracted.
✓ The amount extracted was 3.15 grams

▶ Periods normally use text.

✓ A five-hour exam, a two-day tour.
✗ A four-months posting abroad. (Use singular form, four-month.)

Combined text and digits are best avoided when this relates to the same subject:

✗ Of the 12 candidates who achieved top grades, eight were girls.
✓ Of the 12 candidates who achieved top grades, 8 were girls.

or:

✓ Eight of the twelve candidates achieving top grades were girls.

but:

✓ Of the 250 applicants, 8 were from the Baltic countries

Combined text and digits may clarify a situation:

✓ Four 15-year-old boys were involved.

Another useful guideline if we are uncertain is to use text for general amounts and numbers for more specific quantities:

✓ They arrived five and six at a time. He was born in the '30s and was now in his seventies.

The argument here is that 'five and six at a time' is general, but 'each packet contained either 5 or 6 grams of heroin' is precise. The '30s refers to a specific decade, but 'in his seventies' is a general statement. We could also write 'one in seven migrated' but the ratio of men to women was 1:3.

▶ Higher value numbers involving *round* hundreds, thousands etc. use text. Note also the short form (eleven hundred) for hundreds under 2000 (rather than one thousand one hundred or 1100).

   ✓ More than nineteen thousand cast their votes. Only eleven hundred votes separated the candidates.

   Units of the next lower order which are rounded may use text or figures:

   More than six thousand eight hundred voted *or* More than 6800 voted.

   The hyphen is used for the tens, e.g. one hundred and twenty-one. US English tends to drop 'and': One hundred twenty-one.

   In a title capitals may be used: The Twenty-First Day

   With the exception of the above, hyphens and commas are not used:

   ✗ six thousand, five hundred; six-thousand-five-hundred
   ✓ six thousand five hundred

▶ Numbers may be used for ranges even though the lowest value would normally be written as text:

   ✓ The numbers sold varied between 5 and 120 pairs per day.

▶ Dates *may* commence a sentence:

   ✓ 1975 was a particularly good year for Beaujolais. 17th May is the Norwegian national holiday.

Scientific texts

Scientific amounts, volume, measures, use numbers. This also applies to values less than 10. Decimals always use numbers.

Numbers should be used in connection with symbols: 212°, 5%, $10. This will, of course, apply to mathematical symbols such as $+$, $-$, $\pm$, $<$, $>$ or similar: -4, ± 6, < 30.

✔ 4 litres were required. 6.3 grams of tetramethylthiuram was added to the mixture. The temperature was then increased by 6º C precisely. The ratio was found to be 1:3.

▶ In scientific or technical texts units of measure are abbreviated, e.g. pct (not 'per cent').

✔ The sacks measured 2 m by 1.6 m and contained 256 lbs of grain. Purity was 99.3 pct.

If references to the units are more general, the units do not require to be abbreviated:

✔ The box was about five cubic feet and contained some ten kilograms.
✔ The consignment was about 150 kilograms short.

Units of measurement should be repeated for each item.

✔ The box was 10 feet by 12 feet. Temperatures ranged from 4º to 29º during the period.
✘ The box was 10 by 12 feet. Temperatures ranged from 4 – 29º during the period.

I have noted that an exception *may* be made for tables, i.e. rather than £0 – £9 etc, use:

£0 – 9
£10 – 19
£20 – 29 etc.

Note: 3-dimensional. 'Three-dimensional' may be used for general texts.

Some other points
▶ Text should normally be used at the beginning of a sentence. But occasionally, emphasis is made by commencing the text with a numerical quantity. Rewriting may diminish the impact (try it).

216 members voted for the resolution: just 3 voted against. 3875 patients had been waiting for a year.

The point will have been made in this section that clarity takes predominance over rules. Numbers should be illustrative and informative. But not a few readers are number-blind!

The school had two hundred and ten pupils. Thirty-three of these were from overseas: 4 were from four different Asian countries, 14 were from nine African countries, and 15 from eleven different European countries.

Can *you* remember any details from the previous paragraph? There is much to be said for listing the above:

> The school had two hundred pupils. Of these, thirty-three were from overseas countries as follows. (Numbers in parentheses show the number of countries.)
>
> Asia   4 (4)
> Africa   14 (9)
> Europe 15 (11).

Ranges

Ranges are often incorrectly defined. > 10 means 'greater than 10', i.e. 10.05, 10.1, 10.5 etc. and above, depending upon the interval used, but *excluding* 10.0. $> = 10$ (greater or equal to 10) will include 10.0 and above, although more conveniently given as a range such as 10.0–19.9. Tables must be precise, each category registering the smallest unit involved, here tenths.

Ideally, 0 should be written as 0.0 indicating that intervals are in tenths. The scale indicates precisely what measurements have been employed.

> 0.0–9.9
> 10.0–19.9
> 20.0–29.9
> etc.

The following is ambiguous and therefore wrong (even if decimal .0 is employed):

> 0–10
> 10–20
> 20–30
> etc.

Avoid 0–10; 11–20; 21–, etc. Keep the tens in the same groups: 0–9; 10–19; 20–, etc.

Technical articles however, may employ:

> 0–< 10
> 10–< 20
> etc.

Do not 'abbreviate' numbers in ranges:

> ✗ An increase in the range 800–900,000 was projected. [Worse: 8–900,000.]
> ✗ Salaries were now £10 – £12,000 p.a.
> ✓ An increase in the range 800,000–900,000 was projected. Salaries were now £10,000 to £12,000 p.a.

£10K to £12K p.a. Seems to be increasingly used in text, but my preference is to keep this for advertisements.

Note also: An increase of between a fifth and a quarter of a point was anticipated. (Here we go from the smaller to the larger.) Likewise we should write 'Between $^1/_4$ and $^1/_3$ ...'. Again, the issue of text or numbers arises. I would suggest clarity as the guideline.

Order in ranges or indexes should preferably go from low to high: The housewives were asked to rank the brands on a scale of 1 (awful – wouldn't even give it to my neighbour), to 5 (I'll put it on my Christmas wish list).

But the following is acceptable: The grades ranged from 5 (excellent) down to 1 (very poor). Avoid, if possible, 1 (excellent) to 5 (poor).

Other

The practice of using # for number is common in the US, but is rarely used (at present) in the UK. *He lives in Block 2, Apt. #5.* This sign should not be used as a noun or adjectival noun:

✗ Variable NOP = # of parents

As mentioned above, it is now quite common to see salaries quoted as 12K, seemingly an inheritance of the data era where K = 1000. In connection with the millennium year 2000, it was not uncommon to see this referred to as Y2K. Thank goodness it's a thousand years to the next time.

Ordinal values (first, second, third etc.) are frequently used to list points to be made. The adverbial forms (firstly, secondly, thirdly etc.) are more colloquial and should be used sparingly.

The apostrophe is not normally found in UK English in the following:

This year, Miss Jones will teach the under 8s.

'The under eights' is also acceptable. The under 8s may be encountered in the genitive form such as the under 8s' books are now available.

In a book from 1921 I found: Edward III.'s reign. The full point is certainly not necessary today: Edward III's reign.

Temperature does not have base zero. Therefore, it is not twice as hot when the temperature is 50° than when it is 25°. Further, although we will encounter this, it is incorrect to write 'The temperature fell by 15º' (using the degree symbol), the correct form being 'the temperature fell by 15 degrees'. (It can fall *to* 15°.)

Height and depth (physical features) are usually expressed in feet and inches in the UK. A recent trend is to use yards for depth. In December 2003 it was reported that the '*Beagle 2* had probably landed in a crater some 600 yards deep'. This was on Mars, however, and perhaps Martians employ yards for depth, something which we earthly mortals do not normally do.

▶ Dash or hyphen? The convention is not to use spaced dashes: Mozart (1765–91); See pp. 45–61. (Use the dash, not the minus sign.)

In tables I have seen: $10– 19; $20– 29, etc., (i.e. a space after the dash). Not advisable.

A hyphen is applied in 'a 5-hour course; a two-minute wash'. Hyphenated terms provide an exception to our rule of text for values under ten.

▶ Apostrophes are used for (1) possession: One's own company is best; (2) omission: Two's a crowd; but not for plurals: They came in ones and twos.

References to chapters in books use numbers, e.g. (See Chapters 1 and 21)

▶ Lesser – fewer.

Lesser, smaller and greater refer to size or importance; fewer and more refer to numbers

✓ It is less important today; no fewer than ten were present.

▶ It is sometimes convenient to consider how the 'quick reader' interprets information. Are we talking numbers, or referring to dates? Consider: The population fell from 2000 to 2002. Someone is not very good at maths. Better with: The population declined between 2000 and 2002 *or* The population declined in the period 2000 to 2002.

Commas, while not obligatory, can occasionally assist the quick reader: The rate increased from 2.5% p.a. in 1984 to 4% in 1995. A simple comma serves to distinguish: The rate increased from 2.5% p.a. in 1984, to 4% in 1995.

▶ Approximate amounts. Use text when referring to volume and similar.

✓ About two per cent of the mice were infected. Approximately half recovered.
✗ Ca. 2 per cent failed, ca. 50% passed.

▶ Do you reduce something by or with?

✗ The price was reduced with 15%. Student numbers fell with two hundred.

Seems obvious, but you wouldn't believe that this is a common mistake.

Negatives

One might have thought it obvious that 'neither' is followed by 'nor', but it is often overlooked that this also refers to 'not'.

✗ It is not possible to take a direct flight, or to travel by train to that destination.

Pages

The standard A4 page is 210 mm × 297 mm. The standard British A4 is $8^1/_4 × 11^3/_4$. Standard margins are 1.27 cm or 1″. Camera-ready copy may require mirror margins where the inside margins are wider to allow for binding.

Parentheses [( )]

See also Brackets, p. 31, Full point, p. 82.

Parentheses is the correct term for curved brackets: ( ). These are used in pairs. Note the position of the period.

✓ (An entire sentence has a single period inside.) Otherwise the final period is outside (as in this sentence).

Similarly, a final period is required here, even though a quotation has a final period, exclamation mark etc.

✓ The Tory leader repeated what he said earlier ('No pain, no gain!').

Parentheses have several uses:

Explanation

✓ Mr Logan told Mr Berrigan that his wife (Mrs Logan) was responsible.
✓ The committee arranged to meet again on the same day next week (Wednesday).

Clarification

▶ Parentheses may be useful in clarifying a point. When a hyphened prefix is involved there is no space following the closing parenthesis:

✓ A (semi-)conductor is used on the template.

▶ Punctuation signs may be placed inside or outside the closing parenthesis depending on the context:

✓ What was the expected increase (in government bonds)?
✓ The election was declared void (because the president lost?).

In preparing this manuscript I wrote 'Sample statistics are used for estimating the parameters of a population, often of unknown size'. This could be understood to mean that the parameters were of an unknown size. Parentheses proved better: '... parameters of a population (often of unknown size)', more so than '... parameters of a population the size of which might be unknown.'

If an *entire* sentence is within parentheses, the final full point is *within* the closing parenthesis:

✓ (He confirmed this later.)

– and with double closing parentheses:

✓ (It had been seen to be incorrect (Jones, 1994).)

– otherwise outside:

✓ She said she had (although later denied this).

Style

In addition to explanation and clarification, the use of parentheses can add to the style of your writing, reducing the need for commas, semicolons.

✓ The market was described as anticipatory (?) but not optimistic!
✓ The shares did rise (slightly) towards the end of dealing following rumours of a merger (later shown to be groundless).

The amount of text in parentheses should be considered. (Sometimes an entire sentence – or even two – is included within parentheses, but this gives the impression that the author is not certain whether to include it or not. Further, this may displace the closing parenthesis such that the reader loses track of where the opening parenthesis lay. This is, of course, a typical example.)

If a sentence ends with an exclamation or question mark within the closing parenthesis, a final full point is required, e.g. She received his card (he remembered!). But then ...

Parentheses in lists

Parenthesised numbers in lists can be appropriate where items are listed:

✓ The following three posts were to be appointed: (1) Chairman, (2) Secretary, (3) Accountant.

Numbers are preferable here, rather than (a), (b), etc., as three specific posts are mentioned.

▶ When used at the beginning of a line, it is a matter of taste whether single or paired parentheses are used for letters.

Several points were mentioned in the debate:

a) the state of the roads
b) alternative financing of the toll roads
c) the establishment of a new Inspectorate.

▶ The full point occurs only at the end of the final item on this list.

If items are contained the text, then rather than single parentheses a) and b), paired parentheses (a) provide more clarity and, (b) are easier for the reader to locate. Lower case letters and Roman numerals are often preferable: (a), (b), (c); (i), (ii), (iii) etc. However, listed items in a text (rather than in rows as above), can be more confusing than revealing:

✗ Twenty-six delegates from four countries attended: 1) The U.K. (12); 2) France (3); 3) Germany (5); and 4) Japan (6).

Why, indeed, bother to number the items at all?

Closing parentheses

Where an *entire* sentence is included in parentheses, the final period is included within the parentheses.

(Slaves also developed parallel 'submissive' personalities.)
(Slaves also developed parallel 'submissive' personalities (Elkins, 1963).)
Slaves also developed parallel 'submissive' personalities (Elkins, 1963).
Provision was made by the establishment of crèches (subsequently closed).

If an exclamation or question mark is included in final parentheses, a period is still required.

> He mumbled something about someone (the boys?).
> Did he mean that (about being out with 'the boys')? Or did he mean her ('Miss Stake'!)?

Other

Parentheses serve as a comma, or at least do not necessarily require separation by commas.

> ✓ He was (and I am satisfied that this is correct) an idealist who felt that ...
> ✗ He was, (and I am satisfied that this is correct), an idealist who felt that ...

Avoid unnecessary material in parentheses – you will annoy the quick reader and upset the slow one who may already be suffering from a complex.

> Frank Sinatra (the singer) was less than frank about his past; Beckham (married to Spice-girl 'Posh') certainly has a spicy history himself; and as for Michael J., his thriller yet awaits us ('Thriller' being his main claim to fame, hitherto).

Credit your readers with some intelligence.

Plurals

> 'The council were not interested; the committee was not interested at all. A global ethics was required.'

▶ Singular or plural, i.e. *was* or *were*? Not really a problem. Did you regard the council as a group of old so-and-so's who didn't have too much to say for themselves? Then they should be regarded as a unit or entity and be considered as singular! (The council was ...) But what if you had regarded them as a bunch of cantankerous individuals, each with a mind of his/her own? Well, o.k., they all reached the same agreement, but now you could well refer to them in the plural: 'The council were ... (they were ...). I did read 'Only one per cent state that they would vote for the change'. Fine, so long as we regard this one per cent as being a group of *individuals*.

In Chapter 22 covering further notes on style, I cite the following sentence: A majority of the firms has given their employees job autonomy. Again, 'a majority has', or 'a majority have'? Look at it like this: 'it has ...', or 'they have ...'. Because this is a number of separate actions carried out by individual firms on their own behalf, rather than a joint action determined in unison, I would go for 'they have ...'.

In a newspaper we might read: Every year 20 million cubic metres of gas is exported through this port. The writer is taking the standpoint that this is an entity and not twenty million separate packages. Strictly speaking we are referring to metres (in the plural) and should be treated as such. Occasionally an apparent plural form may be treated as singular: Russian politics is a subject much discussed today.

▶ Data. 'The data was analysed ...' (singular), or, 'the data were analysed ...' (plural). Data was originally and almost exclusively a plural term. Today, this has changed and 'data' is normally regarded as a collective noun, hence 'the data was analysed ...'. Exceptions are when data are (!) considered to be separate units as in The data were collected from a number of sources. Nevertheless we would normally say: The data was compiled over many years. Technical papers still tend to use the plural form.

▶ 'None' may be either singular or plural idiomatically, but 'none' means 'not one'. 'None of them says that it is a satisfactory contract' rather than 'None of them say that ...'

This also illustrates the point that an intervening phrase may displace the association between the subject and the verb: The impression was that the contents of the Act, in spite of the vociferous opposition of Labour members as well as that of a number of Liberals, was acceptable. (The *contents* ... *were* acceptable.)

Losing sight of the verb can result in syntactic disasters. The issue of pollution, which included such varied factors as run-off from farmyards, exhaust from diesel-driven vehicles, fumes from cattle pyres, were all secondary features of the foot-and-mouth epidemic. (The *issue* ... *was*.)

But even simple phrases can catch us out such as: student evaluation of the course ...'; students' evaluations ...; student evaluations ...; students' evaluation ...'. Any of these might apply, but do they all apply to the same thing?

▶ Plurals of abbreviations *may* employ a full point where the singular form uses a full point: ed. but eds and chs without a full point. However, there is no consistency in this among the standard dictionaries. Indeed, you will encounter eds. for 'editors'. We should mention here that you will also encounter ed. for 'edition', especially in US publications.

Apostrophe s

▶ Plural nouns can be a problem. There is a clear distinction between 'armament agreements' and 'armaments agreement'. The problem otherwise is often the apostrophe. Where the term is *descriptive* rather than *possessive*, no apostrophe should be used:

✗ Crisis' theory was the theme of the seminar.
✓ Crisis theory was the theme of the seminar.
✗ The armament's agreement was vetoed by France.
✓ The armaments agreement was vetoed by France.

The 'boy's tent' and 'the boys' tent' clearly relate to singular and plural respectively. The same applies to 'the lady's room' and 'the ladies' room'. But certain words ending in 's' require the apostrophe at the end, even though the term may be considered as singular:

The student of physics' opinion was that savings could be made; the student of economics' view was that this was a mistake.

Latin plurals

Those of us who are old enough remember the teacher's instructions: –us becomes –i in the plural. We were then asked to think of words where this would apply, and to raise our hands and enlighten the teacher: crocus – croci, radius – radii, omnibus – ? 'No, Taylor, that is not funny. But modernity has found its way into Latin. Yes, the plural of *abacus* is *abaci* (*Chambers Dictionary*), but thankfully *abacuses* is also acceptable in line with *croci* or *crocuses, radii* or *radiuses* and *styli* or *styluses*. My Latin fails me at this moment (as it has done for fifty years), but I do not recall the plural of *bonus* (a Latin word) as being *boni*. ('The staff were given summer and Christmas boni.' I don't think so.) The same applies to *apparatus* and where *Chambers* confirms the plural as *apparatuses*.

Generally, Latin words ending in –*us* may have the plural form –*uses*. The exceptions are words ending in –*eus*. These retain the –*i* plural: *nucleus* – *nuclei*; *aureus* (a Roman gold coin) – *aurei*. Not to be confused with the French (as if we would): *milieu*, the plural of which is *milieus* or *milieux*. My never-failing proof-reader points out that English–French dictionaries only give the latter.

Other

Some words can be treated as singular or plural. This applies to most collective nouns (government, committee etc.). There are other terms where the choice of verb form is more dependent upon the predicate. For example: Ethics is a subject which really interests me. But it is also acceptable to say: Ethics are the moral principles of write and wrong.[8]

---

8   It's about time you recognised my sense of humour.

Sometimes we are faced with two objects of the verb, one singular and one plural: What is the outlook and measures to be taken by the government? What are the prospects and the minister's policy? It may be better to rewrite: What is the outlook and what are the measures But this can become long-winded. We know what is meant and the simple way out is to fit the verb to the first-mentioned object.

We often think of 'a' something as singular, but this is not necessarily always so. A leading Sunday newspaper reported 'Belarus at a crossroads'. Probably correct, but I would have thought 'a crossroad' or 'the crossroads'. Nevertheless, *COD* clarifies the matter defining 'crossroads' as *an* intersection.

Other cases are also food for thought. Consider the following which I encountered:

> A semi-transparent orthography like the Norwegian, and the deep orthographies like the French and English, has few invitations in the script itself to integrate phonological accuracy with meaning.

We could have placed the phrase 'and the deep orthographies like the French and English' in parentheses. The result would be the same; it is a complementary phrase. One argument would thus be that the main subject is *a* semi-transparent orthography. We are considering each orthography individually. If these were to be considered jointly, then 'have few invitations' would be appropriate. But, if we change the text to read:

> A semi-transparent orthography such as the Norwegian, like the deep French and English orthography, has few invitations in the script itself to integrate phonological accuracy with meaning.

– then the singular is correct. This is indeed one area which needs careful thought and where rewriting should leave the reader in no doubt about the grammar.

▶ It was reported in the *Daily* and *Sunday Telegraphs* that ...

> I forgot to note the source of this, but my intuition is to avoid plurals with proper nouns: '... in the *Daily* and the *Sunday Telegraph*...'. Better still, of course: 'It was reported in both the *Daily Telegraph* and the *Sunday Telegraph* that ...'.

▶ Those words ending in *s* such as dynamics, statistics and (many) others – singular, or plural. By way of example the *Collins Cobuild* gives:

> Dynamics are forces which produce power or movement.
> Dynamics is the study of motion, energy and forces.

Generally, *studies* of forces ending *–ics* are singular (kinetics, acoustics etc.). 'Dynamics' is one of the few terms which takes on a slightly different meaning when used in the singular or the plural, as the above examples show. Another is 'acrobatics': in the singular this is the art of the acrobat, but in the plural means acrobatic performances.

▶ One grammatical conundrum I was faced with arose in a paper on 'the elite', some of whom held just one position as chairman of a board; others held the position of chairman on several boards. In three different places in the paper these were referred to as (i) chairman of the boards; (ii) chairmen of the board; (iii) chairmen of the boards. We can note that (ii) must be an error as a board will only have a single chairman. Likewise (iii) *could* mistakenly be interpreted as several boards each with more than one chairman. In the given context we had: 'Characteristic of the business elite is that they occupy several posts as chairman.' Further in the text we encountered: 'As chairman of the board he wielded some power.' 'As chairman of the boards of several companies his influence was considerable.' 'As chairmen of the boards of the leading companies in the district, they wielded more power than the local council.'

It is really a question of logic and expressing this clearly. But do credit your reader with the ability to interpret what you are saying even if nitpicking may result in questionable syntax. It may be that we are tempted to make the subject and the object both singular or plural. The error of this can be seen in the following which I encountered in a business report: A scrutiny of the companies' reports revealed discrepancies in the budgets – when what was meant was: A scrutiny of the company's reports revealed discrepancies.

▶ And while we are discussing plurals: Potato – plural potatoes: hero, pl. heroes.

Prefixes and Suffixes

See Chapter 13, Prefixes; Chapter 14, Suffixes

Prefixes

A prefix is an affix such as un-, anti, co-, etc. The following is a selection of the most commonly encountered prefixes and suffixes. A number of adjectives and adverbs may also be used as a prefix, under-, over-, etc., to form compound words. The main problem for the writer is to know when prefixed words should be hyphenated. Such hyphenation is referred to as 'hard hyphenation' in contrast to 'soft hyphenation' which occurs when the word processor divides a word in connection with wrap-around at the end of a line. The problem arises in that the spellchecker does not distinguish between a hard and a soft hyphen.

Prefixes

amphi – both/round (amphibious, amphitheatre)
anti – against
arch – chief (archbishop)
auto – self (autobiography)
bi – two (biennial)
circum – around (circumscribe)
contra – against (contradict)
de – separate (decompose); reversal (decontaminate)
demi – half (demigod)
dis – reversal (disconnect)
for – away/without (forgo
fore – in advance (forefront)
homo – alike (homogenous)
hyper – excessive (hyperactive)
il – not (illegal)
juxta – close (juxtaposition)
im – not (impossible)
in – not (incontrovertible)
mal – bad (malcontent)
meta – change (metamorphic)

mis – wrong (misdeed)
mono – one (monoplane)
multi – many (multitude)
over – beyond (overextend); excess (overspend)
per – through/by (perennial)
post – after (postpone)
pre – before (precede)
pro – forward/support (protagonist)
pseudo – false (pseudoclassicism)
re – back (retreat); repetition (reinstate)
retro – backward (retrograde)
semi – half (semitone)
sub – under (subterranean)
super – above (superintendent)
trans – across (transport)
tri – three (triangle)
ultra – beyond (ultrasonic)
un – reverse (undo)
under – lower (underneath)
uni – one (universal)
vice – in place of (viceroy)

An overview of prefixed words is given in Chapter 13.

Some generalisations can be made about the use of a hyphen:

1 Prefix ends with vowel; word commences with the *same* vowel. Normally hyphenated:

anti-imperialist, pre-engage, co-ordinate (or coordinate).

Normally applies to different vowels: pre-operative

The general exception is the prefix re- which is not normally hyphenated (e.g. redistribution), nor before a vowel (reassign, reinstate, reoccupy, reuse) except before 'e': e.g. re-elect. (US English does not hyphenate reentry.)

2 Prefix ends with vowel; word commences with consonant. Hyphenated.

anti-fade, anti-racism

3 Prefix ends with consonant; word commences with vowel. No general rule.

over-abundance, over-emotional, to overachieve, overindulgent

4 Prefix ends with consonant; word commences with consonant. No general rule, but verbs often conjoined, adjectives and nouns hyphenated.

overhear, underbid, over-sexed, under-jaw

5   'Double-consonant rule'. If the final consonant of the prefix is the same as the first letter of the following word, a hyphen is *normally* used, but there are many exceptions to this rule.

under-represented, out-tray; overreact, midday, outthink

7   mis- does not use a hyphen: misuse, misspelled or misspelt (US misspelt).

8   A hyphen is used where a prefix is used before a word with a capital (i.e. a proper noun):

✓ pre-Christian.

9   A hyphen is used to separate a suffix where this would result in a triple character, or where the suffix commences with the same letter as the stem: She was childlike with a doll-like face; his brain was ball-like – round and rubbery! The off-fore leg.

▶ Most texts maintain that when a prefix such as anti-, pre-, pro-, etc. is applied, then all three elements should be hyphenated.

a) The Stone Age sites were designated as ancient monuments.
The boundaries of the pre-Stone-Age sites had yet to be determined.
b) The women priests' lobby adopted a new approach.
The anti-women priests' lobby was defeated when it came to the vote.

However, when a hyphenated term is affixed with 'non-', for example, the original hyphen *may* be dropped. Wages were originally gender-related. The new regulations stipulated that these were to be non-gender related.

The prefix co- is normally hyphenated in both UK and US English (e.g. co-chairman), but there is no consistency between dictionaries for words such as cooperation (co-operation) or coordinate (co-ordinate). Some recommend one version; others accept both.

Suffixes

The following suffixes are the most commonly encountered.

–able: capable of (predictable)
–age: place/state (marriage)
–ance/ancy: state/action
  (resemblance/buoyancy)
–asm: state/being (enthusiasm)
–dom: state/jurisdiction (martyrdom)
–eer: occupation (auctioneer)
–ence: state/action (independence)

–ent: existing (evident)
–ency: state/action (dependency)
–eous: pertaining to (advantageous)
–escence: act of becoming (convalescence)
–escent: becoming (obsolescent)
–fold: many (threefold)
–genous: yielding/generating (exogenous)
–hood: state/nature (childhood)

–ible: capable of being (possible)
–ile: pertaining to (bibliophile)
–ise: to make/do (idolise)
–ish: resembling (childish)
–ism: state/doctrine (egoism)
–ist: one who believes or does (atheist)
–ite: supporter (Israelite)
–ity: state of (accountability)
–ize. Mainly US for –ise.
–kind: sort (mankind)
–less: without (topless)
–like (resembling) child-like
–logy: study (geology)
–ly: in the manner of (quietly)
–ment: state of (endorsement)

–mony: state of (matrimony)
–most: superlative (uppermost)
–ness: state of (illness)
–ory: pertaining to (obligatory)
–ose: full of /possessing (verbose)
–ous: state of (perilous)
–pathy: state of feeling (sympathy)
–scope: aiding sight (telescope)
–ship: state (friendship)
–some: full of (loathsome)
–tion: state/action (continuation)
–tude: state of being (magnitude)
–ward: direction (eastward)
–wards: direction (homewards)
–wise: manner (clockwise)

▶ Prefixes and suffixes provide excellent opportunity for the imaginative. Words such as remakeable; productivist; maximalist; flexibilisation etc., but where '–ism' seems to offer the best opportunity. Here are some from a single chapter in a book I had to look at: clientelism, consumerism, majoritarianism, personalism, solidarism, inter-classism. There were probably others. Be colourful, yes, but do not dazzle our minds with gobbledegookisms.

When a word is affixed to another, this may be referred to as a compound word. These may be separate words, hyphenated or conjoined: even out; worn-out, hideout. The general rule is: nouns conjoined, adjectives hyphenated, verbs separate words.

Chapter 14 provides a comprehensive overview of words often encountered as suffixes.

Proofreading

Proofreading is the final stage in publication when the draft is checked to see that this complies with the house regulations relating to layout, fonts, spelling, hyphenation, running heads, indexing and so forth.

In 1976, The British Standards Institute published guidelines for *Copy preparation and proof correction* (BS 5261:2:1976). This has been widely reproduced and may be found for example, in *Writers' & Artists' Yearbook*. These guidelines were compiled at a time when typesetting was undertaken by the printer and thorough checking of the proof was required by the author. Text requiring correction had to be indicated by marks in both the text and in the margin. This 'double' indication was necessary as the printed proof was frequently single-spaced using a small font. The final array of text and marginal correction signs frequently resulted in many authors failing to correctly indicate the changes that the typesetter was required to make. Some sixty different proofing marks are recommended by BSI. Mathematical proof correction is covered in another BSI publication (BS 5261:3:1989). All-in-all there is much to be said for assigning proofreading to a professional. Few publishers require familiarity with BSI standards, and some have even adopted their own set of proof marks.

It is important to distinguish between proofreading and 'language washing'. Many authors make the mistake of assuming that the proof-reader will carefully read the text, checking for all minor mistakes of grammar, phrasing, syntax and logic. My first manuscript (not of this book) was returned with the terse comment: 'Too many exclamation marks!'. This was evidence enough to show that the proof-reader was indeed observant, but that it was not her job to correct my *style*. Spelling is normally checked to ensure standardisation of forms, as are obvious pitfalls such as placement of full points inside/outside inverted commas as necessary. But in general refinements of style are not taken into consideration.

Style, logic, syntax, and punctuation are the responsibility of the author. The structure of the article, chapter and even the paragraph, the logic of the argument and its presentation and development are the features which a referee will consider. Without his or her blessing, the publication won't even come in the vicinity of the proof-reader's desk. But the referee will not correct any errors or weaknesses in language, syntax or style. Indeed, he may have been irritated by poor punctuation. A referee is basically interested only in the content, but the fact that your manuscript comes back with a request to carry out a number of changes to the presentation of the argument and to resubmit may also imply that the argument was unclear due to poor punctuation as well as logic.

All authors are proud – and a few are arrogant. Normally the latter are well-established writers who can afford to be arrogant. But the rest of us are proud, sometimes too proud to go to a colleague and ask him to 'just glance through this when you get a moment, can you?'. But a second opinion is always valuable. Colleagues do not pronounce directly that the basic hypothesis is flawed, but their comments on the subject matter may well be heeded. Very handy if they are familiar with the 'Comments' feature on the word processor. It is amazing what one dares to comment upon using this feature as opposed to the more personal pencilled note in the margin. A cautionary note, however. Colleagues may be experts on the subject matter, but frequently miss those niceties of punctuation.

There is one stage between the 'collegial comment' and the day of judgement by a referee. This is 'language-washing'. This process encompasses all those tidying-up operations required prior to submission. A few authors are able to undertake this task themselves, but they have probably spent so long writing and rewriting the paper that they become blind to many slips of the keyboard, incorrect punctuation, placement of footnote numbers and so on. They also fail to register that a sentence which should have been cut and pasted was copied and pasted. Words such as percent may have also been spelt as per cent, the former being the US version although accepted by the UK spellchecker. Controlling for all these elements and more is the function of the 'language-washer'. There are now professionals who undertake these tasks and who, in addition, check many of the features undertaken by the proof-reader. Language-washers are not experts in all fields but are not inhibited from making comments such as 'this sentence apparently assumes that your target group is familiar with the Theory of Relativity'. My experience is that the author questions the reason for such a statement and may well choose to divide a sentence or rewrite a section in order to clarify a specific point. It is not uncommon for authors of technical or academic papers to forget their target group, and assume familiarity with the field when in fact this group may comprise undergraduates new to the study.

Question Marks [?]

Questions are never indiscreet; answers sometimes are. – Oscar Wilde.

Questions

The question mark is used in direct speech.

✓ How could he have known that he would nominated?

▶ In a quotation the question mark is placed within the inverted commas.

✓ She asked him directly: 'Are you available for re-election?'

No final full point is required.

✗ She asked him directly: 'Are you available for re-election?'.

In the following, the question mark relates to what is actually being asked. For example:

✓ How do you say in Lithuanian '*I love you*'?
✓ How do you ask in Lithuanian '*What time is the train?*'

Note that only one question mark is necessary, but two different punctuation marks may be used as required:

✓ Did I hear him exclaim 'damn it!'?

The question mark should be placed at the end of a list. It should not be repeated:

✓ How frequently do you participate: weekly, monthly, quarterly, never?
✗ How frequently do you participate? Weekly, monthly, quarterly, never?

▶ In indirect speech the question mark is not used:

✓ She enquired whether he was available for re-election.
✗ He asked her if she could make herself available?

In a cheap novel I read: 'Larry knocked on the door and said who the guests were and when was I coming down?! I replied ...'

I leave this punctuation to the reader's own judgement, but might add that the book was a bestseller.

▶ A final full point is required in the following:

✓ The publisher said the material was 'not suitable' for the journal (meaning it was nonsense?).

But not if the entire sentence is within parentheses:

✓ (What were the reasons for this?)

▶ Some sentences may permit the use of several question marks. This is really a question of style.

✓ Are you interested in re-election? – in leading the opposition? – or just going into retirement?

▶ If listed or bulleted, only a final question mark is required:

✓ Was he interested in standing for (a) Chairman, (b) Secretary, (c) Registrar?

▶ An apparent question which is essentially a comment or remark still requires a question mark.

'You don't really believe that, do you?', the lawyer muttered, not expecting any response.

But Shakespeare wasn't too fussy:

'To be, or not to be, that is the question.' (*Hamlet.* III. i. 56)

This should not be confused with the so-called tag question:

'I understand you have something to report, Mr Holmes?'

'An attack of brain-fever, for example?'

Note that these tag questions completely change the emphasis. Without the question mark, the interpretation would have been something else. But Arthur Conan Doyle was a master of punctuation: 'An accident, I presume!' No, this was no presumed accident. Conan Doyle's punctuation was: 'An accident, I presume?' How interesting. Presuming something does not normally imply a question. The presumption is made upon the answer. Not so Conan Doyle. We can also add that this renowned author deliberately poses a question as a statement: 'You have been in New Zealand.' –'Right again.'

▶ Probably the most common error is to confuse the direct and the indirect question. The latter requires no question mark. I recently read:

✗ In the fourth section, we ask to what extent and how we can define and measure the effectiveness of EU environmental policy?

This would be correct if we were to place the actual question in quotation marks: ..., we ask: 'to what extent ... ?'

▶ In speech, a question mark may be encountered even though, strictly speaking, a statement rather than a question is presented:

'I must be wrong in thinking that there was a signed contract?'

This draws attention to the fact that there was some doubt behind the statement and is quite permissible.

Can more than one question mark occur in a sentence? I read this in *Famous trials of Marshall Hall* by Edward Marjoribanks: 'Was there any means of avoiding the settlement? or, if not, did that make each will irrevocable?' Unusual, but effective. In a thesis I also read: Several questions had to be asked: Were the parents informed?, What was the child's response?, Did the results come up to expectation?

And another example – effective and unusual:

Police officer: 'He said he had only drunk eight, ma'am.'
Wife: 'Eight?! He has that for breakfast.'

Editorial questions

Questions concerning dates and names (for example) may be in parentheses.

✓ He was originally elected in March(?) 1933.
✓ The new member was called Dick W(illie?) Hampton.

Quotations

Sometimes it seems the only accomplishment my education ever bestowed on me, the ability to think in quotations. –Margaret Drabble, English novelist (1939–)

(See also Quotation marks, below)

Collins English Dictionary defines a quotation as 'a phrase or passage from a book, poem, play, etc., remembered and spoken, esp. to illustrate succinctly or support a point or an argument'.

▶ Short quotations are normally retained within the text. To illustrate the point one might quote 'anything that is written to please the author is worthless' (Blaise Pascal ca.1650). Note that the final full point comes after the author/date.

▶ As a general rule, longer quotations of three lines or more (called an 'extract') form their own paragraph and are normally indented throughout. (Some publishers keep the left margin flush with the main text.) They also use a point size smaller than the general text and employ single line spacing. Extracts are not placed in inverted commas unless these comprise the spoken word.

> In this text we are referring to quotations as a sentence or part thereof, contained within the text. These will employ quotation marks (inverted commas). A longer quotation – extract – will appear as an indented paragraph (as this). The final full point occurs not at the end of the ext but following the author reference which is given in parentheses (Taylor, 2001).

When reverting to the normal text, the first line of the subsequent paragraph is not indented even though initial lines of subsequent paragraphs may be indented.

Quotation Marks [" ",' ']

(See also Quotations)

Quotation marks are also referred to as inverted commas. Some texts also refer to these as 'quotes'. In the first section we are essentially concerned with the typographical application.

General usage – typing

As the name suggests, quotation marks encase the quoted word – that which

is spoken. The spoken word may be placed in either single ['] or double
[" "] quotation marks. UK publishers generally use single quotation marks as
the norm; US publishers use double quotation marks. Newspapers frequently
use the US form. That being said, I prefer the *spoken* word to be in double
quotation marks, and the exceptional use of a word or a special term to be
in single quotation marks:

> Don Herald, the American humorist, once quipped: " 'The more articulate, the
> less said' is an old Chinese proverb which I just made up myself" – What today
> is described as a typical 'Bushism'.

Strictly speaking quotation marks are known as single prime and double
prime quotation marks. It is important to be consistent in their use.
Sometimes double inverted commas are referred to as sixty-six ["] and ninety-
nine ["]. These are also known as 'smart quotes' as opposed to 'straight
quotes' [' and "]. The single and double quotes shown on the keyboard are
straight quotes and appear as such in sans serif typefaces (e.g. Arial). It is with
serif typefaces such as Times Roman that both smart quotes and straight
quotes are available. The latter have special uses (see below).

The primes '6' or '9' [' '] appear automatically, dependent whether the
inverted commas are preceded by a space or not. This means that typing the
phrase *it was a 'hit'/'miss' affair*, has produced a '9' instead of a '6' before
'miss'. This is clearly not what is required. Type this using a space following
the slash: The wedding was a 'hit'/ 'miss' affair. Now delete the space
following the slash giving: The wedding was a 'hit'/'miss' affair.

Early versions of WordPerfect had straight quotes as standard. Sometimes
conversion between two systems or over the Internet can result in straight
quotes. These may be corrected using: Replace ' with ' . This is not quite as
stupid as it may appear. The straight quote is the symbol on the keyboard; it
is also the symbol which will appear in the 'Find what' and 'Replace / with '
fields. But the result will be normal quotes as long as the current typeface is
a serif font. The same applies to the double apostrophe ''. Remember,
however, that straight quotes are needed for feet and inches: 5' 2". If you are
using Times Roman, then you will have to use Insert – Symbols for these (or
change the font to Arial, for example).

It may be useful to know that straight quotes (default) may be set to
automatically convert to smart quotes. Use Tools – AutoCorrect –
AutoFormat as you type and click the appropriate box.

Quotes within quotes

Where the main quotation employs double inverted commas, the quote
within the quote employs single inverted commas. (see Quotation marks)

✓ 'I told you,' Mary repeated, 'that the author's words were "success comes before excess", although "pride comes before a fool" might have been more appropriate.'

The first internal quote ("success ...") is the author's words: the second ('pride ...") is an unreferenced citation that Mary has used to make her point to the person she is addressing.

The final full point precedes the final quotation marks indicating the close of Mary's statement.

✓ 'I told you,' Mary repeated, 'that the author's words were "success is usually followed by excess".'

Note the comma after 'you' in the above and which is placed *inside the quotation mark*. Logically, a comma following the quotation mark ['I told you', Mary repeated] – would appear to be more logical, but this is one of those inexplicable points of English punctuation.

Nested quotes

Quotes within quotes within quotes! Yes, these can be found. Alternate the single and double inverted commas at each level.

✓ 'Well,' he said, 'I distinctly heard Tom say "The Director's exact words were 'Get out of here',", and I have no reason to doubt his word.'

Better to use italics:

✓ 'Well,' he said, 'I distinctly heard Tom say "The Director's exact words were '*Get out of here*',", and I have no reason to doubt his word.'

▶ A final full point is not included inside the quotes as well as at the end:

✗ I commented (in French): 'The Dijon train is late – again.'.

The single quotes (apostrophes)

▶ Inverted commas are often used to emphasise particular words or unusual use of words, or even 'constructed' words!

✓ Milton Berle once described a committee as a group of men who keep minutes and waste hours (and 'ours')!

✓ Her parties were large as was her physique. She was indeed the hostess with the 'mostest'.

▶ If an unusual term or word used in a manner contrary to normal understanding is placed within inverted commas, this punctuation is required only for the first time of use:

Blair's speech had an 'attractivity' about it. The essence of this attractivity lay not in the appeal of the presentation, but in the attraction of the content to the voter.

Some authors have a tendency to put many words and phrases in quotes apparently with the sole purpose of emphasising them. Here is an example from an article I once read:

✗ In sum, it appears that a 'model' which stresses the institutions' authority ...

The term 'model' is not being used metaphorically or in any unusual sense. Why, then, the inverted commas? The flow of the sentence is interrupted, leaving the reader to wonder exactly what the author really meant if he did not mean a 'model'!

▶ Book and article titles should be in italics. Chapter titles are given in single inverted commas.

✓ In Child's book, *The Essentials of Factor Analysis*, Thurstone's theory of simple structure is discussed in Chapter 4, 'The rotation of factors'.

'. or .' – Where to place the full point

The other question is the placement of the final prime – before or after the full point? Complete sentences concluding with the full point or other punctuation are contained within the quotes. This also applies where the spoken word is preceded by a colon.

She told them straight out: 'He's got a speech impediment; she's as deaf as a post.'
He said: 'The shares have recovered.'
'Yes,' she replied, 'I've had the chairs re-covered.'

Some time ago I received instructions from one publisher stating: Punctuation should follow the British style, e.g. 'quotes precede punctuation'. This was aimed at standardisation, but for the majority of publishers the following would be incorrect:

✗ He said: 'The shares have recovered'.

Where the spoken word is included within a sentence, the period comes at the end.

What he wanted to say was that 'the bonds were doing nicely'. But the last time he mentioned this she had replied that 'bondage was not her style'.

Incidentally, when terms such as 'he said' are inserted in a sentence, it is not necessary to use a period. Either of the following is correct:

'Alright, alright,' he said somewhat agitated, 'it was a misunderstanding.'[9]
'Alright, alright,' he said somewhat agitated. 'It was a misunderstanding.'

But if a question mark or exclamation mark is used, then a new sentence is required.

✗ 'Alright, alright!' he grunted, 'it was a misunderstanding.'
✓ 'Alright, alright!' he grunted. 'It was a misunderstanding.'
✗ 'Is that so?' he replied, 'I don't believe you.'
✓ 'Is that so?' he replied. 'I don't believe you.'

A period is not used here, only a comma.

✗ 'That is not correct.' he remarked.
✓ 'That is not correct,' he remarked.

Note the order of inverted commas when a term employing these concludes the spoken word.

He maintained he had been out with 'the boys'.
'What do you mean by 'the boys'?' she asked.
'You know who I mean by 'the boys',' he responded.
'I know who you mean by 'Miss Understanding'.'

As the above illustrates, we have to distinguish between the spoken word (requiring no final period or other punctuation mark), and a quotation (which does).

She wanted to know. 'Isn't that pure nonsense?'
He reflected briefly. Did she really mean that it was 'pure nonsense'?

If a punctuation mark is included in a *quotation*, then a final period will also be required:

✓ She asked herself: 'The boys?' She knew exactly what he meant by 'the boys!'.

▶ If an exclamation mark is included in a quotation which itself is within quotation marks, punctuate as follows:

9   It has been suggested that a comma should be used after 'said'. Modern practice would not demand this.

✓ He quoted them both: 'Russell stated: "Better Red than dead" but I am not certain who said "Better bed than Red!".'

▶ Where special words or terms are placed within inverted commas, the comma (if required) is always outside the inverted commas:

✓ The decision was described as 'intolerable', but was tolerated nevertheless.

A final comment. A number of publishers of the 1920s and 1930s put a space after opening quotation marks, and before the closing marks: ' I am downstairs,' he called out. Strange – and not unproblematic on the PC as a space before the closing quote mark will produce an opening quote (try it).

▶ I note that Penguin Books place a reference *after* the closing quotes, but *before* the final period:

He confirmed this. 'The figure was four times higher' (Evans, 1969, pp. 121 ff..)

Prime and double prime

As stated above, primes ('... and "...) as given on the keyboard will appear as smart quotes ('... and "...) in serif typefaces, but straight quotes in non-serifed typefaces. The modern word processor will also convert straight to smart quotes (or vice versa) if a typeface is changed for a document or passage. However, we may have to control for these as primes are required in certain cases. Note also italics for feet ['] and inches ["].

✓ The box was exactly 4' 2" wide. (Four feet, two inches.)
✓ North Cape is located at N 71° 7' 59". (North, seventy-one degrees, seven minutes and fifty-nine seconds.)
✓ The cyclist reached the mile mark in 1' 24.18". (One minute, 24.18 seconds.)

When using serif typefaces (Times Roman for example), the 'straight quotes' ['"] – here used to denote measurement – will have to be inserted using the 'Insert – Symbols' feature. If you are using a lot of primes and a serif typeface, you may want to make a macro for these. See Chapter 18, Word – Some useful tips).

Other

▶ Quotation marks are not required in a discourse, or account of court proceedings, etc. The spoken word is assumed:

Q: You were asleep? I thought you said that you suffered from insomnia.
A: Yes, I used to until ...
Q: Until what?

A: Until my wife bestowed on me a night-hood.

Q: And that's what gave you the blackout I suppose.

▶ It is not necessary to use quotation marks when the spoken word is being quoted rather than cited as direct speech:

✓ The psychiatrist asked a number of questions. How did it occur? What was the relationship between the parents? Did they quarrel frequently?

▶ One common mistake is to enclose text other than the spoken word in quotation marks. The examples assume the speaker is referring to himself.

✗ He confirmed to the court that 'he had been out with friends'.

The actual words were 'I have (had) been out with friends'. It is quite probable that wrong placement of the inverted commas resulted in a change of tense. The correct punctuation is:

✓ He confirmed to the court that he 'had been out with friends.'

References

References to authors' works in the text, literary sources, further reading and references are important elements in your book or paper. There are a number of rules and standards for references within the body of the text, and in the literature list. These are dealt with comprehensively in Chapter 4.

Roman Numerals

Upper case should be used for chapters. (e.g. Chapter VIII). Lower case is used for the prelims pages (i, ii, iii, iv, etc.). It is unusual to find values over 100 in lower case (c = 100; CC = 200).

i	I	1
v	V	5
x	X	10
l	L	50
c	C	100
	D	500
	M	1000

In principle, symbols commence with the highest value. The values for thousands, hundreds, tens and units are treated in sequence.

Up to three similar characters may be adjoined. (III = 3; CCC = 300) although IIII (4) can be observed on church clocks, and even CCCC (400), as opposed to CD, is occasionally encountered.

A symbol with a lower value 1, 10, 100, 1000 etc. may be placed before the next higher value indicating that this lower value is to be subtracted, IV = 4, IX = 9; XC = 90. XCIV = 94. XCIX = 99 (and not IC. IX is an exception to the 'next higher value' rule). There are nevertheless different ways of writing certain numbers, and even the Romans weren't too strict about the method used (see below).

A bar may be found over the character increasing the value by 1000. $\overline{\text{D}}$ would be 500,000.

Finally, when listing Roman numbers, they are *right* justified.

Most writers will be concerned with numbering the prelims, so we may summarise:

i	1	vi	6	xi	11	xvi	16
ii	2	vii	7	xii	12	xvii	17
iii	3	viii	8	xiii	13	xviii	18
iv	4	ix	9	xiv	14	xix	19
v	5	x	10	xv	15	xx	20

Sans serif typefaces may not produce Roman numbers satisfactorily, e.g. III rather than III.

The full point, formerly used, is now rarely encountered in the possessive form: Edward VIII.'s abdication (with or without period).

Having explained all this I have just discovered (by chance) that Roman numbers may be obtained in Excel using the ROMAN function. This is useful in that it shows the available options. The more complex the number, the more abbreviated versions available.

1900	MCM			
1950	MCML	MLM		
1990	MCMXC	MLMXL	MXM	
1995	MCMXCV	MLMVL	MXMV	MVM
1999	MCMXCIX	MLMVLIV	MXMIX	MVMIV	MIM

The Excel ROMAN function only converts from Arabic to Roman numerals, not vice versa.

Semicolon [;]

See also Colon, p. 43

In many foreign languages, the semicolon is seldom encountered. It has a more specific role in English and is frequently used to combine two sentences which are closely related, or to divide a long sentence where the contents comprise a sequence or list.

Dividing sentences

If many commas appear in a long sentence, a semicolon may be introduced at an appropriate place, particularly if this is preferable to rewriting as two or more sentences. In general only one semicolon should be used within the sentence for this purpose.

✓ There were two views. The government emphasised the importance of monetary policy as an essential element in reviving the economy which, according to virtually all indicators, was now at the low-point of a depression; but the advisory committee – comprised of government-appointed economists – disagreed, and pointed out the need to introduce measures which, in the short term, would reduce unemployment as a first step on the road to recovery.

The semicolon can be used to clarify the different elements in a sentence:

✓ The distribution of appointments was as follows: Sociology, two new lecturers – one of whom was to be a woman; Philosophy, a research assistant – provided that funds were made available for the new project; and two secretaries to the Faculty of Arts.

Lists

The semicolon is used to separate items in a list which contain one or more commas:

✓ The following cities had applied to hold the International Bricklayers Championship for 2008: London, U.K.; Paris, France; Oslo, Norway; Tirana, Albania.

A semicolon may be used in a sequence:

✓ Two maids a-milking; three French hens; four turtle-doves. Two maids, fine: three chickens?

Clauses

The semicolon is used between independent clauses joined by however, indeed or nevertheless, where an association remains. Note that the clause also comprises a complete sentence. This requirement does not apply to the colon.

✓ The government attached importance to monetary policy; however, this remained secondary to issues of employment.
✓ He was acquitted of the charge; nevertheless, the public remained sceptical.

Similarly, the semicolon is used in dividing complementary clauses, particularly where these are sequential or explanatory:

✓ The Opposition supported the Government in the debate; the bill was nevertheless defeated by backbenchers of all parties.

✓ Look before you leap; he who hesitates is lost.

✓ 'I will not say that women have no character; rather, they have a new one every day.' (Heine, 1797–1856)

The semicolon may also replace a comma where more emphasis is required, but where a period could have a disjointing effect:

✓ The documents were missing; yet the safe was still locked.

Expressions

The semicolon may be used between two independent clauses in a spoken sentence interrupted by an expression:

✓ 'What we need is a monetary policy,' the Minister emphasised; 'there is no alternative.'

It may be considered that a full point should follow 'emphasised'. Nevertheless, the words spoken suggest that the basis is a divided sentence: 'What we need is a monetary policy; there is no alternative.' The semicolon contributes to the flow of the text.

Sentence Connectors

Style (or lack of it) is often manifested by repeated phrases, particularly sentence connectors. It is surprising how many times some authors use 'however' when other connectors or adverbs will add a little variety. Consider using some of the alternatives given below. Sentence connectors, where indicated, are defined as such in *Collins Dictionary*, but many adverbs, conjunctions and phrases may also serve as connectors. Avoid colloquialisms such as 'anyway' and 'anyhow', the latter being an adverb but often used as a sentence connector. Other colloquialisms are 'at any rate', 'in any case'. The latter, being more precise in meaning, is acceptable. There are a number of colloquial phrases such as 'among other things' which are vague and should be used with discretion.

While sentence connectors can assist the flow of the text, consider the following: 'In addition, however, to the other elements we also found ...', or even 'In addition to the other elements, however, we also found ...'. The sentence connector 'however' is no longer a connector. In fact, what is its purpose? Nevertheless, consider the following as aids to style:

accordingly	Adverb
although	Conjunction
but	Adverb. Sentence connector. (Also preposition. Verb transitive when used to present an objection (But for that) See *Chambers Dictionary* for examples.
by contrast	Connecting phrase
by way of illustration	Connecting phrase
consequently	Adverb
consequentially	Adverb
despite (that)	Prepositional phrase
even so, if	(= nevertheless. Adverb)
for example	Connecting phrase
further	Adverb
furthermore	Adverb
hence	Adverb. Sentence connector. (But avoid 'hence also'.)
however	Adverb. Sentence connector
howsoever	Adverb. Sentence connector
in spite of (that)	Connecting phrase
likewise	Adverb
meanwhile	Adverb.
more so	[Note: two words]
moreover	Adverb. Sentence connector
nevertheless	Adverb. Sentence connector
nonetheless	Adverb. Sentence connector
notwithstanding	Preposition, adverb
on the contrary	Connecting phrase
on the other hand	Connecting phrase
otherwise	Conjunction. Adverb. Sentence connector
regardless	Adverb. Sentence connector
still	Adverb. Sentence connector
thereby	Adverb. Sentence connector
therefore	Adverb. Sentence connector
though	Conjunction. Adverb. Sentence connector. ('Although' may be preferable)
thus	Adverb. Sentence connector
yet	Conjunction Adverb. Sentence connector

There are, of course, many others. I would avoid the more colloquial of these. 'Whatever,...' – sounds like you didn't really know what point you were trying to make in the previous sentence. But even this may be better than a monotonous 'However...'.

Slash/Backslash [/,\]

Forward slash

The forward (or oblique) slash [/] is used to separate alternatives.

✓ The Chairman and/or The Secretary will be present during the counting of votes.

The forward slash can also mean 'and/or' (both):

✓ New factory opening. Skilled/unskilled workers needed.

But this could be ambiguous, meaning 'either'.

The tenure may be freehold/leasehold by agreement.

Consideration should be given to rewriting the text when such ambiguities may arise.

The forward slash may also mean just 'or':

✓ The name of the winner be announced at 12.30 p.m. He/she will be formally installed on Monday.

Avoid using s/he for she/he.

The forward slash may also indicate 'and – also':

✓ The London/Birmingham/Liverpool train is diverted to Coventry/Stafford/Liverpool.

▶ The oblique slash also means 'per' as in 'per hour'. It should only be used in advertisements and lists in this form. Room to let: £50/week. Fresh cod $10/lb. In scientific articles we may encounter: Fat content 5.6g/100g.

It is also referred to as the solidus in dates: 10/12/58. Whilst the solidus may be used in, for example, 2003/4, this is preferably expressed as 2003–4. The latter clearly suggests the period 2003–2004 whereas the slash (or solidus) might be interpreted as 'or', or 'and'.

The solidus is also encountered in mathematics: $10/2 = 5$.

▶ Other uses include abbreviations such as c/o (care of), I/O (Input/Output).

A double slash is used in Internet addresses: http://jgtaylor.com

▶ Do not 'space' the dash:

✗ The Israel / Palestine border.

This example also illustrates the misuse of the forward slash. Where two words or items are to be linked the dash is more appropriate: The Israel–Palestine boundary; the private–public debate; the Peking–Shanghai train. (Observe that this is a dash and not a hyphen.) However, where it is perfectly clear that 'and' is implied, then avoid using the slash:

✓ Both national and international flights were affected.

✗ The licence covered only wines/beers, not spirits.

Backslash

▶ The backslash [\] is not frequently encountered but has become familiar to Internet surfers:

✓ Our Home Page: http://www.microflop.com\progs\help

Sorting

Sorting records, not only bibliographic material, can present some difficulties and may be an important part of the preparation of your manuscript. A description of a routine for sorting diverse records is given in Chapter 18.

Spelling

Spelling is no longer a major problem for many writers in that all major word processors include a spellchecker. We no longer have to struggle with *–able* or *–ible* and *-ability* or *–ibility*![10] Naturally, the fewer mistakes in your manuscript, the less time taken to correct it. Further, certain errors will not be discovered such as typing *further* for *farther,* or *farther* for *father,* and indeed, dropping the 'h' in *farther* may not be amusing reading in the Company's Annual Report! (This will not be detected by the spellchecker.) Unfortunate typing errors can occur with a number of words, either when a letter is dropped, changed or added. A common problem with the PC keyboard is that keys can 'stick', as I found out when checking an article I had translated about middle class women. Unfortunately, they came out as 'idle class women' (but were reinstated during proofreading!). I do not have to point out the necessity of checking the spelling of *public places*.

The first draft of this book contained a comprehensive guide to spelling where I tried to accumulate all the 'rules'. It did not take long to discover that exceptions to the rule outnumbered the norm in many instances. I was recently asked about the use of double 'll' in English. A colleague supplied the following guide:

> The 'l' is doubled in British English after a single unstressed vowel, e.g. travel, traveller, travelled, travelling (compare US English traveler, traveled, traveling). In both UK and US English, if the final syllable is stressed 'll' is mandatory, e.g. compel, compelled, compelling. In both

10 See Burt, Angela (2000) for some excellent tips on spelling and usage.

variants of English a single 'l' is used after a double vowel, e.g. fail, failed, failing.

I am sure that this is correct – but don't ask me to remember the rule for this. I'll continue to rely on my spellchecker!

Of course, the spellchecker cannot be relied upon for distinguishing between 'maybe' and 'may be'. Consider for example: 'Maybe he will arrive later. It may be that he took the bus instead.' Neither is the grammar checker much help here! Incidentally, the first is an adverb, the second 'may' an auxiliary verb.

For those intent on learning the rules, there are a great number of textbooks where several sections, if not an entire chapter, will enlighten the curious reader. See, for example, Swan (1991, §§568–579), and Phythian (1998, Ch. 9). Marion Field's book in the *How To* series, *Improving Your Spelling*, is a very readable text covering many aspects.

One source of inconsistency in UK/US spelling is *–ise/–ize*. A general rule used to be that UK English used *–ise* while US English used *–ize*. There were a few exceptions in both languages. Today, even the oh-so-conservative CUP has yielded and informs authors that 'In British style either *–ise* or *–ize* may be used, but one form should be used throughout. In American style *–ize* or *–yze* should be used'. *Chambers Dictionary* (1997 edn) gave both as alternatives, but in their 21st Century edition, a distinction is made between UK/US spellings. But as CUP indicates, times are changing, making consistency all the more important.

There are a few differences in US and UK grammar which may be of interest. These are discussed in Chapter 16.

Unrecognised words

Your spellchecker will probably react to a number of words that you consider to be o.k. There may be several reasons for this. Apart from the fact that you had actually misspelt the word, you may have invented a new word! Now this is not such an infringement of the rules as might be thought. Elsewhere in this text I have pointed out that new words may be encountered the whole time, and indeed, it is to be expected of a living language. Proofreaders frequently encounter new 'inventions'. As a proofreader I have learnt that it is unwise to pounce on every word which the spellchecker reacts to and to inform the author that 'this word does not exist'. The mere fact that you have just read it suggests that it *could* exist. Some words encountered in a recent article were 'bilateralist'. The full expression was 'the bilateralist Barents Sea regime' and referred to the agreement by which Norway and Russia regulated fish stocks in this ocean.

This is interesting as it is the suffix which appears unusual. But when we consider the use of the suffix, then it may be acceptable.

> -ist *suff.* 1.a. One that performs a specified action: lobbyist. ... 4. One that is characterized by a specified trait or quality: romanticist *–American Heritage Dictionary*

But what about *fishable*! This arose in the same article. Now, something capable of being fished, using rod, line, net or trawl, is precisely that, i.e. 'fishable' – capable of being fished. But in the context of this article, which was concerned with fish stocks and fishing agreements, the term was used to mean fish stocks that were economically exploitable. Almost any sea creature is capable of being fished, but whether they are 'fishable' in an economic sense depends upon the market conditions. (I have since heard this word on the BBC.) The suffix 'able' is defined in one dictionary:

> -able or -ible *suff.* 1. Susceptible, capable, or worthy of a specified action: *debatable.* 2. Inclined or given to a specified state or action: *changeable.* *–American Heritage Dictionary*

In other words, do not discount the unusual word. As a writer, you may feel that there is something appealing about the unusual. If you are in doubt, place it in inverted commas the first time you use it.

✓ To what extent capelin was 'fishable' was dependent upon market prices. It was certainly as fishable as herring at that time.

If you are coining a new expression, check that the prefix or suffix is appropriate. See Prefixes and suffixes. Finally, consult *The Oxford Dictionary of New Words* or *The New Oxford Dictionary of English*. These are rich sources of new material, the latter also being available on CD-ROM. See also Chapter 23 for useful Internet sites.

Foreign letters and symbols

Foreign words, where less familiar, employ italics. Absorption into the English language may have resulted in the italics and often the accents disappearing (although I have retained both here). Nevertheless, the correct spelling should be retained: *café* rather than *cafe,* and even *mêlée*. Retaining the original French can reflect your personal style. It is still possible to encounter an *hôtel* rather than a *hotel*. And we have all been to a *fête*, of course. Other original spellings are also endearing: *Aesop's Fables* should preferably be written as *Æsop's fables*. We can find *fetus* or *foetus* rather than the more correct *fœtus*. While the single word is not normally italicised, phrases such as *œufs en cocotte* (boiled eggs) should be italicised. Occasionally the diaeresis [¨] should be used in such words as *naïve*. While given in most dictionaries (including

US dictionaries), many writers overlook this. A diaeresis is defined as a mark placed over a vowel indicating a change in the quality of the vowel. We find this in the name of Emily Brontë, author of *Wuthering Heights*. Foreign characters and symbols are obligatory in proper names. A number of words employing foreign symbols have become archaic such as *cañon* (*canyon*).

If a long quotation from a foreign text is given, then the original punctuation marks should be retained. For example, quotations in French are often enclosed in guillemets [«....»]; exclamations and questions in Spanish are contained in pairs of question marks: *¿Qué?*

Foreign letters and symbols can be a headache for the writer. A summary of the keystrokes in WordPerfect and Word is given in Chapter 5.

Plurals

Your spellchecker will pick up many of the following, but it may be of interest to note the following words ending in *o* which become *–oes* in the plural. However, my proof-reader informs that some dictionaries also allow *–os*. *Collins* is more liberal here, for example.

The following lists are not comprehensive, but include some of the most commonly misspelt words in the plural (e.g. potato – potatoes). (Incidentally, my spellchecker reacts to 'misspelt'. The *COD* permits 'misspelt' or 'misspelled'.)

The following nouns end in –o in the singular The plurals (given) are irregular in so far as some may be either –os or –oes.

banjos or banjoes	embargoes	Negroes
bravadoes	flamingos or flamingoes	pedalos or pedaloes
bravoes (hired killer)	ghettos or ghettoes	politicos
buffalo or buffaloes	grottos or grottoes	potatoes
calamancoes	heroes	salvos or salvoes
calicoes	jingoes	tomatoes
dagos or dagoes	lavabos	tornados or tornadoes
desperados or	mangos or mangoes	torpedoes
desperadoes	manifestos	volcanos or volcanoes
dingos or dingoes	mosquitos or mosquitoes	whackos or whackoes
dodos or dodoes	mottos or mottoes	yobbos or yobboes
dominoes	mulattos or mullatoes	

The following nouns end in –y in the singular; –ies in the plural (plural given).

allies	eulogies	novelties
apothecaries	fifties	nudities
batteries	flies	nunneries
bodies	forties	pleasantries
bogies	friendlies	preliminaries
butterflies	guppies	probabilities
candies	halfpennies	sundries
cries	hostilities	supplies
dries	ladies	tries
effigies	mercies	twenties
eighties	monies	
empties	mysteries	

Note also taxis or taxies. I suppose it is natural to ask whether there are any words where the singular ends in *y* and the plural is *–ys*. Apart from a couple of abbreviations, *Emmy* (the award) and *poly* (polytechnic), I found the following: *jansky* (the strength of a radio wave), *storey* (as in building) with the plural *storeys* or *storys*, *trilby* (as in hat), and *zloty* (as in Polish banks and nowhere else).

Misspelt words

Spellcheckers do not recognise errors when the misspelt word comprises another word. For example, when proofreading some of the most common examples encountered are *fir – for*, *my – may*, and *form – from*. But also many three-letter words may be erroneously typed as a two-letter word and accepted by the spellchecker such as *to* for *two*.

Inversion of vowels is another source of such errors, for example, *lion* and *loin*. It could be noted that there are a number of words where adjacent letters on the keyboard can result in misspelt words. For example, the vowels *u, i, o* are located consecutively and may result in mistyping *fun* for *fin*, *firm* for *form*, etc. It is also possible to hit two keys virtually simultaneously giving *suit* for *sit*, *moist* for *most*, etc. Another error is to misplace the consonant in certain words, e.g. *bread* for *beard*.

I keep a note of those words which I have a habit of typing erroneously and take a final check of my manuscript. The following list covers those which I have discovered to be among the most common.

The following two letter words are accepted by the spellchecker, but the intention may well have been a three letter word. For example, *bi* might have been a mistype for *bib, bid, big, bim, bin, bio, bis, bit* or *biz* – all accepted by my spellchecker!

au	fu	me	to
bi	ha	mi	vi
ca	hi	mo	vu
co	ho	no	we
cu	ka	pa	xo
de	la	pi	ye
do	le	se	
ea	lo	so	

All of these are the stem of at least one, and often several three- (and four-) letter words. There is no quick remedy for checking these, but if you are writing an article on the great auk, then it may prove fruitful at the end to check for any typing errors *au* or even *uk*.

The following words are easily mistyped and, clearly, not detected by the spellchecker.

Intended	Mistyped	Intended	Mistyped	Intended	Mistyped	Intended	Mistyped
avid	avoid	fins	fine	mist	moist	sit	site
avoid	avid	first	fist	mist	most	sit	suit
beard	bread	foe	for	mist	must	site	sire
bread	beard	for	foe	most	mist	slat	salt
but	buy	form	from	most	most	tale	teal
buy	but	from	form	must	moist	tan	than
cerate	create	fun	fin	my	may	tat	that
calm	clam	gaol	goal	none	neon	teal	tale
clam	calm	goal	gaol	not	jot	tem	them
corp	crop	hale	heal	our	out	ten	then
dairy	diary	hat	that	out	our	that	hat
dale	deal	he	the	pale	peal	the	then/m
deal	dale	heal	hale	peal	pale	there	three
dependant/dent		is	us	pour	pout	thin	tin
diary	dairy	jot	not	pout	pour	three	there
eat	east	kick	lick	pref.	perf.	tin	ton
except	expect	lair	liar	relies	replies	ton	tin
expect	except	lair	lair	replies	relies	tow	two
fair	fiar	lick	kick	sail	sial	two	tow
fiar	fair	lion	loin	sale	seal	us	is
field	filed	loin	lion	seal	sale	vale	veal
fin	fun	mat	may	sial	sail	veal	vale
fine	fins	may	mat	salt	slat	with	wit

In addition to the above we have those irritating phrases 'not able' so easily mistyped as notable and 'not every' which emerges as 'not very'. Not much to do here except to read every word in the manuscript very carefully.

What used to be the standard pitfalls are less of a problem today as the spellchecker will trap many. Oh, those painful homework assignments we longed to avoid, learning lists of words ending in *–able* and *–ible*. Having finally mastered those we were given *–ant* and *–ent*. The pitfalls are still there but the pits are not as deep. So how many words are there which may be spelt with either suffix? My electronic dictionary and a sorting routine found the following. With the exception of certain words ending with *–ant* or *–ent* these are all alternative spellings. Nevertheless the Word spellchecker still reacted to some. *These are shown in italics.* What is interesting is that neither version of a few words is found in the Word dictionary. A few variations mean quite different things, *distant* (far away) and *distent* (swollen), for instance.

–able, –ible

ascendable	ascendible	impassable	*impassible*
avertable	*avertible*	*intenable*	*intenible*
classable	*classible*	*inventable*	inventible
collapsable	collapsible	preventable	*preventible*
constructable	constructible	*rejectable*	*rejectible*
descendable	descendible	transmittable	transmittible
discussable	discussible	*unascendable*	*unascendible*
gullable	gullible	unavertable	unavertible
ignitable	*ignitible*	undescendable	undescendible
impartable	impartible	undiscussable	undiscussible

–ance, –ence

repellance	repellence
valance	valence

–ancy, –ency

repellancy	*repellency*

–ant, –ent

ascendant	ascendent	*inexistant*	inexistent
co-dependant	co-dependent	pendant	pendent
confidant	confident	*pretendant*	*pretendent*
currant	current	propellant	*propellent*
dependant	dependent	recant	recent
descant	descent	*repallant*	repellent
distant	*distent*	talant	talent
extant	extent	vant	vent

–ice, –ise

advice	advise
device	devise

In UK English *practice* is a noun; *practise* is a verb. In US English *practice* is used for both although *practise* is also used as a verb.

–ise, –ize

Oh yes! UK vs. US. But actually not as simple as that. When that revolutionary program WordPerfect v.4.2 made its appearance in the mid-80s it provided the opportunity for spell-checking in several languages. It was as a labour of love that using the spellchecker I compiled a list of all *–ise* and *–ize* words in both UK and US English which could or should be spelt using either or both suffix forms. Naturally, many words fell into their geographical habitat, but whereas even *advertize* is still not listed in many of my dictionaries (including OUP publications), this form is in general use. But *readvertise* does not permit the *–ize* form (in UK English).

I had intended to use the list mentioned above in this publication, but a check soon revealed that many changes have taken place over the last ten years or so. Virtually every verb ending in *–ise may* employ *–ize*. It depends upon which dictionary you use: *Chambers* allows most; *Collins*, a large number; *Longmans* appears more reserved; the *OUP* is decidedly conservative. The list below shows those words where there is no choice: it is either *–ise* or *–ize*. Accordingly, the normal spelling, *franchise*, is not given: I would not really expect anyone to use *franchize*, but the possibility is there. However, *disenfranchise* uses only the *-ise* form (and is consequently listed). I also encountered some curiosities: *tranquilize, tranquillise* and *tranquillize*. How strange the single-l version only permits the *z* form. I suggest no preference for any of these versions, or indeed for *computerise* or *computerize*; this is just a list extracted from dictionaries. If the term is not found below, then the choice is yours although it might not be the choice of the spellchecker. But it may also be that the word does not exist in the spellchecker dictionary.

There are also a few nouns which may employ *s* or *z*, but beware, these may not be the same thing. Maize is a corn, of course, but a maise is a measure used historically for a quantity of herring.

The following words do not have alternative *–ise/-ize* spellings:

advise	comprise	hazardize	previse
aluminize	covetise	imparadise	readvertise
arise	disenfranchise	improvise	readvise
assize	disfranchise	incise	reappraise
bise	disthronize	maise	rearise
brandise	exercise	maize	rebaptize
brize	fortunize	malaise	supervise
camise	franchise	metalize	surmise
casualize	galliardise	overprize	surprise
catalogize	gallize	precognize	uprise
chastise	gourmandize	presurmise	

Other

In Chapter 2 I quoted Kingsley Amis on the snobbery of using 'x' in words such as 'connexion' instead of 'connection'. But writer beware. I don't think that many of us would write 'transfiction' for 'transfixion' or even misspell 'crucifixion', but reflexion is the scientific term even though your spellchecker may have a hiccup. Strangely, mine showed no reaction to 'praxis'.

Symbols

There are a wide number of symbols available in the modern word processor. These may be used for many purposes such as:

a) currencies   £ $ Pts € ¥ ¢
b) foreign letters   å ø æ ç
c) bullets   ● ○
d) typographical symbols: § ¶
e) mathematical signs etc.: $\sum \sqrt{} \approx {}^1/_3 \ {}^7/_8$
f) business symbols: © ® ™
g) Dingbats, a printer's symbol. Word has several defined as:
   i) Webdings, e.g.:   1 ♪ ℗
   ii) Wingdings, e.g.:   ☻ ✂ ✐

– and others. None of my dictionaries explain the difference between Webdings and Wingdings, but the term 'Dingbats' seems to cover all of these.

Formerly, footnotes and other references used a variety of typographic symbols. Conventionally, they appeared in the following order: *†‡ § ¶. The advent of the word processor seems to have made this historical, particularly as the ASCII values of these symbols produces another order. Avoid using the asterisk [*] as a bullet as it is normally superscripted (or raised a half-line).

Tenses

▶ A common error is to mix tenses in the same sentence.

✗ Even though the resolution is now approved, it had been subject to long debate.

This should read: 'Even though the issue has now been approved ....'

Care should also be given to changing tenses in the same paragraph, although rules concerning mixed tenses are not so strict as previously. Of course, there may be good reason to change tense in mid-paragraph.

Time, Periods

Time

Use of the 24-hour clock is now common practice in those countries which previously used a.m. and p.m. The British originally regarded the 24-hour clock as 'continental' and something to be shunned. The 24-hour clock has made certain inroads in recent years in the U.K., probably because of the influx of cheap Swiss watches whose dial showed both 12- and 24-hour times. The colonies and the USA (not a colony, I hasten to add, rather the reverse), still appear to hold on to the 12-hour system.

The 24-hour clock should preferably use the full point: 08.45, 19.50 rather than 0845, 1950, although the latter is common in timetables.

The dash means 'to' and should not be used following 'between' or 'from':

  ✗ The museum is open between 14.00–17.30. The shop is open from 9.00–17.00.
  ✓ The museum is open between 14.00 and 17.30. The shop is open from 9.00 to 17.00.

A spaced dash is occasionally encountered. Personally, I think this form is clearer.

  Closed 12.30 – 14.00.

A definitive no-no is: Training took place from 17h. to 20h. (I actually read this).

▶ a.m. and p.m. may also be encountered as 'am' and 'pm. This should be avoided although may be accepted in brochures and timetables:

  Brochure: The coach departs Victoria at 9 am, arrival in Paris 2 pm.
  Article etc.: The meeting commenced at 11 a.m. and was concluded at 1.20 p.m.

Previously, capitals were encountered: A.M. and P.M. These always used full points. This format is seldom used today. (Note that AM = anno mundi, in the year of the world; PM = Prime Minister.)

▶ The term 'o'clock' is colloquial and should be reserved for informal literature. Either 4 o'clock, or four o'clock may be used although numbers seem to be the most common. The form 8.30 o'clock (of the clock) can be found in older literature. In any case, avoid writing half past eight o-clock.

▶ Whereas units should be attached to both values in technical articles (between 4 cm and 6 cm), it is perfectly acceptable to write: Between 8 and 9 o'clock.

▶ Times using the 24-hour clock may employ a colon: 12:45, 16:30, particularly where attached to dates: 10.12.58, 13:34.

▶ Per year or per annum? The former normally applies to a calendar year, from January 1 to December 31. 'Per annum' is mainly used in connection with finance and relates to any twelve-month period. For example, the tax year in the UK is the year ending April 5th.

▶ Note the difference between a few minutes later he returned and after a few minutes' conversation he returned. The apostrophe is frequently forgotten as in 6 hours' wait.

Periods

Periods have been mentioned elsewhere (see Dates). But it is worth reminding ourselves of some essential points such as the sin of writing: Between 1990–1995 ... By now we all know that we should write: In the period 1990–1995 ...

But I also encountered an interesting variant: These birds have been returning every year for the last seven to eight years. My impression is that as this is an annual event, it should be: ... for the last seven or eight years. Now if this was an on-going event, then we could write: I have been jogging for the last seven to eight years.

Typefaces and Fonts

A **typeface** is a specific type design such as TIMES ROMAN, ARIAL, COURIER NEW, *Palace Script*, etc. Modern word processors contain 150–200 different typefaces, but many of these, such as the script typefaces shown above, are only suitable for particular purposes such as brochures, guides, handbooks and similar. Some pleasing typefaces may be downloaded over the Internet. Note that certain of these may be a proprietary name requiring you to apply for the rights to use these.

Typeface style may be normal, **bold**, *italic*, or ***bold italic***; and underlined normal, **bold**, *italic*, or ***bold italic***. Typestyle may be small or large, indicated by the point size: This is 10-point; this is 14 point;

this is 18 point.[11]

---

11 Point size is technically defined as a multiple of a twelfth of a pica, theoretically one twelfth of an inch. (72 points = 1 inch). The higher the point value, the larger the typeface.

A font is a specific typeface, style and size; 'a complete assortment of types of one sort, with all that is necessary for printing in that kind of letter (Chambers). ***This font is Times Roman 14 pt bold italic.*** This is Century Gothic 12 pt font.

Frequently, the publishing house will require a serif typeface for the text such as Times Roman 12 pt. It has to be stated, however, that certain non-serif (proportional) fonts such as Arial or Gothic are attractive and easy to read, particularly in smaller point size. The latter are especially useful in figures and diagrams.

I find it irritating that Word provides autoselection for point sizes 12 pt, 14 pt, 16 pt etc., but not 13 or 15 pt. However, these may be selected by typing in the value in the Font Size box. It is also possible to select 12.5 pt. This, or 13 pt is an ideal default font size. Easy solution – make macros for your required point sizes.

Typefaces and PCs

PCs have annoying habits: for the man they have the temperament of the girl-friend – unpredictable! For the woman, they are like the man who forgets the anniversary – irritating! Transferring a file from one PC to another is something like sending a woman into a hat shop. Trimmings are removed and others added, and in the end it isn't quite the same hat! And neither might your file be. Certain typefaces have a frustrating habit of not being accepted or converted easily with the result that Greek symbols may appear instead of italic apostrophes, for example. You may find that you have to change the typeface, but try transferring as a bitmap (PDF-file) as a last resort. This can result in the file size increasing threefold or even more.

If you decide to change the basic typeface of a manuscript, or even a part of it, or to transfer it to another PC or word processor, then it is advisable to make an experimental file, especially where you are using a font not commonly encountered. Include in it a number of normal symbols. I use the following test file, initially written in Times Roman:

Here is a test text (..); [..]; {..}. Here are the symbols which have been used:
– (en-dash);
$ (dollar);
@ (alpha);
© (copyright);
£ (GBP);
€ (Euro).
check ".." and '..' (inverted commas).

Of course, insert any other symbols that you may have used. Now mark and copy this text, inserting it at the end of the file above. Mark this new section and convert to italics. Next, mark and copy the entire file and change to the proposed typeface. This file should now be 32 lines long. Save the file under any name. Close it, and then open it again and check the fonts. Of course, emailing it to yourself may reveal some problems, but it is the recipient's PC and system which are the key factors.

▶ Punctuation following a change in font in a sentence should be the same! The exclamation mark is also in italics. This principle also applies to the typeface! For example, the inverted commas 'must also be Arial font' and not Times Roman.

Underlining (Underscoring)

Generally, <u>underlining should be avoided</u>. It is an indication to the typesetter that the underlined text is to be printed in italics. This dates back to the days of the typewriter although the more 'modern' of these latter-day machines had interchangeable wheels and spherical attachments such as the IBM 'golf-ball' enabling italics to be typed. Some publishers still require that text to be italicised in the printed document is underlined in the manuscript.

▶ Underlining might be used where a phrase is already in italics in order to emphasise a particular word:

Caution: *It is <u>essential</u> to renumber the pages after editing.*

▶ There are a few limited uses for the underscored text, particularly in emphasising the initial letters of an acronym for example, UNESCO (<u>U</u>nited <u>N</u>ations <u>E</u>ducational, <u>S</u>cientific, and <u>C</u>ultural <u>O</u>rganization).[12]

▶ A line can be drawn across the page to 'underline' a section by entering three minus signs: and then < Enter >.

Similarly, typing three asterisks and < Enter > produces the following:

■ ■

There is a little quirk with these that they may be difficult to remove. If this is the case place the cursor at the end of the previous line and click twice on the box symbol on the Format menu at the top of the screen.

12 Acronym: a pronounceable name made up of a series of initial letters or parts of words.

4
Bibliographies, Literature Lists, References

The difference between literature and journalism is that journalism is unreadable and literature is unread. – Oscar Wilde (1856–1900). Irish dramatist and poet.

Bibliographies, Literature Lists

The terms 'bibliography', 'references' and 'literature list' are frequently used synonymously. They are normally used to refer to material consulted when writing the article, book, etc., i.e. the primary sources. A 'literature list' may refer to all material including further reading. Indeed, some student texts contain both a bibliography and literature list, the latter sometimes referred to as 'Further Reading'.

The are numerous variations in the presentation of bibliographic material. For example, references to a volume and page numbers might appear as any of the following, or combinations of the various elements:

Vol. 23, pp. 40–53.
vol. 23 p. 40 ff.
(23) 40–53.
23: 40–53.
XXIII: 40–53.

While there is a broad similarity between the individual publishing houses today, largely arising from the use of the PC, you will still find variations will nevertheless be encountered such as pp. 230 ff., and 230ff. (no space), pp. 40–43 and pp 40–53 (no period after pp). Vol. is not normally capitalised.

There are two main types of referencing systems: a) the author–date system, also known as the Harvard system; b) the Vancouver system, a citation-sequence system. The latter was particularly developed for biomedical journals where many references are to other journals. References appear in the order they are cited rather than alphabetically. This system is not discussed here. The former has become the normal style for many books and journals in the social and political sciences and the humanities.

The Harvard (author–date) system

There are three possible locations for bibliographic material:

1 the main body of the text. Typical entries in the text might be:

    (Wigginbotham 1940:3)

Less commonly:

    (Wigginbotham (1940, p.3)).

Of course, the full bibliographic information will be given in the bibliography at the end of the publication. It is worth mentioning here that *ibid.* and *op. cit.* should not be used for references in the *main text*. Further discussion of references in the main body of the text is given in section B.

It should be said here and now, and I repeat this caution later, that references should be comprehensive. Publisher's *Notes for authors* frequently insist on page numbers being given as in the above examples. Wigginbotham (1940) does not say much, except that you may have read part of the book.

2 Footnote references. These are often an alternative to the brief author-date reference in the main text, indicated by a footnote number.[1] These normally commence at 1 for each new chapter. The first time a reference is given it should comprise the full bibliographic information. Example:

    Wigginbotham, J. 1940. *What Chamberlain should have done with his piece of paper.* London, Notso Press. pp. 12–23.

Subsequent references to Wigginbotham (1940) in the footnotes may use op. cit or ibid. The advantage of the footnote reference is that it may be annotated. Clearly, the footnote reference number is less disruptive to the text than constant author–date information. The original footnote reference still needs be repeated in the bibliography, but without the page references. The fact that the footnote reference can be annotated leads us to the inherent risk in all footnotes, that of relegating to the footnote material which should be retained in the main text.

Occasionally, endnotes are used instead of footnotes. These will be numbered continuously throughout the book. Endnotes are generally inconvenient for the reader, and may well be overlooked – by the reader, and the author.

3 The main bibliography. This will occur at the end of the book although anthologies and article collections may have a bibliography at the end of each chapter. Whilst not obligatory, especially where full references have

---

1 This being an example.

been given in footnotes and accompanied by an author index, repetition of the complete bibliographic information at the end of the publication is clearly advantageous.

The following is based on the Harvard (author–date) system.

Basic principles

In the following I have suggest a norm for each type of publication in the reference list based on common usage. For convenience these are shown in boxes. The fact that I 'suggest a norm' immediately indicates that there are no hard-and-fast rules. The Harvard system permits some flexibility and this is reflected in the variety in detail which will be encountered. Some publishing houses have very strict rules which are required to be followed rigidly. Many seem to leave it to the whim of the author however, although will come down heavily on inconsistency. I am inclined to think that there is a degree of latitude today by publishing houses to allow for the fact that many writers now use a PC reference program. These programs frequently allow a choice of format.

Authors. In the main body of the text just the surname is used. 'Et al.' is used where there is more than one author: (Bogdin 1978; Smorgas et al. 1998). Some publishers require 'et al.' to be used for three or more authors, both names being given in the case of two authors. Medical journals often require all authors to be given in the references.

In the literature list, more detail is given although in general only initials are required: Jackman, W.T. Occasionally two authors with the same surname and initial may be encountered. In this instance to avoid confusion one may use Smith A(nne), for example.

Joint authors. Style usually: Nyman, S. and Ziderman, A. Some 'conservative' publishers reverse the second and subsequent authors: Fledghelem, G.C., P.S.Langley and A.D. Smith (1977)...

Date follows in parentheses, no comma after author names. Normally comma after closing parentheses of date (before title). Some publishers do not place the date in parentheses. In this instance the date is not normally followed by a comma or period. Dates originally used to be placed at the end of the reference. This is not practised today.

Titles of *books* italicised (but not journals). The italicised book title is capitalised.[2] A title of a paper is neither italicised nor capitalised if it is

---

2   Meaning that the first letters of nouns, verbs, adjectives and adverbs (but not prepositions) are capitalised.

unpublished (e.g. a thesis) and consequently not generally available through libraries.

The title of the *journal article* is neither italicised nor capitalised. It may be placed in single quotes. There are advantages in this and it is to be preferred.

Title followed by comma prior to *publisher information* (books), or journal title.

Page numbers are not given with the exception of reference to a chapter in a book. Bibliographic references are general. Specific references to a particular page in a book are given in the reference in the main body of the text or a footnote reference.

Clearly, there are many combinations of author–date styles. The following examples utilise the most common patterns.

Books

Little, R.J.A. and Rubin, D.B. (1987), *Statistical Analysis with Missing Data*, New York: Wiley.

or (first names):

Kalbflesch, John D. and Prentice, Ross L. 1980, *The Statistical Analysis of Failure Time Data*, New York: Wiley.

Notes:

Comma after *surname*; Period after initials but no space between initials. *Second author* name normally inverted as above. A few publishers use a comma before 'and': Little, R.J.A., and Rubin, D.B. This is not really necessary. A few publishers still use an old-fashioned style of only reversing the first author: Little, R.J.A., and D.B. Rubin ...

Very few publishers retain the authors' names in upper case (whole word), popular in the 1970s (as used by Penguin Books, for example). The Open University used boldface for authors as did Penguin for a period. Neither of these are necessary and seldom encountered today.

Many publishers prefer the full name in which case it is preferable to use semicolons between authors rather than commas, e.g. Goldstein, Richard; Anderson, Jennifer; Ash, Arlene ... and. If selected, use full names for *all* references, otherwise initials: Goldstein, R.; Anderson, J.; Ash, A. and ...

Date always given following author(s), or editor(s). Historically the date was given at the end. Sorting with the aid of the computer requires the date after the author(s). A few publishers put the date in parentheses as in the first example above.

Several publications by same author ... (1987a); ... (1987b) etc. Blank space normally used after date where date in parentheses, otherwise period, comma or colon.

Title in *italics*. Normally capitalised throughout (particularly US, e.g. *Transport Systems in Rural Communities*); occasionally just first word (more common in UK, e.g. *Transport systems in rural communities*).

Place. Publisher's main seat. Not London and New York (for example). Distinguish where necessary: Cambridge, MA.; Cambridge, UK. Place name followed by colon.

Publisher. Allen & Unwin; Thames and Hudson Ltd. Use the publisher's official title: and/&. A few publishers omit the place; others state the publisher then the place. e.g. Academic Press, London.

Previously, it was common to see the number of pages given at the end, e.g. 348 pp. This is rarely given today. On the other hand it seems to be a growing practice to give the ISBN reference.

Edition, if other than the first (where required to be given), is normally placed after the title:

Hays, W.L. (1998), *Statistics*, 4th edn. Chicago, IL: Holt, Rinehart & Winston.

Date refers to the edition date. A reprint of the original should state the original date of publication at the end:

Malthus, T.R. (1970), *An Essay on the Principles of Population,* Harmondsworth, Penguin. (First published in 1798).

The US abbreviation for edition is ed. (with a full point). However, the preferred abbreviation is edn (no full point) to distinguish this from ed. as the abbreviation for editor.

Journal Article

Wright, S. (1921), 'Correlations and causation', *Journal of Agricultural Research*, 20: 557–85.

Notes:

Date follows author(s). If date not placed in parentheses use period or comma. If placed in parentheses, a blank space is normal, although a comma is commonly found.

Title of article may be placed in single quotes (some publishers uses double quotes), non-capitalised, comma before journal.

Journal title in italics followed by comma, volume number, colon, space, pages (dash), e.g. pp 557–85. No space around dash. Use dash, not minus sign! Avoid, where possible, references of type 20: 557 ff. (for following pages).

Abbreviation: *Jour.* (Journal) acceptable abbreviation.

Volume and page number may use: vol. 20, pp. 557–85. (vol. not normally capitalised). space after pp. Page numbers may be shortened: 557–9; 557–85; 557–602.

Where a **volume** is issued quarterly (for example), use: 20(2), pp. 557–85. Do not repeat the year of publication (already given after the author), e.g. 1921, vol. 20(2) ...

Some journals have more than one series. Italicise the series as well: *Journal of the Royal Statistical Society, Series B,* 39: 1–38.

A number of publishers formerly placed the series number in boldface, e.g. **Professional Geographer, 33,** 302–10.; *Journal of the Royal Statistical Society,* **B,** 39: 1–38. I have not seen this for several years.

Anthology (Edited Anthology)

Devan, J. (ed.) (1994), *Southeast Asia Challenges of the Twenty-First Century.* Singapore: Institute of Southeast Asian Studies.

Notes:

ed. lower case, period, normally in parentheses. No following comma. If more than one editor use (eds) – no period; no comma after closing parenthesis before date. 'eds.' (with period will be occasionally encountered, but is incorrect).

Paper/Article/Chapter in Anthology

> McIntyre, A. (1993), Indonesia, Thailand and the Northeast Asian Connection, in R. Higgott, R. Leaver and J. Ravenhill (eds), *Pacific Economic Relations in the 1990s,* St. Leonards, Allen & Unwin, pp. 120–35.

Or with title in single quotes, but less frequently used than a decade ago:

> Tuma, Nancy Brandon (1985), 'Effects of labor market structure on job-shift patterns', in James J. Heckman and Burton Singer (eds), *Longitudinal Analysis of Labor Market Data, Cambridge: Cambridge University Press.* pp. 327–63.

Notes:

Date refers to anthology, not date of the original article.

Title. Capitalised. May be in single quotes (see also journal articles); followed by comma.

'In' occasionally preceded by period. [... patterns: In R. Higgott ...]

Anthology editors not inverted. Anthology title in italics, capitalised.

Place: (colon), Publisher. (period).

Pages preferably given. Avoid 327 ff. (following). Space after pp. Dash between numbers [327–63], not minus sign [327-62].

Occasionally a reference such as 'Chapter 6' may be given *instead* of page numbers but is not to be preferred.

Reprinted Journal Articles in Anthologies

An anthology may have been compiled from articles previously published. It is advisable to give the original source. Include the anthology as a separate entry.

> Ullman, Edward (1941) A Theory of Location for Cities. *The American Journal of Sociology*, 46: 653–63. Reprinted in Ambrose, Peter J. (1969), pp. 135–147.

[Reference is to:]

> Ambrose Peter J. (ed.) (1969) *Concepts in Geography, (2) Analytical Human Geography.* London, Longworth.

Alternatively, the latest source may be given together with original source, in a single reference.

> Ullman, Edward (1969) A Theory of Location for Cities, in Peter J. Ambrose (ed.) (1969) *Concepts in Geography, (2) Analytical Human Geography.* London, Longworth, pp. 135–147. (First published in *The American Journal of Sociology*, 1941, vol. 46.)

Notes:

If **page numbers** are given, the term 'vol.' (or 'Vol.') is not used. E.g. ... (First published in *The American Journal of Sociology*, 1941, pp. 63–79)

Volume in Series (Irregular)

> Parkinson M. (1986) *Decision making by Liverpool City Council: Setting the Rate, 1985–86,* The Conduct of Local Authority Business, Research Vol. 4, London, HMSO.

Notes:

The original source gave: Parkinson M. (1986) 'Decision making by Liverpool City Council: Setting the Rate, 1985-86', *The Conduct of Local Authority Business*, Research Vol. 4, London, HMSO.

Here are three elements – the publication title (Decision making ...), the Series title (The Conduct ...), and the Volume name (Research). Rather than the series title being the name of a publication, it is the name of a project and where publications, while being numbered, appear at irregular intervals. These are more akin to Working papers which, even though numbered, are published during a limited period.

Working Papers

This includes working papers, project reports, circulars, etc. appearing at *irregular* intervals. These may be numbered or unnumbered. Where these are generally available from the institute or responsible institution (and therefore may be ordered through a library), these are given as follows:

> Friedman, M. (1970), *The Counter-Revolution in Monetary Theory*. Institute of Economic Affairs, Occasional Paper 33, London: IEA.

Notes:

Title italicised and capitalised.

Name of series *not* italicised (but see following entry).

If the ***name of the institute*** appears as part of the series title (numbered), the series is treated as a journal and italicised as in the following example.

> Maybey, C. (1973), 'Social and ethnic mix in schools and the relationship with attainment of children aged 8 and 11', *CES Research Paper 9*, London: Centre for Environmental Studies.

Congress Papers; Occasional Papers (Unnumbered)

This category covers a variety of miscellaneous publications not generally available through a library. These include congress and seminar papers. Examples are:

> Jaffe, I. (1995) 'Our own invisible hand: antipolitics as an American given'. Seminar paper. Glasgow, University of Strathclyde, Department of Government.
>
> Johnson, M., Cross, M., and Parker, R. (1981), 'Ethnic minorities and the inner city'. Unpublished paper presented to the Institute of British Geographers Conference.

> Party, R. (1982), 'Who runs Scottish social policy?' Paper presented to Political Studies Association Work Group on United Kingdom Politics.
>
> Huinink, Johannes, J., and Tuma, Nancy Brandon (1988), 'An intercohort comparison of postwar patterns of family formation in the Federal Republic of Germany.' Paper presented at the Annual Meeting of the American Sociological Association, Atlanta.

Notes:

Title not italicised (indicating unpublished). May use single quotes.

Where known, a place should be given for the responsible institution, society etc.

Note order – Institution, Department (or Faculty), Institute ('from the whole to the part'): e.g. University of Reading, Faculty of Social Sciences, Institute of Economics.

Date refers to the congress (month given at end).

Information. Title may be followed by comma: ... 'Ethnic minorities and the inner city', unpublished paper presented to the...

Some publishers consider it irrelevant to state 'unpublished paper, for example:

> ... 'Ethnic minorities and the inner city'. Institute of British Geographers Conference, London

Thesis

> Romanov, Allyn Lea (1983) 'Performance and promotion: a stochastic model of decision-making by performance evaluation'. PhD dissertation, Stanford University. (Unpubl.)
>
> Wiggins, L. M. (1955) Mathematical models for the analysis of multi-wave panels, PhD dissertation, Columbia University. Ann Arbor: University Microfilms.

Notes:

Title neither capitalised nor italicised (as unpublished or not generally available). May be given in single quotes.

The *source* such as microfilm, microfiche should be given where possible. (Unpublished).

Occasionally the *institute* may be given after the university: ... PhD dissertation, Columbia University, Institute of Mathematics, Ann Arbor.

Many publishers refer to the *degree* after the place rather than before it, e.g. Columbia University. Unpublished PhD dissertation.

Unpublished theses may be published later elsewhere as in this example.

> Poulsen, C. S. (1982) *Latent Structure Analysis with Choice Modelling Applications* (PhD dissertation, University of Pennsylvania). Aarhus: Aarhus School of Business Administration and Economics

Notes:

Treated as a published book, title in italics, capitalised. Italicised titles indicate general availability through libraries.

Distinguish between dissertation study seat and publishing institution as in the above example.

Newspaper Article

General references to newspaper articles or contributions are best left to footnotes. These will appear:

> Galbraith, J.K. (1989) *The Guardian*. 28 July.

alternatively:

> *Daily Telegraph* 19.1.2003, p. 4, col. 5.

An alternative form of column/page reference is: 19.1.2003, 4/5. As this may be confused with page references the former is preferred.

Notes:

Newspaper in italics. Include 'The' only if part of the newspaper title, *The Times, Daily Telegraph*.

Special editions covering a theme may be given as follows. The newspaper is then regarded as 'the author'.

> Newsweek (1983). *Japan (Special edition)*. 18 May.

Reprint

Reprinted material may relate to (a) a new issue of previously published material or (b) a reprinted extract.

Trotsky, Leon (1974), *The Revolution Betrayed: What is the Soviet Union and where is it going?*, New York, New Park Publications. (First published in 1937).

Wirth, L. (1963) 'Urbanisation as a Way of Life', in P. K. Hatt and A. J. Reiss (eds), *Cities in Society*, Free Press, pp. 46–63. (First publshed in *American Journal of Sociology*, 1938, vol. 44.)

Notes:

Specify if further details available: First published by...; First published in Russian in 19..., Translated from the German, etc.

Government Publications

Where a Ministry or Department is the author, there is no problem:

> Department of the Environment (1984) *Neighbourhood Councils in England*, London, HMSO.

Some publications may be more complicated:

> *Report of the Royal Commission on Local Government in Scotland 1966–1969* (the Wheatley Report), 2 vols., Cmd 4150, HMSO, 1969. Avoid restructuring the title so as to make this the 'author', e.g. *Royal Commission on Local Government in Scotland 1966–1969; Report of.*

Use a cross reference if the report is known by a popular name.

> Wheatley Report (1969), see *Report of the Royal Commission on Local Government in Scotland 1966–1969.*

Avoid making the HMSO (or similar body) the author. It is, in fact, the publisher.

> HMSO (1986), *Paying for Local Government*, Cmnd 9714, London.

Use instead:

> *Paying for Local Government*, (1986) Cmnd 9714, London, HMSO.

Some official reports may not require a place of publication, the implication being that it is a public or parliamentary document available from HMSO.

> Gupta, S.P. and Hutton J.P. (1968) *Economies of Scale in Local Government Services*, Royal Commission on Local Government in England, Research Studies No. 3.

Acts of Parliament

> Local Government (Scotland) Act 1973.

Notes:

The ***title*** of the Parliamentary Act is not italicised (even though the publication may be available in libraries).

The ***date*** is not contained in parentheses as this is part of the title. By implication it is also the date of publication.

Other official publications where the publisher is stated are italicised.

Institution, Society, Local Authority as Publisher

Institutions, local authorities or societies may appear as the publisher. These used to be referenced as follows: *Rhetoric and Reality.* Society of Education Officers, 1982.

The modern approach is to present the publisher as author:

> Society of Education Officers (1982), *Rhetoric and Reality, London.*

While an abbreviation might be suitable for an organisation or institution as publisher, it should be given its full title when functioning as the author. The place of publication should be given.

> Institute of Local Government Studies (INLOGOV), (1987) *The Future Role and organisation of Local Goverment*, London.

General publications do not require italics:

> Lloyds Bank, Annual accounts

Law Cases

> *Regina* v. *Hindley.* Court of Appeal: Criminal Division, 17 October 1966.

Notes:

The ***names*** of plaintiffs and defendants should be italicised. 'v.' with period. Further bibliographic details may follow if relevant.

Chapters in Books

Specific chapters of a book are given only very occasionally. Specific information of this type really belongs to references in the text or is included in a footnote where the page numbers will be given. If there is a particular reason to include this in the bibliography, the chapter title should be given.

> Fielding, N. G., and Lee, Raymond M. (1988), *Computer Analysis and Qualitative Research*. Ch. 5, 'Analystic Pathologies', London: Sage, pp. 119–128.

Reprint

Occasionally a chapter may be issued as a reprint. This information is then included at the end:

> .... Ch. 5. 'Analytic Pathologies', London: Sage, pp. 119–128. (Reprint 2002.)

The Internet

Internet addresses are now frequently included in reference lists and footnotes. Give the whole location in full:

> http://www.yourdictionary.com/cgi-bin/mw.cgi

If your paper is distributed electronically, you may establish hyperlinks such that the reader may click on an address and go straight to a site. Otherwise remove the hyperlink.

Miscellaneous Material

There is a danger of including *everything* which we have consulted when writing a paper or book. Some material may be useful as an indicator of source material.

> Save the Whale Action Group (n.d.). 'The statistical evidence'. [Pamphlet.]

Other material belongs to footnotes:

> Bill Themill (personal communication, 8.12.2003)

Notes:

First name or initials? Might be relevant in a research document. But ask yourself 'who cares anyway?'

References in the Text

A reference in the main body of the text is a pointer to the full bibliographic information given in the bibliography. In technical publications with many annotated references or in anthologies, references are often given in the footnotes or (rarely) endnotes, with just a footnote/endnote reference number in the text. Where the bibliographic information is transferred to the footnote, the bibliographic information may be more comprehensive and annotated. The footnote bibliographic information is not, of course, a substitute for a bibliography at the end of the publication.

Reference formats

The following formats are in general use:

(Smith, J., 1997: 22)	Initial letter only if several authors with same surname.
(Doulgie, 1982a: 55)	Comma between name and date. Comma *may* be omitted.
(Pearson et al., 1987: 22)	'et al.' (not italicised). Applies where three authors or more. [No full point after et!] Name all authors in the reference list or footnote.
(Jackson, 1976: 34; Black, 1992a: 9)	Semicolon between works. References listed chronologically and not alphabetically by author.
(Jackson 1976: 34, Black 1992a: 9)	Comma between works. No comma after author's name. Some publishers prefer this tidier style.
(Peters 1998, p. 273)	Space after p. p and pp (pages) may not use a period.

The ampersand should not be used for author references, whether in the text or the bibliography, e.g. (Bone & Head 1977). That being said, I am told that a few publishers do now require this.

Where several author references are for the same year, use: Smith 2001a, 2001b. Avoid Smith 2001a, b.

References may occasionally be found at the end of the sentence, even where the author's name was repeated:

> Holly contrasts this interview-situation with Bernstein's interviews with boys from private schools (Holly, 1973: 103).

This repetition of the author's name, both in the text and the reference is somewhat superfluous. Some journals, I notice, omit the author's name, but these 'hanging' references may then require some searching, especially if the original reference containing the author's name was in the previous paragraph or even on the previous page.

> Holly contrasts this interview situation with Bernstein's interviews with boys from private schools (1973: 103).

There is also the problem of ambiguity. Did (1973: 103) refer to a publication by Holly or Bernstein? There is much to be said for the preference of most publishers for placing the reference immediately after the author's name:

> Holly (1973: 103) contrasts this interview-situation with Bernstein's interviews with boys from private schools.

Where the 'colon form' is not used, I have even seen:

> Mandel (1968) describes how capitalism has resulted in the increasing interdependence of producers (p. 170).

Splitting a reference, as opposed to a hanging reference, is clumsy, the following being preferable:

> Mandel describes how capitalism has resulted in the increasing interdependence of producers (1968, p. 170).

Care is required where the author's name is replaced by a pronoun:

> He compares this to previous criticism (1973: 67).

It is often preferable to repeat the author's name. But neither will it have evaded many readers' minds that ibid. could be an alternative:

> He compares this to previous criticism (ibid.: 67).

Some publishers, including Cambridge University Press, do not like 'ibid.' in the main text, preferring either the full reference again or a footnote. CUP notwithstanding, 'ibid.' at least refers to the **last** reference made and will normally be found within the same or previous paragraph. 'Ibid.' should certainly be avoided where the last reference was in the previous chapter. A problem can nevertheless arise when the last reference was located several paragraphs back, in which case better to repeat the full reference. On the other hand 'ibid.' does not clutter up the text with repeated references of the order (Donnington-Smythe and Worthington 1972: 168–72). Incidentally, a no-no is Bloggs, ibid., p.28, or even Bloggs, ibid.

The use of 'op. cit.' in the main text is also generally frowned upon today as it refers back to the last reference *by that author*, which again may be several pages previously, and a number of other authors might have been mentioned after this initial reference. As with 'ibid.' it should not be used where the last reference was in the previous chapter, but consider dropping it altogether and repeat the reference.

It is worth pointing out here that when references are made in bibliographic footnotes (or endnotes), the problems with ibid. and op. cit. are not so pressing. It is very easy to glance back through endnotes – and to a lesser extent footnotes – to the last reference made by 'ibid.', and even when 'op. cit.' is applied. But those words of wisdom have to be repeated: 'Consult your publisher.'

Personally, I dislike references such as...theory of sustained development (see, for example, S. Wiggens jr, 2001). Few references are unique – they are all examples. Further, with reference just to the year of publication this is indeed very general. If reference is being made to a specific observation or remark in the book, then a precise location should be given. Who is even going to bother reading Wiggens just to find out whether his viewpoints on sustained development were so revolutionary? Nevertheless, there are occasions when a general reference is in order and 'e.g.' (or preferably 'for example') are appropriate.

✓ ... has been discussed by several (e.g. Smith, 1984).
✓ This is discussed in Smith (1994), for example.

The following is an example of the incorrect use of e.g. (for example).

✗ This is discussed in, e.g. Smith (1994).

A real 'X-certificate' I encountered was: ...for e.g. Cuba, Afghanistan, Iraq, etc. Not only the '... for e.g.' is painful and superfluous; we can also do without the even more superfluous 'etc.'

There is no reason why a combination of references in the text and footnote references should not be used. Indeed, references in the text are probably generally less disruptive to the reader than a footnote to be consulted. But there are occasions when the latter are definitely advantageous:

Smith (1994) reached his initial conclusions after studying the parliamentary debate (Hansard, April 7, 1989: 1216–1228). His findings were particularly criticised in a number of subsequent articles (Bradshaw 1995a: 18; 1996: 242–247).This criticism was found to be justified when the Minister at the time published his memoirs (Smythe-Aitchison 1997), and which subsequently led to a re-evaluation by Smith (1997a, 1997b).

– as opposed to:

Smith (1994) reached his initial conclusions after studying the parliamentary debate.[1] His findings were particularly criticised in a number of subsequent articles.[2] This criticism was found to be justified when the Minister at the time published his memoirs[3] and which subsequently led to a re-evaluation by Smith.[4]

Note that the footnote reference numbers come **after** the comma, full point or other punctuation sign.

If you are referring to your own (the current) book, use the full text commencing with the chapter:

✗ It was mentioned in Ch. 7, p.122, that this theory was weak at best.
✓ It was mentioned in Chapter 7, (page 122), that this theory was weak at best.

Unknown Sources

Occasionally, a source is not known. In this case it is sufficient to include the author's dates of birth and death where known. As the sources to these quotations are unknown, no reference will appear in the bibliography.

Someone once said: 'When in Rome, do as the Romans do.' Possibly Balzac (1799–1850) had it right when he said: 'When in Turkey, do as the turkeys do.' However, when in Ireland, avoid *anything* that Irish do! (Taylor 1937–)

The above raises an interesting point of punctuation. The text concludes with an exclamation mark. The ensuing reference does not need a closing full point. Otherwise the full point follows the closing parenthesis.

Foreign Works

The titles of *foreign* works and organisations mentioned in the text should be in italics. But where an institution or organisation is the author, the reference should be in normal font.

In Norway, public building construction is supervised by a state authority, *Statsbygg* (The Directorate of Public Construction and Property). A number of publications show how this authority is closely engaged in environmental protection during construction (Statsbygg, 2002a, 2002b).

Quotations, Parentheses and References

It will have been observed that the final period comes after the closing parentheses of a reference placed at the end of a sentence (irrespective of the form of the reference):

✓ Bernstein also suggests that the organization of the curriculum affects the internal school hierarchy (Bernstein, 1975).

If the *entire* sentence is placed in parentheses, the closing parenthesis will come *after* the final period:

✓ (Slaves also developed parallel 'submissive' personalities (Elkins, 1963).)

If a *part* of the sentence is in parentheses and relates to the reference, punctuation is as follows:

✓ The introduction of the category of contradictory class positions seems to be little more than a device for dealing with the problem of indeterminacy, albeit in a plainly functionalist way (also, for criticism of deskilling theory, see Wood (1982)).[1]

References in the text should refer directly to the author and the year of publication. Avoid superfluous instructions and excessive parentheses.

✗ This model is widely used (e.g. Jones (1978), Black & Green (1979)).
✓ This model is widely used (Jones, 1978; Black and Green, 1979).

Where the genitive case is used, place the reference date at the most convenient point after the object:

✗ Smith's (1996: 22) point was that it had not been proved.
✓ Smith's point (1996: 22) was that it had not been proved.

– or even:

✓ Smith's point was that it had not been proved (1996: 22).

▶ Avoid familiarity: the surname is sufficient. However, the initials may be useful for clarity. But the following is a bit condescending (even for a woman):

✗ The historian, Jacqueline Bywaters (1972), disputes this finding.

---

1 Example from Philip Cooke (1983) *Theories of Planning and Spatial Development*, London, Hutchinson, p. 230.

✓ This finding is disputed by Bywaters (1972).

Nevertheless, where an author is widely known by his full name, the familiar approach is occasionally better:

✓ It was disputed by James Joyce, but not by Shakespeare!

A note relating to a reference in a footnote (see previous footnote) may use the familiar form.

▶ Several authors of a single work are referred to as Smith et al. (1970). Avoid, however, the genitive *s* as in:

✗ Smith et al.'s theory was ...
✓ The theory advanced by Smith et al. was that ...

Where several authors are included in the text these should be in chronological, and not alphabetical, order:

✓ ... found extensively in work on special development in Italy (Paci, 1973; Bagnasco, 1977, 1981; Arcangeli et al., 1979; Mingione 1979, 1984; Brusco, 1982).

▶ References in footnotes occasionally include the term 'passim', e.g. Smith, Ch. 11, *passim*. This term means 'throughout'.

▶ The abbreviations *ibid., idem,* and *loc. cit.* should **not** be used in the main body of the text. Quote the author and reference again in full or use the forms of reference given above.

Op. cit. (but not *ibid.*) may be used to refer to a previous reference, e.g. (op. cit. p. 62). However, because the author is not named this can only refer to the **last** reference cited (and thus serving the function of **ibid**.). There would be little point in writing (Woogy, op. cit. p. 62) when (Woogy, 1999: 62) is shorter and clearer. So why even bother to write (op. cit. p. 62)? Why not just (p. 62)? This is exactly what CUP suggests. Several references in the same paragraph or section referring to the same book may use this simple reference.

Dates

The following forms may be used:

Taylor (1937–)	Author still living (in spite of everything)
Purcell (1623– ?)	Date of death unknown
Tacitus (55?–130?)	Date of birth and date of death uncertain
Aristotle (384 BC?–322 BC)	Date of birth uncertain
Oscar Wilde(?)	Indicates uncertain *source* (not date).

The spaced dash may be considered more appropriate for some of these. While there are no rules about dates any omission of BC may appear to imply AD. Therefore (384 BC? – 322 BC) seems preferable to (384? – 322 BC) in the above. Do not think that omission of 'AD' automatically implies 'in the year of our Lord. Whereas (55 BC–AD 23) is perfectly clear (55 BC– 23) is certainly not.

Superfluous References

Well worth a separate heading. I find many references somewhat superfluous and irritating. For example, in a recent text I read 'Oil prices fell again towards the end of the year (Withers, 2000).' Now, my immediate reaction is to enquire as to why this reference should be so very important. There is nothing to indicate this. If the sentence had been '... end of the year due to conflicts between the OPEC members (Smithers 1999: 44)', then I would immediately have understood that this was something of interest had I been a student of oil politics.

The golden rule is to use references in the text with discretion. Here is a gem from a manuscript I received whilst assembling material for this book:

Historical studies of certain phases in history, focused on a specific time and place, typically generate singularising questions and answers. Marx's answer to the question of how money can beget money (1867: chs 4, 5, 6) and Weber's (1956: chs 3, 10, 11) and Dahl's (1970) answers as to what constitutes legitimate power are examples of answers which have a high degree of generality. According to Aubert, sociology as a science must work to achieve a coherent view of all social behaviour and the entire structure of society (1979: 14) ... He is reducing 'experience' to 'immediate impressions of the senses' (1943: 178, 180–181, 190, 193, 195–196).

The above illustrates how the visual appearance of the text is broken up by continual reference to other works. It will also break up your reader's concentration. Sometimes the impression is given that the author is saying to the reader: 'just see how well read I am – how much I know about my subject.' What he should be asking is whether the reference really is necessary. I also recently read a paper where many statistics concerning the Norwegian metallurgical industry were presented. These had been obtained from another book where the original author had manifestly obtained these from an official source. It was clearly not necessary to quote the source and the page number for this information at the end of **every** sentence containing a statistic (which this article did). As a general rule, use only references which are specific and necessary, preferably with the relevant page numbers. In fact, I find that many publisher's guides for authors specifically state that page numbers *shall* be given.

References in Footnotes

The point of footnotes is to provide information, including bibliographic references, without cluttering up the text. While there is reason not to have bibliographic information in the text and in footnotes as mentioned above, it is preferable to elect one or the other. The advantage of references in footnotes is that it does permit more information to be included, the title of a work for example.

The bibliographic material in footnotes (endnotes) is also a pointer to the full bibliography at the end of the chapter or book. As a footnote, the reference to source material may be a little more detailed than a reference in the main body of the text, but not as comprehensive as the bibliography. What is *not* required is a mixture where some references are given in the text, and others are referred to by a footnote number.

Where bibliographic references are given in footnotes, some publishers require a full reference to be given the first time a book or paper is mentioned. This, of course, duplicates the main entry in the bibliography. Other publishers do not regard this as essential and accept a shortened, instantly recognisable form whereby the main entry is easily understood. Examples (using the above references), and including the footnote reference number would be:

> 12. Fielding, N. G., and Lee, Raymond M. (eds.) (1991), *Using Computers in Qualitative Research.* pp. 119–128.

The shortened form for any subsequent references to this book contains:

Authors, date, short title, page number(s).

> 14. Fielding and Lee (1991) *Using Computers.* p. 162

Other publishers allow the briefest of references using author, date and page (omitting the title) as discussed above. This form is identical to that used when the reference is given in the main text.

Material in footnotes may contain a wide variety of information in addition to bibliographic notes. For this reason some writers, albeit very few, prefer to keep bibliographic material as endnotes and other information as footnotes. This necessitates a double system of reference numbering (1, 2 ...; i, ii ...). There really is little point in this except possibly in scientific articles where supplementary information may be comprehensive and desired to be kept separate from the main text. An example here might be an explanation to a theory, statistical formula or similar. Footnote numbering should recommence in every new chapter. The same applies to endnotes if these appear at the end of each chapter rather than at the end of the book.

Endnotes

I have referred briefly to Endnotes in the above. I really fail to see the point of these in many publications. Occasionally, it is useful to assemble all information at the end of a document. For example, one might imagine a paper which discusses various acts of parliament and where the annotation states the date of the act together with any other relevant documents, a brief outline of the intention of the act and so forth. It may well serve a purpose to have all such material assembled in a set of endnotes rather than dispersed in many footnotes. Other than this, readers do not generally turn back and forth between the main text and endnotes, and my impression is that little purpose is served by endnotes.

There is also the additional problem that if footnotes are used in addition, numbering may become confusing. Endnotes should be numbered consecutively throughout the book. If these are used then footnotes could be numbered using lower case alphanumeric characters, commencing with ^{i} or ^{a} – either on each page or commencing with each new chapter.

I note that some publishers require endnotes to be submitted as a separate file – I know not why. But it pays to follow the rules.

The Latin Terms

▶ *ibidem* (ibid.)

In footnotes ibid. (not normally italicised) is used meaning 'in the same book'. This refers to the book cited in the *immediately preceding* literary reference. In this case the author's name is **not** restated. Some publishers do not approve of using 'ibid.', preferring the whole reference to be repeated. This is, of course, necessary when the cited source is *not* the immediately preceding literary reference. Another restriction is that ibid. (which does not repeat an author's name) cannot be used if the previous literary reference is a footnote where two authors are mentioned. Ibid. is not used in the main text.

▶ *opere citato* (op. cit.)

Op. cit. as in Waldorf (op. cit.) refers to the last reference made to the work by Waldorf. This may be even be in a footnote on a previous page. Originally, being Latin terms, they were italicised. Not so today. Convention is that foreign terms in everyday use are no longer italicised. Here is a sample set of footnotes to illustrate the principle:

1. Waldorf (1997: 12). The internal split ultimately led to a cabinet reshuffle.
2. The Upper House was unanimous on the issue, but only 67 members were in attendance.

3. Jones (1996) considers that trade union membership declined as a result of the vote
4. A similar workers' reaction to the EU regulation occurred in Denmark (ibid.)
5. Waldorf (op. cit. p. 55) bases his statement on conversations with the Minister (now retired).

Here, ibid. [4] refers to Jones (1996) [3] and op. cit. [5] refers to Waldorf (1997) [1]. Where possible, these should give precise references to page(s).

▶ *loco citato* (loc. cit) means 'in the place cited'.

▶ *passim* means at various/several places throughout the whole section (e.g. chapter) cited.

▶ *idem* means 'as mentioned before'.

These terms are normally adequately covered by ibid. and op. cit., and not generally encountered. But we also find publishers, e.g. Cambridge University Press (CUP), who state that **only** ibid. shall be used. As mentioned above, this assumes that the last literary reference only mentions one author. If the previous reference source was:

14. Smith (1995: 23–4) and Woogy (1999: 31 ff.) both discuss this point

then we would have to give the shortened reference again. I do have some sympathy with avoiding op. cit. The previous reference to Woogy (1999) might well have been a dozen pages previously. Far better to cite the reference again. Indeed, one could also do this with ibid. even where the last reference to this literary work was on a previous page.

Finally, this chapter has discussed various alternatives for bibliographic information, and you should have no difficulty in finding almost all of these. The list at the beginning of the chapter summarises the most frequently encountered formats. Much work may be involved if you have to change the style on account of the publisher's preferences. These must be checked first. Otherwise select your own choices and stick to them.

Other Latin terms used in the text are discussed in Chapter 12.

Author Index

One occasionally encounters an author index with brief pointers to all references by individual authors. An example might be: Mitroff, I., 27, 63n, 92–103. Thus, on page 27 we would expect to find an author–date reference in the text; pages 92–103 could be devoted to a discussion of Mitroff's theory. The affix **n** indicates footnote reference. For example, the footnote on page 63 might read: Mitroff (1974) challenges this viewpoint. The need for a separate, additional, author index is really a matter of choice. If such references are to be made I prefer these to be contained within a separate index rather than being included in the subject index.

The standards adopted by many publishing houses are available on the net but may be changed from time to time. Try searching (for example) author, guide, publishing. Several thousand hits may be made, but I found all the essential information among the first thirty. Indeed, try adding OUP or CUP to the search terms Cambridge University Press has useful information on: https://authornet.cambridge.org/information/productionguide/hss/text.asp

Technical Journals

It is worth repeating the comments about technical journals, most of which have their own house rules. An article appearing in a social science journal may appear:

> Parkin, D.M., Clayton, D., Black, R.J., et al. (1996) 'Childhood leukaemia in Europe after Chernobyl: 5 year follow-up'. *British Journal of Cancer* (vol. 124), pp. 980–3.

The same reference in a medical journal might be:

> Parkin DM, Clayton D, Black RJ, Masuyer E, Freidl HP, Ivanov E, et al. Childhood leukaemia in Europe after Chernobyl: 5 year follow-up. Br J Cancer 1996; 124:980–3.

The latter form should only be used where the publisher specifically requires this. It is often found in the citation–sequence system.

5
Characters and Symbols

Those who read the symbol do so at their peril. – Oscar Wilde

Typographic Symbols

There are a number of general typographic symbols where it is convenient to know the name. These are frequently associated with foreign words but also encountered in general usage. These include:

á, é	acute accent
&	ampersand
'	apostrophe
*	asterisk
{ }	braces
[ ]	brackets
^	caret
ç	cedilla
^	circumflex
:	colon
,	comma
†	dagger
°	degree
ä, ï, ö	diæresis (dieresis)
‡	double dagger
—	em dash
–	en dash
&c.	et cetera (obsolete)
!	exclamation
à, è	grave accent
¶	line return (paragraph)
.	full point (period)
?	question mark
§	section/legal paragraph
;	semicolon
~	tilde

The following sets of symbols are found in Word, but virtually all modern word processors have an extensive range.

- Latin (but does not include D-bar [$\overline{D}$] for 5000, for example)
- Greek
- Cyrillic
- Hebrew
- Arabic
- General punctuation symbols
- Currency symbols
- Number forms (including fractions)
- Mathematical operators
- Miscellaneous Dingbats
- Specials
- Area for inserting own symbols.

Each typeface has its own set of symbols, but these are often limited. There is no difficulty in applying the 'normal text' symbols to any font although some are not particularly suited.

Generally speaking, the characters available on the monitor are printable. However, certain characters may appear on the screen as □. These will also be printed correspondingly.

Modern word-processors allow programming of key-strokes for selected symbols. This might be useful for the mathematician who is constantly using $\sum \sqrt{\ } \Phi$ and so forth.

There are two sets of symbols which one should be aware of: Webdings and Wingdings. Otherwise known as Dingbats, these are printer's symbols where those such as telephone symbol may be useful [☏] or the confirm box ☑. There is a considerable variety here. Many may be downloaded from the web.

If you wish to see all of the available symbols in Word, go to the toolbar at the top of the screen which shows the typeface currently in use (probably Times Roman). Click on the down arrow (bottom right frame), or slide the square button down to any font which will then show the available typefaces. According to your version of Microsoft Word these may include:

- Common bullets
- Holidays MT
- Monosorts
- Monosorts 2
- MS Outlook
- MS Reference 1
- MS Reference 2
- Symbols
- Webdings
- Wingdings
- Wingdings2
- Wingdings3
- Vacation MT

Select the font required, for example Wingdings2. Now type all the keys on the keyboard! Next, repeat these holding down the shift key!! For example, hitting the (capital) letter 'R' (with the shift key) on Wingdings2 will produce ☑.[1] You might need to use a larger font size for a better effect. However, it is worth noting those symbols for which you have regular use. Many of these will not have a shortcut key. If a shortcut key does exist, you may find this out by going to Insert – Symbol, selecting the Font (here Wingdings2), and clicking the symbol on the screen. If no shortcut key is given, then you can define your own. Designating your own short cut key as described below, will further simplify production of these characters, not least by eliminating the necessity of using the 'Insert (symbol)' procedure.

Pre-programmed Symbols

The previous section outlined symbols that could be inserted. This demands quite a bit of activity with the mouse. It is possible to programme keystrokes for those symbols used regularly. However, many foreign letters and punctuation signs are already pre-programmed

The following table shows the keys to be entered to print the character shown.[2] In Word the keys in the first column in the table below are held and released, and the keys in the second column are then entered where required. Where Ctrl + : is required (for example), this will also require the Shift key to obtain the colon (the ' + ' sign is *not* entered). In other words you will have to hold down two keys the Ctrl key and the Shift key, and while doing so tap the colon key. If you continue to hold down the Ctrl and Shift keys while tapping the colon key and then another key, for example *A*, you will get Ä. If, however, you release the Ctrl and Shift keys immediately after tapping the colon key and then tap *A*, you get ä. Dependent upon this last key, you may achieve: ä Ä ë Ë ï Ï ö Ö ü Ü ÿ Ÿ. You may need to experiment to get the hang of this. Not every key is pre-programmed. In the following table, numbers following Alt + must be entered on the *number pad* (press Num Lock first). The AltGr key is the same as Alt + Ctrl. This does not apply to the three symbols achieved by using Alt + Ctrl + 2. Here you use the '2' at the top of the keyboard. (Confused? Remember, this is hands-on.)

The keystrokes for any symbol may be changed. This may be particularly useful where a given symbol is used regularly but the default keystrokes are a bit demanding! You can enter your own selection in the column to the right.

1   It is possible that some versions of Word use different keystrokes, although I cannot confirm this.
2   The previous edition also showed symbols for WordPerfect and Corel Perfect in addition. I never receive manuscripts using these programs today – regrettably.

Change this by going to Insert – Symbol, highlighting the symbol. The present shortcut keys are shown lower right. Hit the shortcut key tab in the lower middle of the frame and then enter your own shortcut keys.

The following table has been sorted on Column 2 then by Column 1 using the Sort feature in Word under Table. Under 'My keys' you may insert your sequence for the existing symbols, or insert your own symbols and keystrokes.

If you find that some of these do not work for one reason or another (these are the latest from Microsoft at the time of writing), then go to Insert – Symbol, find the symbols required and see what the given shortcut keystrokes are. You may change these if required.

Symbol	Word	My keys	
	Hold these, release then press	Symbol	Shortcut keys
~	Alt +~		
ƒ	Alt + 0131		
Ž	Alt + 0142		
˜	Alt + 0152		
ž	Alt + 0158		
a	Alt + 170		
¯	Alt + 0175		
±	Alt + 0177		
¬	Alt + 0178		
2	Alt + 0178		
3	Alt + 0179		
¶	Alt + 0182		
·	Alt + 0183		
1	Alt + 0185		
°	Alt + 0186		
¼	Alt + 0188		
½	Alt + 0189		
¾	Alt + 0190		
þ	Alt + 0254		
¥	Alt + 165		
¦	Alt + 166		
Š	Alt + Ctrl +^ Shift + s		
š	Alt + Ctrl +^ s		

Symbol	Word *Hold these, release then press*	*My keys* Symbol	Shortcut keys
Ã	Alt + Ctrl + ˜ Shift + a		
ã	Alt + Ctrl + ˜ a		
Ñ	Alt + Ctrl + ˜ Shift + n		
º	Alt + Ctrl + 2 < space >		
Å	Alt + Ctrl + 2 Shift + a		
å	Alt + Ctrl + 2 a		
ñ	Alt + Ctrl + n n		
¡	AltGr + !		
…	AltGr + .		
¿	AltGr + ?		
Õ	AltGr + ˜ Shift + o		
õ	AltGr + ˜ o		
©	AltGr + c		
µ	AltGr + m		
—	AltGr + Num-		
®	AltGr + r < space >		
™	AltGr + t		
"	Ctr + ' "		
É	Ctrl + Shift + e		
Œ	Ctrl + & Shift + o		
œ	Ctrl + & o		
ß	Ctrl + & S		
Æ	Ctrl + & Shift + a		
æ	Ctrl + & a		
˒	Ctrl + , < space >		
Ç	Ctrl + , Shift + c		
ç	Ctrl + , c		
¢	Ctrl + / c		
Ø	Ctrl + / Shift + o		
ø	Ctrl + / o		
¨	Ctrl + : < space >		
Ë	Ctrl + : Shift + e		
ë	Ctrl + : e		
Ï	Ctrl + : Shift + i		

Symbol	Word	My keys	
	Hold these, release then press	Symbol	Shortcut keys
ï	Ctrl + : u		
Ÿ	Ctrl + : Shift + y		
ÿ	Ctrl + : y		
Ü	Ctrl + : Shift + u		
ü	Ctrl + : u		
Ä	Ctrl + : Shift + a		
ä	Ctrl + : a		
Ö	Ctrl + : Shift + o		
ö	Ctrl + : o		
^	Ctrl + ^ < space >		
Â	Ctrl + ^ Shift + a		
â	Ctrl + ^ a		
Ê	Ctrl + ^ Shift + e		
ê	Ctrl + ^ e		
Î	Ctrl + ^ Shift + i		
î	Ctrl + ^ u		
Ô	Ctrl + ^ Shift + o		
ô	Ctrl + ^ o		
Û	Ctrl + ^ Shift + u		
û	Ctrl + ^ u		
'	Ctrl + ` '		
«	Ctrl + ` <		
»	Ctrl + ` >		
À	Ctrl + ` Shift + a		
à	Ctrl + ` a		
È	Ctrl + ` Shift + e		
è	Ctrl + ` e		
Ì	Ctrl + ` Shift + i		
ì	Ctrl + ` u		
Ò	Ctrl + ` Shift + o		
ò	Ctrl + ` o		
Ù	Ctrl + ` Shift + u		
ù	Ctrl + ` u		
´	Ctrl + ' < space >		

Symbol	Word		My keys	
	Hold these, release then press		Symbol	Shortcut keys
' '	Ctrl + '	"		
Á	Ctrl + '	Shift + a		
á	Ctrl + '	a		
Đ	Ctrl + '	Shift + d		
ð	Ctrl + '	d		
é	Ctrl + '	e		
Í	Ctrl + '	Shift + i		
í	Ctrl + '	u		
Ó	Ctrl + '	Shift + o		
ó	Ctrl + '	o		
Ú	Ctrl + '	Shift + u		
ú	Ctrl + '	u		
Ý	Ctrl + '	Shift + y		
ý	Ctrl + '	y		
–	Ctrl + Num-			
§	Shift + |			
¤	Shift + 4			

In addition to the above, a considerable number of editing functions are pre-programmed. Many of the alphabetic keys are used in conjunction with the Ctrl key. For example Ctrl + p provides the Print options; Ctrl + A highlights the entire text; Ctrl + b, i. u give boldface, italics and underlining respectively. If you are defining your own key strokes you may well be advised to avoid using the Ctrl key as this key is widely used by Word. On the other hand, only Alt + a, e, h, i, o, t, v and w (lower case) and just Alt + Shift + I (upper case) are pre-programmed. This means that all the other letters (upper and lower case) and numbers (1...0) are available with the Alt keys for your own selected symbols. I discuss below how to programme shortcut keys. Here are the most important pre-programmed Alt, Ctrl and Shift keys. There are some duplicates, but before programming your own key strokes, check these first.

You will have to consult your 'bible' for a closer explanation of some of the above.

The following are some of the 'normal text' symbols which are not pre-programmed in Word but for which you may have frequent use in some texts. You may assign your own shortcut keys. The table below will show which shortcut keys are already programmed, but you will be warned if you try to assign shortcut keys already assigned.

Alt + a	Table menu	Ctrl + H	Replace
Alt + e	Edit menu	Ctrl + N	New document
Alt + f	File menu	Ctrl + O	Open
Alt + F4	Save/Exit	Ctrl + P	Print
Alt + F6	Switch documents	Ctrl + Q	Remove para.formats
Alt + F7	Language/spelling	Ctrl + S	Save
Alt + F8	Macros	Ctrl + Shift + F5	Boomark
Alt + h	Help menu	Ctrl + Shift + F6	Switch documents
Alt + i	Insert menu	Ctrl + Shift + Z	Clear formatting
Alt + o	Format menu	Ctrl + Spacebar	Clear formatting
Alt + Shift + I	Mark citation	Ctrl + X	Cut
Alt + t	Tools menu	Ctrl + Y	Repeat
Alt + v	View menu	Ctrl + 1	Single line spacing
Alt + w	Window menu	Ctrl + 2	Double line spacing
Ctrl + Alt + F2	Open file	Ctrl + 5	1.5 line spacing
Ctrl + C	Copy	Shift + Alt + F4	Save/Exit
Ctrl + CC	Clipboard	Shift + Alt + F6	Switch documents
Ctrl + D	Delete	Shift + Enter	Create line
Ctrl + Enter	New page	Shift + F10	Language/spelling
Ctrl + F6	Browse workbook	Shift + F7	Thesaurus
Ctrl + G	GoTo		

^{n} $c/_o$ $^1/_3$ $^2/_3$ $^1/_8$ $^3/_8$ $^5/_8$ $^7/_8$ ϑ Δ Π Σ $\sqrt{}$ ∞ $\cap$ $\int$ $\approx$ $\neq$ $\leq$ $\geq$ ♀ ♂ ♠ ♣ ♥ ♦ ■ □

In addition there are a number of statistical signs which may be programmed (see below).

Paragraph Symbols

The paragraph mark for typographic purposes is ¶. In legal and other documents the section mark § is often referred to as the paragraph symbol. This may be used where paragraphs are numbered: See §6. This is also referred to in §§2, 9, 12–13. In some countries a space follows the § sign [see § 6]. This practice is occasionally encountered in the UK and USA. Note that §§ means 'paragraphs'.

The paragraph icon [¶] is also used by Word to indicate a 'hard return'. (See Chapter 5, Characters and Symbols)

The Greek Alphabet

The statistician will have considerable use of Greek characters. A number of other symbols will also be of interest to the mathematician. (Yes, maths and stats are two different academic fields.) Many articles use only symbols for the mean (µ), and standard deviation (σ). These are not pre-programmed in Word and must be inserted from the symbols function. However, they are easily programmed as shortcut keys. Don't forget to check whether the sequence is already in use.

Certain fonts, particularly non-serif fonts, are not always suitable for Greek characters, for example:

Times Roman: Γ Λ Ξ Ψ γ π ψ
Arial: Γ Λ Ξ Ψ γ π ψ
Courier: Γ Λ Ξ Ψ γ π ψ

In the following table you may note the key combinations you prefer for selected Greek characters. Consult the previous table for a summary of pre-programmed keys. You could, for instance, programme the available Alt keys as mentioned above.

Character	Upper case	My keys:	Lower case	My keys:
alpha	A		α	
beta	B		β	
gamma	Γ		γ	
delta	Δ		δ	
epsilon	E		ε	
zeta	Z		ζ	
eta	H		η	
theta	Θ		θ	
iota	I		ι	
kappa	K		κ	
lambda	Λ		λ	
mu	M		µ	
nu	N		ν	
xi	Ξ		ξ	
omicron	O		o	
pi	Π		π	
rho	P		ρ	
sigma	Σ		σ	
tau	T		τ	
ypsilon	Y		υ	
phi	Φ		φ	
chi	X		χ	
psi	Ψ		ψ	
omega	Ω		ω	

Mathematical Symbols and Notation

Mathematical analysis

$\lvert a \rvert$	absolute value of a
$\angle$	acute angle
$\measuredangle$	angle
$\approx$	approximately equals
$\frown$	arc
$\because$	because
$\bigcirc$	circle
$/$	divide
$\div$	divide
$\Leftrightarrow$ or $\leftrightarrow$	double implication
$\cong$	equal or nearly equal to
$=$	equals
$\equiv$	exactly equals
Δ	finite difference
$\int$	function
$\geq$	greater or equal to
$>$	greater than
$\Leftarrow$ or $\leftarrow$	implied by
∞	infinity
f	integral
$\in$	is an element in
$:$	is to
$\leq$	less or equal to
$<$	less than
Π	mathematical constant, pi $= 3.14159265$
$\log_e$	mathematical constant, base of natural logarithms $= 2.71828$
$\mp$	minus or plus
$N!$	N factorial
$\neg\, a$	not a
$\neq$	not equal to
$\parallel$	parallel
$\perp$	perpendicular
$\pm$	plus or minus
Π	product
$::$	proportion, so is
$,$	quadrant
$\Rightarrow$ or $\rightarrow$	results in, implies
$\llcorner$	right angle $(90°)$
$\sqrt{}$	root
$\square$	square
$-$	subtraction (minus)
Σ	sum
$\therefore$	therefore
$\neq$	unequal to/different to
δ	variation
$\propto$	varies as, proportional to
$\top$	vertical

Statistical Symbols and Notation

A surprisingly large number of articles which I am required to look at contain statistical symbols which are not used according to custom. By definition a *statistic* is a measure calculated on the basis of a sample. *Statistics* is the analysis of data by which estimates are made about the *parameters* of a *population* (often of unknown size), the basis of the estimate frequently being a *normally distributed representative sample.*

There are a number of statistics which may be used to describe a sample, for example, the sum, mean, standard deviation and so forth. *Latin alphabetic characters* are used to denote the *sample statistics. Greek symbols* are used to denote the *population parameters*, i.e. the sum, mean, etc., of the population. Statistical formulae are given in *Dictionary/Outline of Statistics* by J. E. Freund and F. J. Williams, Dover Publications 1966. Definitions and examples are given in *Dictionary of Statistics* by Roger Porkess, Collins Reference 1988.

The following statistical symbols are normally encountered. For convenience a number of common abbreviations are also included.

Symbol[3]	statistic
χ^2	chi square statistic
(x, y)	a joint event where x is paired with y
$\lvert AD \rvert$	MAD = mean absolute deviation
μ	estimated population mean
ANCOVA	Analysis of covariance
ANOVA	Analysis of variance
cf	cumulative frequency (= running total)
cov(X,Y)	covariance of two random variables X and Y
e	error or a measurement
$E(X)$	expectation of a random variable
F	F-ration computed from a sample
f	frequency (of a variable or class)
G^2	likelihood ratio test statistic
i	used as a subscript for the i_{th} variable
K or κ	kappa statistic
MANOVA	Multiple analysis of variance
MS	Mean Square in ANOVA
n	size of a sample
N	size of population (occasionally used for sample size!)
p	probability of a given event
Q	proportion of classes in the upper tail of a sampling distribution
Q, Y	Yules' index
r_s	Spearman's rank-correlation coefficient

---

3 This list has been sorted using Word Sort routine. The order may differ using other sort procedures.

s	standard correlation coefficient (corrected) for a sample
S	standard correlation coefficient for a sample
S	standard deviation of a sample
S^2	sample variance
SS	Sum of Squares in ANOVA
t	Student's t-statistic
T	Total number of potential observations in a finite population
$\text{var}(X)$	variance of the random variable X.
w	a weighting factor
X	a random variable; independent variable
x	a value which a random variable X may assume
Y	a random variable; the dependent variable
z	standardised score
Z	value of Fisher's r- to Z transformation
α	Type I error (Probability of rejection of H_0 when it is true)
β	Type II error (Probability of failure to reject H_0 when it is true)
θ	theta. General symbol for a population parameter
θ_2	Value of θ specified by the null hypothesis
λ	lambda – measure of asymmetric association
ρ	intraclass correlation coefficient for a population
σ	standard deviation of a random variable
σ^2	variance of a random variable
$\sigma_{\text{diff.}}$	standard error of the difference between two means
τ	tau. Kendall's coefficient of rank-order agreement
ϕ^2	index of mean square contingency for a sample contingency table
Φ^2	index of mean square contingency for a population contingency table

Shortcut Keys

If you use the formula function in Word then most of the above symbols will be available. But if you are describing the results of a statistical test, then you may program keys to produce any symbol. For example, θ_2 is a bit of a hassle to type. But you could assign this to a simple keystroke such as Alt + 1. Incidentally, I have described macros elsewhere, but these are so rarely compiled by many authors and yet so very useful, I make no apologies for showing how useful and simple this is in the present connection. First, type θ_2 the hard way, i.e. normally selecting the symbol and entering '2', changing this to the subscript font. Now highlight this [θ_2] and copy onto the clipboard with Ctrl + C. Record a macro using Tools – Macro – Record New Macro – Name macro [e.g. theta2] – Assign to keyboard – New shortcut key [here you could hold down Alt + 1, for example] Assign – Close – Ctrl + V [to recall memory] – End macro [click the ∎]. Every time you need θ_2 just key in Alt + 1. This is the basic principle for making any macro.

Other Symbols

AutoCorrect

It is possible to use the AutoCorrect feature to make symbols. Word includes several examples. For example, a colon will nearly always be followed by space and we are unlikely to meet an opening parenthesis immediately following a colon, such as :(. The AutoCorrect feature automatically changes :(to ☹ while :) is automatically changed to ☺. So how did I manage to print :(and :)? Just use the delete back key (top right of the alphabetic keyboard) and the characters reappear. You may also switch off the AutoCorrect feature to do this. Using the autocorrect feature you can programme any sequence of letters to produce any symbol that you may be using regularly. As described earlier, another method is to programme the ALT keys. (See Chapter 18. Word – Some practical tips.)

Overstrike

In WordPerfect for DOS it was possible to superimpose (overstrike) two characters such as O and / to make Ø. There is no overstrike equivalent in Word although it is possible to compile a Visual Basic program to do this which may then be run as a macro.

Euro symbol

The Euro currency symbol [€] is included in Windows 98 and shown on modern keyboards where one may use the AltGr + e, or AltGr + 5 keys (Alt + 4 on some systems). This feature is not available in earlier versions of Windows or Word.

Warning!

When exporting files to another user, by email or on diskette, you should ensure that he/she has the same, similar or convertible fonts. *This is 'Palace Script' – and may appear attractive on a brochure for the church bazaar*, but it may appear as gobbledegook on another PC, even though this too has Word, or whatever. Different versions of Word or WordPerfect may not necessarily contain the same set of fonts as your PC. If you are planning to use a special typefaces and/or symbols, first send a trial email file to the recipient first as an attachment. I describe this under Typefaces and Fonts.

6
Tables, Charts and Diagrams

Tables

The table is the only place where a man is never bored during the first hour. – Anthelme Brillat-Savarin, (1755–1826). French politician and lawyer

Of course, the 'table' in the above quotation was not exactly what Brillat-Savarin had in mind at the time of writing, but somehow it seems applicable to the point I wish to make. It is surprising how many manuscripts omit the use of tables as well as figures and diagrams where these could be usefully employed. This is very largely the result of ignorance as to how to produce these on the word processor. A half-hour using the 'help' menu will cure this ailment and will add 'life' to your manuscript. The intention behind four or five lines of confusing text is readily assimilated when presented graphically or in a table.

A frequent mistake on the part of many academic authors is to insert too much statistical data in the text, confusing the reader. Not only may the main point be lost, but other, apparently minor, information may also be omitted. Even where only a few statistics are to be described, they may be usefully summarised in a table. Take the following, for example:

In 1931, Norwegian landings of salmon amounted to 879 tons. Landings of plaice were four times greater, totalling 3484 tons, while halibut exceeded 5200 tons. In 1941 salmon landings had declined to 823 tons while both halibut and plaice landings were only about a quarter of the level of a decade earlier at 1352 tons and 880 tons respectively.

We had lost the trend at the end of the second line, I suspect. Now glance at the first two columns in Table 1. The point is readily understood.

The layout of the table will make the task easier for the reader to grasp the essential points. Modern word processors provide a number of alternative layouts whereby your table will be formatted automatically. These may include colour and fancy fonts, but keep in mind your readership. If you are designing a report to be presented to the Women's Institute, a 'modern' design might be appropriate, but a table in a Ph.D. thesis will probably require a more conservative approach.

Headings for tables and figures

Normally, table headings will be *above* the table; figure headings, *below*. Curiously, a number of publishers place the title of the figure in italics whereas the title of the table is not. Further, the font size for either or both headings may be one point smaller than the normal text.

Numbering tables etc.

Tables and diagrams may be numbered consecutively throughout the book, or by chapter: *Table 1-1, 1-2;* (or as a decimal) *2.1, 2.2*, etc. The same applies to diagrams (figures). If the publisher is converting your text from a standard word processor file, then tables and diagrams may be have to be supplied as a separate file. The text should then include a note: [*Table 1-5 about here*]. This will enable the typesetter to insert the table at the most appropriate place to avoid an unnecessary page-break or white space.

I used to prefer a colon between the table number and the heading:

Table 6: Fishing catch 1970 – 1990

although a single or double space seems to be generally preferred, the title often employing italics. No period at the end:

Table 6.2 *Fishing catch 1970 – 1990*

Table design

Very frequently we get carried away, both with the detail to be included in tables and the layout. The result is that we may have to use a smaller font which, when reduced to the book page-size, is scarcely readable. Further, excessive vertical lines in a table do not contribute to the appearance; horizontal lines should also be kept to a minimum. It is important to keep in mind the scale of reduction required, and where necessary divide a table into two.

Broad tables may be printed 'landscape', that is, turned anti-clockwise 90° such that the top of the table is on the left-hand margin of the page. But this is not an ideal solution. It is often better to redesign and split the table and then to present it on facing pages in normal ('portrait') layout.

It should not be forgotten that the table is frequently a summary of what may or could have been written as text as well as supplying supplementary information. A detailed table is useful in this respect but should be designed such that the essential statistics and trends are easily observed. Some comments should be given in the text drawing attention to the main trends, but excessive detail may cloud over the main issue. There is little point in describing every small change from one period to the next when these may be of minor importance and in any case easily observed in the table.

Commence by constructing a framework: use the 'Table' function in the menu bar to define the number of rows of columns. You can easily add or delete columns and rows as required. The table framework is automatically adjusted to the width of the margins. At this stage we are concerned only with entering data; formatting comes later. Here only four rows are shown (the complete table is given later). Time series should be on the horizontal scale (row); species, amounts etc. on the vertical scale. Care should also be given to the title. Short statements make for clarity. These should summarise the column (here, species) and row (time series) information, and the measurement used (unless the table contains diverse information and units).

Table 6.1 Norway. Fish landings by species 1931–1971. Tons.

	1931	1941	1951	1961	1971
Halibut	5293	1352	5273	4292	1981
Plaice	3484	880	1414	1424	520
Salmon	879	823	896	1335	1704

You do not need to boldface the row and column titles at this stage, but should highlight the *data* (using mouse left click on the cell 5923 and dragging to the cell 1704), and give this area a *right margin alignment* using the icon in the Standard Tool Bar. If the table comprises percentages or values which are similar (all tens, hundreds, thousands etc.) you could try centring the data in the highlighted area. Column headings (here the dates) may be centred. You may also want to change the font for the table. Arial is a good font for numbers and tolerates reduction.

Data can be entered in any order and sorted by row or column later using Tools – Sort. For example, rather than alphabetically it might serve a purpose to sort data high to low for the '1971' column. This would serve to show the dominant catches in 1971 and to emphasise the changed structure of the catch at the end of the period. I sorted the above table alphabetically by species, and by chance this was also the same as the ranked catches for 1931. The full data in Table 2 was sorted by 1931 catches and where the species are not alphabetical. Don't get confused. When we choose to sort by the 1931 *column* all the rest of the table will be changed such that all the data for herring and all other species remains on the same row.

There is nothing complicated about sorting. Highlight the whole table or just the rows containing the species name and data. Using Tables – Sort you will be asked about the sorting criteria. If you have highlighted the entire table make sure that you have indicated that the table has a Header row (i.e. this is table information for years, not the size of the catch).

We resume formatting. It is preferable to set equal column widths and centre the table. Here is the result for the full table, data sorted high to low for 1931, data right-oriented, years (top column) centred.

Table 6.2 Norway. Fish landings by species 1931–1971. Tons.

	1931	1941	1951	1961	1971
Herring	305446	214475	888006	69042	6894
Cod	106834	129686	149070	77580	169457
Haddock	22435	12768	18260	46677	35595
Mackerel	8388	4760	18490	14973	229825
Halibut	5293	1352	5273	4292	1981
Plaice	3484	880	1414	1424	520
Salmon	879	823	896	1335	1704

Now highlight the entire table and select one of the autoformats using Table –Autoformat. The first choice, 'Simple 1', is a useful format, easily modified. Note that the table width is automatically reduced to a convenient size. In our example we now have:

Table 6.3 Norway. Fish landings by species 1931–1971. Tons.

	1931	1941	1951	1961	1971
Herring	305446	214475	888006	69042	6894
Cod	106834	129686	149070	77580	169457
Haddock	22435	12768	18260	46677	35595
Mackerel	8388	4760	18490	14973	229825
Halibut	5293	1352	5273	4292	1981
Plaice	3484	880	1414	1424	520
Salmon	879	823	896	1335	1704

Modern processors provide a variety of autoformatted tables, but you may find that it is worth spending some time adding information and applying your own shading to selected columns in order to distinguish between the variables. Using Table – Insert column to right, I added the percentages manually, i.e. using a pocket calculator. It is possible to use the formula function on Tables, but sometimes a pocket calculator is just as quick. It may also be easier to do the table in Excel and import it into Word, but I found it quicker to insert the column and then calculate the percentage. You may want to right justify this percentage. A 15% density shading is used in Table 4 as the finishing touch.

Table 6.4 Norway. Fish landings 1931–1971. Tons and Per cent of total, by species.

Species	1931	%	1941	%	1951	%	1961	%	1971	%
Cod	106834	23.6	129686	35.6	149070	13.8	77580	36.0	169457	38.0
Haddock	22435	5.0	12768	3.5	18260	1.7	46677	21.7	35595	8.0
Halibut	5293	1.2	1352	0.4	5273	0.5	4292	2.0	1981	0.4
Herring	305446	67.5	214475	58.8	888006	82.1	69042	32.1	6894	1.5
Mackerel	8388	1.9	4760	1.3	18490	1.7	14973	7.0	229825	51.5
Plaice	3484	0.8	880	0.2	1414	0.1	1424	0.7	520	0.1
Salmon	879	0.2	823	0.2	896	0.1	1335	0.6	17	04
TOTAL	452759	100.0	364744	100.0	1081409	100.0	215323	100.0	445976	100.0

The following shows the various shades of grey and white on black. These subtleties may not, however, appear on all laser printers (better on an inkjet printer). These effects are easily achieved by highlighting the column and selecting the background colour. Then choose the font colour (black or white).

Table 6.5 Shading: Percentage grey shading.

0%	5%	10%	15%	20%	25%	30%	35%	W/Gr	W/B
106834	23.6	129686	35.6	149070	13.8	77580	36.0	169457	38.0
22435	5.0	12768	3.5	18260	1.7	46677	21.7	35595	8.0
5293	1.2	1352	0.4	5273	0.5	4292	2.0	1981	0.4
305446	67.5	214475	58.8	888006	82.1	69042	32.1	6894	1.5
8388	1.9	4760	1.3	18490	1.7	14973	7.0	229825	51.5
3484	0.8	880	0.2	1414	0.1	1424	0.7	520	0.1
879	0.2	823	0.2	896	0.1	1335	0.6	1704	0.4
452759	100.0	364744	100.0	1081409	100.0	215323	100.0	445976	100.0

The white on grey (W/Gr) is quite effective, here on a 50% shading. This seems to be more effective than the solid black background (W/B).

By this time it should be clear that Excel is not an ideal substitute for the Tables feature in Word. The same applies to other word processors and associated spreadsheets. The latter are programs for executing calculations and constructing charts. It is a simple matter to import tables into Excel from Word using copy and paste, and vice versa, but do your formatting in Word.

Charts and Diagrams

Even when tables are used, it is surprising how authors fail to go that extra step and provide a few illustrations which summarise the essential data in easily comprehended diagrams. Previously, special chart programmes were necessary and were fairly demanding in setting up diagrams. Remember Harvard Graphics? Once mastered, users often got carried away and produced material more akin to graffiti than a graphical presentation of data. Excellent charts are now available in most spreadsheet programs and which may be compiled in a matter of minutes, thereafter easily transferred to your article using 'copy-and-paste'.

It is essential to remember the purpose of a diagram (or chart – I use these terms as synonyms): this is to give a visual presentation of the main elements of statistical information, often – although not necessarily included in a table accompanying the text. It draws the reader's attention to the main features, distribution pattern, trends and changes over time, etc. In fact, a good chart is often better than a table. If it is trends you wish to emphasise, don't fog up the issue with unnecessary data.

Excel contains 14 basic types of diagram of which just six cover all the essential forms of graphic presentation (the others are largely 'decorative'). The six basic forms are: Column, Bar, Line, Pie, Scatter, Area. While several types of data may be presented using more than one of these styles, some forms of presentation are suited to a particular type of data. For example, time series can be shown using columns or lines (sometimes called a flow chart); correlation and regression must be illustrated using a scatter plot. Finally, each chart type contains several options relating to information to appear on the chart as such; some are suited to absolute values, others to relative amounts (percentages), etc. This is discussed below.

Where historic data is to be plotted the year is given along the horizontal (X) axis. The vertical (Y) axis, is normally used for volume, price, percentages etc.

By way of illustration we shall use the data in Table 6.1, reproduced here:

	1931	1941	1951	1961	1971
Salmon	879	823	896	1335	1704
Halibut	5293	1352	5273	4292	1981
Plaice	3834	880	1414	1424	420

Either a) type the above table into the Excel spreadsheet, or b) type it into a table in Word and then copy it into a new Excel spreadsheet.

Charts in Excel

A hands-on exercise

My examples are based on Excel as this seem to be the most popular spread sheet. If your table is written in Word you can copy it directly into Excel. Files from some other word processors may have to be transferred using the import-export command. How to import tables is conveniently explained in the Word Help menu. In the following we assume that you have entered the above information into an Excel worksheet. Reading the following text won't get you very far – but twenty minutes of follow-my-instructions will reveal your hitherto unknown talents in Excel. We will then construct the diagrams below.

Step 1. Highlight the *entire* data and labels (dates, fish species, data) to be charted. Click on cell A1 and drag to the bottom right cell, thereby highlighting the active work area. Do not highlight 'total' rows or columns.

Step 2. Click on Insert on the toolbar. Select Chart. This now shows 'Chart Wizard – Step 1'. In the Standard Type click Column.

Step 3. Click, Next, Next, Next, Finish. We now have a coloured chart with all the information. This information is contained in a number of hidden fields on the chart. Clicking on any field as described below enables us to edit that particular field. We could have edited information before clicking 'Next', but I prefer the following method as I can see the finished chart before I undertake any necessary editing of text, layout etc.

Placing (not clicking) the cursor on any data or symbol will reveal the name of the field. These are:

Value axis (Y-axis, here with tons although 'tons' not stated)

▶ Category axis (X-axis, time scale)
▶ Plot Area (grey at present)
▶ The Value Axis Grid Lines,
▶ Legend. We can *right* click on any of these fields and edit them.
▶ Series data (here different coloured columns).

Experimenting is the easiest way forward at this stage. Double click on Chart Area (the white area inside the frame). Nothing needs changing here, but you could change the font, for example.

Double clicking on Category Axis or Value Axis enables you to change font, and also the scale. Sometimes we might wish to show data restricted to a certain range – an option observed here.

Right Click Plot Area. Select Format Plot Area. Select white as the Fill Effect as we will normally require a black and white diagram. OK.

Right click again on Plot Area. Select Chart Options. Select Titles and enter these. Select Gridlines and uncheck the Y axis gridlines if not required. Click Legend and relocate if you want.

This will be sufficient. However, you may find that your diagram has lost its shape or size. When you click on any field you can locate the cursor on any of the points indicated on the frame and drag it to the shape you require or even relocate it. Do this now if necessary.

There is just one feature remaining which requires change for a black and white diagram, that is the Series columns. Double click *twice on* any column, for example, Salmon. You now have a frame entitled Format Data Series. Click 'None' under 'Area'; click Fill Effects. Now click 'Pattern' and make sure that Foreground is in black and Background is white. Select a pattern, preferably one that is fairly dark as the Salmon data column is small and needs to be seen. Click OK, OK.

Make any adjustments to the size of the outside frame or the Plot Area frame using click and drag. And now we have it. Quite painless, wasn't it? And for those of your who tried to read the above text you will have learnt little. I did emphasise that this was hands on. And if something did not work quite as described, you will have learnt the principle of clicking on the various elements so that you may then customise your diagram to requirements.

▶ We can now turn to the main types of chart and their properties.

Column diagram

The **vertical column** is used to show relative quantities for each period. Generally a maximum of 6 or 7 groups (here, fish species) is recommended.

A broad variety of shading textures is available, but you may find that these are not distinctive in the diagram keys or in small diagrams. Think more in terms of gradations of a grey scale. Black shading should generally be used only where one of the groups involves very small quantities throughout. The larger the quantity, the larger the area representing the value – or taller the column, and the lighter the shading required. But try to arrange the data such that there is a satisfactory contrast between adjacent columns as in Fig. 1. Nevertheless, the shading could be changed so as to provide a better contrast in the key. The overall effect of your diagram will be dependent upon the visual effect – i.e. the shading. For this reason I have added a note on shading patterns at the end of this chapter.

Gridlines (extending horizontally from the value scale) are optional, as are most features on this chart and all others. Even the frames are optional. Although the titles have been entered in the spreadsheet, it is often more convenient to exclude these and write these above the diagram using the word processor as the figure number and title are then more easily entered and changed.

Norway. Fish landings by species 1931 - 1971

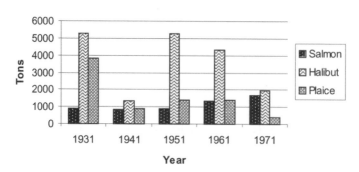

Stacked columns are best when the relative proportions need to be emphasised. Place the larger units at the base of the columns. The flow lines can assist in showing the relative changes if only three of four elements are plotted. More than this and the impression is a confusing display of columns, sectors and lines.

Norway: Fishing catch 1931-1971. Relative proportions

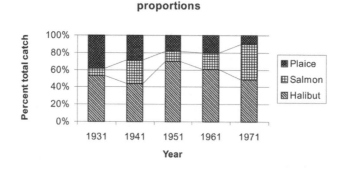

Other varieties of column diagrams are very decorative. Avoid the 3-dimensional charts – they can be more confusing than informative.

Bar charts

The bar chart refers to the column diagram turned 90 degrees. Rather than being used for absolute numbers bar charts are useful for showing relative proportions and where the percentage scale would now be on the X-axis. An example could be the percentages voting for political parties in different cities. Any number of cases (cities) may be given, but for practical purposes should be related to the page size.

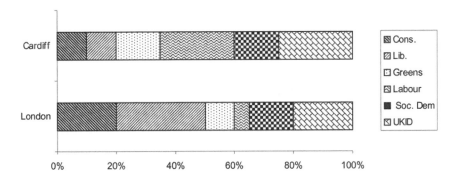

Line charts

Percentage poll at local government elections, by authority type.
1945 - 1964

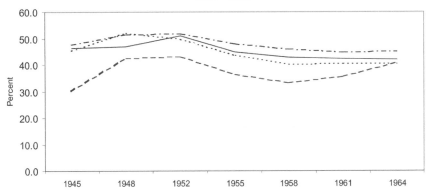

The line chart is useful for showing trends, either continuously – or as here, through a sequence of periods. Note that the information is not cumulative as in the case of total fishing catch by species. Rather, this chart enables a comparison to be made between the categories, showing here the relative increase in interest in county elections towards the end of the period. If one is going to draw any conclusion from this particular chart it must be that the local government reforms of the late sixties were well overdue.

Generally – and especially if there is overlapping – the number of lines (categories) should be limited. Ideally, line diagrams are best coloured.

Stacked area charts

Where trends are required and the elements may be cumulated, the area chart is useful. In many ways this is an alternative to stacked columns. Here again is the trade-off that the relative amounts are not always easy to read. The 'show gridlines' option has been used in this chart. The order of the series is important. Place those species which show little variation over time on the bottom. This will result in less 'distortion'. You will probably agree that it may have been better had 'Halibut' been placed at the top.

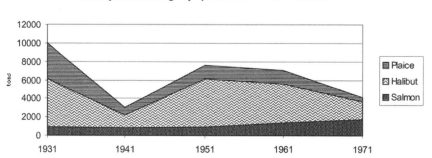

Norway. Fish landings by species 1931 - 1971. Volume

The following chart shows the same data but by proportion (percentage) of the total catch.

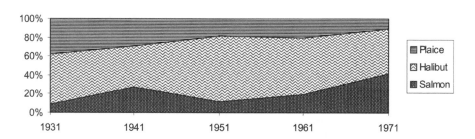

Norway. Fish landings by species 1931 - 1971. Percentage of total catch

Pie charts

Pie charts are an appealing way to show the relative proportions of elements. Depending upon the relative sizes of the elements, up to eight 'slices' may normally be used. More become confusing. Occasionally, two proportional or percentage pie charts may be presented adjacently to show the structure for two different years or subjects, but this is difficult in Excel necessitating two columns in the word processor and a good bit of hassle getting the proportions right.

The largest section should commence at 12 o'clock. It is possible to revolve the pie such that this falls into place as the automatic chart process might choose another sector to commence at this point. Choose a lighter shading for this segment. You may also have to set the background to white and the foreground to black as the default colours may not be distinguishable when printed in black and white. Either percentages or values may be shown, but unfortunately not both.

Norway. Fishing catch 1931. Tons

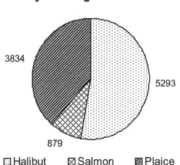

Scatter plot diagrams

Scatter plot diagrams

When there are two or more pieces of information (variables) per case, any two may be shown as a scatter plot. *Correlation* shows the *strength* of the relationship between two variables (see Chapter 7), given as the correlation coefficient Pearson's r. In correlation it does not matter which variable is plotted on the X or Y axis. In the diagram below, Pearson's $r = 0.68$, showing a fairly strong association between fertiliser applications and crop yield. (Pearson's r value is not shown, although R^2 is – we return to that.). The higher the absolute value or r, the closer the correlation. Why 'absolute value'? This is because r can be negative in some studies, showing that as the value of one variable decreases so the other increases. Example: the less money spent on controlling pollution, the more pollution will increase. So r can range from −1 to +1. (0 would indicate no correlation between the two variables.)

Whereas correlation showed us the strength of the relationship between the two variables measured by the coefficient r, we may also be interested in a *causal* relationship. It is here that we use *regression analysis*. Let us assume a fertiliser manufacturer is testing out a concentrated chemical and selects a number of fields at random. Some fields are given a low application; others a large amount. This is the causal or independent variable shown on the X-axis. The Y-axis is the dependent variable. Here is part of the data (originally entered in two columns in the Excel worksheet, but data may also be entered in rows).[1]

```
Fertiliser. Application lbs per acre 1  3   2  2  3 .....    9 10 10
Yield. Cwt. per acre.                9 13 12 19 25 .....   60 59 62
```

Most will be familiar with the formula $Y = aX + b$ which shows the gradient of a line. Y is the yield. b is the value of Y where, if extended, the line crosses the Y axis and when X = 0. We see on the diagram this Y would be about 3.5 at this intercept, confirmed in the formula in the diagram. We see that a has a value of 6.17. This is the change in units of Y resulting from a change in one unit of X. The increase of one pound of fertiliser over an acre would result in an increase of 6.17 cwt. in the crop yield.

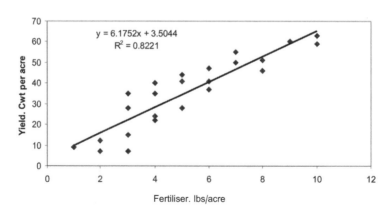

Fertiliser experiment

$y = 6.1752x + 3.5044$
$R^2 = 0.8221$

1   This is based on actual data from an experiment conducted half a century ago. Hence pre-metric units. But the principle is the same whether these were kg/ha application and tonnes/ha yield.

The other piece of information given here is R^2. A simple interpretation is that this is the percentage of total increase in yield due to the fertiliser, here 82%. The remaining 18% may be due to temperature, rainfall, humidity, acidity in the soil and so forth. These would be tested in a multiple regression analysis.

Here we return to hands-on! The initial plot produced by Excel is just a scatter diagram. Double click anywhere on the Chart area or Plot area. Format chart area allows you to select the colours for either area. If the default of the Plot area background is grey, it is better to change this to white. Chart options on this menu allows you to add the titles. You may prefer to remove the grid lines. Just select the appropriate tab on this menu. I find little use for the Series box. Click on it and then Del to remove.

The scales on the axes may be changed. It is not always necessary that these commence at 0. Place the cursor on the axis to be changed, *right* click. On the Format axis menu select Scale and enter the appropriate maximum and minimum values. These should be lower and higher than the minimum and maximum values respectively in the data.

The trend line is useful in regression analyses (it is not required for correlation). Place the cursor on any of the *plot points* on the chart. The coordinates of that point will be given. Now *right* click. Click Add Trendline and select type (of trend). If r was positive the line will slope up to the right; if r was negative is will slope down to the right. You may experiment to see which trend line (except moving average) gives the best fit, i.e. highest value for R^2. This is because the relationship might not be linear, i.e. a straight line, but sloping off (curvilinear) as seen in the next diagram. But ideally, we are looking for a straight line and it may be that the relationship is logarithmic

To examine this (left) click on the trend line. On the Format Trend Line menu select options. Check the Display equation and Display R-squared boxes. Click Type (of trendline). Select logarithmic for example. See whether this gives a notably higher R^2. We are normally interested in linear relationships and a small variation in R^2 may be ignored. Finally, you may want to relocate the equation on the chart. Just click and drag.

Just to remind you, only interval data and not ranked or ordinal data are used in correlation and regression. Techniques are used for correlation involving ordinal and nominal variables are described in Chapter 7.

Other diagrams

There is a wide range of diagrams available on Excel – and even wider on many statistical programmes. As indicated above, several types are decorative more than informative and possibly useful in preparing a brochure on soap powder or cat food. In Excel these are called 'Custom charts'. I have never had use for any except one called 'Smooth lines' where different types of trend line may be superimposed – here a polynomial trend line for a single variable. We note that traffic pollution increases rapidly in the early stages of rush-hour around 7 a.m., and continues to do so, but at a slower rate until about 10 a.m.

Pollution levels

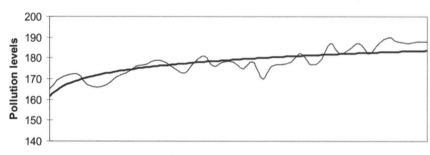

But by all means experiment with those diagrams named B&W Area, Column and Timescale. You may find an effect you like, but ask yourself whether it says anything about the statistical information behind the diagram.

It is possible to plot two or more data sets on a scattergram. This necessitates common elements. For example, another type of fertiliser might also have been applied. But these complex diagrams are seldom informative:

Fertiliser. Comparative study

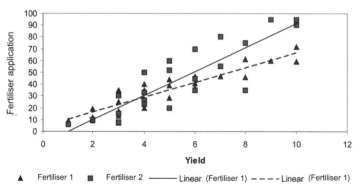

Clearly better with two separate plots.

A note on shading diagrams

One major function of a chart is to present an impression of the main distribution of data in a table. In order to do this successfully the shading of the various segments in the diagram (column, bar, etc.) must be carefully selected. The segments reflect the values of the different series, e.g. cod, herring etc. Different patterns and densities of shading will be used to show each series. The following diagram shows patterns for six series in each column. The names of each style or pattern are shown when selecting from the Fill effects – Pattern menu in Excel. You will find information on this in the Excel Help menu.

Column 1 in the following shows (1) Dots (shading). The density of these varies from 5% to 90%. Those providing best contrast are 10%, 25%, 50% and 80%; (2) Diagonal lines (L/R and R/L i.e. upward/downward). These are found in three thicknesses giving varying densities.

Column 2 uppermost is the small chequer board followed by diamond grid then divot, zigzag, diamond brickwork and large chequer board at the bottom.

Column 3 shows patterns based on horizontal and vertical lines. These are generally not satisfactory and should only be used when other options have been exhausted.

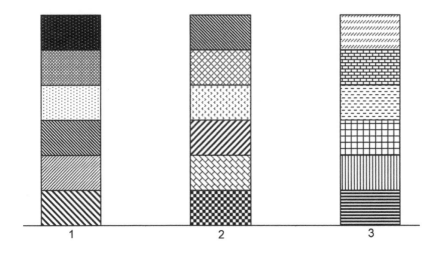

Normally data values will result in segments of varying heights (or widths on a bar chart) reflecting the different values in a series. You may have to experiment to see which patterns give the best effect. Generally, small segments should be darker. Fill these in first. Adjacent segments should show contrast both in patterns and density. An effective manner to look at contrasts is to squint. Try this on the above. You will then see any adjacent segments which should be changed. As is happens, the contrast in column 1 is good even though dots were placed adjacent to each other for demonstration; contrast in column 3 is poor. Note that some patterns may no longer be clear and distinguishable from others when the diagram is reduced in scale. Rather than changing the patterns for the various segments it may be more convenient to reorder the segments, i.e. place them in a different sequence with the aim of improving contrast .(See Help menu in Excel. Keyword 'Sequence', then 'Change the plotting order'.)

Finally, an example of effective (left column) and ineffective (right column) shading. Incidentally, if you have grey-shading on your printer you may also use 'solid shading' black, dark grey, light grey, etc.

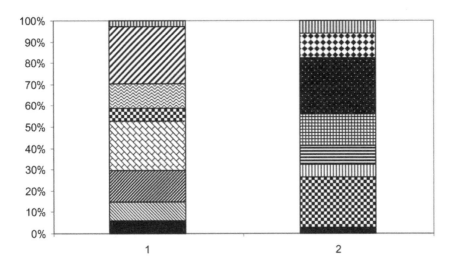

While we have concentrated on shading using Excel, it is also possible to use the Drawing Toolbar in Word to change patterns. This is identical to the Excel procedure described above. For a description, type the keyword 'graphic' on the Word Help menu, then select 'Ways to enhance graphics'.

Finally, you may find problems in importing Excel diagrams into older versions of Word, for example Excel 2003 diagrams into Word 2000. Ensure that both programs are of the same vintage.

7
Statistical Measures and Statistical Tests

It is now proved beyond doubt that smoking is one of the leading causes of statistics. Fletcher Knebel (1911–1993). American writer.

When someone says 'statistics are Greek to me', they may well know what they are talking about. But it is precisely the use of Greek symbols which is the 'scary element' in statistics. This myth may be briefly disposed of in the following, although it must be emphasised that this is not an introduction to statistical method. Rather, it is an aid to understanding the principles of statistics for those who don't know, or those who did know and have forgotten. I have been constantly aware of this when preparing this chapter. At the very least you will have been introduced to the essential terms and principles in statistical method. Better, you may well find yourself able to produce some essential statistical information using Excel. Better still, you will feel encouraged to take the plunge and purchase a book on statistical method. A few are given in the references.

There was a time when the slide-rule, pencil and paper were the tools of the statistician (I remember it well). Today, many useful analyses may be made using spreadsheets; in addition there are a number of excellent statistical programmes in addition to the universal programmes such as SPSS (Statistical Package for the Social Sciences).

Given the fact that these statistical packages are universally found and, under Windows, are very easy to operate, it is rather surprising that so many researchers appear reluctant or unable to present the simplest statistics and *interpret* them. Statistical methods are essentially concerned with (a) describing a data set (descriptive statistics), or (b) making estimates about a population based on a sample (predictive or inferential statistics).

That's all there is too it. So why all this paranoia about statistics? My theory (hypothesis) is that statisticians in general are good with numbers, but weak on words. Now, few are bad but few are brilliant. It is possibly also a problem of packing too much stuff into a book leaving limited space for really explaining the essentials. In the following I am restricted to the essentials, but not to space. If you know nothing about statistics, good. Just imagine you are reading *Harry Potter*. If you know something, well imagine you are reading *The Lord of the Rings*. If you know it all, then go and read a statistics text.

We commence with a brief summary of the different types of data.

Data Types

The following variables from a theoretical study serve to illustrate the main types of data.

Variable	Label	Type
1. Gender:	Male/female	dichotomous
2. Age:	May use decimals or registered in whole years. May also be grouped data (0–9, 10–19, etc.)	continuous or discrete
3. Family size:	Total parents, children, relatives residing in house	discrete
4. Income:	Monthly income in dollars and cents	continuous
5. Residence:	1. Detached; 2. semi-detached: 3. terrace; 4. high block; 5. other	nominal
6. Political preference:	Communist, Socialist, Greens, Liberal, Christian Democrat, Conservative, Radical	nominal, may be treated as ordinal
7. Views on Govt. transport policy	1. Excellent; 2. Very Good; 3. Fair; 4. Poor; 5. Very poor	ordinal

Interval or quantitative data

Quantitative data may be measured in discrete or continuous units of fixed interval.

▶ 'Family size' is *discrete,* that is it may only be given in *whole* numbers. There are no decimals, only when calculating averages such as 2.4 children, for example.

▶ 'Income' is *continuous*, or may be regarded as such. Height, weight and temperature are examples of other variables measured on a continuous scale. If the scale has true zero as the point of origin then the scale is a *ratio scale* in that it is possible to say that a family of 4 is twice as large as a family of 2, or A's income is 10 percent higher than that of B.

Temperature does not have zero as the point of origin. A day with the temperature at 20°C is not twice as warm as a day when the temperature is only 10°C.

▶ 'Age' is strictly speaking continuous, but often registered as discrete data, parts of a year being rounded down (ignored). But what do you do with the baby of just a few months? Clearly, rounding up might be advantageous.

It is often convenient to group quantitative data into classes such as age groups (0–19; 20–29; and so forth). It depends what we want to find out. We can do the same with income classes and possibly even family size (small, medium, large). This is particularly convenient when we are compiling tables.

We should mention that many interval and continuous variables are characterised by a so-called 'normal distribution'. If we plot shoe sizes of a thousand adult shoppers, we will probably find that a high percentage have sizes close to the mean,[1] 41–43 (or 8½ to 9½); quite a lot will have sizes 39–40 or 43–44; very few have under 36 or over 48. If we plot this frequency distribution we have a bell-shaped pattern, known as a normal distribution This may be flat or peaked, depending on the range around the mean (indicated by the standard deviation, discussed below), but nevertheless essentially bell-shaped. Not all distributions are symmetric: some are skewed. Income is a good example of a skewed distribution where many have an income just below the mean and a few have an income far above it.

Categorical or qualitative data

As the name suggests categorical data comprises information registered by category. It registers certain qualities. In the above, gender, type of residence, political preference and views on government immigration policy are examples of categorical or qualitative variables.

▶ 'Gender' is a *dichotomous variable* – it may be either of two categories, male/female. Many variables may be dichotomised. For example a variable which registers heavy smoker, light smoker, non-smoker can be dichotomised into smoker/non-smoker. Yes/no variables are very common. There are special statistical methods which refer to dichotomised variables.

▶ 'Type of residence' is a *nominal* variable. It does not matter what order these are – block, semidetached, terrace, detached – they do not progress from good to bad, expensive to cheap, for example, unless we are putting them into such categories.

---

1   'Average' is a bit more colloquial: 'on the average...'. Statisticians like to use the 'mean'.

▶ 'Political preference' is also *nominal* but could be treated as *ordinal (ranked)* in so far as it goes from the political left to the political right, but it could easily be sorted from right to left. Indeed, there might even be some controversy as to whether Liberals were more 'left' than the Christian Democrats (in our theoretical constituency). And the 'Greens'?

▶ 'Views on government transport policy' – might just as well be views on a brand of butter – are clearly *ordinal* or *ranked* data. However, 'Poor' (4) can hardly be said to be twice as important as Very Good (2), even if the ranking went from 5 down to 1. There is no suggestion that the ranks are 'evenly spaced' and this sort of data has to be analysed carefully. A common mistake is to treat ranked data as numerical or quantitative.

Descriptive statistics for qualitative (categorical) data are quite limited and largely restricted to counts in the various groups. As such we cannot describe the mean or median although we may have a modal group (that with the highest number of counts or N). If 50 per cent of the electorate vote Conservative and 50 per cent voted Labour, we cannot say that on average the electorate favours the Social Democrats.

It is very often convenient to present categorical data graphically. Because we cannot define a mean, statistical tests which assume a normal distribution are not applicable. Consequently these data sets are occasionally referred to as 'distribution free' data. We may also encounter the terms 'parametric statistics' relating to interval data with a normal distribution, and 'non-parametric statistics' relating to ordinal and categorical data.

Useful to say what we mean by a 'parameter' even though we have used the term several times. It is one of those misused terms loved by football managers: 'Within the given parameters I expect England to beat France 2–0.' What a lot of hoo-ha.

Let us take the *OED* definition: 'a numerical characteristic of a population, as distinct from a statistic of a sample.' The point is that when we take a sample we can measure all the data and calculate the statistics. We use this to estimate the population parameters; we can never be absolutely sure as we can't measure all the data in the whole population. By the way, the population means the *entire* set of variables we are considering – *all* pupils taking statistics, all pensioners, all wine drinkers, and so forth.

Parametric statistics cover data that can be measured: ages, income, temperatures and so forth. Here, among other statistics, we can calculate the mean. But we cannot measure the mean of tastes (like, not like), preferences (apples, pears, oranges) or voting behaviour. Here we use non-parametric statistics.

Descriptive Statistics

Descriptive statistics describe variables in a data set. Which statistics are appropriate depends upon the data type. Analysis of qualitative categories largely concerns the class counts or frequency distribution among the categories.

Quantitative data may be analysed using a considerably larger number of statistics methods. These include number of cases (N), the mean, the median, mode, standard deviation and others. These can be exemplified using four data sets. Let us consider the following cases, assuming these to be the ages of children born to a sample of four families, each of whom have been married 12 years. (I am aware that some families will have several children within the first few years of marriage, but the following will serve to illustrate descriptive statistics.)

Age of child / Data set (family no.)	1	2	3	4	5	6	7	8	9	10	11
1		■	■				■	■		■	
2	■			■		■			■	■	
3		■	■ ■		■	■					■
4		■			■ ■		■				■

The mean values for each data set are shaded in the above. Thus, the mean age of the children in three of these families is 6, and 5 for the family number 3 which, incidentally, is the only family with six children. Many of the following statistics indicate the spread of the ages (or dispersion) of all the children around the mean.

Statistical summary:

	Note	Family 1	Family 2	Family 3	Family 4
Data (children's ages)		2 3 7 8 10	1 4 6 9 10	2 3 3 5 6 11	2 5 5 7 11
Number of cases (N =)		5	5	6	5
Sum		30	30	30	30
Mean (Sum/N)		6	6	5	6
Minimum value		2	1	2	2
Maximum value		10	10	11	11
Range (Max. − Min.)		8	9	9	9
Mid-range (Max. + Min.)/2	1	6	5.5	6.5	6.5
Median	2	7	6	4	5

Mode	*3*	-	-	3	5
1. quartile (Q1)	*4*	3	4	3	5
2. quartile((Q2)	*5*	7	6	4	5
3. quartile(Q3)	*6*	8	9	5.5	7
Interquartile range (Q3-Q1)	*7*	5	5	2.5	2
Low spread (Q2-Q1)		4	2	1	0
High spread (Q3-Q2)		1	3	1.5	2
Quartile devn (Q3-Q1)/2		2.5	2.5	1.25	1
Quartile central tendency (Q1 + Q3)/2	*8*	5.5	6.5	4.25	6
Quartile coeff. of relative dispersion	*9*	.45	.38	.29	.17
Mean absolute deviation	*10*	2.8	2.8	2.3	2.0
Coeff. of mean deviation	*11*	0.47	0.47	0.46	0.33
Standard Deviation (SD)	*12*	**3.39**	**3.67**	**3.29**	**3.32**
St. Error of the mean	*13*	**1.52**	**1.64**	**1.34**	**1.48**
Coefficient of variation	*14*	0.565	0.612	0.658	0.553
Moment coeff. of skewness	*15*	**-0.19**	**-0.35**	**1.47**	**0.69**
Moment coeff. of kurtosis	16	**-2.23**	**-1.29**	**2.21**	**1.13**

Statistical measures in **boldface** above are obtainable in Excel using Tools – Data Analysis – Descriptive statistics (OK) – Summary statistics. Other statistics may be calculated using a formula in the spreadsheet. Virtually all the above statistics (and some others) are available in programs such as SPSS, SAS, SYSTAT, MINITAB, etc.

Notes:

1. The **mid-range** is that value located at the mid-point between the lowest and highest values.

2. The **median** is the value of the middle case (i.e. the third case in a data set of five). If there is an even number of cases, the mean of the two middle cases is calculated, i.e. the mean of the third and fourth cases in a data set of six).

3. The **mode** is that value which occurs most frequently in the data set. If the data set is symmetrical the mode will approximate the median (and the mean). A J-shaped distribution will show the mode towards one end. Example: travel time to work. Most travel about 30 minutes; increasingly fewer numbers travel 1 hour, 2 hours, etc. The mean may be about 50 minutes, but the mode may only be 30 minutes. Of course, many data sets may be bi-modal or have several values occurring an equal number of times.

4. Quartiles are useful measures of the dispersion of data around the mean, especially for skewed distributions. The **1. quartile** indicates that value for which one fourth *or fewer* of the cases are below. Where N is divisible by 4,

this is easily calculated. For other values of N, Q1 = $1(N+1)/4$. For data sets with a large number of cases, this is easily calculated. For small data sets it is doubtful that the quartiles mean so much. For Data set 1 Q1 is $(6/4)$ = 1.5. We round this *up* to 2. Q1 is thus the value of the 2nd case ($=3$). Q3 = $3(N+1)/4$ = 4.5. This is rounded *down* to 4. Q3 is thus the value of the 4th case ($=8$). Some programs use other conventions and statistics involving the quartiles when these are very unreliable with low N. (See Note 9).

5. The 2nd **quartile**, Q2, is the median, that value where 50% of cases lie above, and 50% below.

6. Q3, the 3rd **quartile.** Similar to Q1, 75% of cases are *below* this value, 25% above.

7. The **interquartile range** is a measure of spread around the mean indicating the range between which the 'central' fifty per cent of cases are located. But this is affected by skewed distributions. For this reason the **semi-interquartile range** is preferred. This is sometimes called the **quartile deviation.** Note the formula (Q3-Q1)/2

8. A measure of *central tendency* (rather than dispersion) is given by (Q3 + Q1)/2, the **quartile central tendency.**

9. The **quartile coefficient of variation** or the **quartile coefficient of dispersion** is given by (Q3-Q1)/(Q3 + Q1). See Note 4.

10. The **Mean Absolute Deviation** (MAD) is the mean of the absolute values of the each case value minus the mean. For Data set 1 this would be the mean of $|2-6|$, $|3-6|$ giving $(4 + 3 + 1 + 2 + 4)/5$ = 2.8. A useful statistic for this type of data. As its name suggests it is a measure of the mean spread of the data around the mean.

11. The **Coefficient of mean deviation** is given by MAD/mean. This is a measure of relative dispersion (spread) about the mean.

12. The **Standard Deviation** is a measure of spread around the mean. Approximately 68% of all cases will lie within the mean 1 SD in a normal distribution.

13. The **Standard Deviation of the Mean** (confusingly also called the **Standard Error**) is used to estimate the true error of the population in predictive statistics. It provides an estimate of the range within which the true (but unknown) mean of the population will lie.

14. The **Coefficient of variation** is the SD/mean, usually given as a percentage ($*$ 100).

15. The **coefficient of skewness** indicates the number of cases to the left (positive skew) or right (negative skew) of the mean. That is the extent to which the distribution is skewed in comparison to a normal bell-shaped symmetrical distribution. A symmetrical (bell-shaped) distribution will have a coefficient of 0. Date set 3 shows is the most skewed. The youngest child is just three years under the mean age; the oldest is six years above.

16. **Kurtosis** is also a similar measurement to indicate the 'peakedness' of a distribution. Another way of expressing this is the degree to which the tail values are spread with respect to the mean. Data set 3 has the highest coefficient suggesting that it has the most 'peaked' distribution. In fact, three of the six children are aged 2 or 3. Data set 1 has the 'flattest' distribution.

Relationship between known sample mean and estimated population mean

Those having a basic knowledge of statistics will be aware that measures of spread around the mean are very useful in predicting population parameters from sample statistics. We do this when the population is large and it is logistically too costly and difficult to measure the entire population. This can be calculated fairly reliably when we have a regular distribution pattern in the sample, particularly if it is 'normal' (bell-shaped). This is because we assume the population to have a similar distribution.

For example, we can calculate the mean age of a sample of persons. We can then use the sample mean (a statistic) to estimate the probability of the population mean (a parameter) falling within a given range around the sample mean. Example: If a sample of 25 pensioners shows a mean age of 71 with a standard deviation of 5, we calculate the mean age of the population (all pensioners) to be 71 ± 3 with a probability of 90% or 71 ± 6 with a 99% probability. In other words, we are 99% certain that the true population mean is between 65 and 77. The wider the range around an estimated mean, the greater the probability that the true population mean lies within these limits. This range might appear to be very wide, but the larger the sample, the more reliable we expect it to be in estimating this range. With a sample of 500 we might well be able to determine the 99% confidence limits as being between 70 and 72. This is a typical example of parametric statistics. This, of course, reflects the fact that the larger the sample, the closer the sample is expected to resemble the population from which it was drawn. That is why we like a sample to be as large as possible.

We have also mentioned several other measures of dispersion: the semi-interquartile range, the quartile coefficient of relative dispersion, the MAD and others. These are more appropriate to descriptions of skewed distributions, but are limited in their ability to estimate population parameters.

Standardised variables. I did say that this was not going to be a chapter on statistical method, but standardised variables (or **standardised scores** as they are known as in educational statistics) are useful for comparing different data sets. The standardised score (z) for any variable is $z = (x - x_{mean})/s$ where s = standard deviation. Let's take a simple example. Here are the results of Smith Minor in his two favourite subjects. It is not important, but we can assume the maximum score was 100.

Subject	Smith Minor's score	Class mean	Class standard deviation	Standardised score z
Statistics	70	60	12	0.83
History	71	64	9	0.78

Although achieving a higher grade in history, Smith Minor is better, relative to the class grades in statistics. Looking at our family data, we could ask whether the eldest child in data set 3 (11 years old) is relatively older than the eldest child of the same age in (11) data set 4. The youngest child in both families is 2 years old.

Family 3: (11-5)/3.29 = 1.82 Family 4: (11-6)/3.32 = 1.51

The oldest child in Family 3 may be said to be relatively older. You may ask why not divide the age (11) by the mean of each group. This would give 2.2 and 1.8 respectively but this only considers one value (the mean) rather than the *spread* of the ages of all family members. In families 1 and 2 the eldest child is 10 and the mean age for both families is 6. This would show no difference, but standard scores for the child aged 10 are 3.39 and 3.67 respectively. Curiously, if we take the mean of all the differences between the eldest child and all the others in each set (e.g. for set 1, this would be the mean of (10-2) + (10-3) + (10-7) + (10-8)), we achieve the same value, 5, for each set. What this says is that the mean difference for the eldest child in each family and his siblings in *absolute* values is the same. This is not quite the same thing as the *relative* difference given by the z scores. Some statistical programs produce standard scores for all data in the set.

The above shows virtually all the descriptive statistics available although few texts contain descriptions of all of these. In many instances it really does not matter which one you use although the standard deviation is widely used, especially for normally distributed data. For highly skewed distributions the MAD or a quartile deviation will be more suitable.

Now that we are in the mood to look at statistics in a bit more detail. let's take a couple of examples of making generalisations based on samples, i.e. predicting the population parameters.

Inferential or Predictive Statistics

In addition to descriptive statistics, we may need to make inferences, i.e. predictions, based on data. Sometimes we are concerned with the correlation between two variables (discussed in the previous chapter). It is only occasionally that we have a full data set – the statistical population – containing *all* wine drinkers but excluding teetotallers (for example), or *all* pupils studying French, *every* pensioner over the age of 70, and so forth. Normally, we have to predict the true situation based on information from a sample. For example, we might be interested in showing that men show a greater preference for one type of wine compared to women. This is our general hypothesis. Hitherto, we have not stated anything about which wine (red or white) preferred by either gender. We may nevertheless refine the hypothesis to state that men show a greater preference for red wine than do women. It is important to be clear that we are concerned with *differences in percentages* of men and women stating that they normally drink red wine. Although we are not concerned with differences in preferences for white wine, it would be natural to ask whether red wine is preferred to white. We will ignore those stating 'no preference'. A simple sketch will show us the results of our (hypothetical) survey which clearly show both men and women prefer red wine to white. However, the hypothesis which we test is the *null hypothesis*. This states that there is *no difference* between the groups, men and women in their preferences. By 'no difference' we mean that the proportions of men and women preferring red wine are the same. Our observation shows 64% of men and 52% of women prefer red wine. If there was no difference in proportions we would expect the same percentage for both to be somewhere between these. In fact if we had equal numbers of men and women, it would be halfway between then, 58%. This is what we would expect to find.

One-tail and two-tail tests

In a one-tail test we are looking in one direction, here whether there is a significant difference in the percentages of men and women preferring red wine. The hypothesis to be tested is that there is no significant difference in the percentages (here 64% and 52%).

A two-tailed test would examine preferences for both red and white wine looking to see whether one gender has a marked preference for one type of wine and the other gender prefers the other type of wine. We might wish to be more specific and state that men generally prefer red wine; women generally prefer white and to ask if the sample shows a significant difference in the genders in this respect. Again, the hypothesis to be tested is that there is no difference in preferences.

The following diagram is based on the results of our survey (presented below) and illustrates the principle of the hypothesis.

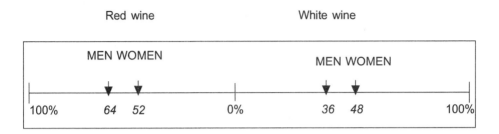

The diagram shows that both men and women have a preference for red wine, but that this preference is stronger among men.

The null hypothesis

In this test the null hypothesis states that there is no difference in the proportions of men and women. But our sample has shown that there is a difference. Nevertheless, we might have drawn another sample showing not 64:52 but 60:55 or even 57:61. In all these, both genders still show a preference for red wine. How do we know that our sample is a true reflection of the population from which it is drawn? And remember, we have only the one sample. We might have been unlucky, but we cannot prove that the sample truly reflects the population choice. What we can do is say: 'If the proportions shown men/women preferences were exactly the same in the population, what was the probability that I could have drawn a sample showing these proportions?' It is similar to having a bag of red and black balls containing equal numbers of each. You take out ten and find that you have six red and four black. You would probably assume that sixty percent of the contents of the bag were red balls and forty percent were black. But this assumption could also be wrong! In fact, had the contents of the bag been 30 percent red balls and 70 percent black, and you had still drawn six red and four black, not knowing the contents you would still have to assume that the distribution on the bag was the same as your sample. How unlucky can you be?

This is just what the test will show us. The null hypothesis assumes equal proportions of black and red balls. In our wine study we are assuming equal percentages of men and women preferring red wine. This is the null hypothesis – no difference. We then find out the probability of drawing a sample with those proportions observed (64:52), if in fact there were no differences (58:58) – the expected proportion. Why 58:58? Because it must be somewhere between 52 and 64, exactly where depending on the proportions of men and women in the sample. We have simplified this by assuming equal numbers of men and women, but in any case the program will calculate this 'expected' percentage at which there is no difference.

The test used for calculating real differences in proportions is the chi-square test. This is used to show the discrepancy between observed and expected proportions and is measured by the chi-square statistic, χ^2. This is all calculated for us, and in fact we don't need to know any more about it. What we do use is the information supplied by this statistic which is the *p*-statistic, the probability value.

Although we only take one sample, the following shows the effect of sample size on the *p*-statistic whereby the larger the sample, the more reliable the results.

	Sample 1				Sample 2			
	Men		Women		Men		Women	
Preference	**Obs.**	Exp.	**Obs.**	Exp.	**Obs.**	Exp.	**Obs.**	Exp.
Red wine	**64**	58	**52**	58	**128**	116	**52**	116
White wine	**36**	42	**48**	42	**72**	84	**48**	84
Total	**100**	100	**100**	100	**200**	200	**200**	200
	Chi-square statistic = 2.596. $p = 0.086$				Chi-square statistic = 5.911. $p = 0.015$			

As we have interviewed 100 of each gender in Sample 1 these figures are also percentages. The actual observations are given in the (Obs)erved column; the expected percentages assuming no difference are shown in the (Exp)ected column. The latter are calculated by the program. Incidentally, the table showing observed and expected values is a called a contingency table, just so that you know!

What we want to know is whether there is a *significant* difference between the observed proportions for the two genders. In other words, does the difference between the observed proportions of men and women preferring red wine differ *significantly* from the expected proportions? Remember that the expected proportions in the null hypothesis are the same for each gender, here 58:58 for red wine. If the observed difference 64:52 is *significantly* different, then we can conclude that there is a difference between men and women's tastes. We return to what we mean by *significantly* below.

Probability and significance

Tests involving predictive statistics, where a sample is used to estimate the population parameters, yield a p-statistic – the *probability* statistic. This is the probability of an event occurring which may be interpreted here as the probability of drawing a sample showing no differences between men and women's preferences when in fact the population contained differences at least as great as that shown in our sample (64:52). Probability theory starts getting a bit heavy here but we can simplify this by saying that assuming the sample to be a true reflection of the population, what is the probability that we could have drawn a sample showing no differences.

As mentioned above, we can forget the chi-square statistic: what we look at is the p-value associate with this statistic. In this example $p = 0.086$. Now an 8.6 percent probability doesn't sound much does it? But is still means that there is about 1 chance in twelve that our sample is misleading us. The question now is, how small do we want that probability to be before we can still say 'I accept that there *is* a difference in the proportions of men/women in the population preferring red to white wine'? Quite possibly we would say a 5 per cent chance, but for some tests it may be 2 per cent or less. In medical research it is likely that we would want to be much more sure, for example $p < 0.00001$ (1 chance in 100,000). This would suggest that if 5 million schoolchildren were going to be given a vaccine against a serious illness (e.g. poliomyelitis), then not only would it probably fail to work for 50 or more children, it could result in some children developing poliomyelitis. I don't think many parents would agree to this injection.

The level which we decide to be important in determining whether there is a real difference in proportions is called the *significance level*, given as α. We usually choose significance levels of 5%, 2% or 1% in the social sciences, i.e. $\alpha = 0.05, 0.02$ or 0.01. Clearly, our value of $p = 0.086$ is larger than any of these. Conclusion: we cannot be confident that this sample does reflect a population with no difference between men's and women's tastes. When $p > \alpha$, we *accept* the null hypothesis[2] and say there is insufficient evidence to show significant differences. When $p < \alpha$, we *reject* the null hypothesis and say there is strong evidence for a real difference.

What value for á do we accept? We must determine this in advance. The smaller the value of á, the more confident we can be of the results. If $p > 0.05$ then we would say that the results were not significant at the 5 per cent level ($\alpha = 0.05$ and $p > \alpha$). With this as our chosen level of significance we are looking for a *smaller* than a 1 in 20 chance.

---

2 Strictly speaking as we can never prove with 100% certainty from a sample, however large, that there is decisively no difference, we say that we 'fail to reject' the null hypothesis.

Sample size and the p-statistic

The larger a sample, the more likely the sample resembles the population from which it is drawn. Therefore we select the largest possible sample that our resources will allow. We would then expect the p-statistic to be smaller with a larger sample even when the proportions are the same. Let us say that our sample had included 200 men and 200 women as in Sample 2 (twice the size of Sample 1). Now, $p = 0.015$. Not only are the results now significant at the 5 per cent level ($p < 0.05$ but also at the 2 per cent level ($p < 0.02$). It is not, however, significant at the 1 per cent level ($p > \alpha$ and where $\alpha = 0.01$). So we would accept the null hypothesis at the 2 per cent level (and the 5 per cent level), but reject it at the 1 per cent level.

Conclusions of tests for samples 1 and 2

Sample 1 (100 observations): $p = 0.086$. Not significant. We accept the null hypothesis of no real difference in the population. Not sufficient evidence at this level to show otherwise.

Sample 2 (200 observations): $p = 0.015$. Significant at 2 per cent level. Reject the null hypothesis at the 2% level and conclude that there is a real difference in the population. But if we have chosen the 'safer' level of $\alpha = 0.01$ then we would have accepted the null hypothesis of no real difference at the 1% level.

The p-statistic in correlation and regression

We can return to the diagram in the previous chapter showing the correlation between fertiliser and yield, although in fact we extended it to a regression analysis. We did not show the p-statistic there which was in fact 0.35. This indicates that the results were significant at the 5 per cent level ($\alpha = 0.05$). We would reject the null hypothesis at this level and state that there we found sufficient evidence to show a true correlation between fertiliser and yield. There was insufficient data from the 40 points plotted for this to be significant at the 2 per cent level and at this level of confidence we would have to reject the null hypothesis stating insufficient evidence – we need more information to be able to draw a conclusion.

What this all comes down to is how much of a risk are we willing to take regarding the reliability of our sample. There are no hard and fast rules here. It depends on whether we are studying crop yields or medicines. We determine *in advance* the level of significance appropriate to our test and what we are willing to accept.

One-tailed and two-tailed tests and probability

We previously described the two-tailed test and gave an example where the hypothesis was that men preferred red wine and women preferred white wine. In other words they would be on either side of the red-wine – white-wine scale in the diagram. It might have been that only a small majority of women preferred white to red wine and a large majority of men preferred red to white. But all we were interested in was whether there was a majority, irrespective of how big, for each gender. Just to remind ourselves, in the one-tail test we were just interested in the red wine preference – a higher proportion of men prefer red wine than the proportion of women. In the two-tail test we consider both ends of the red–white wine scale and state that one gender prefers red, the other white. In a two-tail test the p-statistic is halved. This means that the requirements are more stringent for the null hypothesis not to be rejected.

Did the results of the wine test for sample 1 show that men preferred one type of wine (red) and women another (white)? A two-tailed test would have yielded $p = 0.043$ (half of 0.086). This is significant at the 5 per cent level. We would reject the null hypothesis and say that there was a clear indication that men preferred red wine and women preferred white. In fact, the statistics bear this out. Of the 116 red wine drinkers 55% are men, but only 43% of the 84 white wine drinkers are men. (The proportions for women are 45% and 57% respectively.)

With the large sample (200 subjects) a two-tailed test would have yielded $p = 0.0075$. We could then reject the null hypothesis at the 1 percent level. In other words our larger sample has shown the differences in preferred tastes even more decisively.

Statistical Tests

Statistical tests in general

Many statistical tests are designed to show the relation between variables. Do distributions show similar patterns. Example: Do girls generally attain higher grades in maths than boys? Is there a correlation between the amount of fertiliser and crop yield? Is yield further affected when we take temperature into consideration? Do Asians, Africans, West Indians and Europeans show different voting patterns? There are tests for virtually every combination of data types. Many are included in the standard statistical analysis programmes and it is just a question of selecting the appropriate test, something which is shown below.

But in all tests, a hypothesis has to be advanced – often the null hypothesis.

Referring to the chosen level of significance, the hypothesis is then accepted or rejected. We have no calculations to do, the PC will do them for us; all we need to do is to interpret the result and ask whether this is significant. And just to remind ourselves:

If $p > \alpha$, then p is not significant. We accept the null hypothesis.
If $p < \alpha$, then p is significant. We reject the null hypothesis.

The observant reader may have realised that using a simple task we risk making an error in our conclusion. We may reject the null hypothesis when in fact it is true (known as a Type I error); alternatively accepting it when it is false (a Type II error). This is a risk we have to take.

In the above example of wine preferences, there was no causal relationship – both variables, men and women, were fully independent of each other in their preferences. But what if our data registered smoker/non-smoker and cancer/no cancer instead of men/women and red/white wine? We would now have good reason to suspect a *causal* relationship: smoking and cancer. In this case we do not use *chi* but another statistic called *phi*. The process is the same: we select the level of significance and look at the p-statistic to see if this is significant or not.

Many hundreds of tests have been designed for the analysis of a wide range of data types and hypothesis testing. A select number may be found on most spreadsheets (correlation, regression, chi-square, etc.), but a more comprehensive programme is preferable in order to select the appropriate test. Which test is appropriate is initially dependent upon a) the type of data; b) whether one variable is dependent on one or several others; c) the number of variables.

Theory – hypothesis – test

In the following we do not go into details of any tests, least of all calculations, but illustrate the appropriate tests for the various combinations of data types and relationships. At this stage we may leave the novice behind although have hopefully whetted his or her appetite. At least, the reader will now be able to glance at the output of a statistical analysis and draw some conclusions from the p-statistic knowing what the null hypothesis test involves.

Useful texts for the beginner are included in the reference list.

Summary

1. Outline the theory, its basis and reasoning.
2. State the null hypothesis [Ho].

3. Specify the sample size (minimum).
4. Specify the required significance level α.
5. Select the appropriate statistical test.

Which statistical test?

Some researchers may have access to a statistician who can assist in selecting the appropriate test and in understanding the results of an analysis. But statistics today are more a question of interpreting computer output than writing commands into a program.

The following will enable you to select the appropriate statistical test for your data (or at least to understand why the statistician found it appropriate).

1. How many variables are involved? 1, 2, several
2. What type(s) of variables? (interval, ordinal, nominal)
3. If applicable to the test, are any variables dichotomous?
4. Is one variable a dependent variable? (i.e. is there a causal relationship)
5. Is a test to be made for association, independence, agreement?

One variable (descriptive statistics)

Data	Feature (distribution)	Statistical measure
Interval	Central tendency: – Symmetric distn. – Skewed distribution	mean median, mode, trimmed mean, winsorized mean
	Dispersion	Standard deviation, coefficient of variation. Standard error of the mean
	Distribution symmetry	Skewness (various measures incl. moment coefficient)
	Peakedness	Kurtosis
	Frequencies	Absolute or Relative frequencies, percentages, quartiles, N-tiles
	Normality	(No measures, but tests for normality: Kolmogorov-Smirnov test, chi-square goodness-of-fit test)
Ordinal	Central tendency	Median
	Dispersion	Inter-quartile deviation
	Frequencies	Absolute or Relative frequencies, percentages
Nominal	Central tendency	Modal value
	Dispersion	Relative frequency of modal class
	Frequencies	Class: absolute or relative frequencies, percentages

Two variables

When looking at two variables we are frequently interested in the association between them. What types of data are we concerned with, interval, ranked, etc.? Is the interval data normally distributed? Is one or both of the variables dichotomous. Does the value of one increase as the other increase (or falls); does an increase in one *cause* the increase or fall in the other. The appropriate test is determined by considering the following:

1. Are the variables interval, ordinal or nominal?

2. Is either or both of the variables dichotomous
   – if so are these naturally dichotomous (e.g. male–female) or constructed (e.g. above–below mean)

3. Are the variables independent, interdependent or is one a dependent variable?

You can now determine the test to be used. It is not the statistic itself which is important but, rather, the *significance* of the statistic. In other words, this will tell you whether there is a significant association between the two variables.

Two interval variables – both independent

	Test for:	Statistical measure	Statistical test
1	Equal means	t-statistic	Student's t-test for paired (or correlated) observations Student's t-test for independent samples
2	Linear relationship	Robinson's A Intraclass correlation coeff. *r* Krippendorff's coefficient of agreement	F-test
3	Covariation: Both interval variables	Pearson's product moment *r*	
4	One variable dichotomous	Biserial *r*	
5	Both variables dichotomous	Tetrachoric *r*, phi	

1. Student's t-test for *paired observations* examines whether there is a significant difference between two sets of data for each case, for example grades in maths and French. This test requires that we have the grades in both maths and French for *each* student. (Do students with high grades in one subject have high grades in the other? The null hypothesis is that there is no association between the grades a student attains in maths and that he attains in French).

2. Student's t-test for *independent samples*. This test examines to see whether there is a significant difference between the means of two independent groups, for example, the maths grades attained by boys as a whole and by girls as a whole. There may be a difference number of cases in the two groups (i.e. boys and girls).

3. The F-test considers the variance (rather than the means as in the t-test). It is frequently called the variance-ratio test and is a test of the equality of two population variances. The F-statistic = t. It is useful where a test of the equality of means of *more than two variables* is involved. For example, is there an association between the mean grades achieved by pupils in maths, French and history?

4. If we plot the grades achieved by all students in French and in maths, we can test whether there is an association between these. In other words, bright pupils in maths are also bright in French. We use Pearson's *r* to measure the correlation between these.

5. If we reduce one of the continuous variables to a dichotomous variable, we use biserial *r*. For example, we might plot grades in French with a variable which is either above the mean or below the mean in that subject. If we reduce *both* continuous variables to two classes, (1) above the mean, (2) below the mean grade, we can then plot the frequencies in a 2 × 2 table and use tetrachoric *r*. If both variables are genuinely dichotomous (men–women; smoker–non-smoker) then we use the *phi* statistic. This has a disadvantage of being able to have a maximum value greater than 1. If one variable comprises more than two groups (non-smoker, light smoker, heavy smoker), then the contingency coefficient C is used. The disadvantage of this statistic is that the maximum value is always less than 1 (depending upon the dimensions of the table). Consequently, many prefer Cramérs V which can attain the value of 1, but not exceed it. But, as in many tests it is not the statistic itself but the significance which is important.

Two interval variables – one dependent

	Test for:	Statistical measure	Statistical test
1	Linear relationship	Regression coefficient (b, $beta$)	F-test ($= t^2$)
2	Curvilinear data	Polynomial regression coeffs.	F-test ($= t^2$)

1. Regression was described above. In some cases of interdependence the regression may be shown by treating each variable as the dependent variable in turn. For example, low petrol prices may result in the number of cars on the road (passing a check point) to be greater than when petrol prices are high – a simple supply and demand situation. But low petrol prices might also be the result of fewer cars on the road, the effect of competition between petrol stations. We may then have to look at a further cause for this (cheap travel offers by bus and train, etc.).

2. Curvilinear data. We might find that although the number of cars on the road increases as the price of petrol falls, the increase begins to tail off. After all, the maximum number of cars cannot exceed those registered. Polynomial regression (also available on Excel) will provide a better fit to this line than a linear distribution.

Two ordinal variables – both independent

	Test for:	Statistical measure	Statistical test
1	Association:	Kendall's *tau a, tau b or tau c* Goodman and Kruskal's *gamma* Kim's *d*	
2	If ranks of categories are treated as interval scale:	Spearman's *rho*	

1. Where the ranked data is given in tables, the following measures of association are appropriate:
    a) Kendall's *tau a* is used when there are no tied ranks in the data for the two variables
    b) Kendall's *tau b* is a symmetric measure (independent or interdependent variables), but has a maximum value of ± 1 for square tables (otherwise $> \pm 1$). It corrects for tied ranks (see *tau a*).
    c) Kendall's *tau c* is used where the number of rows and columns differ in a table.
    d) *Gamma* is symmetric and suitable where the relationship between the

variables is consistent. The interpretation of gamma values +1 or −1 is problematic in so far as these may not necessarily indicate perfect positive or negative association. Gamma excludes consideration of tied ranks. (You will have to consult your statistics text on this one.)

2. Spearman's *rho* is a correlation coefficient based on ranks (and differences in the ranks) of matched pairs. Example, a comparison of the rank attained by each pupil (rather than the grade) in the maths and French exams. While this statistic can be used for tables it is particularly appropriate where there are many categories (i.e. ranks).

Two ordinal variables – one independent

	Test for:	Statistical measure	Statistical test
1	Association	Somer's *d*	

1. Somer's *d* is used in tables where one variable is a dependent variable. Consequently, it is an asymmetric measure meaning that it is sensitive as to which of the variables is the dependent variable.

Two nominal variables – both dichotomous

	Test for	Statistical measure	Statistical test
1	Symmetry		McNemar's test of symmetry
2	Covariation	Yule's Q, phi	Fisher's exact test Pearson's chi-square

Clearly, these statistics apply to 2 × 2 tables.

Two nominal variables – both independent

	Test for:	Statistical measure	Statistical test
1	Agreement	Scott's *pi*; Cohen's *Kappa*	
2	Symmetry		McNemar's test of symmetry
3	Covariation. based on cases in each category b) based on cases in modal category	Contingency coefficient C Cramér's V Symmetric *lambda*	Pearson's Chi-square

Two nominal variables – one dependent

Test for:	Statistical measure	Statistical test
Covariation a) based on cases in each category b) based on cases in modal category	Goodman and Kruskall's *tau b* Asymmetric *lambda*	

Two variables: one interval, one ordinal – ordinal variable dichotomous

Treat as an interval scale variable (i.e. both treated as interval scale variables).

Two variables: one interval, one ordinal – ordinal variable not dichotomous

Test for:	Statistical measure	Statistical test
Strength of relationship a) ordinal variable has normal distribution b) ordinal variable is a transformed interval scale variable	Jaspen's coefficient of multiserial correlation. Mayer and Robinson's *M*	Fisher's *r* to *Z* transformation; refer critical ratio of *Z* to normal curve

Two variables: one interval, one nominal – both independent variables

Treat as an interval variables.

Two variables: one interval, one nominal – interval variable dependent

Test for:	Statistical measure	Statistical test
Strength of relationship a) Descriptive b) Estimate population parameter	$Eta\ (\acute{\eta}^2)$ $Omega^2$; Intraclass correlation coeff. Kelly's epsilon^2	F test F test
Interval scale variable normally distributed in the population	Analysis of variance	Bartlett's test Levene's *W*
Interval variable non-normal distribution in the population – matched cases – independent samples		Walsh test Randomization test for matched pairs Randomization test for independent samples

Two variables: one ordinal, one nominal – ordinal variable dependent

Test for:	Statistical measure	Statistical test
Association a) Nominal variable dichotomous – matched cases – independent samples	– Somer's *d*	Sign Test; Wilcoxon signed-rank test Median Test Mann-Whitney U test Kolmogorov-Smirnov two-sample test Runs Test
b) Nominal variable not dichotomous – matched cases – independent samples	– Freeman's coefficient of differentiation	Friedman Test Kruskal-Wallis test Median Test if more than two groups

The *Runs test* is occasionally encountered but not found in many of the statistical programs. It measures the sequence of events involving two groups. For example, which football team is better at passing the ball – is one team significantly better than the other at keeping the ball before losing it to the other team? This does not necessarily show any correlation with goals scored (unless you are a Leeds United fan).

The *Wilcoxon matched cases signs test* uses the magnitude of differences within the matched pairs. For example, in a study of the age differences of husbands and wives, the actual ages would be involved. Importance is attached to the difference between the ages. The Signs test ignores the actual ages but focuses only on whether the man is older or younger than the wife (or vice versa). The test is whether there are significantly more couples where the husband is older than where he is younger.

More than two variables

Tests involving more than two variables soon become complicated although multiple correlation and regression where all variables are interval may be more easily comprehended. Here reference must be made to one of the standard texts.

Other tests

There are a number of other tests available in statistical programmes. Excel contains the essential tests and statistics but is not the easiest programme to operate. In any case it requires that the Toolpack supplementary programme is installed and which may then be accessed under Tools – Data analysis.

One test which is only found on a few programs but which seems to be very popular among social scientists in recent years is Chronbach's alpha. This is a measure of reliability of scores. Unlike the medical laboratory where precision and accuracy of science may be applied and measured, social scientists need a different measure as they cannot repeat the same tests with the same degree of precision each time; subjects (persons interviewed) vary widely. Briefly, this measure shows the ratio of the true score to the measured score. Actually it is a bit more complicated than that, but surprisingly, it is easy to calculate. Researchers look for a reliability of at least 0.8 (80%) in the alpha measurement. There are several articles on this measure on the Internet including a brief description by John A. Ward PhD on www.bamc.amedd.army.mil/DCI/articles, and a more advanced paper by Joseph and Rosemary Gliem. (Search using Cronbach and alpha).
I have included a number of very readable texts in the reference lists which provide useful introductions to statistics for the non-statistician. (See Chapter 24, References)

Statistical Analysis Programs

The simplest way to learn about statistics is to enter data into a programme and press the 'analyse' key when using Excel. Researchers will almost certainly have access to one of the following: SPSS (Statistical Package for the Social Sciences), SAS (Statistical Analysis Systems), Minitab, BDMP, MedStat, or others. The Windows versions of these programs are first-class aids in learning statistical method.

Spreadsheets have developed over the years from being simple aids to calculations to becoming sophisticated analytical programmes, often assisted by quick and easy graphics. but covering, as they do, financial analysis, engineering and general statistical functions, quality seems to have yielded to quantity (there are more than 150 functions in Excel). Chi-square, for example is clumsy as are several other standard statistical procedures. It is not surprising, therefore, that there are a number of add-on programs specifically designed for Excel. One of the best is xlSTAT by Thierry Fahmy. Another is Analyse-It (produced by the company of the same name). Email addresses are given below.

There are a number of other commercial programmes available to the individual at very modest cost, and many free demos are available. A note of caution – demos are nearly always restricted in the size of the data base they can handle, advanced statistics are not included, the program often expires after 30 days – or even less.

For biomedical statistics, Arcus Quickstat is superb (but also excellent for many other statistical purposes). A comprehensive list of statistical software producers and distributors (with direct links to the individual sites and free downloads – where available) is on: www.stats.gla.ac.uk/cti/links__stats/software.html

One superb program, ModStat, developed by Prof. R. C. Knodt, is probably one of the easiest yet most comprehensive programmes available with a step-by-step guide to choosing the correct statistical test. All the tests listed in the chapter are found there plus many more – all for a one-time payment of just $22. Go to members.aol.com/statware for a free 60-day trial.

Finally, in case you miss it, a very comprehensive on-line statistical glossary is available on the www.StatSoftinc.com site. Go to 'Electronic Statistics textbook'.

Further reading

A number of elementary and standard texts are included in the Literature List in Chapter 24.

8
Metric Conversion

Five out of four people have trouble with fractions. – Anon.

There always seems to be one problem when converting data – one can never find the conversion factor required. The British steadfastly retain their pint, and indeed the pound weight as well as the pound in their pocket. Conversions involving population density, miles per gallon, hectares, etc., always seem problematic. This is reflected in the fact that many authors do not even add a footnote explaining the continental or U.S. equivalents. I have found the following to be a convenient aid to conversions – it is alphabetical. One unit of the first column represents so many units of the third, the middle column being the conversion factor. A number of non-metric units are also included. Observe that U.S. abbreviations may differ from the UK equivalents.

unit	abbreviation	equiv. to	unit
acre	a. *or* A.	0.404856	hectares
are (100 sq. m)	a	119.6	sq. yards
centigrade	c	$\times 9/5) + 32$	Fahrenheit
centimetre	cm	0.3937	inches
cubic centimetre	cc *or* c.c.	0.06102	cubic inches
cubic foot	c.f.	0.0280	cubic metres
cubic inch	cu.i	16.380	cubic centimetres
cubic metre		35.3147	cubic feet
cubic metre	cu. m *or* m^3	1.3080	cubic yards
cubic meter		227.020	US dry gallons
cubic meter		264.173	US fluid gallons
cubic yard	cu. yd	0.7650	cubic metres
Fahrenheit	F	$-32 \times (5/9)$	centigrade
fathom	f.	1.828	metres
fluid ounce	fl.oz.	29.573	millilitres
foot	f.	0.3048	metres
gallon (UK)	gall.	1.2010	gallons (US)
gallon (UK)	gall.	4.5461	litres
gallon (US)	gal.	0.8327	gallons (UK)
gallon (US)	gal.	3.7854	litres
gram	g	0.0353	ounces
hectare	ha	2.4711	acres
hundredweight	cwt	50.8020	kilograms

inch	in.	2.5400	centimetres
kilogram	kg	0.0197	hundredweight (cwt.)
kilogram	kg	2.2046	pounds
kilogram	kg	0.1575	stones
kilometre	km	0.6214	miles
kilometre	km	0.5400	nautical miles
kg per sq. cm	kg/cm^2	14.2233	psi (lbs per sq. in.)
knot	kn	1.151	miles per hour
lbs per sq. inch	psi	.07031	kg per sq. cm
litre	l	0.2200	gallons (UK)
litre	l	0.2642	gallons (US)
litre	l	1.7596	pints (UK)
litre	l	2.1133	pints (US) – liquid
litre	l	0.8798	quarts (UK)
litre	l	1.0567	quarts (US) – liquid
litres per mil (10 km)	[lm]	$\dfrac{1}{(\text{lm} \times .0354)}$	miles per gallon
metre	m	0.547	fathom
metre	m	3.2808	feet
metre	m	1.0936	yards
metres/sec.	m/sec.	2.2369	miles/hour (wind speed)
metric tonne	t	0.9843	tons
metric tonne	t	1.102	short tons
mile	m. (mi. *USA*)	1.6093	kilometres
miles/hour	mph	0.4470	metres/sec. (wind speed)
miles/hour	mph	0.869	knots per hour
miles/gallon	mpg	$\dfrac{45.461}{(\text{mpg} \times 1.6093)}$	litres per mil (10 km)
millilitre	ml *or* mL	0.0338	fluid ounces
nautical mile[1]	n.m.	1.8520	kilometres
ounce	oz *or* oz.	28.3400	grams
pint (UK)	p. *or* pt	0.5883	litres
pint (UK)	p. *or* pt	1.243	pints (US)
pint (US) – liquid	pt *or* pt.	0.8043	pints (UK)
pint (US) – liquid	pt *or* pt.	0.4732	litres
pint (US) – dry, liquid	pt *or* pt.	ca. 35	cubic inches
pound	lb *or* lb.	0.4536	kilograms
quart (UK)	q. *or* qt	1.1766	litres
quart (UK)	q. *or* qt	69.355	cubic inches
quart (S) – dry	⎫	67.201	cubic inches
quart (US) – liquid	⎬ q. *or* qt *or* qt.	57.749	cubic inches
quart (US) – liquid	⎭	0.94635	litres
short ton	sh t.	0.907	metric tons (tonnes)
square centimetre	sq cm *or* cm^2	0.1550	square inches
square foot	sq ft	0.0929	square metres
square inch	sq in	6.452	square centimetres
square kilometre	sq km	0.3861	square miles
square metre	sq m	10.7639	square feet

square metre	sq m	1.195	square yards
square mile	sq mi	2.5900	square kilometre
square yard	sq yd	0.8361	square metres
stone	st.	6.3500	kilograms
ton	t.	1.0160	metric tonnes (abbrev. t)
yard	y. *or* yd	0.9144	metres

One UK nautical mile = 6080 feet, i.e. the mean distance on the earth's surface subtended by one minute of latitude. Continentals are less fastidious and round this to 1852 m – deemed the International nautical mile. The UK nautical mile = 1.00064 International nautical miles (i.e. 46.6 inches longer), although hardly an argument for bigger is better!

A note on tons, tonnes and tonnage.

Collins English Dictionary provides useful definitions:

1. **long ton.** *Brit.* a unit of weight (avoirdupois) equal to 2240 pounds or 1016.046 kilograms.
2. **short ton, net ton.** *U.S.* a unit of weight equal to 2000 pounds or 907.184 kilograms.
3. **metric ton, tonne.** A unit of weight equal to 1000 kilograms (2204.62 pounds). Incidentally, a **metric hundredweight** is 50 kg.
4. **shipping ton** or **measurement ton.** Unit of volume in transportation by sea, commonly equal to 40 cu. ft (1.13 cu. m).
5. **freight ton.** *Mainly U.S.* A unit of volume for freight which weighs 1 ton, e.g. 40 cu. ft oak timber, 20 bushels of wheat, etc.
6. **displacement ton.** 2240 lbs or 35 cu. ft (1 cu. m) of seawater.
7. **register ton.** A unit of internal capacity of ships, 100 cu. ft (2.83 cu. m).
8. **kiloton.** 1000 tons

tonnage or tunnage
> The capacity of a merchant ship expressed in tons, for which purpose a ton is considered as 40 cubic feet of freight or 100 cubic feet of bulk cargo, unless such an amount would weigh more than 2000 pounds in which case the actual weight is used. (Dictionary definition – not mine!)

So now we know!

A note on miles

British and U.S. mile = 1760 yards or 5280 feet
Nautical mile: UK = 6080 feet (1.8532 km); U.S. = 6076.1 feet (1.852 km).

A note on gallons

1 gallon (imperial) UK = 4.546 litres (277.4 cubic inches); U.S. = 3.785 litres (231 cubic inches). As a UK gallon and a US gallon each contain 8 pints, the US pint is correspondingly smaller. See below.

A note on fuel consumption

In all their wisdom the continentals measure fuel consumption in litres per mil (10 km) rather than km per litre. So a double conversion is required: mil into miles, and litres into gallons using the formula 0.22 galls per 6.214 miles. 0.22/6.214 = 0.0354. But we have to invert this. 1/(lm x 0.0354) = mpg where lm is fuel consumption in litres per mil. 1 litre per mil is equivalent to 28.25 mpg. The reverse is calculated as 1/(mpg x 0.0354). 45 mpg = 0.6 litres per mil.

A note on US measurements

The above tables and conversions have included U.S. measurements but it is appropriate to include a more detailed summary of U.S. measurements at this point. The British Imperial System pint (and quart) is used for liquid and dry measure. Not so the U.S. Customary System.

	Volume	Litres	Equiv.
1 U.S. pint, *liquid* measure	35 cu. in	0.473	16 ounces
1 U.S. quart, *liquid* measure	57.749 cu. in.	0.946	32 ounces
1 U.S. pint, *dry* measure	40.728 cu in.	0.551, ($1/16$ peck)	–
1 U.S. quart, *dry* measure	67.201 cu in.	1.101, ($1/8$ peck)	–
1 U.S. gallon	–	3.785	

Source: *Webster's Random House Dictionary*

▶ A very comprehensive conversion programme is to be found on www.accelware.com

9
Growth Rates

Rates of growth are an element in many studies, not only finance. The following table shows the factor growth yielded on a principal amount at various rates of interest compounded over a given number of periods. For example, a 10% growth rate (or interest) will result in the capital having doubled after just over 7 years (a factor of 1.95 in exactly 7 years). The formula is given by $F = K*(1 + i/100)^P$ where F = factor growth, K = capital (or principal), i = interest, and P the number of periods. If the world's population is increasing at 5% p.a., it will almost double every 14 years.

Periods   Annual Rate of Growth (per cent)

	1.00	1.50	2.00	2.50	3.00	4.00	5. 00	6.00	8.00	10.00
1	1.01	1.02	1.02	1.03	1.03	1.04	1.05	1.06	1.08	1.10
2	1.02	1.03	1.04	1.05	1.06	1.08	1.10	1.12	1.17	1.21
3	1.03	1.05	1.06	1.08	1.09	1.12	1.16	1.19	1.26	1.33
4	1.04	1.06	1.08	1.10	1.13	1.17	1.22	1.26	1.36	1.46
5	1.05	1.08	1.10	1.13	1.16	1.22	1.28	1.34	1.47	1.61
6	1.06	1.09	1.13	1.16	1.19	1.27	1.34	1.42	1.59	1.77
7	1.07	1.11	1.15	1.19	1.23	1.32	1.41	1.50	1.71	1.95
8	1.08	1.13	1.17	1.22	1.27	1.37	1.48	1.59	1.85	2.14
9	1.09	1.14	1.20	1.25	1.30	1.42	1.55	1.69	2.00	2.36
10	1.10	1.16	1.22	1.28	1.34	1.48	1.63	1.79	2.16	2.59
11	1.12	1.18	1.24	1.31	1.38	1.54	1.71	1.90	2.33	2.85
12	1.13	1.20	1.27	1.34	1.43	1.60	1.80	2.01	2.52	3.14
13	1.14	1.21	1.29	1.38	1.47	1.67	1.89	2.13	2.72	3.45
14	1.15	1.23	1.32	1.41	1.51	1.73	1.98	2.26	2.94	3.80
15	1.16	1.25	1.35	1.45	1.56	1.80	2.08	2.40	3.17	4.18
16	1.17	1.27	1.37	1.48	1.60	1.87	2.18	2.54	3.43	4.59
17	1.18	1.29	1.40	1.52	1.65	1.95	2.29	2.69	3.70	5.05
18	1.20	1.31	1.43	1.56	1.70	2.03	2.41	2.85	4.00	5.56
19	1.21	1.33	1.46	1.60	1.75	2.11	2.53	3.03	4.32	6.12
20	1.22	1.35	1.49	1.64	1.81	2.19	2.65	3.21	4.66	6.73
50	1.64	2.11	2.69	3.44	4.38	7.11	11.47	18.42	46.90	117.39
100	2.70	4.43	7.24	11.81	19.22	50.50	131.50	339.30	2199.76	13780.61

It is also possible to read the table in another manner. If the population of a country has increased by 50 per cent in ten years, what is the mean annual growth rate? The factor growth will be given as 1.5 (150% of the base level). Look along the horizontal row for the 10-year period until we come to 1.5. The nearest value is 1.48 indicating an annual growth rate of about 4 per cent (the value at the top of the column). For the curious, the formula is:

$$i = [(T/P)^{(1/Y)} - 1]* 100$$

where: i = nominal interest rate
P = amount at beginning of period
T = amount at end of period
Y = number of periods

Interest Rates

Using the above we can calculate the realised amount (R) after x years. For simple interest this is given by:

$$R = P(1 + i) \times Y$$

For £1000 invested at 6% over 5 years, this gives:

$$£1000 (1 + 0.06) \times 5 = 1060 \times 5 = £1300$$

For compound interest the formula is:

$$R = P(1 + i)^y$$
$$£1000 (1 + 0.06)^5 = £1338.2$$

Using a hand calculator

The latter may be calculated on a hand calculator with a memory function. Enter 1.06 into M+ (the memory, where .06 is the interest rate, then add 1) The screen shows 1.06.
Now enter 1000 × MRC (Memory Recall) = .[1] The screen shows 1060, i.e. the yield at end of year 1.
For year 2, press × MRC = . The yield after year 2 is 1123.6 (i.e. 1060 × 1.06)
For year 3, press × MRC = . The yield after year 3 is 1191.0 ...
For year 4, press × MRC = . The yield after year 4 is 1262.5 ...
For year 5, press × MRC = . The yield after year 5 is 1338.2 (i.e. 1262.5 × 1.06)

In other words, each time we enter × MRC = we see the yield for the following year (or period).

1 On some pocket calculators this may be shown as MR.

10
Currencies, Prices, Finance

Money can't buy you friends, but you can get a better class of enemy.
– Spike Milligan (1918–2002). Humorist and Goon.

Currencies and Prices

Prices are normally given using the symbol or abbreviation for the currency: e.g. Gold is now $290 per ounce; silver is around £3 per ounce.

The normal form for U.S. dollars used to be $US. This appears to be changing and US$ is now used, corresponding to Can$, HK$, NZ$ and S$ (Canada, Hong Kong, New Zealand and Singapore, respectively). Only the Australian dollar remains as $A with the symbol placed first.

Currencies are often required to be referred to in financial and economic articles, company reports, and so forth. Some years ago international three-letter currency codes (ICC) were introduced. It has become popular to use these in financial documents, currency conversions, world market prices. etc. The norm appears to be that these are placed after the amount e.g. The value of French exports of nitrates to Spain was 2 million FRF. There is also a tendency in financial documents to place M in front for millions:

Norwegian exports rose to 250 MNOK (21.5 MUSD) in January.

In some countries the new international currency code appears on price labels in tourist shops, menus in restaurants and brochures rather than the currency symbol, and normally before the amount: NOK 250. While this list contains references to a number of currencies now replaced by the Euro, these may be useful for historical studies. You may want to enter rates of exchange for your own use in the right-hand column.

Country	Currency	ICC	Symbol	Rate of exchange
Algeria	dinar	DZD	DA	
Australia	Australian dollar	AUD	A$	
Austria*	schilling	ATS	AS	
Belgium*	franc	BEF	BF	
Bulgaria	lev	BGL	Lv	

Canada	dollar	CAD	Can$
China	Yuan	CNY	yen
Cyprus	Cypriot pound	CYP	Can$
Czechia	koruna	CZK	Kc
Denmark	Danish krone	DKK	DKr
EMU	Euro (ECU)	EUR	€
Estonia	Estonian kroon	EEK	EEK
Finland*	Marrka	FIM	M
France*	French franc	FRF	F
Germany*	Deutsche Mark	DEM	DM
Greece*	drachma	GRD	Dr
Hong Kong	Hong Kong dollar	HKD	HK$
Hungary	forint	HUF	Ft
Iceland	Iceland new króna	ISK	IKr
India	Indian rupee	INR	Re
Ireland*	Irish pound (punt)	IEP	Ir
Israel	New Israeli shekel	ILS	NIS
Italy*	Lire	ITL	L
Japan	Yen	JPY	yen, ¥
Korean, South	Won	KRW	W
Kuwait	Kuwaiti dinar	KWD	KD
Latvia	Lat	LVL	LVL
Lithuania	Litas	LTL	Lt
Luxembourg*	Lux. Franc	LUF	Luxf
Malaysia	Ringgit	MYR	M$
Malta	Maltese lira	MTL	LM
Morocco	Moroccan dirham	MAD	DH
Netherlands*	guilder/florin	NLG	f.
New Zealand	NZ dollar	NZD	NZ$
Norway	Norwegian krone	NOK	NKr
Poland	Zloty	PLN	Zl
Portugal*	Escudo	PTE	Esc
Russia	Rouble	RUR	R
Saudi Arabia	Saudi riyal	SAR	SR
Singapore	Singapore dollar	SGD	S$
Slovenia	Tolar	SLT	SLT
South Africa	Rand	ZAR	R
Spain*	Peseta	ESP	Pta
Sweden	Swedish krona	SEK	SKr
Switzerland	Swiss franc	CHF	SFR
Tunisia	Tunisian dinar	TND	TD
Turkey	Turkish lira	TRL	TL
U.K.	pound	GBP	£
USA	dollar, cent	USD	US$

Countries marked with an asterisk * adopted the Euro on January 1, 2002. A comprehensive list is found in *The Economist Style Guide,* Profile Books, London.

Currency rates may be found on www.bloomberg.com/markets/currency/ currcalc.html, or xe.com However, a very comprehensive site with a range of currency tools is found on www.oanda.com

Euro Conversions

Conversion to the Euro (previously known as the ECU) was effective in the following countries as from January 1, 2001. This also applied to territories of Euro-zone countries (mainly French and Spanish colonies). Andorra, San Marino and The Vatican City also adopted the Euro.

The following table shows the (fixed) conversion rates between the *former* currencies and the Euro. By way of example 1 Euro = 13.7603 ATS; 1 ATS = 1/13.7603 Euro (= 0.0726€). The table will be useful in historical studies comparing finance before and after the Euro as well as rates between countries at the time of conversion. For example, 1 ATS = 40.3399/13.7603 BEF (= 2.936 BEF).

Austria	Schilling (ATS)	13.7603
Belgium	Franc (BEF)	40.3399
Finland	Markka (FIM)	5.94573
France	Franc (FRF)	6.55957
Germany	Deutsche Mark (DEM)	1.95583
Greece	Drachma (GRD)	340.75
Ireland	Punt (IEP)	0.787564
Italy	Lira (LTL)	1936.27
Luxembourg	France (LUF)	40.3399
Netherlands	Guilder (NLG)	2.20371
Portugal	Escudo (PTE)	200.482
Spain	Peseta (ESP)	166.386
Vatican City	Lira (VAL)	1936.27

Finance

Money is better than poverty, if only for financial reasons. –Woody Allen (1935–)

Authors of economic and financial papers will almost certainly be familiar with financial terminology. But even the specialist may require to check on the definition terms such as strike bonus system, or ratio spread. A very comprehensive dictionary is to be found on www.amex.com Go to the bottom of the page and click on 'Dictionary'. You may also search for terms in this info base. This website also contains useful links to other sites some of which are given here.

AmexTrader www.amex.com/amextrader
American Stock Exchange Company Guide wallstreet.cch.com/
AmericanStockExchange/welcome.asp
American Stock Exchange Constitution & Rules wallstreet.cch.com/
AmericanStockExchange/welcome.asp
Annual Report Service – World Investor Link amex.ar.wilink.com
The Depository Trust Company (DTC) www.dtc.org
Federal Reserve Board www.federalreserve.gov
NASD (NASDAQ) www.nasd.com
National Securities Clearing Company (NSCC) www.nscc.com
The Options Clearing Corporation (OCC) www.optionsclearing.com
The Options Industry Council (OIC) www.888options.com
Secure Financial Transaction Infrastructure (SFTI) sfti.siac.com
Securities and Exchange Commission (SEC) www.sec.gov
Securities Industry Association (SIA) www.sia.com
Securities Industry Automation Corporation (SIAC) www.siac.com

11
Weights and Measures

When the weight of the paperwork equals the weight of the plane, the plane will fly. – Donald Douglas (1892–1981). Aircraft designer and manufacturer.

General Measurements

Measures of length, mass, etc., are rapidly becoming standardised. There are nevertheless special areas where traditional measures remain. The English pint of beer remains a pint and has not been converted to 0.473 litres. The European commissioners attempted to do this, but had failed to consider that the Englishman was not going to change the habits of a lifetime. European law was such that if a customer asked for a pint, he could expect a pint – alternatively a long explanation as to why not! Barmaids have other things to talk about.

Read along until the required column is reached (12 inches = 1 foot). Only the main equivalents are shown.

Measures of length

	1 foot	1 yard	1 rod/pole	1 chain	1 furlong	1 mile
Inches	12	36				
Feet		3	16½	66		5280
Yards			5½	22	220	1760
Rods/Poles				4	40	160
Chains					10	40
Furlongs						8

The *pole* (also known as a *rod* or a *perch*) is scarcely used today although may be encountered in the building industry where a *square pole* of brickwork of standard 1½ bricks thickness is equivalent to 272 square feet. It is also encountered as a square measure where a *square rod* (or *rood*) = 30.25 square yards.

Historically, *Gunter's chain* was in fact a chain of 22 yards (66 feet) comprising 100 links (each link being 0.66 feet or 7.92 inches). 10 chains = 1 furlong; 10 square chains = 1 acre.

There is also an *engineer's chain* comprising either 50 or 100 links each of 1 foot. Rarely encountered today, so mainly of historical interest

The *furlong* (1/8 of a mile; 0.201 km) is seldom used but still to be seen on signposts and older road maps in the U.K. I seem to recall seeing a signpost with furlongs somewhere in the West Indies on my travels in bygone youth.

Mariners' measures

	Fathom	Cable length	Nautical mile	League
Feet	6	720	6080	
Fathom		120	1000 (approx.)	
Nautical mile				3

A nautical mile is also known as an Admiralty knot.

A *league* (historic) was about 3 miles, mainly used in nautical measurement. A *nautical mile* is 6080 feet or 1.152 miles.

Area

	1 sq. foot	1 sq. yd	1 sq. pole	1 rood	1 acre	1 sq. mile
sq. inches	144	1296				
sq. feet		9				
sq. yards			30.25	1210	4840	
sq. poles				40	160	
Roods					4	
acres					640	

Cubic or solid measure

	1 cu. foot	1 cu. yard
cu. inches	1728	46656
cu. feet		27

5 cubic feet = 1 *barrel bulk shipping*; 40 cubic feet = 1 *ton shipping*. A *cargo* or *last* was about 4000 lbs.

Troy weight

	1 pennyweight	1 ounce	1 pound
grains	24	480	5760
pennyweights		20	240
ounces			12

Pearls and diamonds are measured in *carats*: 1 carat = 4 grains (= 3.2 Troy grains). Thus, the Troy ounce is equivalent to 150 Diamond carats.

Gold *quality* is measured in carats. 24 carat gold is pure gold. 18 carat gold contains 6 parts alloy; 14 carat gold contains 10 parts alloy.

Avoirdupois weight

	drams	1 ounce (oz.)	1 pound (lb.)	1 stone (st.)	1 quarter (qu.)	1 hundred-weight (cwt)	1 ton
grains	$27^{11}/_{32}$	437½	7000				
drams	16	256					
ounces		16					
pounds				14	28	112	2240
stones					2	8	160
quarters						4	80

A *dram* is also known as a *drachm*.

In Scotland, a stone was occasionally 24 pounds; in Ireland a stone was occasionally 16 pounds. Further, historically a stone depended on the product being weighed – 24lb for wool, 22lb for hay, 16lb for cheese, etc. (I read that. You didn't think I made it up did you?)

100 pounds = 1 short hundredweight; 20 short hundredweights (2000 lbs) = 1 short ton.

Apothecaries' weight

	1 scruple	1 dram	1 ounce	1 pound
grains	20	60	480	5760
scruples		3	24	288
drams			8	96
ounces				12

These measurements are still used for dispensing drugs

Apothecaries' fluid measure

	1 dram	1 ounce	1 pint	1 gallon
minims	60	480		
drams		8	160	1280
ounces			20	160
pints				8

Capacity (dry weight)

	1 pint	1 quart	1 gallon	1 peck	1 bushel	1 quarter	1 load
gills	4	8	32				
pints		2	8				
quarts			4				
gallons				2			
pecks					8	64	320
bushels						8	40
quarters							5

The latter, 5 quarters = 1 *load*, is historical as is 36 bushels = 1 *chaldron*. A gallon contains 10 pounds avoirdupois of distilled water.

Liquid measure (US)

	1 pint	1 quart	1 gallon	1 barrel	1 hogshead
gills	4	8	32		
pints		2	8		
quarts			4		
gallons				31½	
barrel					2

Other

A *barrel* (abbrev. bbl) is used for various weights and volume.

Oil: 1 barrel = 35 imperial or 42 US gallons, 159 litres.

Beer or ale, 36 imperial gallons. Just to confuse us the *Encarta* (U.S.) dictionary states that 1 barrel in the U.S. brewing industry is equal to 31 U.S. gallons (approximately 164 litres). I suspect that someone had been tasting the goods before writing that as Random House adds that for most liquids a barrel is the equivalent to 31½ U.S. gallons (119 litres!), as in the table above. For dry materials a barrel is 105 U.S. *dry quarts* (115 litres).

A *butt* is a cask used occasionally for dry products but mostly for wine and beer. 1 butt of wine = 126 gallons (approximately 573 litres), a beer and sherry butt properly = 108 gallons (approximately 491 litres). This seems to be quite different in the United States. *Random House Dictionary* states the volume of a butt to be the equivalent of about two *hogsheads*. A hogshead according to *Encarta* is 63 U.S. gallons or 54 imperial gallons. Returning to the U.K., *Chambers* defines a hogshead as a measure of capacity = 52½ imperial gallons, or 63 old wine gallons; of beer = 54 gallons; of claret = 46 gallons; of tobacco (US) = 750 to 1200 lb. I think I'll stick to my pint. At least I know where the Americanism 'Mind your butt' comes from.

Trade Measures

A number of trade measures are still occasionally encountered.

Cloth

(*Never mind the quality; feel the width.* – BBC radio programme)

2¼ inches   = 1 nail
4 nails   = 1 quarter or 9 inches

4 quarters   = 1 yard or 36 inches
5 quarters   = 1 ell or 45 inches

Cotton yarn

120 yards   = 1 skein
7 skeins   = 1 hank or 840 yards
18 hanks   = 1 spindle or 15,120 yards

Linen

300 yards   = 1 cut
2 cuts   = 1 heer or 600 yards
6 heers   = 1 hank or 3600 yards
4 hanks   = 1 spindle or 14,400 yards

Wool weight

14 pounds   = 1 stone
2 stones   = 1 tod
6½ tods   = 1 wey
2 weys   = 1 sack
12 sacks   = 1 last

Curiously, sometimes a sack was given as 3½ cwt and a last as 29 cwt.

Grain

A bushel of barley weighs (on average) 47 pounds
A bushel of oats weighs (on average) 40 pounds
A bushel of wheat weighs (on average) 60 pounds

Printing paper

24 sheets   = 1 quire
21½ quires   = 1 ream or 516 sheets
2 reams   = 1 bundle or 1032 sheets
5 bundles   = 1 bale or 5160 sheets

Writing paper

24 sheets   = 1 quire
20 quires   = 1 ream or 480 sheets

Wood measure

Timber exporting countries such as Norway and Sweden still use imperial measurements in everyday use reflecting this history of this trade with the U.K. A piece of two-by-three is readily understood as being 5 cm by 7.6 cm, which is what we would ask for in the U.K. Export timber is, of course, by volume and both the U.K. and the U.S. use the following:

```
16 cubic feet   = 1 cord foot
8 cord feet     = 1 cord (128 cu. feet)
```

The Force of Nature

It was not intended that this book should be an almanac, but during preparation I was fascinated by the following and thought them worth including.

Beaufort scale

The Beaufort scale is used for wind speeds. I have added approximate speeds in metres per second in this table.

Code No.	Description	Pressure lbs per square foot	Wind speed miles per hour	Wind speed knots	Wind speed ca. m/sec	Observable effects on the environment
0	Calm	0	less than 1	less than 1	less than 0.5	Smoke will rise vertically.
1	Light air	0.01	1–3	1–3	1–1.5	Rising smoke drifts, weather vane is inactive.
2	Light breeze	0.02	4–7	4–6	1.5–3	Leaves rustle, can feel wind on your face, weather vane is inactive.
3	Gentle breeze	0.28	8–12	7–10	3–5	Leaves and twigs move around. Light weight flags extend.
4	Moderate breeze	0.67	13–18	11–16	6–8	Moves thin branches, raises dust and paper.
5	Fresh breeze	1.31	19–24	17–21	8–11	Trees sway.
6	Strong breeze	2.30	25–31	22–27	11–14	Large tree branches move, open wires (such as telegraph wires) begin to 'whistle', umbrellas are difficult to keep under control.
7	Moderate gale	3.60	32–38	28–33	14–17	Large trees begin to sway, noticeably difficult to walk.
8	Fresh gale	5.40	39–46	34–40	17–20	Twigs and small branches are broken from trees, walking into the wind is very difficult.
9	Strong gale	7.70	47–54	41–47	21–24	Slight damage occurs to buildings, shingles are blown off of roofs.
10	Whole gale	10.50	55–63	48–55	25–28	Large trees are uprooted, building damage is considerable.
11	Storm	14.00	64–75	55–65	29–34	Extensive widespread damage. These typically occur only at sea, and rarely inland.
12	Hurricane	above 17	above 75	above 65	35 and above	Extreme destruction.

Saffir – Simpson Hurricane Scale

Category 1. Winds 74–95 mph.   Storm surge generally 4–5 ft above
                                          normal.

Category 2. Winds 96–110 mph.   Storm surge generally 6–8 feet above
                                          normal.

Category 3. Winds 111–130.   Storm surge generally 9–12 ft above
                                          normal.

Category 4. Winds 131–155 mph.   Storm surge generally 13–18 ft
                                          above normal.

Category 5. Winds more than 155 mph.   Storm surge generally greater than
                                          18 ft above normal.

Fujita Tornado Damage Scale

The Fujita Tornado Scale, usually referred to as the F-Scale, classifies
tornadoes based on the resulting damage. This scale was developed by Dr. T.
Theodore Fujita (University of Chicago) in 1971. Frequency 1950–1994.

F-Scale	Winds	Type of Damage	Frequency
F0	40–72 mph/ 64–116 km/h	Minimal	29%
F1	73–112 mph/117–180 km/h	Moderate	40%
F2	113–157 mph/181–253 km/h	Major	24%
F3	158–206 mph/254–332 km/h	Severe	6%
F4	207–260 mph/333–418 km/h	Devastating	2%
F5	261–318 mph/419–512 km/h	Incredible	< 1%

Several interesting websites may be found using search words Fujita scale.
These give in detail the type of damage encountered.

The Richter scale

The Richter scale for earthquake magnitude is logarithmic, implying that each
whole number step represents a ten-fold increase in amplitude or severity. It
is also an open ended scale although the most severe earthquake registered is
9.2 in Alaska 1964.

Richter magnitudes	Earthquake effects
Less than 3.5	Generally not felt, but recorded.
3.5–5.4	Often felt, but rarely causes damage.
Under 6.0	At most slight damage to well-designed buildings. Can cause major damage to poorly constructed buildings over small regions.

6.1–6.9	Can be destructive in areas up to about 100 kilometres across where people live.
7.0–7.9	Major earthquake. Can cause serious damage over larger areas.
8 or greater	Great earthquake. Can cause serious damage in areas several hundred kilometres across.

See: http://www.zephryus.demon.co.uk/geography/home.html

Useful handbooks

Liflander, Pamela (2002), *Measurements and Conversions.* London, Running Press.
Cassells Dictionary of Weights and Measures

Much information is available on the Internet. Search weights; measures, for example. The following contain useful links to other sites:
www.ex.ac.uk [*A Dictionary of Units* by Frank Tapson]
www.refdesk.com
www.infoplease.com (Also useful for other information)
www.home.clara.net (Contains interesting historical information).
www.convertme.com (Conversion of almost anything to everything else. Works like a calculator.)

12
Abbreviations

Cdnt fnd anthng appr f. ths ch. Suggns wlcm fr nxt edn.

Earlier editions of *The Concise Oxford English Dictionary* contained a list of several hundred abbreviations covering everything from military terms (H.L.I.: The Highland Light Infantry), organisations (L.G.U.: Ladies' Golf Union), membership (F.S.A.: Fellow of the Society of Antiquaries), medical terms (A.I.D.: artificial insemination by donor), miscellaneous (w.a.f. – with all faults!) These are now published separately in *The Oxford Dictionary of Abbreviations*.

It should not be assumed that standard abbreviations in a particular area such as NPM (New Public Management), MBO (Management by Objectives) are familiar to all readers. These abbreviations should be stated in the text or a footnote at the first occurrence. On the other hand some abbreviations are more familiar than their root:

The plants recovered after I dusted them with dichlorodiphenyltrichloroethane (DDT)

It is often convenient to use one's own abbreviations where a term is used constantly throughout an article. The popular mode is to use an acronym for certain types of abbreviations: BAMMO – The Battered and Maltreated Mistresses Organisation! It is essential that these are defined at the first time of use, preferably in a footnote as this will be easy to locate.

Upper and lower case

Some abbreviations require capital letters whereas others do not. For example, plc (public limited company) [lower case], Inc. (Incorporated) [upper case], Ltd or ltd (Limited or limited) is optional. No fast rules here!

A number of energy units are named after their discoverer/inventor: W (Watt), J (Joule). The abbreviations retain the capital (15 kW, 10J), but the terms watts and joules do not. The symbol for megahertz (no capital) is MHz (with a capital).

The full point

Not all abbreviations use a full point. For example, Ltd (Limited) does not require a full point (although is often given one); Co. and Inc. do. A general rule is that if the abbreviation concludes with the final letter of the word, then a full point is not normally required. But there are exceptions here as in Coy. (military company). If the abbreviation comprises the initial letters of two or more words, then a full point is not required, e.g. MP (Member of Parliament). The exception here is where this might cause confusion. Thus, M.P. means Military Police. Previously IBM (International Business Machines Corporation) could have been confused with I.B.M. (Intercontinental Ballistic Missile). The latter is now formally abbreviated ICBM.

Metric measurements do not use a full point: m is used for meters, while m. indicates million. The former abbreviation for 'miles per gallon' was m.p.g. It is normally encountered today as 'mpg', and similarly mph for 'miles per hour' although some dictionaries still retain the full point (m.p.h.).

Naturally, the full point is required at the end of the sentence. Should an abbreviated term occur at the end of a sentence confusion might occur, for example: 'The distance was only 6 m.' (miles or metres?). Use the full term.

Mr and Mrs do not now use a full point although was previously the practice. (It remains so in U.S. English.) The same also applies to other titles today: OBE, DSO, etc. It has been suggested that the full point here was originally dropped as a war-time measure for saving ink! Believe that and you'd believe anything. But there is a general tendency towards dropping full points for abbreviations in general such as USSR rather than U.S.S.R. Dr. and Rev. may be encountered with and without a full point.

Where the singular from employs a full point (ed., ch.), some publishing houses employ a full point for the plural, others do not: eds. (eds), but chs (no full point).

Recently, I was glancing at a publication by Collins covering abbreviations. It was interesting to observe that not a single full point was used throughout. *The Cassell Dictionary of abbreviations* is also pretty sparing in its use of the full point.

Single letter abbreviations

Many single letter abbreviations may be found in upper and lower case where they are abbreviations for different things. A small number of single letter abbreviations may employ either upper or lower case. Some end with a full point, others do not. Thus, we may have p (pence); p. (page, pint); P (Permian, phosphorous (chem. symbol)); P. (Pope, perennial (horticultural)).

We also have italicised forms: *p* (probability (statistics)) and boldface ***p*** (symbol for electric dipole moment (physics)). We also observe that the capitalised abbreviation may refer to a noun which is not capitalised.

Coastal site in Brittany for sale, 23 a, FF 200,000.

Sounds like a bargain, all those acres at that price! But 23 a for a Frenchman means 23 *ares*. An *are* is 100 sq. m and is signified without the full point. The abbreviation for *acre* is a. (with a full point), although it might be preferable to use the alternative ac. or A. (upper case with full point). This is one of the few single letter abbreviations employing either upper or lower case.

The following is a summary of the most common abbreviations encountered. Commonly used Latin abbreviations do not employ italics; other less frequently encountered Latin abbreviations and terms employ italics. However, some dictionaries may not indicate italics at all.

Measures (Abbreviations)

There used to be a general rule that metric measurements did not use the full point in abbreviations whereas imperial and UK measurements did. However, there is tendency to drop these in the UK, although the US still retains the full point in some measurements (e.g. feet; UK = ft, US = ft.). Some scientific journals tend not to use the full point for measurements where these may be given in the following.

Imperial and other UK measurements

area

acre	a., ac. or A.	4840 square yards

capacity

gallon	gall. or gal. (occ. g)	8 pints
gill		¼ pint
pint	p. or pt or pt.	
quart	q. or qt or qt.	2 pints

length

chain	ch.	Gunter's ch. = 66 ft.; engineer's ch. = 100 ft.
foot	ft or ft.(US)	12 inches
furlong	f. or fur.	1/8 mile; 220 yards
inch in.	(not i.)	
mile	m. or mi.	1760 yards; 5280 feet
nautical mile	naut. m. (or mi.)	(UK) 6080 feet, ca. 1.15 miles
yard(s)	yd or yd. (yds)	3 feet; 36 inches

It is important to use the correct sign (straight quotes) for feet and inches: 2′ 6″ and not the single and double quotation marks (smart quotes): 2' 6''.

mass

grain		1 oz = 437.5 grains
hundredweight	cwt or cwt.	112 lbs
ounce	oz or oz.	
pound	lb or lb.	16 oz.
quarter	qr.	28 lbs
stone	st.	14 lb.
ton	t or t.	20 cwt; 2240 lbs

temperature

Fahrenheit	F

volume

bushel	bsh. or bus.	8 imperial gallons (but mainly used for grain, ca. 15.5 cu. ft)

Metric measurements

area

are	a	100 sq. m.
decare	da	1000 sq. m; 10 ares
hectare	ha	10 000 sq. m; 100 ares

capacity

centilitre	cl
decilitre	dl
litre	l or lit.

length

centimetre	cm
kilometre	km
metre	m
millimetre	mm

mass

centigram	cg
gram	g
hectogram	hg
kilogram	kg
kilotonne	kt (1000 tonnes)
tonne tonne	

temperature

Celsius; centigrade	C

Organisations

The following is a list of major international and selected national and commercial organisations where the abbreviated form is often encountered. It should not be assumed that all readers of your manuscript are familiar with these and a footnote is recommended the first time the abbreviation is used. Many thousand acronyms are to be found on www.acronymfinder.com

AEA	Atomic Energy Authority (UK)
AEC	Atomic Energy Commission (USA)
AEC	African Economic Community
AFL	American Federation of Labor
ANC	African National Congress
ANSI	American National Standards Institute
ANZUS	Australia-New Zealand-United States Security Treaty
AONB	Area of Outstanding Natural Beauty
AP	Associated Press
APEX	Association of Professional, Executive, Clerical and Computer Staff
ASA	American Standards Association
ASCII	American Standard Code for Information Interchange
ASE	American Stock Exchange
ASEAN	Association of South East Asian Nations
BCIE	Central American Bank for Economic Integration
BDEAC	Central African States Development Bank
BIS	Bank for International Settlement
BSEC	Black Sea Economic Cooperation Zone
BSI	British Standards Institution
CACM	Central American Common Market
CAEU	Council of Arab Economic Unity
CAP	Common Agricultural Policy
CARICOM	Caribbean Community
CARIFTA	Caribbean Free Trade Area
CBI	Confederation of British Industry
CBSS	Council of the Baltic Sea States
CCC	Customs Cooperation Council
CCJ	Council of Christians and Jews
CCTA	Central Computer and Telecommunications Agency
CDB	Caribbean Development Bank
CDC	Commonwealth Development Corporation
CE	Council of Europe
CEI	Central European Initiative
CEMA	Council for Mutual Economic Assistance
CEMAC	Monetary and Economic Community of Central Africa
CENTO	Central Treaty Organisation
CEPGL	Economic Community of the Great Lakes Countries
CERN	European Organisation for Nuclear Research
CERN	Organisation Européene pour la recherche nucléaire (formerly, Conseil)
CHAPS	Clearing House Automated Clearing System

CHIPS	Clearing House Interbank Payments System
CIA	Central Intelligence Agency
CIO	Congress of Industrial Organisations
CIS	Commonwealth of Independent States
COBOL	Common Business Oriented Language
COCOM	Coordinating Committee on Export Controls
COMECON	Council for Mutual Economic Assistance
CP	Colombo Plan
EADB	East African Development Bank
EAPC	Euro-Atlantic Partnership Council
EBD	European Bank of Development
EBRD	European Bank for Reconstruction and Development
EBU	European Broadcasting Union
EC	European Community (or European Communities)
ECA	European Commission on Agriculture
ECGD	Export Credits Guarantee Department
ECM	European Common Market
ECO	Economic Cooperation Organisation
ECO	European Coal Organisation
ECOSOC	Economic and Social Council (of the United Nations)
ECOWAS	Economic Community of West African States
ECSC	European Coal and Steel Community
ECTG	European Channel Tunnel Group
ECU	European currency unit
EDC	European Defence Community
EDF	European Development Fund
EEOC	Equal Employment Opportunity Commission
EFC	European Forestry Commission
EFTA	European Free Trade Association
EIB	European Investment Bank
EMS	European Monetary System
EMU	European Monetary Union
EP	European Parliament
EPA	Environmental Protection Agency
ESA	Environmentally Sensitive Area
ESA	European Space Agency
ESCU	European Space Operations Centre
ESRO	European Space Research Organisation
EU	European Union
EURATOM	European Atomic Energy Community (Européene pour la recherche nucléaire)
FAO	Food and Agriculture Organisation
FLS	Front Line States
FSU	former Soviet Union
FTC	Federal Trade Commission
FZ	Franc Zone
GATT	General Agreement on Tariffs and Trade
GCC	Gulf Cooperation Council
GMC	General Medical Council

GMT	Greenwich Mean Time
IADB	Inter-American Development Bank
IAEA	International Atomic Energy Agency
IBRD	International Bank for Reconstruction and Development
ICAO	International Civil Aviation Organisation
ICC	International Chamber of Commerce
ICFTU	International Confederation of Free Trade Unions
ICJ	International Court of Justice
ICRC	International Committee of the Red Cross
ICRM	International Red Cross and Red Crescent Movement
IDA	International Development Association
IDB	Islamic Development Bank
IEA	International Energy Agency
IEA	International Environmental Agreement
IFAD	International Fund for Agricultural Development
IFC	International Finance Corporation
IFRCS	International Federation of Red Cross and Red Crescent Societies
IGAD	Inter-Governmental Authority on Development
IHO	International Hydrographic Organisation
ILO	International Labour Organisation
IMF	International Monetary Fund
IMO	International Maritime Organisation
IMO	International Migration Office
InOC	Indian Ocean Commission
Interpol	International Criminal Police Organisation
IOC	International Olympic Committee
IOM	International Organisation for Migration
ISO	International Organisation for Standardisation
ITU	International Telecommunication Union
IUCN	International Union for the Conservation of Nature and Natural Resources
IWC	International Whaling Commission
LAES	Latin American Economic System
LAFTA	Latin American Free Trade Association
LAIA	Latin American Integration Association
LCE	London Commodity Exchange
LDCs	Less developed countries
LEA	Local Education Authority
LIFFE	London International Financial Futures Exchange
LLDCs	Least developed countries
LME	London Metals Exchange
LSE	London Stock Exchange (also London School of Economics)
MNE	Multi-national Enterprises
Mercosor	Southern Cone Common Market (Mercosur) or Southern Common Market
MINURSO	United Nations Mission for the Referendum in Western Sahara
MIPONHU	United Nations Civilian Police Mission in Haiti
MONUC	United Nations Organisation Mission in the Democratic Republic of the Congo

NAFTA	North American Free Trade Association
NAM	Nonaligned Movement
NASA	National Aeronautics and Space Administration
NASDA	National Space Development Agency
NASDAQ	National Association of Securities Dealers Automated Quotation
NATO	North Atlantic Treaty Organisation
NC	Nordic Council
NEA	Nuclear Energy Agency
NHS	National Health Service
NIB	Nordic Investment Bank
NICs	Newly industrialising countries
NIEs	Newly industrialising economies
NIS	New independent states
NSG	Nuclear Suppliers Group
NYFE	New York Futures Exchange
NYSE	New York Stock Exchange
OAPEC	Organisation of Arab Petroleum Exporting Countries
OAS	Organisation of African States
OAS	Organisation of American States
OAU	Organisation of African Unity
OECD	Organisation for Economic Cooperation and Development
OECS	Organisation of Eastern Caribbean States
OEEC	Organisation for European Economic Co-operation
OIC	Organisation of the Islamic Conference
OPCW	Organisation for the Prohibition of Chemical Weapons
OPEC	Organisation of Petroleum Exporting Countries
OSCE	Organisation for Security and Cooperation in Europe
PAC	Pan-African Congress
PCA	Permanent Court of Arbitration
PFP	Partnership for Peace
RG	Rio Group
SACU	Southern African Customs Union
SADC	Southern African Development Community
SHAEF	Supreme Headquarters Allied Expeditionary Force
SHAPE	Supreme Headquarters Allied Powers, Europe
Sparteca	South Pacific Regional Trade and Economic Cooperation Agreement
SPF	South Pacific Forum
SAARC	South Asian Association for Regional Cooperation
TUC	Trades Union Council
UAE	United Arab Emirates
UDEAC	Central African Customs and Economic Union
UN	United Nations
UNAMSIL	United Nations Mission in Sierra Leone
UNCED	United Nations Conference on Environment and Development
UNCTAD	United Nations Conference on Trade and Development
UNDC	United Nations Disarmament Commission
UNDOF	United Nations Disengagement Observer Force
UNDP	United Nations Development Programme
UNEP	United Nations Environment Programme

UNESCO	United Nations Educational, Scientific and Cultural Organisation
UNFAO	United Nations Food and Agriculture Organisation
UNFICYP	United Nations Peace-keeping Force in Cyprus
UNFPA	United Nations Population Fund
UNGA	United Nations General Assembly
UNHCR	United Nations High Commissioner for Refugees
UNHRC	United Nations Human Rights Commissioner
UNICEF	United Nations Children's Fund (formerly UN International Children's Emergency Fund)
UNIDO	United Nations Industrial Development Organisation
UNIFIL	United Nations Interim Force in Lebanon
UNIKOM	United Nations Iraq-Kuwait Observation Mission
UNITAR	United Nations Institute for Training and Research
UNMEE	United Nations Mission in Ethiopia and Eritrea
UNMIBH	United Nations Mission in Bosnia and Herzegovina
UNMIK	United Nations Interim Administration Mission in Kosovo
UNMOGIP	United Nations Military Observer Group in India and Pakistan
UNMOP	United Nations Mission of Observers in Prevlaka
UNMOT	United Nations Mission of Observers in Tajikistan
UNMOVIC	United Nations Monitoring and Verification Commission
UNO	United Nations Organisation
UNOMIG	United Nations Observer Mission in Georgia
UNPREDEP	United Nations Preventive Deployment Force
UNRISD	United Nations Research Institute for Social Development
UNRWA	United Nations Relief and Works Agency for Palestine Refugees in the Near East
UNSC	United Nations Security Council
UNSG	United Nations Secretary General
UNTAET	United Nations Transitional Administration in East Timor
UNTSO	United Nations Truce Supervision Organisation
UNTT	United Nations Trust Territory
UNU	United Nations University
UPU	Universal Postal Union
WAEMU	West African Economic and Monetary Union
WAQDB	West African Development Bank
WBG	World Bank Group
WCL	World Confederation of Labour
WEU	Western European Union
WFP	World Food Programme
WFTU	World Federation of Trade Unions
WHO	World Health Organisation
WIPO	World Intellectual Property Organisation
WMO	World Meteorological Organisation
WP	Warsaw Pact
WToO	World Tourism Organisation
WTrO	World Trade Organisation
ZC	Zangger Committee

British Academic Titles

A number of the following are historic but may be found in the literature. The modern tendency is to use the short version BSc rather than B.Sc. (for example). No space after full point.

When I began compiling these I thought where were about fifty, but I had forgotten the Iron Lady. Mrs Thatcher was renowned for a statement that she would like everyone to be able to have a degree, even dustmen. She didn't make it particularly clear whether she meant that they could earn a degree in emptying dustbins (B.dust.), or whether the should be given the opportunity to take a degree in quantum mechanics. But it has to be admitted that the range and variety of degrees now available must be regarded as another of her controversial legacies. I have included those found in a number of dictionaries – but I suspect there are others. Indeed, a historical study of these might well provide the basis for a research degree MBMD(H) – Master of Bachelor, Master and Doctoral studies (History). Not quite as funny as it sounds. BD is not only a Bachelor of Divinity but also the abbreviation for bomb disposal. While a BBA is a Bachelor of Business Administration, it is also abbreviation for Born before arrival (as a B.Obstetrics would know – if that degree exists). There a few which must be queried such as DCrim. Now instinct would suggest Doctor of Criminology. Oh no – Doctor of Criminality. The *OED* gives this as a derivative of 'criminal', i.e. someone who has committed a crime. Al Capone must have been awarded several such degrees, and not honorary degrees either. The mind boggles!

I have not accredited the degrees to specific universities but there does seem to be some competition here when we find that one university uses BSPhar and another BSPharm (Batchelor of Science in Pharmacy). Possibly the latter university claims that their degree must be better as it contains more letters.

My first draft also included diplomas. A Dip. seems to be pretty common for everything from a weekend course to an alternative to a knighthood, the sort of thing one is required to acknowledge with a surreptitious nod of the head but cannot resist saying 'Oh yes, my cousin has two of those'. Associates and Fellows are also very numerous. I rather suspect that these are awarded on the basis of a contribution to a political party, 'Associates' for a single contribution, 'Fellows' for five years on the trot or a down payment of a ton. Dips, Asses and Fellows are not included in the list.

Those degrees employing the period are mainly pre-Thatcher; the short versions are more recent.

Advanced Certificate in Education	ACE
Bachelier ès arts	BèsA
Bachelier ès lettres	BèsL

Bachelier ès sciences	BèsS; BèSc
Bachelor in Agricultural Science	BAS; BASc
Bachelor in Dental Science	BDentSc
Bachelor of Accountancy	BAcc
Bachelor of Acupuncture	BAc
Bachelor of Agricultural Economics	BAgEc
Bachelor of Agriculture	B.Agr.
Bachelor of Applied Arts	BAA; BAppArts
Bachelor of Applied Mathematics	BAM
Bachelor of Applied Science (Medical technology)	BAppSc(MT)
Bachelor of Applied Science	BAppSc; BAS; BASc
Bachelor of Architectural Engineering	BArchE
Bachelor of Architecture	BArch
Bachelor of Arts in Administration	BA(Admin)
Bachelor of Arts in Art	BA(Art)
Bachelor of Arts in Economics	BA(Econ)
Bachelor of Arts in Education	BA(Ed)
Bachelor of Arts in Environmental Design	BAED
Bachelor of Arts in Journalism	BA(J)
Bachelor of Arts in Music	BA(Mus)
Bachelor of Arts in Music	BAM
Bachelor of Arts in Physical Education	BA(PE)
Bachelor of Arts in Theology	BA(Theol)
Bachelor of Arts	B.Arts
Bachelor of Building Science	BBldg(Sc)
Bachelor of Business Studies	BBA
Bachelor of Canon Law	BCL
Bachelor of Chemical Engineering	BCE; BChE; BChemEng; BE(Chem)
Bachelor of Chemistry	BC
Bachelor of Civil Law	B.C.L.; BCL
Bachelor of Commerce	BC; BCA; BCom; BComm
Bachelor of Commercial Science	BComSci
Bachelor of Dental Science	BDSc; BScD
Bachelor of Dental Surgery (*Baccalaureus Chirurgiae Dentalis*)	BCh(D)
Bachelor of Dental Surgery	B.D.S.; BDS: BChD
Bachelor of Design	BDes
Bachelor of Divinity	B.D.; BD
Bachelor of Domestic Arts	BDA
Bachelor of Dramatic Art	BDA
Bachelor of Economics in Industrial Administration	BEcon(IA)
Bachelor of Economics in Public Administration	BEcon(PA)
Bachelor of Economics	BEc; BEcon; BE
Bachelor of Education	BE; BEd
Bachelor of Education in Commerce	BEd(Comm)
Bachelor of Education in Educational Science	BEd(Sc)
Bachelor of Education in Home Economics	BEd(HEc)
Bachelor of Education in Nursing	BEd(N)

Bachelor of Education in Physical Education	BEd(PE)
Bachelor of Education in Science	BEd(Sc)
Bachelor of Education	B.Ed.
Bachelor of Engineering (*Baccalaureus Artis Ingeniariae*)	BAI
Bachelor of Engineering (Dublin)	BEI
Bachelor of Engineering Science	BES
Bachelor of Engineering	B.Eng.; BEng; BE
Bachelor of Engraving	BEngr
Bachelor of Environmental Science	BES
Bachelor of Fine Arts	BFA
Bachelor of Food Technology	BTechFood
Bachelor of Forestry Science	BForSc
Bachelor of Forestry	BF; BFor
Bachelor of Home Economics	BHE
Bachelor of Horticultural Science	BHortSc
Bachelor of Horticulture	BHort
Bachelor of Hygiene	BHy
Bachelor of Indian Medicine	BIM
Bachelor of Industrial Design	BID
Bachelor of Industrial Engineering	BIE
Bachelor of Interior Design	BID
Bachelor of Land Management	BLM
Bachelor of Landscape Architecture	BLA
Bachelor of Law	B.L.; BL
Bachelor of Laws (*Legum Baccalaureus*)	LL.B.; LLB
Bachelor of Laws	B.LL; BLL
Bachelor of Letters (*Baccalaureus Litterarum*)	BLitt
Bachelor of Letters or Literature (*Litterarum] Baccalaureus*)	LittB
Bachelor of Letters	B.Litt.; BL
Bachelor of Liberal Arts	BLA
Bachelor of Library Science	BLS
Bachelor of Literature (*Bachelier ès Lettres*)	B. ès LL.
Bachelor of Literature	BLit; BL; Litt.B.
Bachelor of Marine Science	BMS
Bachelor of Mathematics	BMath
Bachelor of Mechanical Engineering	BME
Bachelor of Medical Science	BMedSci; BScD; BScMed
Bachelor of Medicine [L *Medicinae Baccalaureus*]	MB
Bachelor of Medicine	B.Med; B.M.
Bachelor of Medicine	BMed
Bachelor of Medicine	M.B.; MB
Bachelor of Metallurgical Engineering	BMetE
Bachelor of Metallurgy	BMet
Bachelor of Mining Engineering	BME
Bachelor of Modern Languages	BML
Bachelor of Music (*Musicae Baccalaureus*)	MusB
Bachelor of Music Education	BME; BMusEd
Bachelor of Music	Mus.B; MusB; BMus; B.Mus.

Bachelor of Natural Science	BNS
Bachelor of Naval Science	BSNS
Bachelor of Nursing Science	BNSc
Bachelor of Nursing	BN; BNurs
Bachelor of Optometry	BOptom
Bachelor of Oratory	BO
Bachelor of Orientation	BOr
Bachelor of Pedagogy	BPd
Bachelor of Pharmacy	BP; BPharm
Bachelor of Philosophy	B.Phil.; BP; BPh; BPhil
Bachelor of Physical Education	BPE
Bachelor of Professional Arts	BPA
Bachelor of Psychology	BPs; BPsych
Bachelor of Public Health	BPH
Bachelor of Religious Education	BRE
Bachelor of Sacred Literature	BSL
Bachelor of Sacred Music	BSM
Bachelor of Sacred Theology	BST
Bachelor of Science in Advertising	BSAdv
Bachelor of Science in Aeronautical Engineering	BSAE; BSAeEng
Bachelor of Science in Agricultural Engineering	BSAE; BSAgE
Bachelor of Science in Agriculture	BSA; BSAgr; BSc(Ag); BScA
Bachelor of Science in Applied Arts	BSAA
Bachelor of Science in Applied Science	BScApp
Bachelor of Science in Architecture	BScArcg
Bachelor of Science in Business Administration	BSBA
Bachelor of Science in Business	BSBus
Bachelor of Science in Chemical Engineering	BSChE
Bachelor of Science in Civil Engineering	BSCE
Bachelor of Science in Commerce	BSC
Bachelor of Science in Dentistry	BSc(Dent)
Bachelor of Science in Design	BSD
Bachelor of Science in Economics	BSc(Econ); BSEc;
Bachelor of Science in Education	BSc(Ed); BSE; BSEd
Bachelor of Science in Electrical Engineering	BSEE; BSEEng; BSEIE
Bachelor of Science in Elementary Education	BSEE
Bachelor of Science in Engineering of Mines	BSEM
Bachelor of Science in Engineering Sciences	BSES
Bachelor of Science in Engineering	BSE; BSEng
Bachelor of Science in Foreign Service	BSFS
Bachelor of Science in Forestry management	BSFM
Bachelor of Science in Forestry	BSF; BSFor
Bachelor of Science in Fuel Technology	BSFT
Bachelor of Science in General Engineering	BSGE
Bachelor of Science in Home Economics	BSHE; BSHEc
Bachelor of Science in Horticulture	BSc(Hort)
Bachelor of Science in Hospital Administration	BSHA
Bachelor of Science in Hygiene	BSHyg
Bachelor of Science in Journalism	BSJ

Bachelor of Science in Library Science	BSLS
Bachelor of Science in Linguistics	BSL
Bachelor of Science in Mechanical Engineering	BSME
Bachelor of Science in Medical technology	BSMedTech; BSMT
Bachelor of Science in Medicine	BSM
Bachelor of Science in Metallurgical Engineering	BSMetE
Bachelor of Science in Metallurgy	BSMet
Bachelor of Science in Mining Engineering	BSME
Bachelor of Science in Nuclear Engineering	BSNE
Bachelor of Science in Nursing	BSN
Bachelor of Science in Nutrition	BSc(Nutr)
Bachelor of Science in Occupational Therapy	BSOT
Bachelor of Science in Pharmacy	BSPhar; BSPharm; BSP
Bachelor of Science in Physical Education	BSPE
Bachelor of Science in Physical Therapy	BSPhTh; BSPT
Bachelor of Science in Public Administration	BSPA
Bachelor of Science in Public Health	BSPH
Bachelor of Science in Radiological Technology	BSRT
Bachelor of Science in Secondary Education	BSSE
Bachelor of Science in Secretarial Administration	BSSA
Bachelor of Science in Secretarial Studies	BSSS
Bachelor of Science in Social Science	BSSS
Bachelor of Science	B.Sc; BSc; ScB; BS (US)
Bachelor of Scientific Agriculture	BSA
Bachelor of Secretarial Science	BSS
Bachelor of Social Science	BSocSc; BSSc
Bachelor of Social Sciences	BScSoc
Bachelor of Social Work	BSW
Bachelor of Surgery (*Baccalaureus Chirurgiae*)	BC
Bachelor of Surgery (Chirurgy)	B.Ch.
Bachelor of Surgery	B.S.; BS; ChB
Bachelor of Surveying	BSurv
Bachelor of Teaching	BT
Bachelor of Technical Education	BTechEd
Bachelor of Technology	BTech
Bachelor of Textile Chemistry	BTCh
Bachelor of Textile Engineering	BTE
Bachelor of Theology	BT; BTh
Bachelor of Town and Country Planning	BTCP
Bachelor of Town and Regional Planning	BTRP
Bachelor of Town Planning	BTP
Bachelor of Veterinary Medicine and Surgery	BVMS
Bachelor of Veterinary Medicine	BVetMed; MVB
Bachelor of Veterinary Science and Animal Husbandry	BVSc&AH
Bachelor of Veterinary Science	BVetSc; BVSc
Bachelor of Veterinary Surgery	BVS
Certificate in Education	CE
Degree of Honour	D of H
Doctor of Medicine	DrMed

Doctor of Science in Economics	DSE
Doctor in Aviation Medicine	DAvMed
Doctor in Guidance Counselling	DGC
Doctor in Orientation	DOr
Doctor in Physical Education	DPE
Doctor in Public Health	DPH
Doctor of Acupuncture	DAc
Doctor of Agricultural Science	DAgrSc; DASc
Doctor of agricultural Sciences (*Docteur en sciences agricoles*)	DScA
Doctor of Agriculture	DAgr; DrAgr
Doctor of Applied Science	DAppSc
Doctor of Applied Sciences (*Docteur en sciences appliqués*)	DScA
Doctor of Architecture	DArch
Doctor of Art	DArt
Doctor of Ayurvedic Medicine	DAyM
Doctor of Canon and Civil Law	JUD
Doctor of Canon Law (*Juris Canonici Baccalaureus*)	JCD
Doctor of Canon Law	DCnL
Doctor of Celtic Literature	DLC
Doctor of Chemical Engineering	DChE
Doctor of Chemistry	DrChem
Doctor of Christian Theology	DCT
Doctor of Civil Law	D.C.L.; DCL
Doctor of Commerce	DComm
Doctor of Commercial Law	DComL
Doctor of Comparative Law	DCompL
Doctor of Criminality	DCrim
Doctor of Dental Medicine	DDM
Doctor of Dental Surgery	D.D.S.; DDS; DChD
Doctor of Divinity or Theology (*Doctor Theologiae*)	DT; D.T.
Doctor of Divinity	D.D.; DD
Doctor of Education	DEd
Doctor of Elocution	DElo
Doctor of Engineering Science	DEngS
Doctor of Engineering	DEng(g); DocEng; DrEng
Doctor of Entomology	DEnt
Doctor of Health Services	DHS
Doctor of Hebrew Letters	DHL
Doctor of Hebrew Literature	DHL
Doctor of Holy or Sacred Scripture (*Doctor Sacra Scripturae*)	DSS
Doctor of Humane letters	DHL; DHumLit
Doctor of Humanities or Literature (*Litterarum Humaniorum Doctor*)	LHD
Doctor of Hygiene	DHyg
Doctor of Jewish Theology	DCT
Doctor of Juridical Science	DJS

Doctor of Law; Jurisprudence (*Doctor Juris*)	DJur
Doctor of Laws (*Legum Doctor*)	LLD
Doctor of Laws	Dr jr; JD
Doctor of letters (*Docteur en lettres*)	DLett
Doctor of Letters (*Doctor Litterarum*)	DLitt; LittD
Doctor of Letters (*Docteur ès lettres*)	DèsL
Doctor of Letters in Economic Studies	DLES
Doctor of Literature	DLit; Litt.D.
Doctor of Literature, Doctor of letters [L *Doctor Litterarum*]	D.Litt.; DLitt
Doctor of Medical Science	DMS; MedScD; MSD; MScD (*US*)
Doctor of Medicine (*Docteur en médecine*)	DenM(ed)
Doctor of Medicine (*Medicinae Doctor*)	MD
Doctor of Medicine and Surgery	DMS
Doctor of Medicine	DMed; M.D.
Doctor of Metallurgy	DMet
Doctor of Meteorology	DMet
Doctor of Military Science	DScMil
Doctor of Ministry	DMin
Doctor of Music (*Musicae Doctor*)	MusD
Doctor of Music	D.Mus.; DMus; Mus. D.
Doctor of Natural Science	Dr rer. nat.; DrNatSci
Doctor of Ocular Science	DOS
Doctor of Pedagogy	DPed
Doctor of Pharmacy	DPharm
Doctor of Philosophy	D.Phil.; DPhil; DP; DPh; DPhil; DrPhil
Doctor of Philosophy	Ph.D.; PhD
Doctor of Political Economics (*Doctor Oeconomiae Politicae*)	DrOecPol
Doctor of Political Economy	DPEc
Doctor of Political Science (*Docteur en sciences politiques*)	DSP
Doctor of Political Science (*Docteur ès science politique*)	DèsScPol
Doctor of Political Science	DPolSc
Doctor of Public Health	DrPH
Doctor of Public Service	DPS
Doctor of Religious Education	DRE
Doctor of Rural Science	DRuRSci
Doctor of Sacred Music	DSM
Doctor of Sacred Theology	DST
Doctor of Science (*Docteur ès sciences*)	DèsS(c)
Doctor of Science in Agriculture	DSc(Agr)
Doctor of Science in Engineering	DScEng
Doctor of Science in Forestry	DScFor
Doctor of Science	D.Sc.; DSc; DS; DSc; ScD
Doctor of Social Science(s)	DSS; DSocSc

Doctor of Social Work	DSW
Doctor of Surgery	DS
Doctor of Technical Science	DScTech
Doctor of Technology	DTech
Doctor of the University of Paris (*Docteur de l'Université de Paris*)	DUP
Doctor of Theology	DrTheol; DTh; DTh(eol)
Doctor of Veterinary Medicine and Surgery	DVMS
Doctor of Veterinary Medicine	DVM; MVD
Doctor of Veterinary Science	DVSc(i)
Doctor of Veterinary Surgery	DVS
Doctor of Zoology	DZool
honorary doctor (*Doctor honoris causa*)	Dr hc
Honorary doctorate (*Doctoris honoris causa*)	Dhc
Master in /of Landscape Architecture	MLA
Master in Agriculture	MSA
Master in Chemical Analysis	MChemA
Master in Dental Science	MDentSc
Master in Engineering	MaE
Master in the Teaching of English as a Foreign Language	MTEFL
Master in/of Social Work	MSW
Master of Accountancy	MAc
Master of Aeronautical Engineering	MAE
Master of Agricultural Economics	MAgEc
Master of Agricultural Science	MAgrSc
Master of Agriculture	MAg
Master of Anaesthesiology	MAneas
Master of Applied Science	MAppSc; MAS; MASc; MScApp
Master of Art Education	MAE
Master of Arts in Economics	MA(Econ)
Master of Arts in Education	MA(Ed); MAE
Master of Arts in Law and Diplomacy	MALD
Master of Arts in Social Science	MA(SS)
Master of Arts in Teaching	MAT
Master of Arts	M.A.; MA.; M.Arts
Master of Building Science	MBdgSc
Master of Business Administration	MBA
Master of Business Management	MBM
Master of Business Science	MBSc
Master of Chemical Engineering	MChE
Master of Civic Design	MVCD
Master of Civil Engineering	MCE
Master of Clinical Science	MClSc
Master of Commerce and Administration	MCA
Master of Commerce	M.Comm.; MComm
Master of Community Health	MCommH
Master of Dental Science	MScD; MDS

Master of Dental Surgery (*Magister Chirurgiae Dentalis*)	MChD
Master of Design	MDes
Master of Diplomacy	MDip
Master of Economics	M.Econ.; MEc
Master of Education	M.Ed.; MEd
Master of Electrical Engineering	MEE
Master of Engineering (*Magister in Arte Ingeniaria*)	MAI
Master of Engineering Science	MESc
Master of Engineering	ME; MEng
Master of Fine Arts in Music	MFAMus
Master of Fine Arts	MFA
Master of Food Science	MFS
Master of Foreign Study	MFS
Master of Gynaecology and Obstetrics	MGO
Master of Home Economics	MHE
Master of Hospital Administration	MHA
Master of International Affairs	MIA
Master of Landscape Design	MLD
Master of Laws (*Legum Magister*)	LL.M.; LLM
Master of Laws in Commercial Law	LLMCom
Master of Laws	ML
Master of Letters [L *Magister Litterarum*]	M.Litt.
Master of Letters of Literature (*Litterarum Magister*)	LittM
Master of Letters	ML
Master of Letters; Literature (*Litterarum Humaniores*)	LitM
Master of Library Science	MLS
Master of Mathematics	MMath
Master of Mechanical Engineering	MME; MMechE
Master of Medical Science	MMedSci; MMSc; MScMed
Master of Medicine	MMed
Master of Metallurgical Engineering	MMetE
Master of Metallurgy	MMet
Master of Mining Engineering	MME
Master of Ministry	MMin
Master of Music (*Musicae Magister*)	MusM
Master of Music Education	MME
Master of Music	M.Mus.
Master of Musical Education	MMusEd
Master of Nursing	MNurs
Master of Obstetrics and Gynaecology	MO&G
Master of Oratory	MO
Master of Orthopaedic Surgery (*Magister Chirurgiae Orthopaedicae*)	MChOrth
Master of Philosophy	M.Phil.; MPh; MPhil
Master of Physical Education	MPE
Master of Professional Accounting	MPA
Master of Psychological Science	MPsSc
Master of Psychology	MPS; MPsych
Master of Public Administration	MPA

Master of Public and International Affairs	MPIA
Master of Public Health	MPH
Master of Regional Planning	MRP
Master of Religious Education	MRE
Master of Sacred Music	MSM
Master of Sacred Theology	MST
Master of Science (Economics)	M.Sc. (Econ.)
Master of Science (US)	MS
Master of Science in Aeronautical Engineering	MSAE
Master of Science in Agriculture	MSAgr; MScA
Master of Science in Architecture	MSArch; MSc(Arch)
Master of Science in Business Administration	MSBA
Master of Science in Business	MSBus
Master of Science in Chemical Engineering	MSChE
Master of Science in Civil Engineering	MSCE
Master of Science in Community Planning	MSCP
Master of Science in Dentistry	MSD; MSDent
Master of Science in Economics	Msc(Econ)
Master of Science in Education	MSc(Ed); MSE; MSEd
Master of Science in Electrical Engineering	MSEE
Master of Science in Engineering mechanics	MSEM
Master of Science in Engineering of Mines	MSEM
Master of Science in Engineering	MSE
Master of Science in Forestry	MSF
Master of Science in Home Economics	MSHE; MSHEc
Master of Science in Horticulture	MSc(Hort)
Master of Science in Hygiene	MSHyg
Master of Science in Industrial Engineering	MSIE
Master of Science in Journalism	MSJ
Master of Science in Library Science	MSLS
Master of Science in Linguistics	MSL
Master of Science in Mechanical Engineering	MSME
Master of Science in Metallurgical Engineering	MSMetE
Master of Science in Music	MSM; MSMus
Master of Science in Nursing	MSN
Master of Science in Nutrition	MSc(Nutr)
Master of Science in Physical Education	MSPE
Master of Science in Public Health Engineering	MSPHE
Master of Science in Public Health	MSPH
Master of Science in Teaching	MST
Master of Science in Pharmacy	MSPhar; MSPharm
Master of Science of Social Service	MS
Master of Science	M.Sc.; MSc
Master of Social Science	MSS
Master of Social Science(s)	MSocSc
Master of Social Welfare	MSW
Master of Statistics	MStat
Master of Surgery [*Magister Chirurgiae*]	M.Ch., M.Chir.; MCh
Master of Surgery	Ch.M.; ChM; CM; M.S.; MS

Master of Surveying Science	MSurvSc
Master of Surveying	MSurv
Master of Technology	M.Tech.; MTech
Master of the Liberal Arts	ML
Master of the University	MUniv
Master of Theological Studies	MTS
Master of Theology	MTh
Master of Town Planning	MTO
Master of Veterinary Medicine	MDV; MVetMed
Master of Veterinary Science	MVetSc; MVS; MVSc
Master of/in Civil Law	MCL
Master of/in Surgery (*Magister Chirurgiae*)	MCh(ir)
Masters Certificate in Education	MCE
Post-graduate Certificate of Education	PGCE
Professional Diploma in Education	PDE

▶ Many first degrees previously suffixed Hons., indicating 'With honours' – a first or second class degree. Regarded as 'snobbishness' by many, it is less frequently encountered today.

▶ Capitals are not used when making general references to degrees and diplomas. He planned to write a doctorate dissertation after he had finished his master's degree.

Commercial Abbreviations

A/C	Account
A/c	account of
APR	annual percentage rate
A/S	account sales
a/d	after date
B/E	Bill of Exchange
B/L	Bill of Lading
B/S	Bill of Sale
CBA	Cost-benefit analysis
CCJ	County Court Judgement
CD	Certificate of Deposit
CEO	Chief Executive Officer
C.O.D.	Cash on delivery
CPI	Consumer Price index
d/a	days after acceptance
d/d	day's date
d/s	day's sight
ENG	Electronic News Gathering
f.o.b. or fob	free on board
GDI	gross domestic income
GDP	gross domestic product

GNP	gross national product
ICC	Internat.Currency Code
ICT	Information and Communication Technology
IEA	International Environmental Agreement
IOU	letter of debt
IRR	internal rate of return
J/A	Joint account
L/c	Letter of Credit
LIBOR	London Inter-Bank Offered Rate
MBO	Management by objectives
Mc	Metallic currency
m/d	month's date
MLM	Multi-level Marketing
m/s	month's sight
NFP	not-for-profit (org.)
NGO	Non-governmental organisation
NPM	New Public Management
NPV	net present value
O & M	Organisation and methods
o/a	on account
OR	Operational research
OTC	over the counter (price, market etc.)
PAYE	Pay-as-you-earn (tax)
PC	Politically correct
P/E	Price-Earnings ratio
PERT	Programme Evaluation and Review Technique
PFI	Private financial initiative
plc or PLC	public limited company
P/N	Promissory Note
PPBS	Planning, Programming, Budgeting System
PPI	Producer Price Index
PPP	purchasing power parity
pv	present value
R&D	research and development
RAMPS	resource allocation and multi-project spending
RPM	resale price maintenance
TQM	Total Quality Management
VAT	Value-added tax
WPI	Wholesale price index
ZBB	zero-base budgeting

Local Government (UK)

I assume that a reasonable proportion of users of this book are concerned with local government. Here is a glossary of terms – some antiquated (e.g. GLC), but which may be encountered.

ACC	The Association of County Councils

AEF	Aggregate External Finance
AMA	The Association of Metropolitan Authorities
APSAS	The Association of Public Service Administrative Staff
CEO	Chief Executive Officer
CIPFA	The Chartered Institute of Public Finance and Accountancy
COG	Chief Officers' Group
COSLA	The Convention of Scottish Local Authorities
DES	The Department of Education and Science
DLO	Direct Labour (use of the council's workforce as opposed to contracted)
DOE	The Department of the Environment
EOC	Equal Opportunities Commission
EPA	Educational Priority Area
FGC	Family Group Conference
GLC	The Greater London Council
GREA	Grant Related Expenditure Assessment
HIPS	Housing Investment Programmes
ICSA	The Institute of Chartered Secretaries and Administrators
ILEA	The Inner London Education Authority
INLOGOV	The Institute of Local Government Studies (Univ. of Birmingham)
LA	Local authority
LASS	Local authority social departments (staff)
LBA	The London Boroughs' Association
LGMB	Local Government Management Board
LEA	Local Education Authority
LIT	Local Income Tax
LRT	London Regional Transport
NALGO	The National and Local Government Officers' Association
NUPE	National Union of Public Employees
OMT	Officers' Management Team
PC	Politically Correct!
PEA	Prescribed Expenditure Allocation
PPB	Programme Budgeting
PPP	Private and Public Partnership
PSS	Personal social services
PTA	Passenger Transport Authority
QUALGO	quasi-local government organisation.
QUANGO	quasi non-governmental organisation
RIPA	The Royal Institute of Public Administration
RSG	Revenune Support Grant
SAUS	The School of Advanced Urban Studies (Univ. of Bristol)
SoLACE	The Society of Local Authority Chief Executives
SSA	Standard Spending Assessment
SSAP	Statement of Standard Accountancy Practice
SSD	Social Services Department (LA)
SSG	Standard Spending Grant
SWD	Social work department (LA)

Latin Abbreviations in a Text

In Chapter 4 mention was made of Latin terms in bibliographic reference. Here we discuss other Latin terms, many of which are among the most used and misused. Normally these abbreviations do not require italics as they are in common use. (The full Latin term is given in italics here.)

Abbreviation

c., ca. circa	circa, about, approximately. Note. In full sentences write text: The war finished about 1245 AD. Do not use with periods as in ca. 1900–1902.
cf or cf. confer	compare with. (Not frequently used).
e.g. exempli gratia	for example. [1]
et al. et alii	and others (authors)
etc. et cetera	and so forth. [2]
et seq. et sequentia	and the following pages
f.	and the next page
ff.	and the following pages
ibid.	*ibidem* in the quoted reference.
id.	*idem* the same
i.a. or ia *inter alia*	among other things (rarely used)[3]
i.e. id est	that is.[4]
loc. cit. *loco citato*	at the place cited
N.B. Nota Bene	note well (capitalise)
op. cit. *opere citato*	in the work already cited
op. opus,	composition number. E.g. Berlioz, opus 21
passim	found at various places throughout the text
q.v. quod vide	which see
v.	see
v., vs.	versus
viz. vidilicet	in other words. Used to introduce an explanation.

Occasionally one encounters abbreviations of English terms. One of these is f.i. – for instance. There may be others, but these are not standard.

And while we are on the subject of Latin terms *ex libris* is an adjective meaning *from the library of...* . The noun *ex-libris* (hyphenated) is a bookplate bearing the coat of arms, name, etc. of the owner.

Notes to the above:

[1] *e.g – exempli gratia.*
This should be understood as meaning *by way of example, such as,* or *including*, thus preceding a list.

✓ The shop sold exotic fruits and vegetables, e.g. stuffed olives, mangoes, sweet potatoes and so forth.

A useful rule is if 'and so forth' can be applied, then e.g. may be used. Incidentally, it is not necessary to use the conjunction *and* before the final item in a list:

✓ He proposed a number of changes, e.g. larger typeface, wider line spacing, broader margins.

Neither do we use e.g. *and* etc.

✗ She ordered unnecessary garments, e.g. corsets, girdles, laced items beyond description, unlaced items beyond comprehension, etc.,

▶ A common error is to use this abbreviation in a phrase such as:

✗ He thought, for e.g. that the font size should be increased.
✗ See e.g. Jones (1953).

instead of:

✓ He thought, for example, that the font size should be increased.
✓ See, for example, Jones (1953).

▶ e.g. is not followed by a colon.

✗ He ordered some basic necessities, e.g.: shirts, jackets, trousers.

[2] *etc. – Et cetera*

'Etc.' is often loosely used when 'and so forth' is better. Frequently 'e.g.' is best substituted by 'such as', 'including', for example', 'as well as'. Some advise against its use in the middle of a sentence, one of the above being preferable.

He considered buying a hat, coat and shoes, etc., but not those his wife wanted.

Caution should be used in consideration of inverted commas. Did he actually say 'etc.'? If it is the spoken word, the write out in full.

'I bought dollars, euros, sterling, et cetera.' He did not mention the rates of exchange.
He stated that he 'had bought dollars, euros, sterling', etc. He did not mention the rates of exchange.

[3] The abbreviation *i.a.* is rarely encountered in English (UK) texts. In fact, the full term is not to be found in all dictionaries. Otherwise we can find the abbreviation in *Encarta Dictionary* (US), but where it means *in absentia*.

The *Oxford Dictionary of Abbreviations* gives 'immediately available'. I did encounter: 'On the 11th, reports were received that Furnace had been seen, inter alia, at Kettering, Guildford and Hastings.' Clearly, this means 'among other places'. I am left with the feeling that this is one of the Latin terms we really can do without.

The Latin preposition *inter* precedes a number of terms: *inter alia* (amongst other things); *inter alios* (among other persons); *inter nos* (between ourselves); *inter partes* (between two parties [legal]); *inter se* (among themselves); *inter vivos* (between living persons, as opposed to a legacy).

In UK English all these should be written in full and in italics.

[4] i.e.

This abbreviation is use to clarify or explain a statement where it means 'that is (to say)':

- ✓ The court was adjourned for a week, i.e. until March 3rd.
- ✓ The flag is yellow, green and red, i.e. reflecting the sun, the forests and the blood of the country's heroes.

In spoken language, the full text meaning 'namely' is best:

- ✓ 'I will phone you on the day at the end of the week, that is to say Saturday.' [namely, Saturday].

Other Abbreviations

(*sic*)	So or thus. Follows text to show that it is correctly quoted although appears doubtful.
A	absolute; ampere; area
A.D.	(previously used for AD)
	Note 1999 AD *or* AD 1999 *but* 1999 BC
a.m.	*ante meridiem*: before noon
abbrev. or abbr.	abbreviation/abbreviated
ABM	antiballistic missile
AD	*anno Domini (In the year of our Lord).*
AGM	annual general meeting
amp	ampere
amu	atomic mass unit
AOB	any other business
APL	A Programming Language
APR	annual percentage rate
ASCII	American standard code for information interchange
ASM	air-to-surface missile

AU	astronomical unit
AV	audio-visual
b.	born [John Smith b.1927]
B.C.	(previously used for BC)
BASIC	Beginners All-purpose Symbolic Instruction Code
BC	Before Christ. See AD
c	cent-; cubic (also cu.)
c.	century; cent(s); circa (also ca.); copyright (also ©)
C.	Conservative (party)
cfi	cost, freight, insurance
c.i.f.	cost, insurance, freight
C.O.D.	cash on delivery
c/o	care of
ca.	*circa* (or circa) about
CAD	computer-aided design
CAI	computer-aided instruction
CAL	computer-aided learning
CAM	computer-aided manufacture
CASE	computer-aided software engineering
CATV	cable television
CBL	computer-based learning
CCD	charge-coupled device
CCR	camera cassette recorder
CCTV	closed circuit television
CD	compact disc
CD-ROM	compact disc read-only memory
cent.	century
c.f.	carried forward
cg.	centigram
cgs	centimetre-gram-second
CGT	capital gains tax
ch.	church; chain (unit of measure)
Co.	Company (e.g. Co. Ltd, limited company)
col.	column
Coll.	College
Coy.	Company (military)
CPU	central processing unit
CRT	cathode-ray tube
CTT	capital transfer tax
D	The first derivative of a mathematical function
d.	died [John Smith d.1992]
DBMS	database management system
DBS	direct broadcasting from satellite
dc	direct current
DCF	discounted cash flow

DDP	Director of Public Prosecutions
dept	department
Dr	Doctor
dr.	drachma
DST	daylight saving time
DTP	desk-top publishing
d.w.t	dead weight tonnage
E	East; English
ed.	editor; edited. Confusingly, this is frequently used for 'edition'.
edn	edition
eds.	editors (also eds – without period)
Eq.	Equerry
eq.	equation
F	franc(s)
f	function (math.) If possible, use symbol $\int$
f.	fathom(s); female; following page (see ff.)
f.o.b.	free on board
FAQ	Frequently asked questions (frequently encountered on the Internet).
ff.	following pages (or FF.); folio
fig.	figure
fr.	francs
Fr.	French
ft.	foot; feet
fur.	furlong
fx	foreign exchange; for example (recently found).
G	giga; gigabytes; gravity (e.g. 3G)
GDI	gross domestic income
GDP	gross domestic product
GMT	Greenwich Mean Time
GNP	gross national product
h.	hour(s); height; hundred; husband [Anne h. John]
h.& c.	hot and cold
ho.	house
hp	horsepower
hr	hour
hrs	hours
HRT	Hormone replacement therapy
I.	Institute; International; Island
i.	interest (finance)
i.a.	*in absentia.* (NOT inter alia = among other things)
i.e.	*id est:* that is (avoid ie, although this is increasingly encountered)
ICT	Information and Communication Technology

i/c	in charge
Inc.	Incorporated
J	joule(s)
j	unit vector along the *y*-axis
J.	Judge (plur. JJ.)
jr	junior
K	kilobytes; Köchel (or K.) [Mozart; K454]
k.	karat(s)
kp	kiloparsec
kv	kilovolt
kw	kilowatt
L	lire
l. (or L.)	length
L.	Liberal (party); Licentiate
l.c.	lower case
LAN	local area network
LED	light-emitting diode
ll.	lines
log	logarithm
long.	longitude
LPG	liquefied petroleum gas
lpt	line printer
Ltd, ltd	Limited
m	meter(s); mile(s); million(s); minute(s)
M	Million, marks
m.	male; married; meridian; month
M.	Monsieur; million
M.P.	Military Police
math.	mathemat/, -ical. (Not maths.)
memo.	memorandum
Messrs	Messieurs
mg	milligrams
MHz	megahertz
misc.	miscellaneous
MM or MM.	Messieurs
MP	Member of Parliament
mpg	miles per gallon (formerly m.p.g.)
mph	miles per hour (formerly m.p.h.)
Mr	Mister (Not Mr.)
Mrs	Refers to married woman (originally abbrev. of Mistress)
Ms	abbreviation for Miss/Mrs (Not Ms.)
ms. or MS.	manuscript
mss. or MSS.	manuscripts
MW, MWh	megawatt(s), -hours
mW	milliwatt(s)

n	nano-
N	North
n.	noon; note; number
N.B.	Please note
n.d. or nd	not dated
N⁰	No.; number
o	used in logic for a negative category
o.	only
O.K. or OK	'all correct'. 'o.k.' may be used, but not 'ok'
o/s	out of stock
ob.	*obit.* died (on tombstones)
p	pence
p.c.	per cent
p.m.	*post meridiem:* after noon
pc	parsec (not ps)[1]
PC	personal computer
per pro	by proxy
PIN	personal identification number
plc	public limited company
pop.	population, occasionally popn
POS	point of sale
POW	prisoner of war
pp	*post procurationem*; for and on behalf of [usually written *per pro*]
pp or pp.	pages
pr	used for *per*; pair (plural prs)
pr.	price
PROM	programmable read-only memory
QC	Queen's Counsel
R	(currency) rand; rupee
R&D	research and development
RAM	random access memory
RDA	recommended daily allowance
recd	received
repr.	reprinted
Rev, Rev., Revd.	Reverend
rms	root-mean-square
ROM	read-only memory
RPI	retail price index
RPM	resale price maintenance
rpm	revolutions per minute
RSVP	Please reply (*Répondez s'il vous plait*) (prev. R.S.V.P.)
Rt Hon	Right Honourable (Prev. Rt. Hon.)
s	second (time)
S	Society; South; (currency) Schilling

s.	semi-; signed; singular
S.	Socialist; Society; Saint (plur. Sts)
s.d.	several dates
sae	stamped addressed envelope
SAS	Statistical Analysis System (data program)
SD	Standard Deviation of a Population (math.)
sd	Standard Deviation of a Sample (math.)
sec.	second (time)
Sec.	Secretary
sect.	section
sic	thus, so (should be printed [*sic*])
Soc.	Socialist; Society
SONAR	sound navigation and ranging
sov.	sovereign (coin)
SPSS	Statistical Package for the Social Sciences
sq.	square
SQL	structured query language
st (or s.t)	short ton (2000 lbs)
St	Saint
St.	Statute, Street, Strait
suppl.	supplement
t	tonne(s)
t.	tare (commerce)
trs.	transpose
U	Unionist; University (or U.)
U.	union (math.); unit
u.c.	upper case
u.d.	undated
u.p.	under proof
US	United States (but USA preferable)
v	velocity; volume (specific v of a gas)
V	volume (capacity)
v.	very; version; volume (series)
VAN	value-added network
VAT	value-added tax
vs.	versus (but v or v. in legal cases: *The Crown* v. *Jones*).
vv.	verses
W	watt; West
w.	with; week; weight; width; wife [John w. Anne]
w.f.	wrong font
W/L	wave length
WMD	Weapons of mass destruction
X	denoting an unknown variable etc.
x ex.	(commerce); algebraic variable
x-i.	ex interest

x-n.	ex new shares
Y	denoting an unknown variable etc.
y.	year(s)
yf	Yours faithfully
yr.	younger
yrs	yours
ys	yours sincerely
Z	zone; denoting an unknown variable etc.
z.	zero; zone

[1] parsec: an astronomical unit of distance equal to 3.262 light years. A parsec is the distance from which the Earth's distance from the Sun would subtend one second of arc (*Encarta Dictionary*). Note however that reference to an astronomical unit means a distance equivalent to the mean distance between the Earth and the Sun, about 150 million km/93 million miles.

It may be of interest to know that I originally used the Microsoft 'Sort' function for the above list of abbreviations, but even though it was set to *case sensitive,* there were still a number of problems. These arose due to the fact that the full point is treated as a symbol. I would have preferred MP to be followed by M.P. However, the full point has a lower ASCII value than the letter 'a' resulting in the above order, and not least placing '(*sic*)' at the head of the list!

Abbreviations in titles and text

Avoid abbreviations or acronyms in titles of books and chapters unless they are very familiar:

✓ THE ROLE OF IBM IN INTERNATIONAL TRADE

but not:

✗ Chapter IV: THE CDM: CHALLENGES AND OPPORTUNITIES

– unless CDM has been previously defined in the book.

Note the following:

The Clean Development Mechanism (CDM) established in the 1997 Kyoto protocol is designed to ... However, it is unclear whether soil carbon sequestration projects will be possible under the CDM.

In the second sentence, CDM stands for The Clean Development Mechanism (i.e. including the definite article). As a general rule the article should be given even if it is already implied in the abbreviation or acronym.

13
Prefixes

Reread before your rewrite and you will avoid rehashing it. – Anon.

Prefix: an element placed at the beginning of a word to adjust or qualify its meaning (e.g. *ex-*, *non-*, *re-*) or (in some languages) as an inflection (*New Oxford Dictionary of English*). There are about 200 prefixes such as un- (unhappy), dis- (disenfranchise), etc. In the following we are concerned with prefixed words and other prefixes which may employ a hyphen.

Where the prefix is a word in its own right, such as 'back', 'cross', 'over', etc., these may form (a) a hyphenated word (*back-door, over-optimistic, under-fed*); or (b) a conjoined word (*backbone, overhasty, underpass*). Further, certain terms are neither hyphenated nor conjoined (*[to] back down, [a] cross compiler, under age*). I prefer to use the expression 'compound term' for these. Are there any 'rules' concerning separate, hyphenated or conjoined terms? A colleague ventured to suggest that terms in occasional use are separate words; those in common use tend to be conjoined. This would also apply where the conjoined term forms a distinct unit, e.g. *semicircle*. A useful guideline perhaps. But beware! The norm may be the exception! For example we have *over-represented* but *underrepresented*. Why? The only reason I can find is that these are the norms! But no-one would deny that *under-represented* is also legitimate.

The following lists have been compiled from several dictionaries and where the most commonly encountered form has been selected. It may be noted that *Oxford* and *Collins* tend to favour conjoint terms more so than *Chambers* which still tends to retain hyphenated versions.

Note: In the following summaries the columns are in alphabetical order vertically.

a, a-
 few words retaining the Old English prepositional form: afire, a-hunting, alike, akin

above
The following terms are hyphenated:

above-board   above-named
above-ground   above-the-line
above-mentioned

Word spellchecker accepts the first four as conjoined words, but I have not found this in any dictionary.

all, all-
Frequently found in compound words and expressions. Adjectival forms are generally hyphenated. Whilst commonly encountered, *alright*, is colloquial and less preferable than *all right* or *all-right*. The most frequently encountered terms using 'all' are shown.

all-American	all-important	all-rounder
All Blacks	all-in	all-seater (stadium)
all-clear	all in all	all square
all comers *or* all-comers	all-inclusive	all standing
all-day	all-or-nothing	all-star
all done	all-out	all-telling
all-electric	all-over	all-terrain bike
All Fools' Day	all-powerful	all-time (high, low, record)
all found	all-purpose	all-terrain bike
All-Hallows	all right *or* all-right	all-to
All Hallows' Day	(alright = coll.)	all-up service
All-hallowtide	all-round	all-weather

ante, ante-, *ante* (Latin: before, prior to). Do not confuse with *anti-*. Latin origin. Latin terms in everyday use are not italicised.

ante lucem	antechoir	ante-Nicene
ante meridiem	antedate	anteorbital
ante mortem	antediluvial	antipasto
ante-bellum	antefix	antependium
antecede	antelucan	antepenultimate
antecessor	antemeridiem	ante-post
antechamber	ante-mortem	anteroom
antechapel	antenatal	anteversion

anti, anti- (Greek: against, opposing, counteracting.) Do not confuse with *ante-*.

Hyphenate before a capital: *anti-American, anti-Establishment, anti-Communist, anti-Zionist*.
Hyphenate before a vowel: *anti-imperialism*
Note: *antichrist, anticapitalist, antifascist* but *anti-roman*.

anti-abortion
anti-abrasion
anti-ageing
anti-aircraft
anti-alien
anti-American
anti-apartheid
anti-aristocratic
antibacterial
antiballistic
antibiblical
anti-Bolshevik
anti-British
anticapitalist
anti-Catholic
anti-chip
antichrist
antichristian
antichurch
anticlassical
anticoagulating
anti-Communist
anti-competetiveness
anticonscription
anticonstitutional
anticorrosive
anti-Darwinian
antidemocratic
anti-devolutionist
anti-ecclesiastical
anti-episcopal
anti-erosion
anti-establishment
anti-Establishment

anti-evolution
antifaction
anti-fade
antifascist
anti-federal
anti-federalism
anti-federalist
anti-feminist *or*
antifeminist
anti-flash
anti-Freudian
antifundamentalist
anti-Gallican
anti-hero
antihumanist
anti-imperialist
anti-inflammatory
anti-inflationary
anti-Jacobin
antilabour
anti-lock
anti-marketeer
antimaterialistic
antimatter
antimicrobial
antimilitarist
antimodernist *or*
anti-modernist
antimonarchist
antinarcotic
anti-national
antinationalist
anti-Nazi
antinoise

antipacifist
antipathogen
anti-personnel
antipolitical
antipollution
anti-predator
antiprohibition
anti-Protestant
antipuritan
antiracism
anti-racist
antirational
antireligious
antirepublican
antirevolutionary
antiriot
anti-roll
antirust
antiscientific
anti-Semite
antishock
anti-social *or* antisocial
anti-Soviet
antispiritual
antisubmarine
anti-tank *or* antitank
antiterrorist
antitheft
antitheist
antivirus
antivivisection
antiwar
anti-Zionist

auto-
(Greek: self, same. e.g. autobiography). All conjoined except auto-suggestion.

back, back-
Adjective (e.g. *back* door) and verb (e.g. *back* down). When hyphenated, may form a noun (e.g. *back-cloth*) or an adjective (*back-door* deal).

backache
back-bench
backbone

backbencher
backbite
backing-down

back-block
back-board
back-slapping

backbreaker	backlash	backslide
back burner	backlift	backspace
back-calculate	back-light	backspin
back-chain	back-load	backstage
backchat	backlog	backstairs
back-cloth	backlot	backstays
back-comb	backmarker	backstitch
back-country	backmost	backstop
backcourt	back-number	back street
back-crawl	back-office	back-stroke
back-cross	backpack	backswing
back-date	back passage	back-to-back
back-door	backpay	back to earth
backdown	back-pedal	back to front
back-draught	backpiece	back to nature
backdrop	back-plate	back-to-nature
back-end	back pressure	back to square one
backfire	back-projection	backtrack
back-foot	backroom	back-up
back-formation	back-rope	backwash
back-friend	back-row	backwater
backgammon	backsaw	back water
background	backscatter	backwoods
back-hair	backscratch	backwoodsman
backhand	back-seat driver	backword
back-handed	back-shift	backwork
back-hander	backside	backyard
back-heel	back-slang	

bi, bi- (Latin: two, twice.) Do not confuse with *by-*
Virtually all words commencing with the affix *bi* do not employ a hyphen
(e.g. *bidirectional, bifocal, bilateral, biplane)*. Exceptions: whereas
biannual, bicentenary and *biennial* do not use a hyphen, the following do:

bi-monthly	bi-weekly	bi-yearly

by, by- (near, aside, subsidiary, incidental). Do not confuse with *bi-*.
Nouns are hyphenated except the following:

bycatch	bypath	byway
byname	byroad	
bypass	bystander	

The following are hyphenated:

by-and-by	by-name	by-product
by-blow	by-passage	by-street
by-election	by-past	by-thing
by-form	by-play	by-time
by-line	by-plot	by-work
by-motive		

Only *bye-law* now uses the historic *bye-* version. But even this is not listed in the latest version of the *OED* which gives *bylaw*.

Nearly all terms and expressions are not hyphenated e.g. *by all means*).

Note compass directions *north by east, north by west* – (also *south by east/ west*, BUT *east-by-north (-south)* and *west-by-north (-south)*).

'by' is found in many expressions: *by the way, by leaps and bounds*. Only *by-and-by (eventually)* is (may be) hyphenated.

co, co- (jointly, mutual)
No fixed rules. Most words beginning with co-or may also use coor (e.g. *co-ordinate; coordinate)*. The following exceptions use a hyphen:

co-agent	co-operate *or* cooperate	co-presence
co-author	co-operative	co-respondent
co-ax (but coaxial)	co-operator	(but correspondent)
co-chair	co-opt *or* coopt	co-routine
co-dependant	co-option	co-star
co-dependent	co-optive	co-starred
co-determine	co-ordinal *or* coordinal	co-starring
co-driver	co-ordinate *or* coordinate	co-tenancy
co-host	co-pilot *or* copilot	co-worker
co-op	co-portion	co-write

contra against
All conjoined except Latin terms, *contra mundum, conra pacem*.

counter, counter- against, counteracting
Used in many compound words, but no hard-and-fast rules for hyphenation.

counteract	counter-attraction	counterbid
counter-agent	counterbalance	counterblast
counter-argument	counterbase	counterblow
counter-attack	counter-battery	counterbluff

counterbond
countercheck
counter-claim
or counterclaim
counter-clockwise
countercondition
counter-culture
counter-current
counterdraw
counter-espionage
counter-evidence
counterfect
counterfeit
counterfoil
counter-force
counter-gauge
counter-guard
counter-influence
counter-insurgency
counter-intelligence
counter-jumper
countermand
countermarch
countermark

countermeasure
countermine
countermotion
countermove
countermovement
counteroffensive
counteroffer
counter-opening
counterpane
counterpart
counter-passant
counterplea
counter-plot
counterpoint
counterpoise
counter-poison
counter-pressure
counterproductive
counterproof
counter-proposal
counter-punch
Counter-Reformation
counter-revolution
counterseal

counter-security
countershaft
countersign
counter-signal
counter-signature
countersink
counterspy
counter-statement
counterstroke
countersubject
countersunk
counter-tenor
counter-terrorist
counter-trading
counter-turn
countervail
counter-view
counter-vote
counter-weigh
counter-weight
counter-wheel

cross, cross- (against, contrary)
Many are conjoined (e.g. *crossbencher, crossroads*). The following are hyphenated. A few exceptions are neither conjoined nor hyphenated (e.g. *cross compiler*).

cross-armed
cross-buttock
cross-border
cross compiler
cross correspondence
cross-country
cross cousin
cross-cultural
cross-current
cross-division
cross-examination
cross-eye
cross-fade

cross-fertilisation
cross-grained
cross guard
cross hairs
cross-hatching
cross-lateral
cross-leaved
cross-legged
cross-linking
cross-match
cross-ply tyre
cross-pollination
cross-purpose

cross-quarters
cross-question
cross-reference
cross-ruff
cross-section
cross-selling
cross-springer
cross-staff
cross-stitch
cross-stone
cross-talk
cross-vaulting

de, de- *de* (Latin: down from, away, reversal)
Few words are hyphenated, e.g. dethrone, demoralise. Apart for Latin terms, most of the others separate two vowels.

de facto	*de profundis*	de-emphasise
de fide	*de règle*	de-energise
de haut en bas	*de rigueur*	de-escalate
de integro	deactivate	de-ice
de jure	de-alcoholise	de-Stalinise
de luxe	de-Americanise	
de novo	de-contextualise	

demi, demi- (French: denoting a half)
Almost exclusively hyphenated. Exception *demigod*

demigod	demi-monde	demi-semiquaver
demi-jour	demi-pension	demi-volt

dis (a reversal, negation) e.g. *disavow*
No hyphenated words.

down, down-
'down' is used as an adverb, adjective, preposition, verb and noun. As such it may be found in many compound words and expressions.

down-and-out	down-line	downstream
down-at-heel	download	downswing
down-at-the-heel	downmarket	down the drain/hatch
downbeat	*or* down-market	down-throw
downbow *or* down-bow	down payment	*or* downthrow
downburst	downplay	downtime
downcast	*but* down-played	down to earth
down-come	downpour	*or* down-to-earth
or downcome	down-quilt	down tools
downdraft	downrange	down town, down-town
down-draught	downright	*or* downtown
or downdraught	downriver	downtrain
downfall	downscale	downtrend
down-going	downside	down-trod
downgrade	downsize	down-trodden
down-haul *or* downhaul	downslide	*or* downtrodden
down-hearted	downstage	downturn
or downhearted	downstairs	downunder
down in the dumps	downstate	downwind
down in the mouth		

duo- (from the Latin *duo* two)
Strictly speaking, not an affix. All words conjoined, e.g. duopoly

eco- (relating to the environment)
Conjoined (e.g. *ecotoxicology*) except the following:

eco-label	eco-management	eco-tourism

ex, ex-, *ex* (Latin: out, from)
A hyphen is used *when this is a prefix* (e.g. *ex*-wife) as opposed to exhume etc. Many Latin terms commence with *ex*. These are not hyphenated. However, both *ex libris* and *ex-libris* are permissible.

ex also implies 'direct from' as in ex works, ex stores (not italicised).

ex-directory	*ex hypothesi*	*ex-librist*
ex-dividend *or*	*ex improviso*	*ex officio*
ex dividend	*ex int*	ex-serviceman
ex dono	*ex lib*	ex stores
ex gratia	*ex libris or ex-libris*	ex works

extra, extra-, *extra* (adjective: extraordinary, additional; adverb: unusual, exceptional)
All conjoined (e.g. *extrajudicial,* extramarital) except the following:

extra-axillary	*extra muros*	extra-special
extra-condensed	extra-parochial	extra-uterine
extra-curricular	extra-physical	extra-virgin (US)
extra-illustrate	extra-solar	extra virgin (UK)
extra modum		

far (remote, most distant)
Adjective, adverb and verb transitive. Hyphenated except in expressions such as '*far and wide*'.

far and away	far-flung	far-seeing
far and near	far-forth	far-sighted
far and wide	Far North	far-sought
far be it	far-off	Far South
far cry	far-out	far-spent
Far East	far-reaching	Far West
far-fetched		

fore- (Old English: previously, former, in front)
Most terms are conjoined: *forehead, foreground*, etc. Exceptions:

fore-advise	fore-brace	fore-end
fore-and-aft	fore-cited	fore-notice
fore-and-after	fore-edge	fore-quoted

geo (relating to, or denoting the earth)
all terms conjoined: e.g. *geophysical*

hemi (Greek: half) Not hyphenated
hemidemisemiquaver   hemisphere

hyper (excessive). Not hyphenated. e.g. *hypersensitive*.

il (the negative form). (E.g. *illegal*)
Not hyphenated

ill (misfortune, evil)
'Ill' is an adjective and not hyphenated when associated with a noun (e.g. ill nature). All non-hyphenated versions are shown. The hyphenated terms are adjectival (e.g. ill-defined, ill-disposed, ill-natured). These are not shown except for the few cases where an adverbial form may be constructed. The one exception occurs when 'ness' is suffixed to the adjective to form a noun (ill-naturedness).

ill blood	ill-natured	ill success
ill luck	ill part	ill temper
ill nature	ill seen	ill-tempered

in, in-, *in* (relating to)
Preposition and adverb. The Latin *in-* form is almost exclusively used to form adjectives.

in-between	in-depth	in-line
in-bond	in-flight	in-service
in-bounds	in-foal	*in situ*
in-built	in-group	in-store *or* in store
in-calf	in-house	in style
in camera	in-joke	in-toed
in capite	-in-law	in-tray
-in-chief	in-laws	in-word

infra (Latin: below, within)
All terms are conjoined, e.g. infrastructure, infrared

inter, inter- (Latin: between, among.) Conjoined (e.g. *interactive*) except the following. Latin terms separate words. These are shown.

inter-arts	inter-collegiate (but	*inter partes*
Inter-Bank (transaction)	interdepartmental)	inter-science
inter alia	*inter nos*	*inter se*
inter alios	*inter pares*	*inter vivos*

intra, intra- (Latin: from the inside.) Conjoined (e.g. *intramolecular*) except the following. Latin terms separate words.

intra-abdominal	intra-departmental	*intra vires*
intra-arterial	intra-Fallopian	*intra vitam*
intra-articular	*intra muros*	

macro- (Greek: long, great) The list shows the most commonly encountered terms. With the exception of those below, all others are conjoined (e.g. *macroeconomics, macroinstruction*).

macro-axis	macro lens	macro-marketing

mega (Greek: large, large scale)
All words conjoined (e.g. *megastore*)

meso- (intermediate). All conjoined, (e.g. *mesolit, Mesolithic*)

meta- (among, change). All conjoined (e.g. *metamorphosis*)

micro, micro- (Greek: small, minute.) No fixed rules. The most common terms include:

microampere	microeconomics	micro-meteorology
microbar	microgram	micro-organism (UK)
micro-brew	micro-manipulation	microorganism (US)
micro-brewery	micro-marketing	microwave
micro drive (PC)	micro-meteorite	

mid, mid-, midi (middle). No fixed rules. The most common terms include:

mid-Atlantic	midmost	midsummer
midday	midnoon	midterm
midfield	mid-ocean	mid-Victorian
midiron	mid-off	midway
midi-skirt	mid-on	mid-week
midi-system	mid-point	Midwest
midland	midrib	mid-wicket
Midlands (The)	mid-season	midwife
mid-Lent	midshipmate	mid-winter
mid-life crisis	midships	mid-year
mid-morning	midstream	

mini, mini- (small, minature). No fixed rules. The spellchecker may react to certain conjoined words. The most common terms include:

minibar	minicomputer	mini-roundabout
mini-budget	mini-dress *or* minidress	mini-skirt *or* miniskirt
mini-buffet	mini-floppy	mini-skis
minibus	mini-flyweight	mini-sub
minicab	minigolf	mini-submarine
mini-car	mini-rocket	

mis (wrong, mistake). All words conjoined (e.g. *mismanage*)

mono, mono- (single)
All words conjoined (e.g. monorail) except:

mono-compound	mono-ski

multi, multi- (many, much)
All words conjoined (e.g. *multiracial*) except the following: multi-access

multi-author	multi-layered	multi-storey
multi-faceted *or*	multi-modal	multi-track
multifaceted	multi-ownership	multi-wall
multi-function	multi-stage *or* multistage	

neo- (Greek: new)
Hyphenated before a proper noun (e.g. *Neo-Darwin*), but some terms conjoined (e.g. *Neopythagoran*):

Neo-Catholic	neologism	neoplastic
Neo-Christian	neologistic	neoplasticism
neoclassic	Neo-Malthusianism	Neo-Plasticism
neocolonialism	Neo-Melanesian	Neoplatonic
Neo-Darwin	neomycin	Neoplatonism
neodymium	neonatal	Neoplatonist
Neofascism	neo-Nazi	Neopythagorean
Neo-Gothic	neo-Nazism	neorealism
Neohellenism	neopagan	neorealist
Neo-Impressionist	neophile	Neo-Scholasticism
Neo-Kantian	neophilia	neotoxin
Neo-Latin	neophobe	Neotropical
neologian	neophyte	neovitalism

no (negative)
The following terms are hyphenated:

no-ball	no-man's land	no-trumps
no-go area	no-score draw	no-win situation
no-good		

non, non-, *non* (Latin: not)
There are well over a thousand words to which the prefix *non* may be attached. There are no hard and fast rules as to whether these should be hyphenated or not. Some dictionaries may give the hyphenated version, others dictionaries suggest the conjoined form. A colleague has suggested that if the term is a commonly accepted word, e.g. *nonhuman*, then it is more likely to be conjoined. Less familiar terms e.g. *non-contentious*, are usually hyphenated. But we do find *non-conclusive* (a familiar term) and *noncontemporary* (hardly a familiar term).

Again, I am not able to find any specific rules or guidelines. In addition to selected Latin terms, the following shows where the conjoined form is the norm or where the hyphenated version is also acceptable. Note hyphenated form before a proper noun (e.g. *non-Catholic*).

Latin terms

non compos mentis
(persona) non grata
non licet
non liquet
non multa, sed multum
non obstante
non placet
non seq
non sequitur

nonacademic
nonacceptance
nonaddictive *or*
non-addictive
nonagricultural
non-aligned
nonattendance *or*
non-attendance
non-attributable
nonattributive
nonauthoritative
nonautomated
nonautomatic *or*
non-automatic

nonbasic
nonbelligerent *or*
non-belligerent
nonbiological *or*
non-biological
nonbreakable *or*
non-breakable
noncarbonated
noncarnivorous
noncausal
noncelestial
noncellular
noncentral
noncerebral
nonchargeable
nonclassic
nonclassified *or*
non-classified
nonclerical
nonclinical *or*
non-clinical
noncoagulating
noncollegiate *or*
non-collegiate
noncombining
noncommercial *or*

non-commercial
noncommissioned *or*
non-commissioned
noncommunicant *or*
non-communicant
noncommunicative
noncommunist
noncompetitive
noncompliance
nonconciliatory
nonconclusive *or*
non-conclusive
nonconcurrent *or*
non-concurrent
nonconductive
nonconfidential
nonconflicting
nonconformist
noncongenital
nonconnective
nonconsecutive
nonconsenting
nonconstitutional
nonconstraining
nonconstructive
noncontagious *or*

non-contagious
noncontemporary
noncontributing
non-contributory
noncontrollable
noncontroversial
non-controversial
nonconventional
nonconvergent
nonconversant
nonconvertible
non-co-operation
noncorroborative
noncorroding
noncreative
noncriminal
noncritical
noncultivated
noncurrent *or*
non-current
nondeciduous
nondeductible
nondelivery *or*
non-delivery
nondemocratic
nondemonstrable
nondenominational *or*
non-denominational
nondepartmental
nondependence
non-destructive
nondetachable
nondetonating
nondictatorial
nondiffusing
nondiplomatic
nondirectional
nondisciplinary
nondiscriminating
nondistinctive
nondivisible
nondoctrinal
nondogmatic
nondomesticated
nondramatic

nondrinker *or* non-
drinker
nondriver *or* non-driver
nondurable
nonearning
noneconomic
nonedible
nonelastic
nonelection *or*
non-election
nonelective *or*
non-elective
noneligible
nonemotional
nonequal
nonequivalent
nonestablishment
nonethical
nonexchangeable
nonexclusive
nonexecutive *or*
non-executive
non-existence *or*
nonexistence
nonexistent *or*
non-existent
nonexplosive
nonfactual
nonfatal
nonfattening
nonfatty
nonfederal
non-ferrous
non-fiction
nonfictitious
nonfinite
non-flam film
non-flammable
nonflexible
non-flowering
nonfluid
nonformation
nonfreezing
nonfulfilment *or*
non-fulfilment

nonfunctional *or*
non-functional
nonfusible
nongaseous
nongovernmental
nongreasy
nonhabitable
nonhazardous
nonheritable
nonhistorical
nonhuman
nonidentical
nonidiomatic
noninclusion
nonindependent
nonindictable
nonindustrial
noninfectious
noninflammable
noninflected
noninformative
noninherent
noninheritable
noninjurious
noninstinctive
noninstitutional
nonintellectual
noninterchangeable
nonintersecting
nonintoxicating
nonintuitive
noninvasive
non-invasive
noninvolvement *or*
non-involvement
nonirritant
non-issuable
nonjury
nonkosher
nonlaminated
nonlethal *or* non-lethal
nonlinear *or* non-linear
nonliterary
nonliturgical
nonlocal

nonlogical
nonluminous
nonmagnetic
nonmalignant
nonmaritime
nonmarried
nonmaterialistic
nonmaternal
nonmathematical
nonmeasurable
nonmechanical
nonmedical
nonmedicinal
nonmelodic
nonmember *or*
non-member
nonmembership
nonmetric
nonmigratory
nonmilitant
nonministerial
nonmountainous
nonmystical
nonmythical
nonobligatory
nonobservance *or*
non-observance
nonoccurrence
nonofficial
nonoperable
nonoperational
non-operational
nonoperative
nonorganic
nonorthodox
nonostensive
nonparallel
nonparasitic
nonparental
nonparliamentary
nonparochial
nonpaternal
nonpaying
nonpayment *or*
non-payment

nonpermanent
nonpermeable
nonphilosophical
nonphonemic
nonphysical
nonphysiological
nonplaying
non-playing
nonpoisonous *or*
non-poisonous
nonpolitical
nonpolluting
nonporous
nonpossession
nonpractical
nonpractising
nonprecious
nonpredatory
nonpredictable
nonprejudicial
nonprescriptive
nonpreservable
nonpreservation
nonprofessional *or*
non-professional
nonprogressive
nonproportional
nonprotective
nonpunishable
nonracial *or* non-racial
nonradical
nonradioactive
nonrational
nonreader *or* non-reader
nonrealistic
nonrecognition
nonrecoverable
nonreflective
nonrefundable
non-regardance
nonregimented
nonregistered
nonreligious
nonrenewable
non-representational

nonrepresentative
non-residence
non-resident
nonresidential
nonrestricted *but*
non-restrictive
nonroutine
nonrural
non-scheduled
non-scientific *or*
nonscientific
nonseasonal
nonsectarian
nonsecular
nonsegregated
nonselective
nonsensitive
non-sequence
nonsexist *or* non-sexist
nonsexual
nonshrinkable
nonsignificant
nonsinkable
nonskilled
nonsocial
nonsoluble *or*
non-soluble
nonspeaking
nonspecialist *or*
non-specialist
non-specific *or*
nonspecific
nonspeculative
nonspiritual
nonsporting
nonstainable
nonstaining
nonstatistical
nonstrategic
nonstructural
nonsubscriber
nonsuggestive
nonsulphurous
nonsuppression
nonsurgical

nonsustaining
nonswimmer *or*
non-swimmer
nonsymbolic
nonsystematic
nontaxable
nonteaching
nontechnical
non-technical
nontemporal
nonterritorial

nontheatrical
nontoxic *or* non-toxic
nontraditional
nontransferable
nontropical
nontypical
non-U
nonuniform
non-union
non-unionist
nonusage *or* non-usage

nonuse
nonuser *or* non-user
nonvenomous
nonverbal *or* non-verbal
nonverifiable
nonvintage
nonvocal
nonvolatile *or*
non-volatile
nonworking

off, off- (away, not in position)

Adjectival forms usually hyphenated (e.g. *the off-and-on relay switch*). Some common phrases are shown which should not be hyphenated (e.g. *His mood was off and on all day*); others conjoined (e.g. *offset, offshoot, offshore*).

off-air
off-and-on switch
off and on
off balance *or* off-balance
off base
off-beam
off beam
off-board
off-break
off-Broadway
off-centre
off-chance
off chance
off colour *or* off-colour
off-come
off-comer
off-cut
off-day
off duty or off-duty
off-fore
off-job

off-key
off-licence
off-limits *or* off limits
off-line
off-load
off pat
off-peak
off-piste
off-plan
off-putter
off-putting
off-ramp
off-reckoning
off-road
off-sales
off-season
off-shake
off-shakt
off-site
off-sorts
off-spin

off-spinner
off-stage
off-stream
off-street
off the air
off-the-job training
off the map
off the mark
off-the-peg *or*
off the peg
off the rails
off the record *or*
off-the-record
off the reel
off-the-shelf *or*
off the shelf
off the wall
off-ward
off-wards
off-white
off-year

on, on-
Used in several expressions. The hyphenated expressions are adjectival *or* adverbial. Others not listed are conjoined (e.g. *ongoing*).

on-and-off
on and off
on board
on-board
on-going
on-job training
on-licence
on-line

on-shore
on shore
on sight
on-stage
on-stream
on stream
on terms

on-the-job training
on the offchance
on the off-chance
on the slate
on the sly
on the spot
on-the-spot

out, out-
Generally conjoined (e.g. outweighed, outplayed). These are not shown. Used in several expressions without a hyphen. The hyphenated terms may be adjectival, adverbial or nouns. The most common are given here.

out and about
out and away
out-and-out
out-half
out-Herod
out-of-date
out of date
out-of-pocket

out of pocket
out of the blue
out of work
out-of-work
out-paramour
out-parish
out-patient

out-pension
out-pensioner
out-porter
out-sentry
out-take
out-tray
out-wall

over, over-
Words commencing with 'over' are normally not hyphenated. This applies to verbs (e.g. overstate, overturn), adjectives (e.g. overdone), and nouns (e.g. overlay, overtime). The exceptions are shown together with certain phrases which are occasionally and mistakenly hyphenated – or vice versa!

over-absorption
over-abundance *or*
overabundance
over-abundant
over-achiever
overactive
over-activity
over-age
overaggressive
overall (n)
over-all
over-and-under
over-anxiety
over-anxious *or*
overanxious
over-anxiously

over-beat
over-breathe
over-breathing
overbulky
overcommon
over-determined
overdiligent
over-drowsed
over-emotional or
overemotional
over-exact
overexacting
overexcitable
over-excite or overexcite
over-exert or overexert
over-exposure or

overexposure
over-exquisite
overextend
overhasty
over-optimistic *or*
overoptimistic
overoptimism
over-precise or
overprecise
overqualified
over-refine
over-representation *or*
overrepresentation
over-represented
over-riding
over-seas

overseas
over-sexed
over-shoe
overspread
over-the-counter
over the counter
over the hill

over the hump
over the moon
over the odds
over-the-top
over the top
over the way
over the wicket

over-trade
over-trading
over-weighted
over-zealous *or*
overzealous
over-60s

para- (Greek: beside)
Not hyphenated (e.g. *paraglider*). Exceptions *para-amino acid, para-compound.*

post, post- (Latin: to place, also used to signify 'after'.) Conjoined (e.g. *postcode, postgraduate*) except the following:

post-bellum
post boy
post-chaise
post chaise
post-communion
post-diluvial
post-doc
post-doctoral
post-echo
post-entry
post-exilian
post-existence
post-free
post-glacial
postgrad *but* postgraduate
poste-haste
post-impressionism

Post-Impressionist
Post-it (label)
post-lingual
postmaster
post meridiem
post-millenarian
post-millennial
post-modern
post-mortem *or*
post mortem
post-Nicene
post-nuptial
post-orbit
post-office box
post-office *or* post office
post-operative
post-paid

post-partum
post-positionally
post-primary
post-production
post-Reformation
post-structuralism
post-synch
post-synchronisation
post-tension
Post-Tertiary
post-traumatic
post-vintage
post-viral illness
post-vocalic
post-war credit
post war *or* post-war
postwar (US)

pre, pre-, Pre- (Latin: in front of, before)
Not normally hyphenated, even before vowels (e.g. *prearrange, preconstruction, prepaid, preoccupied*). Exceptions given below. Hyphenate before proper names (e.g. *pre-Christian, pre-Gothic*).

pre-buy
pre-Byzantine
pre-Carboniferous
pre-conquest
pre-elect
pre-election
pre-eminent

pre-empt
pre-engage
pre-engagement
pre-enlistment
pre-establish
pre-estimate
pre-examination

pre-examine
pre-exist
pre-expose
pre-glacial
pre-ignition
pre-industrial
pre-judicial

pre-position	pre-set	pre-tax
pre-qualify	pre-senile	pre-tension
pre-school	pre-shrink/shrunk	pre-war *or* prewar
pre-sell		

pro, pro- (Latin: before, supporting.) Hyphenate before a proper noun (e.g. *pro-Catholic*). All other words are not hyphenated (e.g. *proactive, procapitalist*, exception *pro-life*).

Latin terms are separate words.

pro hac vice	*pro patria*	*pro tanto*
pro indiviso	*pro rata*	*pro tempore*
pro memoria	*pro re nata*	

Note *pro forma* (a matter of form), and *pro-forma invoice*. The latter (adjectival form) is also found unhyphenated.

pseudo (spurious, deceptive). All conjoined also before a vowel, except pseudo-archaic. Hypohenated before a proper noun, e.g. pseudo-Gothic.

quasi (Latin: as it were.) Hyphenated.

quasi-contract	quasi-historical	quasi-stellar

re, re- (Latin: repeat, do again)
Not hyphenated, even before a vowel (e.g. *reabsorb, reinstate, reopen, reuse,* etc., except before e: *re-elect, re-encounter* etc.). The exceptions are shown below. Latin terms are separate words, e.g. *re infecta*

re-ally	re-ignite	re-route *or* reroute
re-alter	re-invent	re-site
re-alteration	re-open *or* reopen	re-train *or* retrain
re-assemble *or* reassemble	re-position	re-type
re-bar	re-release	re-unite *or* reunite
re-e... (all words)	re-roof	re-use

When the hyphen is omitted the following terms take on a different meaning as a noun or as a verb.

re-act	re-dress	re-lay
re-cede	re-form	re-make
re-collect	re-formation	re-mark
re-count	re-formed	re-order
re-cover	re-fund	re-present

re-press	re-solve	re-treat
re-print	re-sort	re-turn
re-sign	re-tread	re-view

retro- (backwards, towards the past) e.g. *retrograde, retrospective*. Not hyphenated except:

retro-operative   retro-rocket

self (personally, oneself)
All words hyphenated (e.g. *self-explanatory, self-indulgence*) except:

selfheal   selfhood   selfsame

semi, semi- (Latin: half.) Normally hyphented before a vowel. There are a few exceptions with 'a'. Thus, *semiarid*. All others conjoined (e.g. *semicircle, semifinal*), except the following:

semi-annual	semi-double	semi-officially
semi-annually	semi-drying	semi-opal
semi-annular	semi-ellipse	semi-opaque
semi-aquatic	semi-elliptical	Semi-Pelagian
semi-Arian	semi-evergreen	semi-permeable
semi-Arianism	semi-finished	semi-precious
semi-arid *or* semiarid	semi-grand	semi-rigid
semi-attached	semi-illiterate	semi-ring
semi-automatic	semi-imbecile	semi-sagittate
or semiautomatic	semi-independent	Semi-Saxon
semi-axis	semi-jubilee	semi-skilled
semi-bajan	semi-liquid	semi-soft
semi-barbarian	semi-log	semi-trailer
semi-barbarism	semi-logarithmic	semi-tropical
semi-centennial	semi-metal	semi-truck
semi-detached	semi-monthly	semi-tubular
semi-diameter	semi-mute	semi-uncial
semi-diurnal	semi-nude	semi-weekly
semi-divine	semi-occasional	semi-yearly
semi-dome	semi-official	

socio (relating to society)
Not hyphenated. However, both socioeconomics and socio-economics are found.

sub (Latin: under, near)
All words conjoined (e.g. *subentry, suboffice, subprovince, subunit*) except:

sub judice	sub-post-office *or*	sub-tropical
sub-editor	sub-post office	*sub voce*
sub-machine gun	(but post-office)	sub-zero
sub-postmaster	sub-species	
sub-postmistress	sub-standard	

A few terms may not necessarily be conjoined nor hyphenated, e.g. sub goal. 'Sub' is also an abbreviation for substitute, submarine

super, super- (Latin: above, superior)
All words conjoined (e.g. *supercharge, supermarket*) except:

Super G	super-flyweight	super-middleweight
super-bantamweight	super-highway	super-rich
super-featherweight	super-intelligent	super-royal

supra (Latin: above)
All words conjoined (e.g. *supralunar, supramolecule*) except:

supra-axillary

tele- (Greek: far)
All words conjoined (e.g. *teleconferencing, telejournalism*) except:

tele-ad(vertisement)

to, to- (preposition)
All words conjoined. Phrases not hyphenated (e.g. *to a fault*)

trans- (Latin: across, beyond)
All words conjoined except the following which are optionally hyphenated. This does not apply to proper nouns. e.g. Trans-Siberian trans-racial

trans-sexual	trans-shape	trans-ship
trans-sonic		

tri, tri-(Latin: threefold)
All words conjoined (e.g. *triaxial, tricolour, tripartite*) except the following:

tri-jet	Tri-State area	tri-weekly

ultra, ultra- (Latin: beyond)
Hyphenated before a proper noun (e.g. *ultra-Conservative*). All other words conjoined (e.g. *ultrafilter, ultrasonic*) except the following:

ultra-distance	ultra-high	ultra-tropical
ultra-fashionable	ultra-modern	*ultra vires*
ultrafiche	ultra-rapid	ultra-virtuous
ultra-heat-treated	ultrasensual	

un, un- (Latin, Greek: against)
All words conjoined (e.g. *unmusical, unnerved*) except:

un-American   un-English

note: unchristian (no hyphen *or* capital).

under, under- (Old English: below)
All terms conjoined (e.g. *underpass,* understeer), with the exception of the following. Note that some occupations are hyphenated (e.g. *under-secretary*), others are not (*underservant*). These are shown.

under-age *or* under age	underpowered	under-serve *but*
under-and-over	under-privileged	underservant
under-board	under-produce *or*	under-sexed
under-bonnet	underproduce	under-shepherd
under-boy	underproduction	under-sheriff
under-clerk *or* underclerk	under-representation	under-the-counter *or*
under-constable	under-represented	under the counter
under-countenance	*or* underrepresented	under the weather
under-craft	under-ring	under-trick
under-declared	under-ripe	under-tunic
under-driven	underripened	under-turnkey
under-fed	under-roof	underwater
under-hangman	under-sawyer	under-workman
under-jaw	under-school	under-16s
under-power	under-secretary	

up, up- (a higher level or state)
This prefix is found in many expressions and phrases. Generally, adjectives and adjectival nouns are hyphenated. Other terms not shown are conjoined (e.g. *update, upgrade, uptake*).

up-and-coming	up-current	up-line
up and down	up-draught	(one) upmanship
up-and-down	up for grabs	up-market
up-and-over	up front	up-tempo
up and running	up-front	up the creek
up-and-under	up hill and down dale	up the pole
up-beat	up in arms	up the wall
up-country	up in the air	up-time (computer)

up to (*not upto*)	up to the hilt	up-to-the-minute
up to a point	up to the knocker	up-town
up-to-date	up to the mark	up-train
up to the eyes	up to the minute *or*	up-wind

vice-, *vice* (Latin: in the place of.) All terms hyphenated except the following:

vice anglais	viceregent	viceroy

It is normal to capitalise when referring to a specific person. The vice-chancellor was present as was Vice-President Johnson.

14
Suffixes

A suffix is an appendix which embellishes the meaning of a term such as 'ch' when added to 'Scot'. – Anon (Irish).

There are about two hundred suffixes ('ch' not being one of them). Many are used to form adverbs or adjectives, occasionally nouns. These include *–ish, –ly, —ess,* etc., which are exclusively conjoined. In this chapter we are concerned with suffixed words which may be conjoined or hyphenated (there are no rules!). Separate words frequently form a verbal phrase and are not generally included.

Example: a) *He went* **over all** the books once more, but failed to find the mistake.
b) *This paint will give an* **over-all** covering with just one coat.
c) *He put on his* **overall** before starting to paint the room.

Likewise, we have *pull over, pull-over, pullover; every day, every-day, everyday; fall out, fall-out, fallout.*

In general:

1. Separate words often comprise a phrasal verb: to *break away, give away, knock down, take away.* These are not included in the following.

2. Hyphenated words are normally:
    – compound nouns: *a hold-all is a large bag; the concert was a sell-out;*
    – adjectives: *stand-up comic; knock-down prices.*

3. Conjoined words usually form:
    – a noun: *he had a breakdown; let's get a takeaway; the disguise was a giveaway; he bought a new pullover.*
    – an adjective: *we bought a foldaway table.*

However, to draw up hard-and-fast rules would be to deny the flexibility of English. Rather, we should look at customary usage. In fact, one standard text dismisses the problem by stating 'use your own judgement'! Indeed, in one dictionary I found *a foldaway table* and in another *a fold-up bed.*

The following summarises suffixes which may be generally encountered together with notes relating to selected affixes.

-able, - ible. Capable of (e.g. *navigable, accessible*). About 2000 words in the English language have the suffix *–able*, and about 300 employ *–ible*. Rely on your spellchecker!

-all takes a hyphen when suffixed to form a noun. Exception is *overall*. *Over-all* is the normal adverbial form.

be-all	end-all	over-all
be-all and end-all	free-for-all	overall
carry-all	hold-all	save-all
cure-all	Jack-of-all-trades	you-all
do-all	know-all	

-away
When used as a separate word *away* is normally an adverb (e.g. *to throw away*). Where conjoined, it may form a noun (*he is a bit of a tearaway*), an adjective (*a throwaway item*) or, what used to be known as an adjectival noun but better referred to as a compound noun (*a foldaway*). Note *give-away* product (two consecutive vowels). The hyphenated suffix is normally an adjective: *a hide-away* dugout.

The following includes those terms where the adverb (a separate) word (e.g. *to give away, to run away*) may be confused with the suffixed term and/or the hyphenated version comprising a noun (a*)* or adjectival noun (e.g. a *giveaway*).

breakaway	give-away product	take-away *or* takeaway
fade-away	going-away outfit	tearaway
faraway	hide-away *or* hideaway	throwaway
foldaway *or* fold-away	home-and-away	walk-away *or* walkaway
getaway	runaway	wash-away
giveaway	straightaway	

-back
back is found in many terms and compound words. Most terms comprising two words are phrasal verbs (e.g. *to play back*), but conjoined words are nouns (e.g. *a playback*). A few nouns use the hyphenated form. Some are optional (e.g. *fallback* or *fall-back*). The following shows those nouns which are hyphenated.

blowback *or*	carry-back	diamond-back
blow-back	centre back	fallback or fall-back
buy-back	or centre-back	fastback

hark-back	laid-back	splash-back
hog's-back	leather-back	swart-back
hump-back	olive-back	swayback *or* sway-back
humpback bridge	pass-back	swing-back
hunchback	pull-back	turnback *or* turn-back
knock-back	razor-back	write-back
ladder-back	rusty-back	

-by

As a suffix, *-by* is largely used to form a noun. In addition there is the adjective *sell-by (date)*. The verbs are not hyphenated (*to lay by, to pass by*).

fly-by	lay-by	stander-by
fly-by-night	passer-by	swing-by

The compass bearings relating to north and south are *not* hyphenated: *north by east/west; south by east/west*. Those relating to east and west *are* hyphenated: *east-by-north/south; west-by-north/south*.

-down

Nouns are mostly conjoined (e.g. a *splashdown, lockdown*). Two separate words are phrasal verbs (e.g. *to splash down*). Adjectival forms (e.g. *slimmed-down*) and some nouns are hyphenated. These are shown.

backing-down	rubdown	top-down
broken-down	rundown *or* run-down	torn-down
draw-down	showdown	turn-down
dressing-down	sit-down	up and down *or*
knock-down	slimmed-down	up-and-down
let-down	slow-down	upside down *or*
mark-down	splash-down	upside-down
paste-down	sponge-down	watered-down
round-down	thumbs-down	

-fold

Preferably not hyphenated: e.g. *twofold, tenfold* etc. (Note, however, *two-handed, four-legged* etc.)

-free
Hyphenate

E.g. *ice-free tax-free* etc.

Exception: *handsfree* (n. or adj. E.g. handsfree set for the mobile phone)

-ible. See –able.

-in
Hyphenated for nouns, e.g. *cave-in, fill-in*, etc.

-less
This affix is only hyphenated after 'll': wall-less. Single 'l' is not hyphenated, e.g. *heelless, recoilless*, etc. Exception *tail-less*, although *tailless* may be encountered. All other words conjoined (e.g. *aimless, fearless*).

-like
There are few rules for forming compound words with the suffix 'like'. When the stem word ends in 'l', a hyphen is used: *bell-like, spaniel-like*. Some texts suggest that those with animal connections are not hyphenated: *crablike, catlike, lionlike*. But there are many exceptions: *lamb-like, ostrich-like*. The same vagueness applies to the human touch: *king-like, queen-like, man-like*, but *princelike, ladylike*. Where the term begins with un– as in *ungodlike, unladylike*, a hyphen does not precede *'like'*, even though the original form was hyphenated. Thus we have *unladylike, unqueenlike*. '-like' words may be formed from many nouns. If your spell-checker reacts to the compound form, then hyphenate it.

-ness
This affix is never normally hyphenated. It is used to form a noun from an adjective for example: severe – severeness. Words ending in 'y' change form: happy – happiness. It may be hyphenated in some constructed words, especially where applied to words ending in 'n', e.g. nation-ness.

-off
Phrasal verbs are not hyphenated (e.g. *to write off*). These are not shown. Nouns and adjectives are normally hyphenated (e.g. *a write-off, a written-off car*). A few adverbial phrases are not hyphenated (e.g. *he was badly off*).

badly-off *or* badly off	jump-off	rake-off
(*but* better off)	kick-off	rip-off
blast-off	lay-off	run-off
blow-off	lift-off	sawed-off
brush-off	mid-off	sawn-off
cast-off	on-and-off	sell-off
cut-off	one-off	send-off
face-off	on-off	set-off
falling-off	part-off	show-off
fall-off	pay-off	shut-off
hand-off	play-off	spin-off
hands-off	push-off	split-off
jumping-off site	put-off	stand-off

stop-off	telling-off	well off
take-off	ticking-off	well-off
taking-off	tip-off	write-off
teeing-off	trade-off *or* tradeoff	
tee-off	turn-off	

-on

Separate words from phrasal verbs (e.g. *to add on*). These are not shown. Hyphenated terms are nouns (e.g. *hanger-on*), or adjectival phrase (e.g. *unbuilt-on land*) and/or adverb (e.g. *end-on*).

add-on	odds-on	spot-on
bolt-on	off-and-on *or* off and on	spray-on
carry-on	pull-on	try-on
clip-on	right-on *or* right on	turn-on
come-on	roll-on	unbuilt-on
end-on	roll-on-roll-off	unsmiled-on
hands-on	run-on	wait-on
hanger-on	side-on	walker-on
have-on	slip-on	walk-on
knock-on		

-out

Phrasal verbs comprise separate words (e.g. *to bail out*). These are not shown. Adverbial phrases (e.g. *they went all out to win*) are separate words. These are shown. Nouns and adjectival phrases are normally hyphenated (e.g. *a hand-out, an all-out strike*). However, there are one or two exceptions (e.g. *spaced out, lookout*), and rather surprisingly (two consecutive vowels), *takeout*.

all-out	dim-out	lead-out
bail-out	down-and-out	long-drawn-out
bug-out	drop-out	lookout
burn-out	fade-out	not-out
buy-out	fall-out	opt-out
call-out	far-out	pay-out
carry-out	fit-out	played-out
check-out	fitting-out	pour-out
chucker-out	fold-out	print-out
clapped-out	freeze-out	pull-out
clean-out	get-out	push-out
clear-out	grey-out	read-out
cop-out	hand-out	rig-out
count-out	hang-out	sell-out
cut-out	hole-out	shake-out

share-out
shoot-out
shut-out
spun-out
stake-out
stressed-out

takeout
try-out
walk-out
washed-out
wash-out

watch-out
way-out
white-out
work-out
worn-out

-over

Phrasal verbs comprise separate words (e.g. *cross over*). These not shown. Adjectives are hyphenated or conjoined (e.g. *all-over paint, takeover bid*). Adverbs are conjoined (e.g. *moreover*). Nouns may be hyphenated or conjoined (e.g. *a push-over* or *pushover, a takeover*). all-over crossover

cut-over
flash-over
flyover
going-over
handover
hangover
holdover
leftover
limited-over
makeover
moreover

once-over
out-over
Passover
pullover
pushover
push-over
roll-over
slip-over
spillover
stopover
switch-over

takeover
tick-over
turnover
twice over
under-and-over
up-and-over
up-over
walk-over
work-over
wrapover

-up

The notes applying to *–over* also apply to this suffix.

all-up
all-up service
back-up
back-up file
blow-up
brew-up
build-up
built-up
buttoned-up
call-up
check-up
cover-up
get-up
get-up-and-go
hard-up
hold-up

hook-up
hyped-up
jumped-up
jump-up
knees-up
knocker-up
lay-up
let-up
lighting-up
lighting-up time
line-up
link-up
lock-up
make-up
mark-up
mess-up

mix-up
mock-up
mop-up
muck-up
paid-up
paste-up
patch-up
picker-up
pick-me-up
pick-up
pick-up head
pin-up
pop-up
press-up
punch-up
push-up

put-up	speed-up	toss-up
put-up job	stand-up	totting-up
roll-up	start-up	turn-up
roll-up fund	step-up	turn-up for the books
round-up	stick-up	two-up
runners-up	stitch-up	used-up
runner-up	stuck-up	wake-up
run-up	take-up	warmed-up
set-up	tarted-up	warm-up
shake-up	tie-up	washed-up
shape-up	tip-up	washing-up
slap-up	ton-up	wash-up
slip-up	topping-up	well-set-up
slow-up	top-up	wind-up
smash-up	top-up loan	write-up

-wise

Conjoined: e.g. *clockwise, coastwise, leastwise, streetwise*. Exceptions: *penny-wise, worldly-wise*.

Other

A number of nouns may be prefixed as conjoined, hyphenated or as a compund term. These are too many to list. The problem (again) is that the spellchecker will not react to those with spaces or hyphens. the term 'room' for example. The following are hyphenated:

barrack-room	harness-room	robing-room
bar-room	lamp-room	room-divider
bed-sitting-room	living-room	room-fellow
breakfast-room	lumber-room	room-mate
chart-room	mess-room	room-ridden
checking-room	morning-room	sitting-room
dining-room	music room	smoke-room
drawing-room *or*	pump-room	spare room
drawing room	reading-room	standing-room
dressing-room	receiving-room	throne-room
elbow-room	reception room	tool-room
engine-room	recitation-room	waiting-room
guest-room	refreshment-room	

All others are separate words: common room, day room, music room, powder room, etc.

15
Hyphenated, Conjoined and Compound Words

Lloyd George didn't hyphenate his name as the hyphen was not popular at the time. This reputedly reduced both his status and income. – Anon.

The following list covers terms comprising separate words known as compound words (e.g. *air freight*); conjoined words (e.g. *airmail*); hyphenated words (e.g. *air-mechanic*). Terms are sorted in this order (most sorting routines ignore hyphens). For reasons of space the **predominant category** for each word is omitted and only the exceptions (where applicable) are given. By way of example, there are about a dozen every-day terms employing 'air' in compound words, just over fifty conjoined words commencing with 'air', and almost seventy are hyphenated terms. The latter, comprising the most numerous group, are therefore not given: it can thus be assumed that the term '*air-intake*' is hyphenated while *airship* and *air letter* are respectively conjoined and separate terms. As the latter comprise the 'exceptional groups', these are shown in the list.

> % all compound words. Exceptions given
> ‡ all conjoined. Exceptions given
> – all hyphenated. Exceptions given

Verbs are not normally hyphenated (e.g. *to fade out*) and are not given. It should also be noted that dictionaries may vary in their use of hyphenation. Spell-checkers do not normally respond to hyphenated words and would not detect *air-terminal* (instead of *air terminal*) or *air-base* (instead of *airbase*).

The previous comments concerning dictionaries particularly apply here and where the *Collins* and *Oxford* use the conjoined form more frequently than *Chambers*.

- **A** -
able-bodied
A-bomb
about-face
above-board
above-mentioned
above-named
absent-minded
accident-prone
account-book
across-the-board
add-on
adjutant-general
ad-lib
ad-man
aero-engine
Afro: –
after-dinner
after-effect
after-life
aftercare
aftertreatment
age-bracket
agent-general
age-old
à go-go
aide-de-camp
AIDS-related
air: –
air ambulance
air bag
air force
air gun
air letter
air rifle
air scout
air support
air taxi
air terminal
airbase
airborne
aircraft
aircraftman
airfield
airflow

airfoil
airframe
airlift
airline
airliner
airlock
airmail
airman
airmanship
airplane
airport
airship
airsick
airspace
airspeed
airstrip
airtight
airtime
airwave
airway
airworthy
air-vice-marshal
aircraft-carrier
airy-fairy
alarm: –
Alice-in-Wonderland
all- (See Prefixes)
alms-house
also-ran
altar: –
ambassador-at-large
analogue-to-digital
angel: –
Anglo: –
Anglo-American
animal-worship
ante-mortem -
anti- (See Prefixes)
apple: –
armour-plate
arm-rest
arms-length (but at arm's length)
arrow-head
Ascension-day

asylum-seeker or asylum seeker
Attorney-General
audio: –
auto: –
avant-garde
awe-inspiring
awe-stricken

- **B** -
baby: –
back- (See Prefixes)
badly-off
bad-tempered
bald-eagle
bald-faced
ball: –
ball and socket
ball lightning
ballet-dancer
ballot-box
ballot-paper
ballot-rigging
balls-up
bank: %
bank-agent
bank-bill
bank-book
bank-cheque
bank-holiday
bank-manager
bank-note or banknote
bank-paper
bankroll
barbed-wire
bar-bell
barber-shop
bar-b-q
bar-chart
bar-code
bare-knuckled
bargain: –
barley-sugar
barrel-organ
base: ‡

base coin
base fee
base jumper
base metal
base rate
base-burner
base-court
base-level
base-line
base-load
basket-maker
bath-house
bathing: –
bathing beauty
bathing belle
baton-charge
battle-axe
bay-window
beach-ball
be-all and end-all
beam-end
bed-and-breakfast
bed: ‡
bed-bath
bed-closet
bed-jacket
bed-linen
bed-plate
bed-rest
bed-settee
bed-sheet
bed-sitter
bed-table
bed-wetting
bed-worthy
beech-oil
beef-tea
bee-moth
beer: –
beer belly
beetle-browed
before-mentioned
beggar-my-neighbour
bell: –
bell end

bellpush
belly: –
below-the-line
belt-tightening
between-decks
Bible: –
big-time
bilge: –
bill-broker
billiard: –
bin-liner
bird: –
bird of prey
bird strike
birdbath
birdcage
birdcall
birdlike
birdman
birds of a feather
birdseed
birdsong
birdwatcher
bird's-eye view
bird's-foot
birthday-suit
birth-rate
bit-map
bi-weekly
bi-yearly
black-and-blue
black-and-tan
blind-alley
blind-drunk
blindman's-buff
blind-side
blood donor
bloody-minded
blotting-pad
blow-by-blow
blow-dry
blow-up
blow-valve
blue-chip
blue-collar

blue-green
board-game
boarding: %
boarding house or
boarding-house
boarding school or
boarding-school
boat: –
boatman
boat people
boatrace
body-bag
body-builder
bog: –
bog down
boiling-point
bold-faced
bomb-disposal
bone: –
bone china
bone marrow grafting
bonehead
boneless
boneshaker
booby-prize
boogie-woogie
boo-hoo
book: –
book club
book out
book price
book sale
book through
book trade
book value
bookbinder
bookcase
booked-up
booking: –
bookkeeper
bookmaker
bookmark
bookrest
bookseller
bookshelf

bookshop
bookstall
bookstand
bookstore
bookworm
booze-up
born-again
bottle: –
bottle bank
bottle neck
bottleneck
bottom-heavy
bottom-up
boulder-clay
bow-legged
bowling: –
bow-wave
bow-window
box: –
box file
box junction
box number
box profits
boxroom
boxwood
boy-meets-girl
brain: %
brainbox
braincase
brainchild
brainpower
brains trust
brainstorm
brainwashing
brain-dead
brain-teaser
brain-wave
branch: –
brand-new
brazen-faced
bread-and-butter
break down
breakdown
break-even
breakfast-room

breakfast-table
break-out
break-up
breast-feed
breathing-space
breeding-ground
brew-up
bric-à-brac
bride: ‡
bride-chamber
bride-price
bride's-cake
bride's-maid (or
bridesmaid)
bridge-builder
bridle: –
brief-case
bright-eyed
brim-full
broad: ‡
broad bean
broad daylight
broad: –
broken: –
broken home
brother-in-law
brush-off
bubble: –
bubble and squeak
bubble bath
buck-rabbit
building-block
build-up
built-in
bull: –
bulldog
bulldoze
bumble-bee
bunny-girl
burial-ground
burning-point
burn-out
burying-ground
bus-conductor
bus-fare

bush-baby
bushy-tailed
butter: –
buy-back
buy-in
buy-out
by- (See Prefixes)
by-and-by
by-corner
bye-bye
bye-law

- C -
cable-car
cab-rank
cacao-bean
call-box
call-up
camera-ready copy
candle-holder
cannonball
cannon-shot
can-opener
captain-general
carbon-copy
car-coat
card-holder
card-table
card-vote
carriage-free
carriage-paid
carry-all
carry-on
car-sickness
cart-horse
cartridge-paper
carve-up
carving-knife
car-wash
case-by-case
case-law
cash-and-carry
cash-book
cash-box
cash-credit

cashew-nuts
cash-register
casting-vote
cast-iron
castle-building
castor-oil
castor-oil plant
cat-and-mouse
cat-burglar
catch-phrase
cat-flap
cathode-ray
cat-o-nine-tails
cave-dweller
cave-in
CD-ROM
cease-fire
cedar-nut
centre-forward
centre-half
centre-rail
cha-cha-cha
chain-smoke
chargé-d'affaires
charge-hand
chart-buster
chat-line
check-in
checkbook (US)
checking-room
check-up
cheque book *but*
cheque-book journalism
chewing-gum
chicken-hearted
chicken-livered
child-resistant
chimney-sweep
chock-a-block
chock-full
chopping-block
chopping-board
Christmas-tide/time
chucker-out
church-parade

cigar-shaped
cinema-goer
clapped-out
class-conscious
clean-cut
clean-living
clean-shaven
clean-up
clear-cut
clear-headed
clear-out
clear-sighted
cliff-face
climb-down
climbing-frame
clip-on
clock-radio
close-down
close-in
close-knit
close-up
clothes-horse
clothes-line
clothes-peg
cloud-cuckoo-land
club-foot
coach-horse
co-agency
co-agent
coal-black
coal-box
coal-fired
coast-to-coast
co-author
Coca-Cola
cocoa: –
cocoanut
coconut: –
code-breaker
code-name
co-dependant
co-dependency
co-dependent
cod-fishing
cod-liver oil

co- (See Prefixes)
co-driver
co-ordinate
coordinates
coffee-maker
coin-operated
cold-blooded
cold: %
cold-blooded
cold-drawn
cold-hearted
cold-rolled
cold-shoulder
cold-weld
colonel-in-chief
come-and-go
commander-in-chief
common-law
communion-cloth
company sergeant-major
computer-aided design
concert-goer
conning-tower
con-rod
conscience-stricken
contra-flow
conveyor-belt
cooling-off period
co-op
co-operate
co-opt
co-ordinate
co-pilot
copper: –
copper nickel
copperhead
copperplate
coppersmith
copperworks
copy-edit
coral-reef
cork-tipped
corn: ‡
corn-beef
corn-cake

corn-chandler
corn-cracker
corn-cure
corn-cutter
corn-dealer
corn-fed
corn-merchant
corn-spirit
cost-accounting
cost-elements
co-star
cost-benefit analysis
cost-effective
co-tenancy
cotton-gin
counter- (See Prefixes)
country-and-western
country-dancing
court-martial
cover-up
cow-dung
crash-proof
cream-bun
crease-resistant
crêpe-de-chine
crêpe-soled
criss-cross
cross- (See Prefixes)
cross-and-pile
crossing-sweeper
country: %
countrywide
country-and-western
country-dancing
country-folk
country-house
country-rock
country-seat
crown-wheel
crystal-clear
crystal-gazer
cuckoo-spit
cul-de-sac
cupboard-love
curly-headed

currant: –
custom-built
customs-house
cut-and-thrust
cut-price

- D -
daddy-long-legs
dairy-farm
daisy-chain
damp-course
damp-proof
dance: –
darning-needle
data-processing
date-palm
date-stamp
daughter-in-law
Davy-lamp
day: –
day by day
day care centre
day centre
day of action
day off
day room
day-to-day
day trip
daybreak
daydream
daylight
daylight robbery
Daylight Saving Time
daylong
daystar
daytime
D-day
dead-end
dead-eye
deaf-and-dumb
death: –
death certificate
death penalty
death row
death squad

death wish
deathlike
deathwatch
deck: –
deck officer
deckchair
deckhouse
deep-freeze
de-ice
delivery-man
demi- (See Prefixes)
depth-charge
devil: –
dew-drop
diamond: –
diamond jubilee
diamond snake
diamond wedding
die-cast
dilly-dally
ding-dong
dining: –
direct-grant school
director-general
dirt-cheap
discount-broker
dish-cloth
dishwater
ditch-water
divan-bed
diving: –
D-notice
dock-labourer
dog-collar
dog's-body
dog-tired
dogtooth
do-it-yourself
doll's-house
donkey-man
Domesday Book
dot-matrix printer
double: –
double act
double axel

double back
double bassoon
double bed
double bill
double bluff
double chin
double concerto
double cream
double dagger
double doors
double Dutch
double exposure
double fault
double feature
double figures
double first
double knit
double negative
double or quits
double play
double pneumonia
double spread
double standard
double star
double time
double top
double up
double vision
double wedding
double whammy
dove-house
Dow-Jones average
down- (See Prefixes)
down-to-earth
draft-dodger
drag-parachute
drag-queen
drag-racing
drawing-paper
draw-leaf table
dray-horse
dress-circle
dressing-gown
dress-rehearsal
drift: –

drill-hole
drink-drive
drinking-up time
drink-money
drip-dry
drip-feed
driving: –
driving licence
driving seat
driving test
drop: –
drophead coupé
drug-addict
dry: %
dry-cell
dry-clean
dry-dock
dry-eyed
dry-fly
dry-goods
dry-iced
dry-nurse
dry-point
dry-rot
dry-shod
dry-stone
dry-stove
dry-wash
dual-control
dumb-waiter
dung-cart
dung-fly
dust: –
dust bag
Dust Bowl
dust cover
dustbin
dustcart
dustman
dustproof
dustsheet
duty-free
duty-paid
dwelling-house
dyed-in-the-wool

- E -
each-way
eagle: –
early-Victorian
early-warning
ear-piercing
earth: –
earth science
earthbound
ear-trumpet
East-ender
easy-going
eating-apple
echo-sounder
eco- (See Prefixes)
egg: –
egg custard
egg white
eggcup
egghead
eggnog
eggshell
eggwash
ego-trip
eider-duck
ejector-seat
elbow-grease
electro: ‡
electro-optic
eleven-plus
e-mail
ember-day
emery-paper
empire-builder
empty-handed
end-on
end-product
end-user
engine: –
environmentally-
friendly
epoch-making
errand-boy
Euro: ‡
Euro-American

Euro-dollars
Euro-MP
Euro-Parliament
Euro-passport
Euro-sceptic
even-handed
evening-dress
evergrowing
every day; everyday
evil: –
ex-directory
exercise-book
ex-libris
ex-serviceman
extra- (See Prefixes)
eye: –
eye bank
eye contact
eye for an eye
eye lotion
eye muscle
eye socket
eye to eye
eye up
eyeball to eyeball
eyebright
eyebrow
eyeglass
eyehook
eyelash
eyeless
eyelet
eyelet-hole
eyelid
eyeliner
eyeshade
eyeshadow
eyesight
eyesore
eyestrain

- F -
face: –
face down
face out

face pack
face powder
face the music
face to face
face-to-face
face value
faceworker
fact-finding
factory-gate sale
fade: –
fail-safe
faint-hearted
fair: –
fair comment
fair enough
fair play
fair trade
fairground
fairway
fair-and-square
fairyland
fairylike
fairytale
fairy-godmother
faith-healer
fall-out
fancy-free
far (See Prefixes)
farm-hand
far-reaching
fast-talking
fast-track
father-figure
father-in-law
fatigue-dress
fault-finding
feather: –
featherweight
feature-length
feeble-minded
feed-pipe
feel-good
fellow: –
fellowship
felt-tip(ped) pen

ferro: ‡
ferro-manganese
ferro-molybdenum
ferro-nickel
ferry-boat
ferry-house
fiddle-bow
fifth-generation
fifty-fifty
fifty-pence
fig-leaf
fig-tree
file-cutter
file-fish
file-leader
fill-in
fill-in flash
film-strip
filter-bed
filter-paper
filter-tip
fine-draw
fine-spoken
fine-spun
fine-tooth(ed) comb
fine-tune
finger-painting
finger-pointer
Finno-Ugric
fir-cone
fire-and-brimstone
fire: –
fire blanket
fire brigade
fire bucket
fire door
fire drill
fire engine
fire escape
fire extinguisher
fire-grate
fire hose
fire sale
fire station
fire up

firearm
fireball
firebox
firebrand
firebrick
firecracker
firefloat
firefly
fireguard
firelight
firelighter
firelock
fireman
firemark
firepan
fireplace
firepot
fireproof
firescreen
fireside
firestone
firethorn
fireweed
firewood
firework
first: –
first cousin
first degree burn/murder
first floor
first gear
First Lady
first lieutenant
first light
first name
first night
first offender
first-past-the-post
first person
first principles
first reading
first refusal
first storey
first strike
first thing
first water

First World
fir-tree
fish: –
fish cake
fish eagle
fish eaters
fish stick
fishball
fishburger
fisherman
fisheye
fishing-tackle
fishmonger
fishskin
fishskin disease
fishwife
fishing: –
fitting-out
five-a-side
five-day week
fixed-interest
flag: –
flagship
flagstaff
flagstone
flame-thrower
flat-footed
flea-bite
flesh: –
flesh wound
fleurs-de-lys
flexi-cover
flip-side
flip-top
flower: –
flower child
flower power
flowerpot
fly-by-night
fly: –
fly front
fly line
fly powder
fly rail
fly rod

fly swat
fly whisk
flycatcher
flyleaf
flyover
flypaper
flytrap
flyway
flyweight
flywheel
f-number
fog-bank
folk: –
folk hero
folk music
folk rock
folklore
follow-on
foot: ‡
foot brake
foot fault
foot-bath
foot-candle
foot-dragging
foot-in-the mouth
foot-passenger
foot-patrol
foot-pump
foot-soldier
foot-stall
foot-tapping
foot-ton
foot-warmer
foot-and-mouth
force-feed
force majeure
fore- (See Prefixes)
fore-and-aft
forest: –
fork-lift truck
fork-tailed
fortune-teller
foster: –
foul-mouthed
foundation-stone

fountain-pen
four-by-four
four-footed
four-foot way
four: –
fourfold
fourscore
foursome
fourth dimension
fourth estate
fowl-pest
fox: –
foxberry
foxglove
foxhole
foxhound
foxtrot
frame-saw
frame-up
Franco: ‡
franking-machine
free-and-easy
free: % (adjective)
free: –
freebooter
freeborn
Freefone
freehand
freehold
freelance
freeman
freemason
freephone
Freepost
freestyle
freethinker
freeway
freewheel
freeze-dry
freezing-point
freight-car
French-Canadian
French-polish
front-bench
front: –

front door
front line
front man
front row
fruit-bat
fruit-tree
frying-pan
fry-up
fuel-injected
full: –
full blast
full brother
full cousin
full dress
full hand
full house
full marks
full moon
full nelson
full of beans
full pelt
full pitch
full sail
full score
full point
full tilt
full time
full toss
full up
fullback
fully-fashioned
fully-fledged
fund-raising

- G -
gambling-house
game-chicken
game-dealer
gaming-table
gang-rape
gaol-bird
gas: –
gas burner
gas chamber
gas cooker

gas engine
gas escape
gas fire
gas fitter
gas fixture
gas furnace
gas heater
gas helmet
gas jar
gas jet
gas lamp
gas leak
gas main
gas mantle
gas mask
gas meter
gas oil
gas oven
gas pipe
gas plant
gas poker
gas ring
gas shell
gas station
gas stove
gas tank
gas tap
gasbag
gasholder
gaslight
gaslit
gate-keeper
G-clef
gear: –
gear ratio
gearbox
gearchange
gearshift
gearwheel
gender-specific
general-purpose
get-rich-quick
get-up-and-go
ghost-writer
glass: –

glass eye
glass fibre
glass paper
glass wool
glasshouse
glassware
glassworker
globe-trotter
glue-sniffing
go-between
go-cart
God-almighty
god-forsaken
god-given
godson
go-getter
going-away kit
gold: –
gold card
gold certificate
gold disc
gold dust
goldfield
goldfinch
goldfish
goldsmith
goldstone
golden: %
goldenrod
golden-crested
good: –
good afternoon
good faith
good for anything
good for you
Good Friday
good gracious
good heavens
good offices
good sense
good turn
goodnight
goodtime
goodwill
good-day

goose: –
goose bumps
goose step
gooseberry
gooseberry-wine
gooseflesh
gossip-monger
governing-body
governor-general
Grace-and-Favour
grass-cutter
gravel-pit
gravel-voiced
great-aunt
Greco-Roman
green-keeper
grey-coat
grief-stricken
gripe-water
ground-beetle
ground-to-air
group-captain
growing-pains
grown-up
G-string
guest-house

- H -
habit-forming
hack-saw
hail-storm
hair-brained
hair-brush
hair-raising
hair's-breadth
hair-splitting
half-a-dozen
half: –
half back
half board
half nelson
half past eight
halfpace
halfpenny
halfway

halfwit
half-yearly
ham-fisted
hand: ‡
hand and foot
hand ball
hand grenade
hand in glove
hand line
hand over fist
hand puppet
hand to mouth
hand-ball
hand-barrow
hand-basket
hand-feeding
hand-glass
hand-held
hand-in
hand-in-hand
hand-knitted
hand-loom
hand-lotion
hand-me-down
hand-mill
hand-out
hand-painted
hand-picked
hand-post
hand-press
hand-screw
hand-sewn
hand-to-hand
hand-to-mouth
hands-free
hang-glider
hang-up
hansom-cab
happy-go-lucky
harbour-dues
hard-and-fast
hard: –
hard bop
hard by
hard card

hard case
hard cash
hard cheese
hard coal
hard copy
hard core
hard court
hard currency
hard disk
hard edge
hard facts
hard feelings
hard hat
hard hit
hard labour
hard landing
hard left
hard line
hard luck
hard of hearing
hard pad
hard right
hard rock
hard roe
hard rubber
hard sauce
hard sell
hard shoulder
hardboard
hardface
hard disk
hardgrass
hardhead
hardline
hardmouthed
hardnosed
hardparts
hardshell
hardship
hardtop
hardware
hardwood
hare-and-hounds
hare-brained
harness-maker

harvest: –
has-been
have-a-go
have-nots
hawk: ‡
hawk-beaked
hawk-eyed
hawk-moth
H-bomb
head-on
head-to-head
hearing-aid
hearing-impaired
heart-failure
heart-free
hearth-rug
heart-to-heart
Heath(-)Robinson
heaven-born: ‡
heavy-duty
heavy-handed
hedging-bill
heir-apparent
hell: –
he-man
hemp-seed
hem-stitch
hen: –
henpecked
hero-worship
herring-bone: ‡
hide-and-seek
high: –
high admiral
high altar
high and dry
high and mighty
high bailiff
High Church
high command
High Commissioner
high court
high explosive
high fidelity
high frequency

high gear
High German
high horse
high jinks
high jump
high life
high living
high mass
high noon
high point
high priest
high profile
high relief
high school
high seas
high season
high sheriff
high society
high spirits
high spot
high street
high table
high tea
high technology
high tide
high time
high treason
high water
high wire
highball
highbrow
highjack
highland
highlight
highlighter
highly: –
highroad
highway
highwayman
hill-billy
hire-purchase
hit-and-run
hitch-hike
hi-tec
hit-or-miss

hit-parade
hog's-back
hold-all
hold-up
hole-in-the-wall
holier-than-thou
holly-oak
home: %
homebound
homebuyer
homecraft
homeland
homeless
home-made
homemaker
homeowner
homesick
homespun
homestead
homeward
homework
home-bred
home-brew
home-coming
home-croft
home-defence
home-farm
home-fire
home-grown
home-keeping
home-life
home-made
home-produced
home-ruler
home-signal
home-straight
home-stretch
home-thrust
home-town
home-truth
homeward-bound
homo: ‡
Homo sapiens
honey: –
honey creeper

honey fungus
honeybun
honeycomb
honeydew melon
honeymoon
honeypot
honeysuckle
hop-vine/bine
horse: –
horse artillery
horse box
horse brass
horse chestnut
horse fair
Horse Guards
horse latitudes
horse mackerel
horse mushroom
horse mussel
horse race
horse sense
horse soldier
horseback
horsecar
horsefeathers
horseflesh
horsefly
horsehair
horsehide
horselaugh
horseman
horsemeat
horseplay
horsepower
horseradish
horseshoe
horsetail
horsewhip
horse-and-buggy
hot-air balloon
hot-tempered
hot-water bottle
house-breaking
house: ‡
house agent

house arrest
house call
house guest
house lights
house martin
house physician
house plant
house sparrow
house surgeon
house-breaker
house-dog
house-father
house-mother
house-party
house-proud
house-to-house
house-trained
house-warming
house-to-house
how-do-you-do
howdy-do
hub-cap
humble-pie
hunger-strike
hunting: –
hurdle-race
hurricane-lamp
hymn-book

- I -
ice: %
iceball
iceberg
iceblink
icebound
icebox
icebreaker
icecap
icefield
icepack
ice-action
ice-belt
ice-blue
ice-cold
ice cream

ice-cream soda
ice-free
ice-ledge
ice-skate
ill- (See Prefixes)
in-between
-in-chief
index-finger
index-linked
Indo: –
in-fighting
in-flight
ink-blot
in-law
in-patient
input-output analysis
in-situ
internal-combustion engine
intra-articular
in- (See Prefixes)
iron: –
Iron Age
Iron Cross
Iron Curtain
iron horse
iron lung
iron maiden
iron ore
iron pyrites
ironing-board
ironmaster
ironmonger
ironsmith
ironstone
ironware
ironwood
ironwork
ivory-black
ivory-palm

- J -
Jack-in-the-box
jail-bird
jerry-builder

jet: –
jet boat
jet engine
jetfoil
jetliner
jetplane
jetsam
jetstream
jewel-case
jewel-house
Jew's-harp
jib: –
joint: –
joint account
joint resolution
joint venture
joint will
joint-stock bank
joy-ride
Judas-kiss
judgement-day
ju-jitsu
juke-box
jump-jet
junior-(weight): ‡
junk-shop: ‡
jury-box

- K -
kerb-crawler
key-ring: ‡
kick-off
kidney: –
kiln-dried
kind-hearted
king: –
king of beasts
king of the castle
king penguin
kingfisher
kingmaker
kingpost
kiss-and-tell
kitchen: –
kitchen unit

kitchenware
kite-flying
kite-mark
knee: –
knee sock
kneecap
kneehole
knife: –
knight: –
knitting: –
knock-down
knock-on effect
know-how (UK)
knowhow (US)
Ku-Klux Klan

- L -
labour: –
labour-saving
lady-in-waiting
lady-killer
ladylike
laissez-faire
lake-dweller
lamp: –
lampholder
lamplight
lamplighter
lamppost
lampshade
lance-corporal
land: –
land grant
land office
Land Registry
landfall
landfill
landform
landholder
landlady
landless
landlord
landmark
landmass
landowner

landscape
landslide
landslip
landwind
landing: –
larger-than-life
last-ditch
last-gasp
last-minute
lattice-work
laughing-gas
laughing-stock
launching-pad
laundry-maid
law: –
law agent
law centre
lawsuit
lawyer
lawn tennis
lawnmower
lawn-party
lawn-sprinkler
lay-by
layer-cake
lay-off
lead-free
leaf: –
leafbud
leaflike
lean-to
leap-frog
lease-lend
leather: –
leathergoods
left-bank: ‡
Left Bank
left guard
left tackle
left wheel
left wing
leg: –
leg break
leg bye
leg side

leg slip
leg spin
leg spinner
leg warmers
legwear
legwork
lemon-grass
lend-lease
let-down
letter: –
letter quality
letterbox
letterhead
level: –
level best
liberty-boat
Lib.-Lab.
lie-in
lieutenant: –
life-and-death
life: –
life annuity
life assurance
life expectancy
Life Guards
life insurance
life peer
life sciences
life sentence
life story
lifebelt
lifeboat
lifebuoy
lifeguard
lifelong
lifespan
lifestyle or life-style
lifetime
life-support system
lift-boy
light: –
light bulb
light engine
light horse
light industry

light infantry
light literature
light meter
light music
light opera
light railway
light up
light welterweight
lighter-than-air
lighthouse
lighting-up
lighting-up time
lightning-conductor
lightship
lightweight
lightly: –
like-minded
lime-green
lime-tree
lime-twig
lime-wood
limited-liability company
limited-over
line: –
line drawing
line feed
line judge
line up
lineman
line drawing
line feed
line judge
line up
line-out
line-printer
link-up
linseed: –
lionlike
lion-hearted
lip: –
lip brush
lip liner
listening-in
litter-bug
litter-lout

live-bait: ‡
live birth
live cartridge
live circuit
live shell
lived-in
livestock
livery-servant
living-room
loan: –
loan collection
loan shark
loan translation
loan word
lobster-pot
lock-keeper
lock-nut
lock-down
lock-up
locum-tenency
log: –
log cabin
log in
log out
log tables
long: %
longboat
longbow
longhand
longhorn
longhouse
longship
longshoreman
longsuffering
longwearing
long-ago
long-chain
long-dated
long-distance
long-drawn-out
long-eared
long-faced
long-haired
long-haul
long-legged

long-life
long-line
long-lived
long-measure
long-range
long-sighted
long-standing
long-stay
long-tail
long-term
long-time
long-wave (adj.)
long-winded
look-alike *or* lookalike
looking-glass
loose-cut
loose-leaf
Lord Justice-General
lotus-eater
love: –
love affair
love game
love life
lovebird
lovebite
lovelock
lovemaking
lovesick
loving-kindness
low: –
Low Church
low comedy
low frequency
low gear
Low German
low life
low mass
low profile
low technology
low tide
low water
lowland
lowlight
lozenge-shaped
lucky-dip

luggage-van
lumber-yard
lump-sugar
luncheon-bar
lynch-law
lynx-eyed

- **M** -
mace-bearer
machine: –
machine gun
machine-gunner
machine code
machine language
machine tool
macro- (See Prefixes)
magneto: –
mail: ‡
mail drop
mail order
mail-boat
mail-car
mail-coach
mail-order
mail-plane
mail-train
maintenance-man
major-general
make-believe
make-do
make-or-break
make-peace
malt: –
malt liquor
malt tea
malt vinegar
malt whisky
man-hours
manic-depressive
man-of-war
man-servant
mansion-house
man-sized
man-years
many-sided

map-pin
map-reading
mark-down
market: –
market cross
market economy
market forces
market garden
market gardener
market leader
market profile
market research
market share
market square
mark-up
marriage: –
marriage bureau
marriage guidance
marriage partner
marsh-gas
Mason-Dixon Line
mass-energy equation
mass: %
mass(-)production
mass-bell
mass-book
mass-energy equivalence
mass-marketing
mass-produced
master: –
master-at-arms
master of ...
master page
mastermind
masterpiece
mastersinger
masterstroke
masterwork
match-maker
match-play
matter-of-fact
means-test
measuring-tape
meat-eater
medico: –

medium: –
meeting-house
melting-point
melt-water
memory-resident
men-of-war
merry-go-round
mess-tin
mess-up
mezzo-soprano
micro- (See Prefixes)
middle: %
middlebrow
middleman
middlemost
middleweight
middle-age
middle-bracket
middle-class or middle
class
middle-distance
Middle-Eastern
middle-income
middle-of-the-road
mid- (See Prefixes)
midi- (See Prefixes)
mile-post
milk: –
milk chocolate
milk of ...
milk round
milk stout
milkfish
milkmaid
milkman
mill: –
millboard
milldam
millpond
millrace
millstone
millstone-grit
millwright
mince-pie
mind-altering

mind: –
mine: –
minefield
minesweeper
mini- (See Prefixes)
minute: –
minute steak
minuteman
mirror: –
mirror symmetry
mirrorwise
mischief-maker
mixed-ability
mock-up
money: –
money belt
money clip
money supply
moneybags
moneylender
monkey: –
monkey-block
moon: ‡
moon daisy
moon-eyed
moon-faced
moon-fish
moon-flower
moon-god
moon-madness
moon-stricken
mooring-mast
morning: %
morning-after pill
morning-glory
morning-gown
morning-prayer
morning-room
mortice-lock
moss: –
moss green
moss stitch
mossback
mossland
mossplant

moth-eaten
mother-in-law
mother-to-be
motor: –
motor car
motor caravan
motor generator
motor home
motor neurone
motorail
motor-cycle
motorcycle combination
motorcyclist
motorway
mounting-block
mourning: –
mouse-colour: ‡
muck-rake
multi- (See Prefixes)
music-holder
mussel-shell
mustard-oil
mutton-suet
mystery-man

- N -
nail: –
nail gun
nail polish
nail punch
nail set
nail varnish
name-calling
name-plate
nanny-goat
narrow-boat
narrow-gauge
narrow-minded
nation building
nation-state
nationwide
nature-cure
near: –
Near East
near gale

near miss
nearside
neck-bone
neo- (See Prefixes)
net-fishing
never-ending
new: %
newborn
newcomer
newfangled
New-Age
new-blown
new-fallen
new-fledged
new-found
new-laid
new-made
new-mown
newly-qualified
news: ‡
news agency
news conference
news fiction
news magazine
news-sheet
news-stand
news-theatre
news-value
news-vendor
news-writer
newly-wed
night: –
night air
night duty
night fighter
night nurse
night out
night safe
night school
night shift
nightbird
nightcap
nightclass
nightclothes
nightclub

nightdress
nightgear
nightgown
nighthawk
nightjar
nightlife
nightlong
nightmare
nightpiece
nightrider
nightshade
nightshirt
nightspot
nightwear
nig-nog
nine-hole
noble-minded
no- (See Prefixes)
non- (See Prefixes)
north-country
north-east
nose-cone
Notre-Dame
now-a-days
nuclear-free zone
nuclear-powered
nut-wrench

- O -
oak-tree
object-lesson
obtuse-angled
obtuse-angular
ocean-going
odd-job
odds-on
off- (See Prefixes)
office-boy
office-girl
oil: –
oil(-)field
oil immersion
oil length
oil of ...
oil paint

oil painting
oil platform
oil rig
oil shale
oil slick
oil well
oilcan
oilcloth
oilfield
oilman
oilskin
oilstone
old: –
old age
old girl
old-age pension
old-fashioned
O-level
on-board
once-and-for-all
once-for-all
once-over
one-of-a-kind
one-man band
one-sided
on-going; ongoing
on-the-job training
open: –
open access
open adoption
open book
open cheque
open circuit
open court
open day
open door
open economy
open fire
open harmony
open house
open letter
open market
open marriage
open mind
open prison

open question
open sandwich
open score
open sea
open season
open secret
open sentence
open shop
open side
open skies
open system
open verdict
opening time
open-and-shut
opera-glasses
orange-blossom
orange-peel
order-book
organ-builder
ostrich-egg
otter-hunting
out-and-out
out- (See Prefixes)
out-of-the-way
out-of-work
outward-bound
oven-proof
over- (See Prefixes)
oxy-acetylene
oyster-bed: ‡
ozone-friendly

- P -
pace-bowler
pack: –
pack ice
packsheet
packing: –
paddle-boat
paddy-field
page-boy
pain-killer
paint-box
palette-knife
pall-bearer

pall-mall
palm: –
palm court
palmhouse
Pan: –
panty-hose
paper: –
paper money
paper profits
paper tape
paper tape reader
paper tiger
paperback
paperboard
paperless
paperware
paperwork
park-and-ride
parking lot
parking meter
parking-place
parking-ticket
parliament-house
parrot: –
partition-wall
part: –
part of speech
part-exchange
partridge-wood
party: –
party line
party machine
party man
party plan
party politics
party sales
party spirit
party-spirited
party wall
pass-book
passe-partout
passer-by
pasture-land
patent-rights
pathbreaking *or*

pathbreaking
patrol-wagon
pattern: –
pay-as-you-earn
pay: –
paymaster
payroll
payslip
peace: –
peacemaker
peacetime
pea-green
pearl: –
pearl barley
pearly king/queen
pear-shaped
pea-soup
pea-stone
pea-straw
peat: –
pebble-stone
pedal: –
peep-hole
pen-and-ink
pencil-case
pen-friend
penny-farthing
penny-pinching
pen-pusher
pepper: –
pepper-and-salt
pepper
pepper tree
peppercorn
peppermill
peppermint
percussion: –
photo: ‡
photo call
photo opportunity
photo-ageing
photo-emission
photo-engraving
photo-etching
photo-finish

photo-process
photo-relief
piano: –
piano roll
pianoforte
picket-duty
pick-pocket
picture: –
picture postcard
piece: –
piecemeal
pied-à-terre
pie-eyed
pier-head
pigeon: –
pigeon's milk
pigeonhole
pig: ‡
pig swill
pigfeed
pig-eyed
pig-faced
pig-fish
pig-iron
pig-lead
pig-lily
pig-rat
pike-perch
pile-driver
pile-up
pile-worm
pill-box
pillion-rider
pillow-fight
pilot: –
pilot burner
pilot engine
pilot jet
pilot lamp
pilot light
pilot officer
pilot project
pilot scheme
pince-nez
pincer-movement

pin: –
pine: –
pine cone
pine kernel
pine marten
pine needle
pine tar
pine tree
pineapple
pinewood
ping-pong
pipe: –
pipe dream
pipe fitting
pipe major
pipe organ
pipeclay
pipefish
pipeline
pitch: –
pit-coal
plain-cook
plain-spoken
plane-polarised
plane-tree
plate: –
plate glass
plate rack
play-acting
player-piano
plea-bargaining
pleasure-giving
pleasure-seeker
plough-iron
plug-in
plum-cake
plus-twos/fours
pocket-handkerchief
point-blank
point-duty
point-of-sale
point-to-point
poison-ivy
poison-oak
poker-faced

police: –
police dog
police force
police inspector
police office
police officer
police state
police station
police trap
policeman
policewoman
policy maker or policy-
maker
polishing-paste
politico-economic
polka-dot
poll-tax
pop-up
portrait-gallery
post- (See Prefixes)
pot-belly
pot-roast
pot-sick
poultry-farm
pound-foolish
poverty-stricken
powdering-room
power-amp
preaching-cross
pre- (See Prefixes)
present-day
preserving-pan
pre- (See Prefixes)
press-button
press-gang
press-up
pressure-cook
pre-stressed
pre-war
price-cutting
price-earnings ratio
price-fixing
printing: –
printing paper
print-out

pro-chancellor
procurator-fiscal
profit-orientated
profit-sharing
profit-taker
pro (see Prefixes)
pro-life
proof-correcting
proof-mark
provost-marshal
psalm-book
psalm-tune
pseudo: –
pub-crawl
public-domain
public-relations
public-school
public-spirited
pudding: –
pug-faced
pull: –
pullover
pulse-rate
pump-room
punch-bag
puppet-show
puppy-dog
puppy-fat
purse-seine
purse-strings
push: –
pushover
pushrod
put: –
putting-green
putting-stone
putty-coloured
putty-faced
putty-knife
putty-powder
put-up
puzzle: –
pye-dog
pyro: –

- Q -
quarter: –
quarter past
quarter to
quarterback
quarterdeck
quarterlight
quartermaster
quartermaster-general
quartz-crystal
quasi: –
queen: –
queen bee
queen mother
question-mark
question-master
queue-jumping
quick: –
quick fire
quick time
quicklime
quicksand
quicksilver
quickstep
quickthorn
quicktrick
quill-pen
quotation-mark

- R -
rabbet-joint
rabbit-hole
raccoon-dog
radar-gun
radial-ply tyre
radio: ‡
radio altimeter
radio amateur
radio astronomy
radio beacon
radio communication
radio compass
radio frequency
radio galaxy
radio ham

radio microphone
radio spectrum
radio star
radio station
radio telescope
radio wave
radio-actinium
radio-frequency heating
radio-gramophone
radio-isotope
radio-strontium
radio-telegraphy
radio-therapy
radio-thorium
rags-to-riches
rail: –
railbus
railcard
railhead
railman
railroad
railway: –
railway station
rainbow-coloured
rain: –
rainbow trout
rainbow-chaser
rainbow-coloured
rainbow-tinted
raincoat
raindrop
rained off
rainfall
rainforest
rainmaker
rainproof
rainstorm
raintight
rainwater
rainwear
rake-off
rally-cross
rapid-fire
rat: –
razor: –

reading-book: ‡
read-only
ready: –
ready-to-wear
receiving-house: ‡
record-player
re-count
re- (See Prefixes)
refreshment-room
Registrar-General
relay-race
remote control
remote-controlled
rent-a-crowd
rent-collector
restaurant-car
rest: –
rest stop
resting-place
Rh-negative
ribbon-development
rib: –
rice: –
ridge-pole
riding: –
riff-raff
rifle-shot
right: –
right-about face
right-mindedness
rig-out
ring: –
ring fort
ring main
ring network
ring road
ring spanner
ring up
ringbone
ringing tone
ringleader
ringmaster
ringside
ringtail
ringway

ringworm
rip-off
rip-saw
risk-money
river: –
river basin
river blindness
river novel
riverbank
rivercraft
riverfront
riverside
road: –
road hump
road manager
road pricing
road rage
road sign
roadblock
roadhouse
roadrunner
roadshow
roadside
roadway
roadworks or
road works
roast-beef
robe-maker
rock: –
rock bottom
rock cake
rock candy
rock crystal
rock drill
rock garden
rock lobster
rock melon
rock music
rock pigeon
rock plant
rock rose
rock salt
rock snake
rock tripe
rock wool

rockfish
rocksteady
rockwater
rockweed
rockwork
rocking: –
rock-'n'-roll
rocket: %
rocket-launcher
role-play
roll-call
roller: –
rolling-pin
rolling-stock
roll-neck
roll-on
roll-on-roll-off (RoRo)
roll-top
roll-up
roly-poly
romper-suit
rood: –
roof: –
roof garden
rooftop
rooftree
room: –
room service
rope: –
rope stitch
rope trick
roper-in
ropeway
ropework
ropeworks
ro-ro ship
rose: –
rose geranium
rose laurel
rose oil
rosebay
rosebowl
rosebud
rosebush
rosefinch

rosefish
rosehip
rosemary
rosewater
rosewood
rosewood-oil
rosy-cheeked
rouge-et-noir
rough: –
rough-and-ready
rough cut
rough diamond
rough grazing
rough house
rough justice
roughcast
roughneck
rough-and-ready
rough-and-tumble
round: –
round about
round dozen
round game
round off
round on
round tower
round up
roundabout
roundhand
Roundhead
roundhouse
rounding error
roundworm
route-march
rowan-berry
rowan-tree
rowing-boat
row-port
rubber-stamp
rubbish-heap
rubble-stone
rule-of-thumb
rum-punch
run-down
run-in

runner-bean
runner(s)-up
run-off
run-of-the-mill
rush-grown
rust-coloured
rustic-work
rust-proof

- S -
Sabbath-day
sabre: –
saddle-shaped
sad-eyed
safe: –
safe house
safe light
safe period
safe seat
safe sex
safeguard
safety: %
safetyman
safety-catch
safety-deposit
sail-maker
sale-catalogue
salmon-fisher
salmon-pink
saloon-keeper
salt: –
salt bath
salt cake
salt dome
salt eel
salt flat
salt lake
salt marsh
salt pan
salt pit
salt spoon
salt spring
saltbox
saltbush
saltcellar

saltchuck
saltfish
saltpetre
saltwater
saltworks
sand: –
sand bar
sand bath
sand bed
sand blow
sand break
sand bunker
sand dab
sand eel
sand flea
sand grain
sand grass
sand grouse
sand lance
sand leek
sand lizard
sand martin
sand mole
sand pipe
sand plough
sand sole
sand trap
sand wasp
sandbag
sandbank
sandblasting
sandbox
sandboy
sandcastle
sandfly
sandglass
sandheap
sandhill
sandiver
sandpaper
sandpiper
sandpit
sandpump
sandshoe
sandspout

sandstone
sandstorm
sandsucker
sandwich
sandworm
sand-binder
sand-blind
sand-cast
sand-casting
sand-dart
sand-devil
sand-dune
sand-flag
sand-hog
sand-hopper
sand-lark
sand-peep
sand-screw
sand-skipper
sand-snake
sand-star
sand-thrower
sapphire-quartz
saucer-eyed
savanna-forest
savoir-faire
saw-frame
scalping-knife
scarlet-bean
scene-of-crime (adj.)
school: ‡
school age
school bell
school board
school book
school doctor
school house
school nurse
school ship
school term
school year
school-age
school-bred
school-friend
school-inspector

school-leaver
school-mate
school-trained
scissors-and-paste
scissor-tooth
scorched-earth policy
scoring-board
scrag-end
scrap-man
scrap-metal merchant
screech-owl
screen-wiper
screw-up
scribbling-book
scrubbing-brush
scullery-maid
scythe-stone
sea: %
seabank
seabed
seabird
seaboard
seaborne
seacoast
seacock
seacraft
seadrome
seafarer
seafaring
seafolk
seafood
seafowl
seafront
seagull
seahawk
seahog
seahorse
seahound
seakale
sealine
seaman
seamark
seaplane
seaport
seaquake

seascape
seashell
seashore
seasick
seaside
seaward
seawater
seaway
seaweed
seawoman
seaworm
sea-bathing
sea-beaten
sea-blue
sea-born
sea-fight
sea-fire
sea-fisher
sea-fishing
sea-going
sea-green
sea-island
sea-like
sea-pig
sea-rocket
sea-roving
sea-wolf
sea-worn
sealing-wax
seal: –
sealskin
sealwax
seal off
seal ring
seal rookery
sealed-beam
searing-iron
seat-of-the-pants
second-class: ‡
second-hand
second-to-none
secretary-general
seed-coat: ‡
seek-no-further
self- (See Prefixes)

sell-by date
selling-price
sell-out
semi- (See Prefixes)
senate-house
send-off
Serbo-Croatian
sergeant-at-arms
sergeant: –
serpent-eater
serpent-lizard: ‡
servant-maid
session-clerk
session-house
set-aside
set-down
se-tenant
set-to
set-up
seven-a-side
seven-day
Seventh-day Adventists
sewage-farm
sewing-machine
sex: –
shadow-boxing
shaft-horse
shaggy-dog story
shape-up
share-capital
share-out
sharp: –
shaving-brush
she-devil
sheep: –
sheep station
sheep tick
sheep's sorrel
sheep's-foot
sheep's-head
sheepcote
sheepdog
sheepfold
sheepshank
sheepshearer

sheepskin
sheeptrack
sheet: –
sheet film
shell: –
shell bean
shell mound
shell ornament
shell out
shell parrot
shell star
shell suit
shelldrake
shellduck
shellfire
shellfish
shellproof
shellshock
shellwork
ship: ‡
ship('s) boy
ship canal
ship carpenter
ship chandler
ship fever
ship letter
ship money
ship railway
ship water
ship-breaker
ship-holder
ship-of-the-line
ship-owner
ship-rigged
shock-absorber
shoot-out
shop-floor
shop-lifter
short: –
short circuit
short cut
short fuse
short hundredweight
short leg
short list

short-lived
short measure
short metre
short odds
short order
short rib
short sale
short score
short sea
short selling
short sheep
short shrift
short slip
short story
short tennis
short time
short ton
short track
shortarm
shortbread
shortcake
shortcoming
shortfall
shorthand
shortstop
shortsword
shoulder-high
shove-halfpenny
shrill-voiced
shrink-resistant
sick-fallen
side-effects *or*
side effects
side-on
sidestep
siege-artillery
sight-read
signal-to-noise ratio
sign-painter
simple-minded
singing-bird
single: –
single cream
single figures
single file

single house
single parent
single soldier
single tax
single transferable vote
singletree
sister-in-law
sit-in
sitter-in
sitting-room
six-footer
six-pack
sixth-form college
skating-rink
ski-jump
skin-deep
skin-diver
skipping-rope
skirting-board
sky: ‡
sky marshal
sky pilot
sky sign
sky troops
sky wave
sky-blue
sky-bred
sky-diving
sky-high
sky-jumping
sky-surfing
sky-writing
slave-driver
sloop-of-war
slop: –
slow-up
small: %
smallholder
smallpox
small-arm
small-bore
small-coal
small-hand
small-minded
small-screen

small-time
small-tooth comb
small-town
smash-and-grab
smear-dab
smelting-furnace
smelting-house
smoke: –
smoke abatement
smoke alarm
smoke detector
smoke helmet
smoke signal
smoke test
smoke tunnel
smokeboard
smokehouse
smokeproof
smokescreen
smokestack
smoketight
smooth: –
snack-bar
snail-paced
snake-oil
snake-pit
snow-hole
snuff: –
snuff mill
snuff movie
snuff spoon
snuff video
snuffbox
so-and-so
so-called
sober-minded
soda-siphon
soft-billed: ‡
Solicitor-General
solid-state
someone
son-in-law
soul-confirming: ‡
soul mate
soul music

soul sister
sound-carrier
south-west
space-age
space-heating
spare-time
speaking-voice
spear-point
speed-cop
speed-up
sperm-whale
spin-bowler
spin-doctor
spin-dried
spin-dryer
spine-chiller
spin-off
split-level house
split-screen
spoon-feeding
spot-check
spot-welder
spray-on
spray-paint
spread-eagle
spring-clean
spring-loaded
spun-out
squadron-leader
square: %
squarehead
square-bashing
square-built
square-cut
square-dance
square-lipped
square-rigger
square-sail
square-shouldered
square-toed
staff-system
staff-tree
stage-manage
stage-struck
stamping-ground

stand-alone
standard-bearer
stand-by
stand-in
stand-off
stand-up
star: ‡
star billing
star fruit
star grass
star map
star sapphire
star shell
star sign
star trap
star wars
star wheel
star-apple
star-bright
star-crossed
star-gaze
star-shaped
star-spangled
star-studded
stark-naked
starry-eyed
state-aided
state-of-the-art
station-manager
station-master
steady-state theory
steam-driven
steam-roller
steel: –
steel band
steel drum
steel erector
steel pan
steel plate
steel wool
steelman
steelworker
step: %
stepbrother
stepchild

stepdancer
stepfather
stepladder
stepmother
stepping-stone
stepwise
step-cut
step-daughter
step-down
step-in
step-parent
step-parenting
step-sister
step-son
step-up
stiff-necked
still-life
stock-farmer
Stone-Age
stone: %
Stone(-)Age
stonecast
stonecutter
stonefish
stonefly
stonemason
stones-cast
stonewaller
stoneware
stonewashed
stonework
stone-age
stone-blind
stone-breaker
stone-broke
stone-cold
stone-coloured
stone-crazy
stone-dead
stone-deaf
stone-hard
stone-lily
stone-still
stop-and-search
stop-consonant

stop-loss
stop-press
straight-cut
strato-cumulus
street-level
stretcher-bearer
strip-poker
strong-minded
sub- (See Prefixes)
sugar-coated
sugar-cube
summit-level
sun: ‡
Sun Belt
sun bittern
sun bonnet
sun dance
sun deck
sun lounge
sun parlo(u)r
sun protection factor
sun room
sun visor
sun worship
sun-blind
sun-clad
sun-dried
sun-god
super- (See Prefixes)
sure-enough
sure-fire
surface-to-air
surf-bathing
swaddling-clothes
swans-down
swan: –
sweat-shirt
sweep-net
sweet: %
sweetbread
sweetcorn
sweetfish
sweetheart
sweetie-pie
sweet-and-sour

sweet-briar
sweet-savoured
sweet-scented
sweet-talk
sweet-tempered
sweet-toothed
sweet-water
swell-headed
swell-mob
swimming-pool
swing: –
swinging-post
swingtail aircraft
switch-over
sword: –
system-built

- T -
table: –
table football
table game
table knife
table licence
table linen
table manners
table money
table napkin
table salt
table tennis
table water
table wine
tablecloth
tablespoon
tablespoonful
tabletop
tableware
tag-end
tail: –
tail wind
tailback
tailboard
tailgate
taillie
tailpiece
tailpipe

tailplane
tailrace
tailspin
tailwheel
tailor-made
take-down
take-home pay
take-in
take-off
take-up
talent-spotter
talk-in
talk show
tally-system
tap-dance
tape-recording
tar-paper
task-force
tax-collector
tax-deductible
tax-exempt
tax-free
taxi-driver
tax-payer
T-bone
tea-cosy
tea-drinker
teatime or tea-time
team-mate
tear-jerker
tee-off
telephone-tapping
telling-off
tell-tale or telltale
tender-hearted
tennis-ball
ten-pounder
ten-score
terror-struck
test-ban treaty
test-bed
test-drive
test-tube baby
tête-à-tête
text-editor

theatre-goer
thick-and-thin
thick: –
thickskin
thickset
think-tank
third-class
thought-reader
thousand-pound
thousand-year
three-colour
three-day event
three-dimensional
three: –
three-four time
three cheers
three deep
three quarters
threefold
threepence
threescore
three-line whip
thunder: –
thunderbolt
thunderclap
thundercloud
thunderflash
thunderstorm
thunderstruck
thunder-and-lightning
tick-over
tide-gauge
tie: –
tie beam
tie clip
tie line
tieback
tiepin
tight-fisted
tile-stone
timber: –
timber hitch
timberline
timberyard
time: %

timecard
timed-release
timeframe
timekeeper
timepiece
timescale
timetable
time-bill
time-consuming
time-expired
time-honoured
time-lapse
time-release
time-saving
time-share
time-thrust
title-holder
T-junction
tobacco-pouch
toffee-apple
toilet-table
toll-free
tone-deaf
tongue-and-groove
tongue-in-cheek
tongue-tied
ton-up
toolbox, toolkit
tooth-picker
toothpick
top: –
top brass
top dead centre
top dog
top drawer
top gear
top hat
top secret
top table
top the bill
top up
topcoat
topfull
topless
topline

topmaker
topman
topmast
topmost
topping-up
topsail
topside
topsoil
topspin
totting-up
touch-and-go
town-dweller
trade-off
traffic-lights
traffic-manager
trail-blazer
train-spotter
tram-stop
transit-trade
travel-sick
trawl-line
treasure-trove
trellis-work
trench-coat
trestle-table
trickle-charge
trigger-happy
tri-jet
trolley-car
troop-ship
trouser: –
truck: –
true: –
true blue
true time
true-love knot
trump-card
trumped-up
trumpet-flower
trunk-call
trunk-road
trust-house
T-shirt
tug-of-war
tumbler-drier

tuna-fish
tuning-fork
turbine-pump
turbo-generator
turning-point
turnpike-road
turn-screw
turn-up
turtle-soup
tusk-shell
tutti-frutti
tut-tut
'tween-deck
twelve-tone
twin: –
twin bed
twin town
twinset
two-by-four: ‡
two-dimensional
type-bar: ‡
type-body

- U -
U-bend
U-boat
U-shaped
ultra- (See Prefixes)
un-[country]
unbuilt-on
uncalled-for
unco-ordinated
under- (See Prefixes)
unheard-of
unlived-in
unslept-in
untalked-of
unthought-of
up- (See Prefixes)
up-and-coming
up-and-down
upper-bracket
upper-case
upside-down
up-till

user-friendly

- V -
vacuum-clean
vacuum-packed
vampire-bat
vaulting-horse
velvet: –
vice- (See Prefixes)
vine-leaf
violin-bow
visiting-card
V-neck
vol-au-vent
V-shape

- W -
wage-earner
wage-push inflation
wages-fund theory
wagon-lits
waist-deep
waiting: –
walkie-talkie
walking: –
walk-on
walk-over
warm-blooded
war-proof: ‡
wash-and-wear
washed-up
washing: –
water: %
waterborne
watercolour
watercourse
watercraft
watercress
watered-down
waterfall
waterfowl
waterfront
waterglass
waterhen
watering

watering: –
waterlily
waterline
waterlogged
watermark
watermelon
waterproof
watershed
waterspout
watertight
waterway
waterweed
water-bearing
water-borne
water-bound
water-breather
water-carriage
water-carrier
water-cooled
water-diviner
water-heater
water-jet
water-parting
water-repellent
water-resistant
water-ski
water-softener
water-soluble
water-spaniel
water-sprinkle
water-worn
watt-hour
wax-proofed
weak: –
weak point
weak side
weak spot
wear and tear
weasel-faced
weather: %
weatherboard
weathercock
weatherman
weatherproof
weather-beaten

weather-bitten
weather-bound
weather-driven
weather-wise
weather-worn
web page, web site *or*
webpage, website
web-toed
weigh-in
weight-lifter
well: –
well and good
well and truly
well-being
well curb
well deck
well-developed
well drain
well hole
well in
well met
well off
well preserved
wellbeing
wellhead
well-educated
wellhouse
wellspring
wet-and-dry paper
whale-fishing
wheel-clamp
whip-round
whistle-stop
white: %
whitebait
whitebass
whitefly
whitehead
whitepot
whitesmith
whitethroat
whitewall
whiteware
whitewash
whitewing

whitewood
white-bearded
white-bellied
white-billed
white-breasted
white-collar
white-crested
white-crowned
white-eye
white-face
white-footed mouse
white-fronted
white-haired
white-handed
white-headed
white-heart
white-hot
white-listed
white-livered
white-out
white-slave traffic
white-supremacist
white-tailed
white-tie
white-water
white-winged
whole: –
whole blood
whole cloth
whole milk
whole note
whole number
whole step
whole-tone scale
wholefood
wholegrain
wholemeal
wholesale
wholestitch
wholewheat
wicket-keeper
wide: –
wide awake
wide boy
wide of the mark

wide open
wide receiver
wide screen
wideawake
widebody
widescreen
widespread
Wild-West Show
wind-chill factor
window-dressing
window-shop
windscreen-wiper
wind-up
(to) wind up
wine: %
wineberry
wineglass
winepress
wine-berry
wine-bibber
wine-coloured
wine-cooler
wine-grower
wine-stone
wine-tasting
winner-takes-all
winter-clad
woman: –
woman-born
woman-hater
woman-suffrage
wonder-struck
wool: –
wool ball
wool card
wool clip
wool comb
wool mill
wool oil
wool shears
wool staple
woolfat
woolman
woolpack
woolsack

woolshed
woolsorter
woolwork
woollen mill
woollen-draper
woollyback
woollybutt
woolly-haired
woolly-hand crab
woolly-headed
woolly-minded
word-association: ‡
word: –
word for word
word memory
word of honour
word order
word picture
wordbreak
wordgame
wordplay
wordsmith
work%
work-to-rule

workout
work-sharing
workplace
working: %
working-beam
working-class
working-day
working-over
world: –
world power
World Series
World War
worldscale
worldwide
world-without-end
worldly: –
worm-eaten
worn-out
worst-case
write-back: –
writing: –
wrongdoing
wrought-iron

- **X** -
X-factor
X-rated
X-ray

- **Y** -
yacht-club
Yankee-Doodle
yard-arm
year-end
year-on-year
yearlong
year-round
yellow: –
yes-man
Y-fronts
you-know-what
young-offenders
institution

- **Z** -
Z-DNA
zero: –
zip-fastener

16
UK English vs. US English

England and America are two countries divided by a common language.[1] – Bernard Shaw (1856–1950). Irish playwright and critic. Oscar Wilde's views were somewhat different: *We really have everything in common with America nowadays except, of course, language.*

A colleague recently remarked that he did not think it important to draw attention to differences between UK or US English – 'we all understand each other'. I think he may be right. US spellings are now widely acceptable. There is hardly an *–ise* word that cannot use *–ize* as my *Chambers Harrap Electronic Dictionary* suggests. I discuss this particular item under Spelling.

Use of words

There are many words used differently or which take on a different meaning in American. A few do exist only in the one language. Examples of different words in UK English and US English respectively are *flat – apartment; taxi – cab* (also used in UK English)*; railway – railroad; autumn – fall.* A *high-riser* is certainly not a term in general use in UK English, but neither is *block of flats* in US English. But there are also more subtle differences. Longmans *Language Activator* informs me that *toward* is US while the UK is *towards.*

Useful lists are given in Swan (1991), Bickerton (1998) and Etherington (1999). It should, however, be noted that most UK speakers know the meanings of the American equivalents due to high exposure to American films on TV and at the cinema.

American grammar

Sufficient examples may be found for a whole book on UK versus US English usage and grammar. There are several books covering this subject. Not least is the situation enriched by the broad variety of dialects found in each country.

---

1 Variously quoted as 'separated by the same language' (see page 3).

There are many differences in grammar related to colloquial language. For example, the use of 'have' is more limited in US English:

I have got a seat reserved at the restaurant (UK).

I got a seat reserved at the restaurant (US).

Note the perfect participle of *get* used in US English: *She has gotten a place at university.* The term *gotten* is only found in the UK in the expression *ill-gotten gains* (plural).

Compound words

There is a tendency in US English to conjoin terms which, currently, are written as two words in UK English, occasionally hyphenated:

UK English	US English
non-profit	*nonprofit*
non-scientific	*nonscientific*
per cent	*percent* (less frequently *per cent*)
pre-exist	*preexist*
trade mark	*trademark*

Spelling, US vs. UK

After having written this section I realised that differences in US and UK spelling are of relatively little importance in this day and age of multilingual spellcheckers. Nevertheless, it is interesting to reflect on a few differences. And differences may well be getting fewer as a number of English dictionaries give both UK and US spellings as alternatives.

One difference, readily observed, is that many words spelt using *z* in US texts are rapidly becoming acceptable in UK texts (e.g. *advertise, utilize*). In fact, *Chambers Dictionary* allows –ise and –ize for virtually all these words. This reflects the tendency towards phonetic spelling in US English: *gray* for *grey*; *specialty* for *speciality; esthetic* for *aesthetic; skepticism* for *scepticsm*. Other examples of different UK – US spellings include: *aluminium* (UK) – *aluminum* (US); *cheque – check, tyre – tire*. The spelling *'programme'* is *'program'* in US English. In UK English, we refer to a *TV-programme*, but a computer *program*. US English uses the shorter version in both instances. But in general US English is much more phonetic. It is not entirely surprising that American drawl causes them to spell *jewellery* as *jewelry*. *Enquire* and *inquire* are acceptable to both UK and US. My proof-reader pointed out that *focussed* is the US spelling, but a number of UK dictionaries permit the double 's' as well as *focused*.

There are a number of generalisations which readily distinguish between UK and US English.

-able   Nouns ending in *e* in adjective form often drop the *e* in American.
ageing (UK) – *aging* (US)
size – *sizeable* (UK) – *sizable* (US)
unshakeable (UK) – *unshakable* (US)

-ae   The *ae* in words derived from Latin and Greek such as *gynaecology* is often written as *e* (*gynecology*) in American. Also *encyclopaedia* (UK) – *encyclopedia* (US).

-ce   *ce* is normally *se* in American. Examples: *license, defense.* However, note *fence* in both countries.

-ise   In preparing this book I compiled a list of UK and US spellings which could use either or both spellings, e.g. *advertise* or *advertize*. *Collins Dictionary* appears to accept both as UK spelling. So, I'll not bother with further investigation. In fact Chambers Dictionary appears to accept *–ize* as a UK alternative to all words spelt with *–ise*. (See Spelling).

-l   English often doubles the *l*:
annul – *annulled* (UK and US, due to the stress being on the final syllable)
cancel – *cancelled* (UK) – *canceled* (US)
council – *councillor* (UK) – *councilor* (US)
counsel – *counsellor* (UK and US) – *counselor* (US)
model – *modelling* (UK) *modelling* (US)
signal – *signalled* (UK) – *signalled* (US)
travel – *traveller* (UK) – *traveler* (US)
wool – *woollen* (UK) – woolen (US)

But some exceptions may be encountered in both English and American:
enrol – *enrolment* (UK and US) – *enroll* – *enrollment* (US)
fulfil (UK) – *fulfil* (US)
instal – *instalment* (UK) – *install* – *installment* (US)
modelling (UK) – *modelling* (US)
rebel – *rebelled* (UK and US)
skill – *skilful* (UK) – *skillful* (US)
wilful (UK) – *willful* (US)

-ge   American normally drops the *e*:
judge – *judgement* (UK) – *judgment* (UK and US). It adds one in *whiskey* (US).

-ise Modern (UK) English dictionaries now give the –ise and –ize spellings for virtually every word using these affixes. A few retain –ise in both languages (concise, coastwise). Apart from 'capsize' or other words ending in -size, I have not found any more which only use –ize in both languages. Even 'standardize' and 'agonize' may employ –ise.

-ou A few English words using *ou* are found using just *o* in American: *mould* (UK) – *mold* (US)

-ogue historical? The *OED* gives *cataloge* (1460), and *catalogue* (1535). Interesting that the US versions *analog, catalog* are not acceptable in the UK while *analogue, catalogue* are alternatives in the US. There are nevertheless a few words using an English-type spelling such as *theologue* (a student of theology).

-our Virtually all English words ending in *our* use *or* in American: *behaviour – behavior; colour – color; favour – favor; harbour – harbor; honour – honor; labour – labor*

-re Many English words ending in *re* are Americanised in the US: *centre – center; metre – meter.*

-yse Retains the 's' form in UK English. The US form is mostly 'z': UK *analyse* – US *analyze*, and so forth.

There are a number of other words which differ in spelling: *plough* (UK) – *plow* (US), *manoeuvre* (UK) – *maneuver (U*S). *Whilst* is still fairly common in English, although perhaps somewhat antiquated. It does not appear in the *Encarta* (US) *Dictionary*. The (indispensable) Longmans *Language Activator* informs me that *towards* is UK; *toward* is US. Finally, we may find alternative spellings in both languages: *enquire – inquire.*

I have observed that there is a tendency in US English to allow compound words more so than in UK English, e.g. *proofreader*[2] (US), *proof reader* (UK); *socio-economic* (US), *socio-economic* (UK). But there is no doubt that US practice is rapidly being adopted into UK English.

A useful summary of English and American terminology is to be found in Bickerton A. (1998) *American English – English American.* Here you will not only be enlightened about such things as a UK *banknote* is called a *bill* in the US, and whereas the English say *loo, toilet*, or *WC*, the Americans – in all their modesty – say *bathroom*, or more colloquially, *john*. In public places in the US the term *restroom* is used. But if you've gotta go, then you've gotta go. It's the same in any language really!

---

2 Word spellchecker hyphenates this: proof-reader.

17
Nations of the World

We meant to change a nation, and instead, we changed a world.
– Ronald Reagan (1911–2004). U.S. motion picture actor and
president.[1]

The following list comprises the official names of the countries of the world
based on information from the Norwegian Foreign Ministry with later
additions. The respective adjectives are shown. The adjectival form also
comprises the noun (person) unless stated: *Afghan*, [*an Afghan*]: *Swedish/a
Swede*. Some countries do not possess an adjectival form and require that the
name of the country is used, for example *New Zealand lamb*. A few
countries do not have a person noun, e.g. *a resident of The Vatican*. One or
two I have not been able to check (emails please).

Nations

AFGHANISTAN: The Islamic State of
Afghanistan – *Afghan*

ALBANIA: The Republic of Albania –
Albanian

ALGERIA: The People's Democratic
Republic of Algeria – *Algerian*

ANDORRA: The Principality of
Andorra – *Andorran*

ANGOLA: The Republic of Angola –
Angolan

ANTIGUA AND BARBUDA: Antigua
and Barbuda – *Antiguan,
Barbudan*

ARGENTINA: The Argentine Republic
– *Argentinean*

ARMENIA: The Republic of Armenia
– *Armenian*

AUSTRALIA: Commonwealth of
Australia – *Australian*

AUSTRIA: The Republic of Austria –
Austrian

AZERBAIJAN: The Azerbaijani
Republic – *Azerbaijani*

BAHAMAS: The Commonwealth of
the Bahamas – *Bahamian*

BAHRAIN: The Kingdom of Bahrain
– *Bahraini*

BANGLADESH: The People's
Republic of Bangladesh –
Bangladeshi

BARBADOS: Barbados – *Barbadian*

BELARUS (WHITE RUSSIA): The
Republic of Belarus –
Belorussian or *Byelorussian*

BELGIUM: The Kingdom of Belgium
– *Belgian*

BELIZE: Belize – *Belizian*

BENIN: The Republic of Benin –

---

1   Microsoft *Encarta Dictionary* (CD ROM version) contains many thousands of quotations,
    including several hundred on nations, nationality and related subjects.

Beninese

BERMUDA: Bermuda – Bermudan

BHUTAN: The Kingdom of Bhutan –
Bhutanese

BOLIVIA: The Republic of Bolivia –
Bolivian

BOSNIA-HERZEGOVINA: Bosnia and
Herzegovina – *Bosnian,
Herzogovinian*

BOTSWANA: The Republic of
Botswana – *Botswanan/
a Tswana*

BRAZIL: The Federative Republic of
Brazil – *Brazilian*

BRUNEI [DARUSSALAM]: Brunei –
Bruneian

BULGARIA: The Republic of Bulgaria
– *Bulgarian*

BURKINA FASO: Burkina Faso.
(Previously Upper Volta) –
Burkinese

BURMA: Union of Burma. See
MYANMAR

BURUNDI: The Republic of Burundi
– *Burundian*

CAMBODIA: The Kingdom of
Cambodia – *Cambodian*

CAMEROON: The Republic of
Cameroon – *Cameroonian*

CANADA: Canada – *Canadian*

CAPE VERDE: The Republic of Cape
Verde – *Cape Verdian*

CENTRAL AFRICAN REPUBLIC: The
Central African Republic –

CHAD: The Republic of Chad –
Chadian

CHILE: The Republic of Chile –
Chilean

CHINA: The People's Republic of
China – *Chinese*

COLOMBIA: The Republic of
Colombia – *Colombian*

COMOROS (The): The Islamic
Federal Republic of the Comoros
–

CONGO: Democratic Republic of the
Congo (The). (Previously Zaïre) –
Congolese

CONGO: The Republic of the Congo
(Formerly Brazzaville) –
Congolese

COSTA RICA: The Republic of Costa
Rica – *Costa Rican*

CROATIA: The Republic of Croatia –
Croatian

CUBA: The Republic of Cuba –
Cuban

CYPRUS: Republic of Cyprus –
Cypriot

CZECH REPUBLIC (The): Czech
Republic (The) – *Czech*

DENMARK: The Kingdom of
Denmark – *Danish/a Dane*

DJIBOUTI: The Republic of Djibouti
– *Djiboutian*

DOMINICA: The Commonwealth of
Dominica – *Dominican*

DOMINICAN REPUBLIC (The):
Dominican Republic (The) –
Dominican

EAST TIMOR: The Democratic
Republic of Timor-Leste –
Timorian

ECUADOR: The Republic of Ecuador
– *Ecuadorian*

EGYPT: The Arab Republic of Egypt
– *Egyptian*

EL SALVADOR: The Republic of El
Salvador – *Salvadorean*

EQUATORIAL GUINEA: The Republic
of Equatorial Guinea –

ERITREA: The State of Eritrea –
Eritrean

ESTONIA: The Republic of Estonia –
Estonian

ETHIOPIA: The Federal Democratic
Republic of Ethiopia – *Ethiopian*

FIJI: The Republic of the Fiji Islands
– *Fijian*

FINLAND: The Republic of Finland –
Finnish/a Finn

FRANCE: The French Republic –
*French/Frenchman,
Frenchwoman*

GABON: The Republic of the Gabon
– *Gabonese*

GAMBIA, THE: Republic of The
Gambia – *Gambian*

GEORGIA: The Republic of Georgia
– *Georgia*

GERMANY: The Federal Republic of
Germany – *German*

GHANA: The Republic of Ghana –
Ghanaian

GREECE: The Hellenic Republic –
Greek

GRENADA: Grenada – *Grenadian*

GUATEMALA: The Republic of
Guatemala – *Guatemalan*

GUINEA: The Republic of Guinea –
Guinean

GUINEA-BISSAU: The Republic of
Guinea-Bissau – *Guinean*

GUYANA: The Co-operative Republic
of Guyana – *Guyanese*

HAITI: The Republic of Haiti –
Haitian

HOLLAND see NETHERLANDS

HONDURAS: The Republic of
Honduras – *Honduran*

HUNGARY: The Republic of Hungary
– *Hungarian*

ICELAND: The Republic of Iceland –
Icelandic/an Icelander

INDIA: The Republic of India –
India

INDONESIA: The Republic of
Indonesia – *Indonesian*

IRAN: The Islamic Republic of Iran –
Iranian

IRAQ: The Republic of Iraq – *Iraqi*

IRELAND: Ireland. (Occ. The Irish
Republic) – *Irish/an Irishman,
Irishwoman*

ISRAEL: The State of Israel – *Israeli*

ITALY: The Italian Republic –
Italian

IVORY COAST (The): The Republic
of Côte d'Ivoire –

JAMAICA: Jamaica – *Jamaican*

JAPAN: Japan – *Japanese*

JORDAN: The Hashemite Kingdom of
Jordan – *Jordanian*

KAZAKHSTAN: The Republic of
Kazakhstan – *Kazakh*

KENYA: The Republic of Kenya –
Kenyan

KIRGISTAN or KYRGYZSTAN: The
Kyrghyz Republic –

KIRIBATI: Republic of Kiribati –

KUWAIT: The State of Kuwait –
Kuwaiti

LAOS: Lao People's Democratic
Republic (The) – *Laotian*

LATVIA: The Republic of Latvia –
Latvian

LEBANON: Lebanon the Lebanese
Republic – *Lebanese*

LESOTHO: The Kingdom of Lesotho
–

LIBERIA: The Republic of Liberia –
Liberian

LIBYA: The Great Socialist People's
Libyan Arab Republic – *Libyan*

LIECHTENSTEIN: The Principality of
Liechtenstein –/a *Liechtensteiner*

LITHUANIA: The Republic of
Lithuania – *Lithuanian*

LUXEMBOURG: The Grand Duchy of
Luxembourg –/a *Luxembourger*

MACEDONIA: The Former Yugoslav
Republic of Macedonia –
Macedonian

MADAGASCAR: The Republic of
Madagascar – *Madagascan* or
Malagasay

MALAWI: The Republic of Malawi –
Malawian

MALAYSIA: Malaysia – *Malaysian*

MALDIVES (The): The Republic of Maldives – *Maldivian*

MALI: The Republic of Mali – *Malian*

MALTA: The Republic of Malta – *Maltese*

MARSHALL ISLANDS (The): The Republic of the Marshall Islands – *Marshallian*

MAURITANIA: The Islamic Republic of Mauritania – *Mauritanian*

MAURITIUS: The Republic of Mauritius – *Mauritian*

MEXICO: The United Mexican States – *Mexican*

MICRONESIA: The Federated States of Micronesia – *Micronesian*

MOLDOVA: Republic of Moldova (The) – *Moldovan*

MONACO: The Principality of Monaco – *Monacan* or *Monégasque*

MONGOLIA: Mongolia – *Mongolian*

MOROCCO: The Kingdom of Morocco – *Moroccan*

MOZAMBIQUE: The Republic of Mozambique – *Mozambican*

MYANMAR: the Union of Myanmar. (Previously Burma) – *(Burmese)*

NAMIBIA: The Republic of Namibia – *Namibian*

NAURU: The Republic of Nauru –

NEPAL: The Kingdom of Nepal – *Nepalese*

NETHERLANDS: The Kingdom of the Netherlands – *Dutch/a Dutchman, Dutchwoman, Netherlander*

NEW ZEALAND: New Zealand –/a *New Zealander*

NICARAGUA: The Republic of Nicaragua – *Nicaraguan*

NIGER: The Republic of the Niger – *Nigerien*

NIGERIA: The Federal Republic of

Nigeria – *Nigerian*

NORTH KOREA: The Democratic People's Republic of Korea – *North Korean*

NORWAY: The Kingdom of Norway – *Norwegian*

OMAN: The Sultanate of Oman – *Omani*

PAKISTAN: The Islamic Republic of Pakistan – *Pakistani*

PALAU: Republic of Palau –

PANAMA: The Republic of Panama – *Panamanian*

PAPUA NEW GUINEA: Independent State of Papua New Guinea – *(Papua New) Guinean*

PARAGUAY: The Republic of Paraguay – *Paraguayan*

PERU: The Republic of Peru – *Peruvian*

PHILIPPINES (The): Republic of The Philippines – *Philippine/ Filipino/a/*

POLAND: The Republic of Poland – *Polish/a Pole*

PORTUGAL: The Portuguese Republic – *Portuguese*

QATAR: The State of Qatar – *Qatari*

RUMANIA: Romania/Rumania – *Romanian* or *Rumanian*

RUSSIA: Russian Federation (The) – *Russian*

RWANDA: The Rwandese Republic – *Rwandan*

SAINT HELENA: Saint Helena –

SAINT KITTS AND NEVIS: The Federation of Saint Kitts and Nevis –

SAINT LUCIA: Saint Lucia –

SAINT VINCENT AND THE GRENADINES: Saint Vincent and the Grenadines –

SAN MARINO: The Republic of San Marino –

SAMOA: Independent State of Samoa

– *Samoan*

SÃO TOMÉ AND PRÍNCIPE: The Democratic Republic of São Tomé and Princípe –

SAUDI ARABIA: The Kingdom of Saudi Arabia – *Saudi Arabian* or *Saudi*

SENEGAL: The Republic of Senegal – *Senegalese*

SERBIA AND MONTENEGRO: Serbia and Montenegro – S*erbian* or *Serb*

SEYCHELLES: The Republic of Seychelles – *Seychellois*

SIERRA LEONE: The Republic of Sierra Leone – *Sierra Leonian*

SINGAPORE: The Republic of Singapore – *Singaporian*

SLOVAKIA: The Slovak Republic – *Slovak* or *Slovakian*

SLOVENIA: The Republic of Slovenia – *Slovenian* or *Slovene*

SOLOMON ISLANDS: Solomon Islands –*/a Solomon Islander*

SOMALIA: Somalia. [Formerly:The Somali Democratic Republic] – *Somalian* or *Somali*

SOUTH AFRICA: The Republic of South Africa – *South African*

SOUTH KOREA: Republic of Korea (The) – *South Korean*

SPAIN: The Kingdom of Spain – *Spanish/a Spaniard*

SRI LANKA: The Democratic Socialist Republic of Sri Lanka – *Sri Lankan*

SUDAN (The): The Republic of the Sudan – *Sudanese*

SURINAME: The Republic of Suriname – *Surinamese/a Surinamese* or *a Surinamer*

SWAZILAND: The Kingdom of Swaziland – *Swazi*

SWEDEN: The Kingdom of Sweden – *Swedish/a Swede*

SWITZERLAND: The Swiss Confederation – *Swiss*

SYRIA: Syrian Arab Republic (The) – *Syrian*

TAJIKISTAN: The Republic of Tajikistan – *Tajik* or *Tadjik*

TANZANIA: United Republic of Tanzania (The) – *Tanzanian*

THAILAND: The Kingdom of Thailand – *Thai*

TOGO: The Republic of Togo – *Togolese*

TONGA: The Kingdom of Tonga – *Tongan*

TRINIDAD AND TOBAGO: The Republic of Trinidad and Tobago – *Trinidadian, Tobagan*

TUNISIA: The Republic of Tunisia – *Tunisian*

TURKEY: The Republic of Turkey – *Turkish/a Turk*

TURKMENISTAN: Turkmenistan – *Turkoman* or *Turkmen*

TURKS AND CAICOS ISLANDS: Turks and Caicos Islands –

TUVALU: Tuvalu – *Tuvaluan*

U.A.E. (The): United Arab Emirates (The) (Formerly Trucial Oman) –

UGANDA: The Republic of Uganda – *Ugandan*

UKRAINE: Ukraine – *Ukrainian*

UNITED ARAB EMIRATES: United Arab Emirates [Formerly Trucial Oman]

UNITED KINGDOM (The): United Kingdom of Great Britain and Northern Ireland (The) –*British/a citizen of* or *a Briton* [slang Brit]

URUGUAY: The Oriental Republic of Uruguay – *Uruguayan*

USA: United States of America (The) – *American*

UZBEKISTAN: The Republic of Uzbekistan – *Uzbek*

VANUATU: The Republic of Vanuatu –

VATICAN (The): Vatican City State (The)/Holy See – *Vatican/a resident of*
VENEZUELA: The Bolivarian Republic of Venezuela – *Venezuelan*
VIETNAM: The Socialist Republic of Viet Nam – *Vitenamese*
WEST-SAMOA: The Independent State of Western Samoa – *(West) Samoan*
WESTERN SAHARA: Western Sahara –
WHITE RUSSIA: The Republic of

Byelorussia – *Byelorussian*
YEMEN (The): The Republic of Yemen – *Yemeni*
YUGOSLAVIA: The Federal Republic of Yugoslavia Serbia and Montenegro – *Yugoslav*
ZAIRE (See Democratic Republic of the CONGO) – *Zaïrean*
ZAMBIA: The Republic of Zambia – *Zambian*
ZIMBABWE: The Republic of Zimbabwe – *Zimbabwean*

The following countries are administered by the nation stated, or have a degree of independence but foreign affairs are administered by the former colonial power. Others may have special administration agreements.

ANGUILLA: Anguilla [British Dependency]
ARUBA: Aruba [Netherlands]
BRITISH VIRGIN ISLANDS: British Virgin Islands [UK]
CAYMAN ISLANDS: Cayman Islands [British Dependency]
CHRISTMAS ISLAND: Territory of Christmas Island [Australia]
COCOS (KEELING) ISLANDS: Territory of Cocos (Keeling) Islands [Australia]
COOK ISLANDS: Cook Islands. [New Zealand]
CORAL SEA ISLANDS. Coral Sea Islands Territory [Australia]
FALKLAND ISLANDS (MALVINAS): Falkland Islands. [UK; Claimed by Argentina]
FRENCH GUIANA: Department of Guiana [France]
FRENCH POLYNESIA: Territory of French Polynesia [France]
GREENLAND: Greenland. [Self-governing; Danish Foreign Affairs]

GUADELOPE: Department of Guadelope [France]
GUAM: Territory of Guam [US]
HONG KONG: Hong Kong Special Administration Region [China]
MACAU: Macau Special Administrative Region [China]
MARTINIQUE: Department of Martinique [France]
MAYOTTE: Territorial Collectivity of Mayotte [France]
NETHERLANDS ANTILLES: Netherlands Antilles [Netherlands]
NEW CALEDONIA: Territory of New Caledonia and Dependencies [France]
NIUE: Niue. [Self-governing; NZ Foreign Affairs]
NORFOLK ISLAND: Territory of Norfolk Island [Australia]
NORTHERN MARIANA ISLANDS: Commonwealth of the Northern Mariana Islands [US]
REUNION: Department of Reunion [France]
SOUTH GEORGIA AND THE SOUTH

SANDWICH ISLANDS: South Georgia and the South Sandwich Islands.

SVALBARD: Svalbard [Erroneously referred to as Spitzbergen] [Norway]

VIRGIN ISLANDS: United States Virgin Islands [US]

WALLIS AND FUTUNA: Territory of the Wallis and Futuna Islands [France]

The following political units of the United Kingdom have their own administrative bodies with defined powers.

GUERNSEY: Bailiwick of Guernsey

ISLE OF MAN: Isle of Man – *Manx*

JERSEY: Bailiwick of Jersey

SCOTLAND: Scotland – *Scottish/a Scot* or *Scotsman, Scotswoman* (not *Scotchman*).

[However, Scotch whisky, a Scotch and soda]

WALES: Wales – *Welsh/a Welshman, Welshwoman*

Useful international information along with excellent maps is given in the *Encarta World Atlas*. But undoubtedly the best reference to countries is the *CIA World Fact Book* which is also kept up-to-date. You will find this on www.cia.gov/cia This contains information on individual countries including conventional and local names (Finland – *Suomi*), former names (e.g. Cambodia – *Khmer Republic*) and abbreviations where applicable. Occasional notes are included where country names are not unilaterally recognised such as Myanmar (Burma). A number of regions and islands enjoying a degree of self-autonomy or under special administration are also included such as Guam, Johnston Atoll, Kingman Reef and others. While the Gaza Strip is mentioned, Kurdistan is not. This data base is updated regularly and contains full information on the population, economy, health (incl. HIV/AIDS) etc.

CIS (USSR)

The former Soviet Union (USSR) comprised 15 republics and ceased to exist in 1991. Twelve Autonomous Soviet Socialist Republics (ASSR) along with Russia (Socialist Federal Soviet Republic, SFSR), subsequently agreed to form the Commonwealth of Independent States (CIS).

The abbreviation FSU is frequently used for *Former Soviet Union*. However, it should be noted that the Baltic states (Estonia, Latvia and Lithuania) did not become members of the CIS and in official documents it is not politically correct to refer to these as FSU countries. The term *Baltic states* should be used.

Membership states (Soviet Socialist Republics – SSR) in The Commonwealth of Independent States (CIS)

Armenia	Kazakhstan	Turkmenistan
Azerbaijan	Kyrgyzstan	Ukraine
Belarus	Moldova	Uzbekistan
Georgia	Tajikistan	

Autonomous Soviet Socialist Republics (ASSR) by SSR.

Russia (SFSR)
Bashkiriya, (Bashkir ASSR)
Buryatiya, (Buryat ASSR)
Checheno-Ingushetiya, (Chechen-
  Ingush ASSR)
Chuvashiya, (Chuvash ASSR)
Dagestan, (Dagestan ASSR)
Kabardino-Balkariya, (Kabardino-
  Balkar ASSR)
Kalmykiya, (Kalmyk ASSR)
Karelia, (Karelian ASSR)
Komi, (Komi ASSR)
Mari, (Mari ASSR)
Mordoviya, (Mordvinian ASSR)

Severnaya Ossetiya, (Severo-Ossetian
  ASSR)
Tatarstan, (Tatar ASSR)
Tuva, (Tuvinian ASSR)
Udmurtiya, (Udmurt ASSR)
Yakutiya, (Yakut ASSR)
Georgia SSR
Abkhaziya, (Abkhaz ASSR)
Adzhariya, (Adzhar ASSR)
Azerbaijan SSR
Nakhichevan, (Nakhichevan ASSR)
Uzbek SSR
Karakalpakiya, (Karakalpak ASSR)

The USA

The United States of America comprise 54 States. The two-letter postal abbreviations are also encountered in a variety of circumstances and are given here.

State	Postal code	State	Postal code
Alabama	AL	Hawaii	HI
Alaska	AK	Idaho	ID
Arizona	AZ	Illinois	IL
Arkansas	AR	Indiana	IN
California	CA	Iowa	IA
Colorado	CO	Kansas	KS
Connecticut	CT	Kentucky	KY
Delaware	DE	Louisiana	LA
District of Columbia	DC	Maine	ME
Florida	FL	Maryland	MD
Georgia	GA	Massachusetts	MA
Guam	GU	Michigan	MI

State	Postal code	State	Postal code
Minnesota	MN	Pennsylvania	PA
Mississippi	MS	Puerto Rico	PR
Missouri	MO	Rhode Island	RI
Montana	MT	South Carolina	SC
Nebraska	NE	South Dakota	SD
Nevada	NV	Tennessee	TN
New Hampshire	NH	Texas	TX
New Jersey	NJ	Utah	UT
New Mexico	NM	Vermont	VT
New York	NY	Virgin Islands	VI
North Carolina	NC	Virginia	VA
North Dakota	ND	Washington	WA
Ohio	OH	West Virginia	WV
Oklahoma	OK	Wisconsin	WI
Oregon	OR	Wyoming	WY

The European union

The European Union (EU) has 27 members. Distribution of the 344 votes (based on population) in the European Economic and Social Committee (EESC) is given. 'S' indicates signatory to the Schengen treaty.

Austria	12	S	Latvia	7	
Belgium	12	S	Lithuania	9	
Bulgaria	12		Luxembourg	6	S
Cyprus	6		Malta	5	
Czech Republic	12		Netherlands	12	S
Denmark	9	S	Poland	21	S
Estonia	7		Portugal	12	
Finland	9	S	Rumania	15	
France	24	S	Slovakia	9	
Germany	24	S	Slovenia	7	
Greece	12	S	Spain	21	S
Hungary	12		Sweden	12	S
Ireland	9		United Kingdom	24	
Italy	24	S			

EFTA members

Iceland	S	Norway	S
Liechtenstein		Switzerland	

All EFTA members, except Switzerland, entered into an agreement with the European Economic Area (EEA) in 1992.

Useful websites

www.europa.eu.int   www.efta.int   www.eurovisa.info

G7/G8

1975 (G6)	*1976* (G7)	*2002* (G8)
France	Canada	Russia
The United States		
Britain		
Germany		
Japan		
Italy		

The G7 has met with Russia since 1994, referred to as P8 (Political 8).

G20

... an informal body in which both industrialised and emerging economies could engage in and develop an open dialogue in a spirit of mutual trust. The G20 was called into being on 15/16 December 1999 in Berlin. Its member countries represent two-thirds of the world's population and generate over 90 per cent of the global gross national product. In short, the G20 is the response of the international community of nations to globalisation.

The members of the G20 are the finance ministers and central bank governors of 19 countries:

Argentina	India	Saudi-Arabia
Australia	Indonesia	South Africa
Brazil	Italy	Turkey
Canada	Japan	United Kingdom
China	Korea	United States
France	Mexico	
Germany	Russia	

Another member is the European Union, represented by the Council presidency and the President of the European Central Bank. The managing director of the IMF and the president of the World Bank, plus the chairpersons of the International Monetary and Financial Committee and Development Committee of the IMF and World Bank, also participate in the talks as ex-officio members.

G77

The Group of 77 (G77) was established on 5 June 1964 by seventy-seven developing countries signatories of the 'Joint Declaration of the Seventy-Seven Countries' issued at the end of the first session of the United Nations Conference on Trade and Development (UNCTAD) in Geneva. Beginning with the first Ministerial Meeting of the Group of 77 in Algiers in 1967 which adopted the Charter of Algiers, a permanent institutional structure gradually developed which led to the creation of Chapters of the Group of 77 in Rome (FAO), Vienna (UNIDO), Paris (UNESCO), Nairobi (UNEP) and the Group of 4 in Washington, D.C. (IMF and World Bank). Although the membership of the G77 has increased to countries, the original name was retained because of its historic significance.

Argentina
Bahamas
Bahrain
Bangladesh
Barbados
Belize
Benin
Bhutan
Bolivia
Bosnia and Herzegovina
Botswana
Brazil
Brunei Darussalam
Burkina Faso
Burundi
Cambodia
Cameroon
Cape Verde
Central African
   Republic
Chad
Chile
China
Colombia
Comoros
Congo
Costa Rica
Côte d'Ivoire
Cuba
Democratic People's
   Republic of Korea

Democratic Republic of
   the Congo
Djibouti
Dominica
Dominican Republic
Ecuador
Egypt
El Salvador
Equatorial Guinea
Eritrea
Ethiopia
Fiji
Gabon
Gambia
Ghana
Grenada
Guatemala
Guinea
Guinea-Bissau
Guyana
Haiti
Honduras
India
Indonesia
Iran (Islamic Republic
   of)
Iraq
Jamaica
Jordan
Kenya
Kuwait

Lao People's
   Democratic
   Republic
Lebanon
Lesotho
Liberia
Libyan Arab Jamahiriya
Madagascar
Malawi
Malaysia
Maldives
Mali
Marshall Islands
Mauritania
Mauritius
Micronesia (Federated
   States of)
Mongolia
Morocco
Mozambique
Myanmar
Namibia
Nepal
Nicaragua
Niger
Nigeria
Oman
Pakistan
Palau
Palestine
Panama

Papua New Guinea
Paraguay
Peru
Philippines
Qatar
Romania
Rwanda
Saint Kitts and Nevis
Saint Lucia
Saint Vincent and the
    Grenadines
Samoa
São Tomé and Príncipe
Saudi Arabia
Senegal
Seychelles

Sierra Leone
Singapore
Solomon Islands
Somalia
South Africa
Sri Lanka
Sudan
Suriname
Swaziland
Syrian Arab Republic
Thailand
Timor-Leste
Togo
Tonga
Trinidad and Tobago
Tunisia

Turkmenistan
Uganda
United Arab Emirates
United Republic of
    Tanzania
Uruguay
Vanuatu
Venezuela
Viet Nam
Yemen
Zambia
Zimbabwe

The Commonwealth

Antigua and Barbuda
Australia
Bangladesh
Barbados
Belize
Botswana
Brunei
Cameroon
Canada
Cyprus
Darussalam
Dominica
Fiji Islands
Ghana
Grenada
Guyana
India
Jamaica
Kenya

Kiribati
Lesotho
Malawi
Malaysia
Maldives
Malta
Mauritius
Mozambique
Namibia
Nauru
New Guinea
New Zealand
Nigeria
Pakistan
Papua
Samoa
Seychelles
Sierra Leone
Singapore

Solomon Islands
South Africa
Sri Lanka
St Kitts and Nevis
St Lucia
St Vincent and the
    Grenadines
Swaziland
The Bahamas
The Gambia
Tonga
Trinidad and Tobago
Tuvalu
Uganda
United Kingdom
United Republic of
    Tanzania
Vanuatu
Zambia

The Organisation of American States (OAS)

Antigua and Barbuda
Argentina

The Bahamas
Barbados

Belize
Bolivia

Brazil
Canada
Chile
Colombia
Costa Rica
Cuba (*)
Dominica
Dominican Republic
Ecuador
El Salvador
Grenada

Guatemala
Guyana
Haiti
Honduras
Jamaica
Mexico
Nicaragua
Panama
Paraguay
Peru
Saint Kitts and Nevis

Saint Lucia
Saint Vincent and the
   Grenadines
Suriname
Trinidad and Tobago
United States of
   America
Uruguay
Venezuela

* Cuba has been excluded since 1962.
Useful website: www.oas.org

The Organisation of African Unity (OAU)

The OAU was dissolved on 25. May 1998 and replaced by the African Union
(see below)

The People's Democratic Republic of
   Algeria
The People's Republic of Angola
The Republic of Benin
The Republic of Botswana
The Republic of Burkina Faso
The Republic of Burundi
The Republic of Cameroon
The Republic of Cape Verde
The Central African Republic
The Federal Islamic Republic of the
   Comoros
The People's Republic of the Congo
The Republic of Côte d'Ivoire
The Republic of Djibouti
The Arab Republic of Egypt
The People's Democratic Republic of
   Ethiopia
The Republic of Equatorial Guinea
The Republic of Gabon
The Republic of the Gambia
The Republic of Ghana
The Republic of Guinea
The Republic of Guinea Bissau

The Republic of Kenya
The Kingdom of Lesotho
The Republic of Liberia
The Great Socialist People's Libyan
   Arab Jamahiriya (Libya)
The Republic of Madagascar
The Republic of Malawi
The Republic of Mali
The Islamic Republic of Mauritania
The Republic of Mauritius
The Republic of Mozambique
The Republic of Namibia
The Republic of Niger
The Federal Republic of Nigeria
The Republic of Rwanda
The Saharawi Democratic Arab
   Republic
The Republic of São Tomé and
   Príncipe
The Republic of Senegal
The Republic of the Seychelles
The Republic of Sierra Leone
The Republic of Somalia
The Republic of the Sudan

The Kingdom of Swaziland
The United Republic of Tanzania
The Republic of Tchad
The Republic of Togo
The Republic of Tunisia

The Republic of Uganda
The Republic of Zaire
The Republic of Zambia
The Republic of Zimbabwe

Useful website: http://www.itcilo.it/actrav/actrav-english/telearn/global/ilo/law/
oau.htm, but you will find this by searching OAU and clicking the site
marked *Organization of African Unity*. (There is another site, *Organization
of African Unity – OAU*, but this is less informative.)

The African Union (AU)

(Replaced the OAU on 25. May 1998)

The following OAU members are not in the AU: The Republic of Guinea (see
below), The Republic of Zaïre (now Congo).

The following members of the AU were not members of the OAU: The
Democratic Republic of the Congo (Previously Zaïre), The Republic of the
Congo (Formerly Brazzaville), The Republic of Guinea (now Guinea-Conakry),
The Republic of South Africa.

Useful website: www.africa-union.org

The New African Partnership for Africa's Development (NEPAD)

The People's Democratic Republic of
   Algeria
The People's Republic of Angola
The Republic of Cameroon
The Democratic Republic of the
   Congo
The Arab Republic of Egypt
The Federal Republic of Ethiopia
The Republic of Gabon
The Republic of Ghana
Useful website: www.nepad.org

The Republic of Kenya
The Socialist People's Libyan Arab
   Jamahiriya
The Republic of Mali
The Islamic Republic of Mauritania
The Republic of Mozambique
The Federal Republic of Nigeria
The Republic of Rwanda
The Republic of Senegal
The Republic of South Africa

Other African organisations

UDEAC	The Central African Customs and Economic Union (1981)
ECCAS	Economic Community of Central African States. An expansion of the above (1983) to include the following:

CEPGL	Economic Community of the Great Lakes States (Burundi, Rwanda, Zaïre) plus São Tomé and Príncipe.
COPAX	Council for Peace and Security in Central Africa (1999)
AEC	The African Economic Community (inactive)
ECOWAS	Economic Community of West African States
COMESA	Common Market for Eastern and Southern Africa
SADC	Southern African Development Community
AMU	Arab Maghreb Union

Organisation of Islamic conferences

Islamic State of Afghanistan 1969
Republic of Albania 1992
People's Democratic Republic of Algeria 1969
Republic of Azerbaijan 1992
Kingdom of Bahrain 1972
People's Republic of Bangladesh 1974
Republic of Benin 1983
Brunei-Darussalam 1984
Burkina-Faso (then Upper Volta) 1974
Republic of Cameroon 1974
Republic of Chad 1969
Union of Comoros 1976
Republic of Djibouti 1978
Arab Republic of Egypt 1969
Republic of Gabon 1974
Republic of The Gambia 1974
Republic of Guinea 1969
Republic of Guinea-Bissau 1974
Republic of Guyana 1998
Republic of Indonesia 1969
Islamic Republic of Iran 1969
Republic of Iraq 1975
Hashemite Kingdom of Jordan 1969
Republic of Kazakhstan 1995
State of Kuwait 1969
Kyrghyz Republic 1992
Republic of Lebanon 1969
Socialist People's Libyan Arab Jamahiriya 1969

Malaysia 1969
Republic of Maldives 1976
Republic of Mali 1969
Islamic Republic of Mauritania 1969
Kingdom of Morocco 1969
Republic of Mozambique 1994
Republic of Niger 1969
Federal Republic of Nigeria 1986
Sultanate of Oman 1972
Islamic Republic of Pakistan 1969
State of Palestine 1969
State of Qatar 1972
Kingdom of Saudi Arabia 1969
Republic of Senegal 1969
Republic of Sierra Leone 1972
Republic of Somalia 1969
Republic of Sudan 1969
Republic of Suriname 1996
Syrian Arab Republic 1972
Republic of Tajikistan 1992
Republic of Togo 1997
Republic of Tunisia 1969
Republic of Turkey 1969
Turkmenistan 1992
Republic of Uganda 1974
State of The United Arab Emirates 1972
Republic of Uzbekistan 1996
Republic of Yemen 1969
Republic of Côte d'Ivoire 2001

The Caribbean Community – Caricom

CARICOM member states

Antigua and Barbuda	Jamaica
The Bahamas	Montserrat
Barbados	Saint Lucia
Belize	St. Kitts and Nevis
Dominica	St. Vincent and the Grenadines
Grenada	Suriname
Guyana	Trinidad and Tobago
Haiti	

Associate Members

Anguilla	Cayman Islands
Bermuda	Turks and Caicos Islands
British Virgin Islands	

ASEAN - The Association of South East Asian Countries

Brunei Darussalam	Philippines
Indonesia	Singapore
Malaysia	Thailand

NATO – The North Atlantic Treaty Organisation

Year of accession in parentheses, otherwise from the foundation in 1949.

Belgium	Hungary (1999)	Poland (1999)
Bulgaria (2004)	Iceland	Portugal
Canada	Italy	Romania (2004)
Czech Republic (1999)	Latvia (2004)	Slovakia (2004)
Denmark	Lithuania (2004)	Slovenia (2004)
Estonia (2004)	Lithuania (2004)	Spain (1982)
France	Luxembourg	Turkey (1952)
Germany (1955)	Netherlands	United Kingdom
Greece (1952)	Norway	United States

Greece and Turkey joined the organisation in February 1952. Germany joined as West Germany in 1955 and German unification in 1990 extended the membership to the areas of former East Germany. Spain was admitted on May 30 1982 and the former Warsaw Pact Countries of Poland, Hungary and the Czech Republic made history by becoming members on March 12 1999.

France is still a member of NATO but retired from the military command in 1966. Iceland, the sole member of NATO which does not have its own military force, joined on the condition that they would not be expected to establish one. Slovenia and the former Warsaw Pact countries of Bulgaria, Estonia, Latvia, Lithuania, Romania and Slovakia officially acceded to NATO on 29 March 2004.

The Euro-Atlantic Partnership Council (EAPC)

The EAPC was set up in 1997 to succeed the North Atlantic Cooperation Council.

Albania	Greece	Russia
Armenia	Hungary	Slovakia
Austria	Iceland	Slovenia
Azerbaijan	Ireland	Spain
Belarus	Italy	Sweden
Belgium	Kazakhstan	Switzerland
Bulgaria	Kyrgyz Republic	Tajikistan
Canada	Latvia	The former Yugoslav
Croatia	Lithuania	Republic of
Czech Republic	Luxembourg	Macedonia
Denmark	Moldova	Turkey
Estonia	Netherlands	Turkmenistan
Finland	Norway	Ukraine
France	Poland	United Kingdom
Georgia	Portugal	United States
Germany	Romania	Uzbekistan

The Warsaw Pact

Treaty of Friendship, Co-operation and Mutual Assistance of May 1 1955 between:

The People's Republic of Albania
The People's Republic of Bulgaria
The Hungarian People's Republic
The German Democratic Republic
The Polish People's Republic

The Rumanian People's Republic
The Union of Soviet Socialist
   Republics
The Czechoslovak Republic

Kyoto

A full list of signatories to the Kyoto Agreement is given on:
www.unfccc.int/resource/kpstats.pdf

The World Trade Organisation (WTO)

Country and date of membership

Albania 8 September 2000
Angola 23 November 1996
Antigua and Barbuda 1 January 1995
Argentina 1 January 1995
Armenia 5 February 2003
Australia 1 January 1995
Austria 1 January 1995
Bahrain, Kingdom of 1 January 1995
Bangladesh 1 January 1995
Barbados 1 January 1995
Belgium 1 January 1995
Belize 1 January 1995
Benin 22 February 1996
Bolivia 12 September 1995
Botswana 31 May 1995
Brazil 1 January 1995
Brunei Darussalam 1 January 1995
Bulgaria 1 December 1996
Burkina Faso 3 June 1995
Burundi 23 July 1995
Cameroon 13 December 1995
Canada 1 January 1995
Central African Republic 31 May 1995
Chad 19 October 1996
Chile 1 January 1995
China 11 December 2001
Colombia 30 April 1995
Congo 27 March 1997
Costa Rica 1 January 1995
Côte d'Ivoire 1 January 1995
Croatia 30 November 2000
Cuba 20 April 1995
Cyprus 30 July 1995
Czech Republic 1 January 1995
Democratic Republic of the Congo
    1 January 1997
Denmark 1 January 1995
Djibouti 31 May 1995
Dominica 1 January 1995
Dominican Republic 9 March 1995
Ecuador 21 January 1996

Egypt 30 June 1995
El Salvador 7 May 1995
Estonia 13 November 1999
European Communities 1 January
    1995
Fiji 14 January 1996
Finland 1 January 1995
Former Yugoslav Republic of
    Macedonia (FYROM) 4 April 2003
France 1 January 1995
Gabon 1 January 1995
The Gambia 23 October 1996
Georgia 14 June 2000
Germany 1 January 1995
Ghana 1 January 1995
Greece 1 January 1995
Grenada 22 February 1996
Guatemala 21 July 1995
Guinea 25 October 1995
Guinea Bissau 31 May 1995
Guyana 1 January 1995
Haiti 30 January 1996
Honduras 1 January 1995
Hong Kong, China 1 January 1995
Hungary 1 January 1995
Iceland 1 January 1995
India 1 January 1995
Indonesia 1 January 1995
Ireland 1 January 1995
Israel 21 April 1995
Italy 1 January 1995
Jamaica 9 March 1995
Japan 1 January 1995
Jordan 11 April 2000
Kenya 1 January 1995
Korea, Republic of 1 January 1995
Kuwait 1 January 1995
Kyrgyz Republic 20 December 1998
Latvia 10 February 1999
Lesotho 31 May 1995
Liechtenstein 1 September 1995

Lithuania 31 May 2001
Luxembourg 1 January 1995
Macao, China 1 January 1995
Madagascar 17 November 1995
Malawi 31 May 1995
Malaysia 1 January 1995
Maldives 31 May 1995
Mali 31 May 1995
Malta 1 January 1995
Mauritania 31 May 1995
Mauritius 1 January 1995
Mexico 1 January 1995
Moldova 26 July 2001
Mongolia 29 January 1997
Morocco 1 January 1995
Mozambique 26 August 1995
Myanmar 1 January 1995
Namibia 1 January 1995
Nepal 23 April 2004
Netherlands – For the Kingdom in
    Europe and for the Netherlands
    Antilles
1 January 1995
New Zealand 1 January 1995
Nicaragua 3 September 1995
Niger 13 December 1996
Nigeria 1 January 1995
Norway 1 January 1995
Oman 9 November 2000
Pakistan 1 January 1995
Panama 6 September 1997
Papua New Guinea 9 June 1996
Paraguay 1 January 1995
Peru 1 January 1995
Philippines 1 January 1995
Poland 1 July 1995
Portugal 1 January 1995
Qatar 13 January 1996

Romania 1 January 1995
Russia (planned) 2004
Rwanda 22 May 1996
Saint Kitts and Nevis 21 February
    1996
Saint Lucia 1 January 1995
Saint Vincent & the Grenadines 1
    January 1995
Senegal 1 January 1995
Sierra Leone 23 July 1995
Singapore 1 January 1995
Slovak Republic 1 January 1995
Slovenia 30 July 1995
Solomon Islands 26 July 1996
South Africa 1 January 1995
Spain 1 January 1995
Sri Lanka 1 January 1995
Suriname 1 January 1995
Swaziland 1 January 1995
Sweden 1 January 1995
Switzerland 1 July 1995
Chinese Taipei 1 January 2002
Tanzania 1 January 1995
Thailand 1 January 1995
Togo 31 May 1995
Trinidad and Tobago 1 March 1995
Tunisia 29 March 1995
Turkey 26 March 1995
Uganda 1 January 1995
United Arab Emirates 10 April 1996
United Kingdom 1 January 1995
United States of America 1 January
    1995
Uruguay 1 January 1995
Venezuela 1 January 1995
Zambia 1 January 1995
Zimbabwe 5 March 1995

Observer governments
Algeria
Andorra
Azerbaijan
Bahamas

Belarus
Bhutan
Bosnia and Herzegovina
Cambodia
Cape Verde

367

Equatorial Guinea
Ethiopia
Holy See (Vatican)
Iraq
Kazakhstan
Lao People's Dem. Republic
Lebanese Republic
Russian Federation
Samoa
São Tomé and Príncipe
Saudi Arabia

Serbia and Montenegro
Seychelles
Sudan
Tajikistan
Tonga
Ukraine
Uzbekistan
Vanuatu
Viet Nam
Yemen

Note: With the exception of the Holy See, observers must start accession negotiations within five years of becoming observers.

International organisations observers to the General Council:

(Observers in other councils and committees differ)
United Nations (UN)
United Nations Conference on Trade and Development (UNCTAD)
International Monetary Fund (IMF)
World Bank
Food and Agricultural Organisation (FAO)
World Intellectual Property Organisation (WIPO)
Organisation for Economic Co-operation and Development (OECD)

The Organisation of Petroleum Exporting Countries (OPEC)

The current Members are Algeria, Indonesia, Iran, Iraq, Kuwait, Libya, Nigeria, Qatar, Saudi Arabia, the United Arab Emirates and Venezuela.

Other

A distinction is made between Great Britain (or Britain) (England, Scotland and Wales) and The United Kingdom (England, Scotland, Wales and Northern Ireland, but excluding the Channel Islands and the Isle of Man). The British Isles includes Britain and the whole of Ireland (Northern Ireland and Eire). The Scandinavian peninsula comprises Norway and Sweden; Scandinavia usually refers to Norway, Sweden and Denmark, but will frequently include Finland, Iceland and occasionally The Færoe islands. Dictionaries vary in their definitions. Your text should make it clear what you mean by 'Scandinavia'. The Nordic countries (occasionally referred to as Norden) comprise Norway, Sweden, Denmark, Finland and Iceland and are closely linked through the Nordic Council of Ministers.

18
Word – Some Practical Tips

To err is human but to really foul things up requires a computer. –
Anon.

There are a number of so-called 'bibles' available in bookshops each with
hundreds, if not thousands, of tips both on how not to foul it up and what
to do once it is. This chapter is not so much on what to do after you receive
the Doomsday report: 'Your file has been destroyed. It is not recoverable'
(Norton Utilities often reveals this to be a fallacy), it is a guide to many of
those things you probably want to know and feel that you ought to know.

Undoubtedly the best tips are available on the Internet, but the Internet is
often a last resort – we normally want to know something here and now! I
don't pretend that this chapter will answer every immediate need, but
judging from the questions I receive from my clients the following will
certainly assist with some of the most useful procedures required for
designing and working with your manuscript.

This chapter is essentially a set of hands-on exercises aimed at assisting you
with some of the essentials in editing, structuring and organising your file.
The Word Help feature contains summaries of several of the following, but it
is difficult to look at the Help menu and carry out exercises simultaneously.
Of course, one of the standard handbooks may be useful, but I find that I
have to wade through thirty pages relating to indexes, section breaks and so
forth, just to clarify a simple point. Hence this chapter. There is nothing
worse than reading about Ctrl + Shift and other keystrokes, but five minutes'
hands-on for each section will save you hours – every week. And before we
begin, Alt + F means hold the Alt key and then hit the F key (do not type the
+). Click = click left mouse unless otherwise stated. If it didn't work, then
double-click probably will.

One other point. This chapter was written at the time when Word 2000 was
standard. Recently (in 2004), Word 2003 has begun to make a small impact.
The fact that it is apparently a year late may well be due to the fact that
none of us like paying out several hundred dollars, pounds or Euros for a
new version of a program every couple of years or so. In fact some of my
clients still use Word 97 as of Anno Domini 2004. Where appropriate I have

included a few comments on Word 2003, otherwise it is so similar to Word 2000 that I question its value to the general user and the value for money.[1]

The Monitor Display

MS Word. The top frame shows the file name and the Application buttons on the right (Restore, minimize, close). Below this is the Menu bar (File, Edit...). Right click on this and you will see the toolbars which are open and those which are available by clicking the name. Normally you will have the Standard toolbar and the Formatting toolbar. It is useful to have the ruler showing below these. This shows you where your tabs are located. Click on this rule and you can locate a new tab (L). These may be moved by click-holding-slide to new position. Right click to remove these.

At the bottom of the screen we have the View buttons, the Status bar (showing page, section, etc), and open files on the bottom frame. We click on these to change between files. Incidentally, the Page is the actual number of the page, not the sequence number of the sides. If you have three pages commencing with Roman numerals before the main text, using the command Print Page 10 will print the tenth page in the file, not page number 10.

Shortcuts and Screen Tips

First of all, you may find it useful to be able to view the shortcut keystrokes when we place the cursor on an icon on a toolbar. Placing this on the Printer icon will show the shortcut Ctrl + P. But not all procedures have an icon, or it might be 'hidden' if you have chosen to have the standard and formatting toolbars on the same line, for instance. Tip: if these shortcut keystrokes do not appear when pointing to an icon, go to Tools – Customize – Options. Check the 'Show ScreenTips on Toolbars' and 'Show shortcut keys in ScreenTips'.

There are several dozen shortcuts in Word using the Ctrl, Shift and Alt keys in various combinations together with other keys, e.g. Ctrl + Shift + Z (clear formatting). Tips for Shortcut Keys: you may print out a list of shortcut keys – very useful when selecting combinations of Ctrl, Alt and Shift with any other key, including the F-keys, for your own shortcuts or macros. Do this with the following: Tools – point to Macro – Click Macros. In the Macro name box type Listcommands (one word). Click run. Your will now see 'Create a new document' which lists current menu and keyboard settings.

---

1 Having said that, MS Office 2003 contains Microsoft Picture Manager, one of the best picture editors on the market in my opinion.

Click OK. Here is your file. Save it and print it if you want. But you will find it necessary to sort it. Use: Table – Sort – Modifiers – Then by Key. All the Alt, Ctrl and Shift keys now come at the end of the table. Highlight this part and print if you want to save paper.

But this list is a gem for revealing all the shortcuts we never knew existed but always wanted to use. Using Microsoft Help enter then search keyword 'shortcut'. You will then see 'Print a list of shortcut keys'. Click this and there on the screen you have the instructions. Tip – print out this page with Ctrl + P. Following the instructions will result in a table of almost 40 pages. We don't want all these as most do not contain shortcut keys. Incidentally, if you have defined some shortcut keys these will be given in the list as well.

My advice is to highlight the column headed 'Modifier' (i.e. Ctrl key etc.). Click and drag to the bottom of the table, then drag it to the right to highlight the 'Key' column as well. In the Menu bar: Table – Sort – By Modifier – Then by Keys. Now go down to the top line to the first entry in the Key column. This is actually Del. The Modifier columns is blank. Highlight the table beginning on this line and drag to the bottom. Click on the Copy icon in the Menu Bar; click on the New document Icon; click the Paste icon. You now have a file showing all the shortcut keys. Save it! If you highlight the entire table with Ctrl + A, you may now reset the font to 9 pt. and the whole table will fit onto 6 pages. Confused? I warned you this was a hands-on chapter. Perhaps I forgot to say that you need an IQ of 155 to comprehend it.

Continuing, the left-hand column shows the Command name. You may want to make a file with these in alphabetic order rather than according to the Modifier. Just click and drag to highlight this column, then sort by column 1.

Here are some of the most useful shortcuts – and I bet you didn't know more than half of them.

Moving around the text

Ctrl →	moves the cursor forward one word.
Ctrl ←	moves the cursor back one word.
Ctrl ↑	moves the cursor to the first word in the previous paragraph or heading.
Ctrl ↓	moves the cursor to the first word in the next paragraph or heading.
Ctrl + Home	moves the cursor to the top of the file.
Ctrl + End	moves the cursor to the end of the file.
Ctrl + PgUp	moves the cursor to the top of the previous page. However, if the previous Browse (GoTo) command was to go to the Previous table, then this will go to the previous table.

Ctrl + L left justifies text; Ctrl + R right justifies, Ctrl + E centres text (useful for titles); Ctrl + J fully justifies text. Applies to text as from cursor position or for highlighted text. Note that full justification may make the text 'airy'. Appearance may be improved using the hyphenation feature (Tools–Language–Hyphenation). But you might not always like the hyphenation!

Ctrl + PgDn   moves the cursor to the top of the next page. See note above.

F5 (or Ctrl + G)   invokes the GoTo [Page, Footnote, etc.] menu.

Moving the text

I cannot find this documented, but Alt + Shift is useful for moving paragraphs. Place the cursor anywhere in the paragraph to be moved. Hold Alt + Shift and then press the up or down arrow. This will then highlight the paragraph and relocate it one paragraph up or down. Repeat this to relocate the paragraph further up or down.

Repeating the last command

F4 repeats the last command, whether this was deleting a word, inserting character, etc.

Drop-down menus

Click on the Menu bar (File, Edit etc.) rather than Alt + F, Alt + V etc. Clicking twice will give the full menu.

Line spacing

Did you know that Ctrl + 1 gave single-line spacing; Ctrl + 2, double-line spacing; Ctl + 5, 1.5 lines spacing? Well, you know now.

Marking and Editing the Text

Ctrl + A marks (highlights) the entire text. Ctrl + click will highlight the sentence; double click twice to highlight a word; three clicks to highlight the paragraph. To highlight several words, paragraphs or pages, place the cursor on the first word and use left click and drag, alternatively Ctrl + Shift and the appropriate arrow, (up or down). Note that if you hold Ctrl and drag using the left mouse beyond the bottom of the page, the text will 'run away' over the page when highlighting so you will have to use Ctrl + Shift and the down arrow.

Alternatively use F8; click this key twice to highlight the word; click once more to highlight the sentence; once again for the paragraph; and yet again the entire text (better to use Ctrl + A for this last feature). Esc then (left) click to cancel highlighting when using F8.

Deleting text

Delete the highlighted text using the Del key.

Typing a text when a word or paragraph is highlighted will automatically delete the highlighted text replacing with the new text.

Copying text

Copy the highlighted text with Ctrl + C; move the cursor to a new place and insert the copied text with Ctrl + V. Ctrl + X will cut the highlighted text. It may be pasted using Ctrl + V. You may find clicking the copy and paste icons easier. The copy command also works if you are transferring text to another file as the copied text is stored in the clipboard.

Using Ctrl + X will only paste the last item copied using Ctrl + C. But the clipboard can contain the last 12 items copied. Right click the menu bar at the top and then click 'Clipboard'. This will reveal how many items are stored on the clipboard. These are in 'historical' order. Click on the icon required. Unfortunately you can't see the contents until you have pasted, but if it is the wrong item just click the undo arrow on the top menu bar (or Ctrl + Z) to remove it.

Ctrl + S. Saves the file. Do this regularly.

Ctrl + B gives **Boldface**; Ctrl + I gives *Italics*; Ctrl + U gives underlining. Applies from the cursor location or to highlighted text. Pressing these again halts the action. These may be used in ___combination___. These are toggle switches, meaning that entering the keystroke again will switch off the feature.

Shift + F5. Returns to last edit point, for example following a paste. The last three edit locations may be found. This also hops between files if the previous edit was in another file which is still active. Incidentally, this also works when opening up a file in a new session enabling you to return to the last entry or correction made during the previous session.

Moving paragraphs

If you highlight a paragraph you may move this to go in front of the previous paragraph or to follow the next one. Handy when editing. Highlight the paragraph, then hold Alt + Shift and use the up or down arrows.

Undoing changes

The curly arrows in the Standard menu bar enable you to undo and re-do the last changes. Alternatively use Ctrl + Z and Ctrl + Y respectively.

Search, search and replace

Ctrl + F, then type in the text to be found, or Highlight the word and Ctrl + F. Case-specific searches may be indicated. Press the 'More' button, check the 'Match case' box. Search and replace with Ctrl + H also offers case-specific searches and case-specific replacements.

Fonts

You may select the fonts from the font and style windows in the Formatting toolbar, but macros may simplify this task if you are using a variety of fonts. Other font features such as superscript, subscript and small capitals may be obtained from the using Format – Font on the Menu bar. Even here a macro saves time (see below). There are a couple of useful shortcuts if you are writing simple formulas, for example. If you want to superscript a number, word or phrase, type this as normal then highlight, Now, use Ctrl + + [Hold Ctrl and hit +]. Repeat this to cancel. Similarly Ctrl + Shift + = gives a subscript. Useful when writing fractions such as $^9/_{16}$.

The 4D mouse

The mouse with a roller button is the easiest way to roll through text. Buy one where Ctrl + [roll] zooms the text in or out. Useful for seeing page set-up and where you can view the set-up for several pages at a time. Well worth the £10–15 these cost.

Comments

'Comments' is a useful feature when preparing your manuscript. You may discover a sentence where you wish to check a fact, insert a reference and so forth, and wish to return to this. Using Insert – Comment, Word will highlight that word closest to the cursor and insert a comment number, for example[21]. Later we will make a macro to insert a comment. Just now we will have to use Insert – Comment.

This opens up a window on the bottom half of the screen where the comment may now be written. Irritatingly, comments cannot be written in footnotes in your file; they may only be made in the main text. Close the window when you have written the comment. The comment number disappears although the commented word remains highlighted. Place the cursor on this highlighted field and you will see your comment without using the View – Comments needed to open up the lower window again. Worth noting: you can highlight a phrase or entire sentence using click (hold left mouse) and drag; then Insert – Comment. The whole phrase is highlighted.

Removing comments

Many people do not appear to use comments because of the hassle in removing them afterwards. Logically we would think that the GoTo and select Comment would take us there, but Word is not constructed on logic alone. This move takes us to the beginning of the highlighted text (the final 'e' of 'example' in the above). DEL will now delete the word and not the Comment. Not what we want.

We need to open up the Comments window with View – Comments, but (important) now place the cursor back in the main text on the top window. This process shows the comment numbers in the text: the lower window shows the comment. Click on the comment number[21].This will now be highlighted. Press DEL and the comment is deleted. If you did not open up the Comments window before doing this, clicking twice on the comments number will open it up for you.

Fine for removing one comment. But what about all of them? Easiest is to make a macro. See under Macros below.

Track Changes

Sometimes it is handy to keep track of those changes have been made. Under Tools – Track changes – Highlight changes, select 'Track changes while editing' and 'Highlight changes on screen'. Under 'Options' you may select the colours for the text which has been added, ~~deleted~~, or where the font has been changed. Deleted text may be indicated by a single-line strikethrough, or a symbol. I prefer the former. Incidentally, a mark can be given in the margin to show where text has been changed. Small changes might not always be clear where, for example, a comma has been added. The margin mark will indicate this. If you wish to view the changed text as it will appear, then unclick the 'Highlight changes on screen'. I have two macros which switch this viewing feature on/off such that I can see the changes made/view the corrected text. Just use Tools – Record macro and repeat the above Track changes sequences to record each macro. I use Alt + S

(Show changes) and Alt + D (Disguise changes). The latter 'disguises' the corrections and shows the corrected copy.

Word 2003 has changed the appearance of changes to the text and deletions by putting these in the margins. Several changes in one line become confusing with a profusion of notes stating 'deleted text', 'added text' and so forth. This is of little help to my clients and Word 2000 remains my standard program. You will definitely find use for the macros mentioned above if you use Word 2003. As stated, we will learn to make these below.

Accepting changes

Once the changes have been made and these are to be permanent, use Tools – Track changes – Accept or Reject Changes with (alternatively without) highlighting. I prefer to use the button 'with highlighting' as I can then observe the text which has been corrected. This choice also shows deleted text. Click the Find button to go to the first correction. There are four buttons 'Accept', 'Reject', 'Accept all', Reject all'. The first two keys allow you to accept or reject each individual change, the third and fourth to accept/reject all. You may undo all the changes here, but even if you exit this menu you may still undo all changes with the 'undo typing arrow' (Ctrl + Z) providing you have not saved the changes with Ctrl + S.

If you replace a Table of Contents, the original will still be there but marked with the strikethrough. This may occupy several pages and not be required. You can delete this superfluous TOC by highlighting it, go to Tools – Accept or Reject Changes, and select the 'Accept' button to the left. This will delete the highlighted TOC but none of the other changes. You will have discovered that you cannot highlight a text marked for deletion with the strikethrough and then press the delete key. Nothing will happen. You can highlight any selected text, table, figure, etc., and use this procedure to accept changes in the highlighted section without accepting any other changes at this point in time.

This has been a heavy chapter thus far, but once you have mastered the simple procedures for entering and deleting comments, even without macros to do this for you, you will soon reap the benefit of this Word feature.

AutoCorrect

This function is a gem for the bad typist. When supplied Word contains several hundred words which are automatically corrected. Incidentally, if you need to correct spelling in more than one language (that of the program purchased), you will have to purchase the Proofing Tools CD-ROM.

Under Tools – AutoCorrect you will find a list of character and letter sequences which are automatically corrected when typed incorrectly: 'acheived' becomes 'achieved', for example. The fact that you may add your own 'errors' (as well as delete from the list) means that you may enter a sequence such as ys and have this 'corrected' to 'Yours sincerely'. This is probably easier than writing a macro. However, a macro able to execute search and replace, for example, as part of a sequence of keystrokes, thereby serving another purpose. Best to keep a record of any personal autocorrections. You could define them all as beginning with 'x' for example, for example xys for 'Yours sincerely'.

The auto-correct function is not ideal for longer phrases. If your paper regularly includes a number of terms which cannot be conveniently abbreviated such as 'global warming and ozone layer depletion', remembering the fact that you will probably be writing the article over several weeks, these terms can be stored in a separate 'term file'. In the main article, enter 'gwoz' or similar (to indicate 'global warming and ozone layer depletion'. At the appropriate time switch to your term file. Highlight the required term (global warming...) and copy this with Ctrl-C. Return to your main file and use Search 'gwoz' and place the cursor on Replace. But you do not have to type the term; just enter the stored term using Ctrl-V. Neither do you have to retype the term the next time you return to work with your article – it's in your own term-bank.

Symbols etc.

If you are using a symbol regularly such as ¶, a shortcut key will enable you to avoid the long-winded Insert – Symbol procedure. We can mention here that every symbol has a character set name and a Unicode number, e.g. Wingdings 61520, which is ¶.

Insert – Symbol – [select symbol] – Shortcut key – Press New Shortcut Key – [Alt + X for example] – Assign – Close – Close.

Hitting Alt + X in this example types the selected symbol. I personally reserve Alt + X (as indicated above) as a temporary shortcut key for that symbol I use regularly, but you may choose whatever you want. You will soon find that you have use for a number of such shortcut keys.

Finding (and Replacing) Symbols

While it is appropriate to include this section here, hop over it if you really don't need it (yet).

You cannot enter a symbol in the Find box using Insert – Symbol, copy/ paste, or a shortcut key. We have to use the Unicode number. To find out what this is for any symbol, use Insert – Symbol and then click the selected symbol (which may be under Webdings or Wingdings, or elsewhere); press the shortcut key on this screen. On the lower left you will now see Description, Symbol: 61538 (or another Unicode number). This character number should be entered into the Find field using the *Numeric pad* on the right of the keyboard (Press NumLock). Hold down the Alt key while typing the number, then release. A symbol will appear in the 'Find' field, but it may not be the symbol you are expecting. Ignore it. Now use Find next, and it will take you to your chosen symbol.

Selecting symbols

Click 'Insert–Symbols' on the Menu bar. In the Font window go to 'Normal font'. Here you will find most of the useful symbols. Try also Webdings and Wingdings as well as the font called 'Symbols'. Others may be found under MS Reference 1 and 2.

Finding and replacing symbols is similar to replacing text, except that we have to use character codes (sometimes called unicodes). To find the character code for any symbol, click on the symbol in the matrix shown. Then click 'Shortcut key'. Under 'Description' you will find the five-digit character code.

Imagine that you want to replace ✗ (Wingdings 2 Unicode 61647) with ✓ (Wingdings Unicode 61520). Click NumLock on (a green signal lamp shows on the keyboard). Open up the Find/Replace window (Ctrl + H). Place the cursor in the 'Find what' field. Hold down Alt and enter the Unicode number of the symbol on the *numeric* keypad, here 61647. Release the Alt key. Don't worry that this may not show the symbol you are looking for. Move the cursor to the 'Replace with' field. Repeat using the character code for the replacement symbol, here 61520. Again, this might show a surprise symbol. Just use the Find next – Replace/all command as normal.

Planning Your Manuscript – Headings, Fonts and More

All basic styles are automatically stored in a template file called Normal.dot and are the default fonts for normal text, headings, footnotes and so forth when you begin a new file. You might want to change these, particularly heading styles, or you may want to define a new set of fonts to apply to a particular set of documents.

As we commence with the Normal.dot default normal font (probably Times Roman 12 pt), we assume that this is satisfactory. But let us assume that we require to set up four levels of headings to our own specifications (or that of our publisher) and save this as a template. We can do the following in a blank document, but here it will serve our purpose if we do this as an exercise. Open a new file and type in the following:

Chapter 1 (Heading 1 level)
Section (Heading 2 level)
Subsection (Heading 3 level)
Subsection (Heading 4 level)

Just for the sake of this exercise, save this as Headings.doc. The text in square parentheses below is a suggestion for font style and size but you may make your own choice. There are several points to be modified in each level of heading.

Go to Format – Style – Heading 1.

Modify the font

Select: Modify – Format – Font [Select Times New Roman – Bold –18 – All Caps] – OK

Modify the paragraph

Format – Paragraph – Spacing After [6 pt] – [Before 0] – Special [none] – By [blank] – OK

The 6 pt spacing puts a half line space between paragraphs. Much better than a whole line (12 pt).

Modify the numbering

Format – Numbering – [Select the frame which shows the correct level numbering] – Customize – Number format [Type 1]

Number style [select 1,2 3] – Start at [1] – OK.

If the 'More' key is shown on the right, click it. If 'Less' is shown then – Follow the number with [Tab character] – OK. This will enable automatic renumbering of chapters and sections when reorganising.

Check and exit

Check the preview. Make any changes by repeating any of the above.

Automatically update [optional] – Add to template [optional] – OK –Apply.

Automatically updating means that if you change the style of the font, for example by clicking the Font Size, this will affect all previous text written in that style (Normal font, Heading 1 etc.). Sometimes you do not need this as you are only changing the font size for a particular paragraph. Likewise, 'Add to Template' will mean that this font will apply for all new documents using this template, here the Normal.dot template.

Now Highlight the top line of this file (Chapter 1...). On the Style window in the toolbar, go to Heading 1. Click this. The heading now appears as defined.

Now do the same for Heading 2, selecting the appropriate font. Here, we check that the numbering is [Start at] 1.1. When formatting the numbering, check the appropriate frame carefully. Applies to this and subsequent levels.

Similarly for Headings 3 and 4, if required. Here are the results

1 CHAPTER 1 (HEADING 1 LEVEL)
1.1 Section (Heading 2 level)
1.1.1 Subsection (Heading 3 level)
1.1.1.1 Subsection (Heading 4 level)

You can select Numbering [none] for the fourth level if you consider four digits to be excessive and unnecessary.

An excellent document on the Internet related to numbering is at: www.shaunakelly.com/word/numbering/OutlineNumbering/

The Outline Feature

A very useful feature when organising a book or an article is the Outline feature. This is in fact a comprehensive set of features but where one or two are particularly useful. Briefly, Outline lets you examine the contents of your paper, not only enabling you to find a chapter or section, but to move a section and all its contents to another place in the file without highlighting, cutting and pasting, or to redesignate a subsection as a section or chapter. Now this differs from Cut and Paste because Outline automatically renumbers the sections and subsections. I found this particularly useful when compiling this book. Imagine that you have Chapter 2 with sections 2.1, 2.2, ... 2.6. Later you find that you wish to add a new section following 2.2. This will necessitate sections 2.3 thru 2.6 now becoming 2.4 thru 2.7. Further, subsections 2.3.1 etc. are now required to become 2.4.1 etc. 'Outline' enables you to do this. An example is the best way to illustrate this.

Click View – Outline. We now have the Outlining Toolbar with a number of arrows. But go first to the numbers in the middle of the toolbar. Click 1 and you see all the Heading 1 levels; click 2 and you see Headings 1 and 2, and so forth. Assume that you wish to make Chapter 3 as Chapter 4. Then click on '1' to view all Heading 1 levels (i.e. the Chapters). Highlight Chapter 1 and then use the down arrow ♦. This will relocate the entire chapter and its contents to the new location, and automatically renumber all the other chapters and subsections.

This command is probably most useful for sorting sections. But not only can you move them within chapters, you may also use this feature to relocate a subsection in another chapter. After this has been done use View – Normal to return to the whole text.

A full summary is found on: www.mvps.org/word/FAQs/Formatting/Using OLView.htm

Saving and Recalling the Template

Having defined the styles we may want to save these either as our default template (Normal.dot) or as a template for a particular document. Remember that when we load a blank document the Normal.dot is the default. We can make changes to this, add new styles, and so forth.

Saving the default Normal.dot template

If this is a standard we are going to use for virtually all our documents, we can modify the Normal.dot file. In fact, we do this if we check the 'Add to Template' box when changing the style using Format–Style–Modify Style–[make modifications]–Add to template.

Saving as a special template

If we wish to save these new styles as our special template (.dot) file for thesis chapters, then we must save these in a blank file. But of course, we do not want the text in the .dot file. Save as a copy under any name – I use xxx (.doc).[2] Then delete all the text with Ctrl + A, Del. Next: Save As –

---

2   I find it convenient to commence the name of any special or temporary files with xxx. It's just that I always foreget the special name attributed to them, and they are easily located using Search.

Document Template – File name [Thesis] – Save. Note that we do not type '.dot' (just as we do not type the extension '.doc' for text files). I now have a special template called Thesis.dot for chapters in my thesis.

Opening a special template

If we wish to write a file using a previously saved special template, then: Tools – Templates and Add-Ins – Attach – [Select the required template, e.g. Thesis.dot] – Open. Note: To apply styles select 'Automatically update document styles'. Click OK.

Replacing a template in an existing file

The file is opened with the Normal.dot unless it was previously saved with another template.

If we have written a file with Normal.dot or other template but wish to replace this with another template, e.g. Thesis.dot, then follow the procedure in the previous paragraph.

If the template you require is not in the checked boxes, click Add – [Select the required template] – Open – OK. (See note in previous paragraph). If you change anything later under Format – style and which this to be included in the template for future use, then check 'Add to Template'. This will not affect the Normal.dot template.

Quick change of font

If you click on Font style or Font size windows on the Formatting toolbar (it is probably showing 'Normal'), you may scroll up or down to any style, for example Heading 1 and may change the style temporarily, for example to type a quotation in another style. But if the 'Automatically Update' box has been checked then all text typed in Normal will now be changed – a ripple effect through the whole file.

Normal text and Body Text

Normal text relates to the whole file; Body Text relates to a specified body of text. If I write something in Font size 18 pt boldface, and this is the same as my Heading 1 font and Update box is checked, then the Styles manager will consider this to be a Heading! So I format this using Body Text style.

Styles in Use

Headings, fonts

You will have noticed that the Formatting toolbar shows the font and style which are you using at the moment of typing, or where the cursor is located. Clicking the arrow by 'Normal' or whatever style is in use, will reveal all the other styles in use for footnotes, comments, TOC (Table of Contents) as well as headings at several levels. It may even show many that you are not using and do not intend to use. This means scrolling through the list every time you want to insert a new heading. It helps to delete the styles that are not in use – they can always be included later.

Deleting styles not required

Go to Tools – Templates and Add-Ins – Organizer. On the left are the styles being used in your paper. You can highlight those not wanted. But if the whole lot is there, then highlight everything (use shift and down arrow), then click the delete button. This will delete most styles not in use in your paper so far (not all may be permissibly deleted). If there are many styles in the Normal.dot file not being used, then delete these as well. You can always add them in again defining them under Format – Style. The result is that it is easy to use the style window.

Macros

A macro is a stored set of commands which are executed on a run command for a given macro file. In fact Microsoft has many pre-programmed macros the names of which are revealed using Alt + F8, then select Macro in Word Commands. The names are fairly self-explanatory. For example, one near the top of the list is AllCaps. Why you would want to run this macro when you have a Caps Lock key I couldn't even guess. But it is often *very* convenient, and very simple, to create your own. The problem is that the shortcut keys are not shown for these existing macros.

I use many short macros for a variety of functions including changing fonts. If my basic font is Times Roman 12 pt and I want to give a quote in Arial 11 pt, then instead of clicking the Font Style and Font Size frames on the toolbar at the top, I press Alt + F8 and then type A11 (this being the name I have given to the macro). Typing is now in Arial 11. I have another macro, T12, to return me to Times Roman 12 pt. We can make these commands even shorter, using shortcut keys, as described in the next section.

Writing a macro

To write a macro: Tools – Macro – Record New Macro. Type in Macro name (A11), click Keyboard and Close. An icon shows that you are recording. Click the Font Style frame and select Arial; click the Font Size frame and click 11. Click the stop bullet ▪.

To run the macro, press Alt + F8 and the name of the macro – here A11 – (or select it from the list now shown). You can highlight a paragraph and run a macro so that it applies to the whole section.

You will have noted that instead of using Alt + F8 and the macro title you could have entered your own shortcut keystrokes to run the macro. Do this after clicking the 'keyboard' icon when defining the macro.

A macro for inserting comments

Click: Tools – Macro – Record new macro. Give the macro a name such as Inscom, or even ic. Click Keyboard icon. Use the key sequence you want to run the macro such as Alt + C. If this sequence is already in use, re-enter another sequence. Assign – Close. Now enter the sequence for inserting a comment: Insert – Comment. The Comment window opens up. Click the stop recording bullet ▪. Now enter your comment and close the Comment window. You can always view the comment just by placing the cursor on the highlighted field. Every time you wish to insert a comment, place the cursor at the appropriate place and hit Alt + C.

A macro for deleting comments

Deleting comments is a bit more complicated. Logically we would think that GoTo Comment – Next would suffice. But Word is not built on logic alone. This move would take us to the highlighted field, not the comment number. Del would then remove the word, not the comment. Do the following:

First, check Tools – Track changes – Highlight changes – Track changes while editing is *off*.

View – Comments (the Comments window opens). Place cursor at head of main text in the top window.

Click: Tools – Macro – Record new macro. Give the macro a name such as Delcom, or even dc. Click Keyboard icon. Enter the key sequence you want to run the macro such as Alt + D. If this sequence is already in use (you will be informed), re-enter another sequence. Assign – Close. Now enter the following sequence: Find (use Ctrl-F) – More (if this is shown at the bottom of this Window) – Special – Comment Mark:^a appears in the search field.

Find next. Close the Search window (use the x on top right of this screen – not the full text screen!). The Comment number is now highlighted, e.g. [21] is now highlighted. Click the Del key. Close the comments window. Click the stop recording bullet ■.

To delete a single or multiple comments open the View – Comments window first, and place the cursor back in the main text. Now press the sequence you chose to run the macro, e.g. Alt + D if that was selected above. You may hold the Alt key, and every time you hit the D key, the next comment will be deleted. You may also hop over those comments you wish to keep until later. All comments are renumbered automatically as each is deleted.

Shortcut keystrokes

A macro is thus a set of keystrokes but may be initiated by a shortcut keystroke. This can be Alt + X, Shift + B, or whatever, and used to run the macro. Well, not quite, because Word uses almost 250 combinations, including some with Alt + Ctrl, Shift + Ctrl along with alphabetic and F-keys. So, avoid using these combinations. You will be warned, for example, that Ctrl + S is used by Word to save your file, and it is doubtful that you want to change that. Also avoid combinations such as Alt + A, E for example. This is because Word uses Alt + A followed by certain letters such as F (for 'Save File As'). Keep to simple keystrokes. Use Alt + any letter except A, E, F, I, O, R, T, V and W. Ctrl is used with almost every letter, so avoid this key in shortcut keystrokes. But you will be warned that a certain combination is used by Word when you try to enter that sequence. I use Alt + S for Show Changes (under Track Changes) and Alt + D to hide (Disguise) them. I reserve Alt + X for temporary macros.

Other shortcuts

Another use for shortcut keystrokes is for symbols. If you are using a symbol regularly then use Insert – Symbols and highlight the required symbol. Click on Shortcut Key. Enter the keystrokes (such as Alt + T) and Close. I use Alt + T for this Tick: ✓. Unfortunately shortcut keystrokes do not work in Find and Replace. There you will have to use the Unicode numbers described on pp. 377–8.

Sectioning – Page Numbering

Probably the most infuriating feature of Word is the page numbering, especially when different sections require no numbers, lower case Roman numbers, or ordinary pagination. (This section really is a hands-on exercise!) Under Insert on the Menu toolbar, we find Break. The important thing to remember is that a break is effective from the next page. If we have no breaks and we use the Insert – Page numbers command, the cursor can be anywhere in the file and pagination will apply from the first page. But, illustration by example is best.

Assume we have a file with the following structure (and you should type this but may omit the text in square brackets):

Section 1	TITLE PAGE	[No pagination]
	BLANK PAGE	[No pagination]
Section 2	PRELIMS First page	[LC Roman i]
	PRELIMS Second page	[LC Roman ii]
	PRELIMS Third page	[LC Roman iii]
Section 3	MAIN TEXT First page	[Ordinary pagination 1]
	MAIN TEXT Second page	[Ordinary pagination 2]
	MAIN TEXT Third page	[Ordinary pagination 3]

Clearly, there are three sections here: Title page (and reverse side) Prelims (TOC etc.) and the Main text. It is optional whether the first page of the two numbered sections is given as *i* and *1* respectively, but here we will assume this. We do have the option to include the number on the first page.

The following may appear tricky, but take it step by step. We are going to leave the Title page unnumbered; apply lower case Roman numerals to the Prelims; number the Main text as normal.

It is reasonable to assume that you have already made a new page with Ctrl-Enter for sections although we will be entering a section break coupled with a next page. So that we can delete the page mark already there, click on the ¶ symbol to show the codes. Begin at the top of the file and move the cursor down. The first code mark we will see is the page break at the foot of the title page: ....Page break................ Just under that will be another showing the page break at the end of the blank second page.

Procedure. Place the cursor at the beginning of this page break, and press DEL. This has removed the former page break. Now, on the menu bar, click Insert – Break – Next Page (under Section break types) – OK. Not only have we inserted a new page but a section break. The cursor is now located in Section 2 on the first line of the prelims.

Next the tricky bit. On the menu bar: View – Header and Footer. We see that the cursor is in the Header frame, but we will want the numbers in the Footer panel. In this menu bar click the fourth icon from the *right* (Switch between header and footer). The cursor is now in the footer panel of Section 2. Now click the next icon to the *left* (Same as previous) which should be *off*. The text 'Same as previous' has disappeared from the footer panel.

Back to the top menu bar: Insert – Page numbers – Alignment (Centre) – Format – Number format (select lower case Roman) – Start at (i) – OK – Show number on first page (check if required) – OK. Close.

That was the tricky bit, except all the file from the first page of the prelims on is now numbered in Roman numerals. We have to restart numbering from the Main text section. Place the cursor on the .....Page break ..... at the end of the prelims sections. Now repeat the process beginning with the paragraph above 'Procedure'. The only difference is that we will select normal instead of Roman numerals.

Click Show/Hide ¶ again to return to the normal view. Sections 2 and 3 are now numbered.

Removing numbers

Click on the page number. This will launch the Header–Footer panel. Click on the page number to highlight it in white/black, Press delete. This will delete the page numbers for the section.

Incidentally, while this panel is open, using the up and down arrows you may proceed to the previous/next header/footer.

Which page am I on?

The information at the bottom of the screen will show the page number of the section as well as the placement in the total number of pages, e.g. 7/152, irrespective of the different numbering of the sections. Using the 'GoTo' command (Ctrl + G) and giving a page number will relate to this page, i.e. the seventh page in the document irrespective of the page number. However, 'GoTo ii' will locate at page ii.

Cross-references (sections, pages) – renumbering

It will not have gone unnoticed that restructuring a paper with Outline or repagination will affect chapter headings, sections, etc. These will be automatically renumbered as will indexed words. But what about cross references such as 'See page 27'? Clearly the reference to page 27 has to linked or cross-referenced to a so-called 'Bookmark' on that page. Let us say that on page 27 the text we are referring to states: 'It was stated that the Foreign Secretary had cautioned Blair about Iraq.'

First, go to this text and Highlight a word or phrase. 'Blair' would be sufficient. Click Insert – Bookmark. As instructed, give this bookmark a name, for example 'Blair1'. Click Add. We can now refer to this bookmark 'Blair1' on page 27 anywhere in the text. Let us assume that we are writing a reference on another page; either before or after page 27. We then type a leading text: '... as mentioned on page'... Here, we click Insert – Cross-reference. Select type [Bookmark]; Insert reference to [Page number] – which bookmark? [Highlight Blair1] – Insert – Close. The page number where the Blair1 bookmark is currently located will now be highlighted in the text: 27.

Assuming that you decide to delete pages 11 and 12, the Blair1 bookmark will now be located on page 25. Mark all (Ctrl + A), then F9. This will update all cross-references to page 25 (Blair1) and to all other bookmarks as well. Experiment with a small file yourself.

This feature may also be applied to cross-reference chapters, tables, sections and so forth. See Help on the standard toolbar. Type keyword 'reference' in the help menu index field. Click on Add cross references (near the top of the list).

Creating an Index

Many find the creation of an index a challenging task. The bibles on Word have around 25–30 pages devoted to the subject. But a very practical index can be made following the guidelines in the following 2–3 pages.

It is very simple to mark every occurrence of every word intended for an index. But this is not what an index is for. A reader should not be referred to every single page where the word 'syntax' occurs. What he is looking for is the meaty stuff.

Before you begin, if it is a long book you are indexing, make a copy first. Disasters can occur.

In the following, an outline is given to enable you to prepare an index. A considerable number of refinements can be made to layout, fonts, subentries and so forth later. Many of these are outlined in the Word Help menu.

There are two main ways to make an index. The normal way is to go through the text and mark a word to be included. You have the opportunity to indicate that this should be included every time it is encountered. Do this by highlighting the word, and clicking Alt + Shift + X. An 'XE' (index entry) field is then placed in the text. Toggle the Show/Hide ¶ icon on the standard toolbar to show or hide this.

The question is one of syntax rather than grammar.

Before compiling the index from these marked words, these must be hidden. If they do not disappear when you click the Show/Hide ¶ icon, go to Tools –

Options – View, and unclick 'Hidden text'.

Let us take an example. I have highlighted (bold-faced) the terms I wish to index, although here this is just for purposes of illustration. We wish to make three types of entry: a main entry, a subentry and a cross reference. In addition we will make an name reference (which can be an author reference). Here is the text:

Various proposals for **reform** of the **rating system** have been made. Given that this is a **tax**, it might be thought that it could be replaced by a supplement on **income tax**. But this would overlook the fact that not all **income tax payers** are **property owners**. Again, there are various types of property to consider: **apartments, bungalows, houses**, and **mansions**. Property may be **rented, owned** or **leased**. The reforms suggested by the **Thatcher (Conservative)** regime were definitely rejected, but **New Labour** under **Blair** has not offered any alternative, being apparently more concerned with **fox-hunting**.

After indexing the file appears on the monitor thus:

Various proposals for reform{XE "reform"} of the rating system{XE "rating system"} have been made. Given that this is a tax{XE "tax"}, it may be thought that it could be replaced by a supplement on income tax{XE "income tax"}. But this would overlook the fact that not all income tax payers{XE "tax payers" \t "See income tax"} were property owners{XE "property owners"}. Again, there are various types of property{XE "property types"} to consider in any tax reform{XE "tax reform"}: apartments{XE "property types:apartments"}, bungalows{XE "property types:bungalows"}, houses{XE "property types:houses", and mansions{XE "property types:mansions"}. Property may be rented{XE "property:rented", owned{XE "property:owned"} or leased{XE "property:leased"}. The reforms suggested by the Thatcher{XE " *Thatcher"} (Conservative{XE "Conservative" \t "See Government"}) regime were definitely rejected, but New Labour{XE "New Labour" \t "See Government"} under Blair{XE " *Blair"} has not offered any alternative reform{XE "reform"}, being apparently more concerned with foxhunting{XE "other reforms: fox-hunting"}.{XE "Government: Conservative"}{XE "Government: New Labour"}

INDEX

*Blair, 1
*Thatcher, 1
Conservative. See Government
    Government
    Conservative, 1
New Labour, 1

income tax, 1
New Labour. See Government
other reforms
fox-hunting, 1
property
    leased, 1
    owned, 1
    rented, 1
property owners, 1
property types, 1
    apartments, 1
    bungalows, 1
    houses, 1
    mansions, 1
rating system, 1
reform, 1
tax, 1
tax payers. See income tax
tax reform, 1

Index of Names
    Blair 1
    Thatcher 1

The numbers refer to page numbers (all 1 in this example) They may be right-flushed if required with or without a leader.

Main entry

Reform is a main entry. Highlight the word 'reform' then Alt + Shift + X to mark the entry. The Mark entry screen appears with 'reform in the main entry field. Mark. Highlight next word or phrase, here 'rating system'. Mark.

Subentry

We will have marked 'income tax' as a main entry. We have decided that 'income tax payers' is to be a subentry. But this appears in the Main entry window. Highlight it, Ctrl + X, locate cursor in Subentry window, Ctrl + V (to paste). In the Main entry window type 'income tax'. Mark.

Cross–references (See)

We can make a cross-reference by highlighting the main word and entering the cross-reference after See in the cross-reference field. Mark. For 'tax payers' we are referred to 'income tax'. But no subentry is given under 'income tax' for 'tax payers'. If we had wanted a reference under 'income tax' to 'tax payers' together with the page number, then we have to make an additional entry by highlighting 'tax payers' again, and then enter 'income tax' as the Main entry, and 'tax payers' as the subentry.

Other entries

We may find that we need to reference a subheading but we have no main heading. For example, 'Conservative' and 'New Labour' are subheadings which we want to go under the Main heading 'Government'.

Place the cursor at the end of the paragraph on a blank space. Alt + Shift + X. Enter. Make 'Government' the Main entry and 'Conservative' as the subentry. Mark. Do the same for 'New Labour'.

To generate a 'Names index' I placed an asterisk before the name (e.g. *Blair) in the Main entry, ensuring that these would be sorted to the head of the index as * is sorted before alphanumeric characters. The * can be removed later.

Editing

You can edit the XE fields for spelling mistakes, wrong case, etc., as well as the generated index. I have deleted the two asterisked references at the head of the table and placed these in a 'Names' index.

Alternative method

An alternative method for compiling an index is to compile a list of words as one reads through the manuscript, typing these into a separate file which we can call Bookidx.doc. This is convenient as the word only has to be typed once. Nor will it be necessary to recompile the index when preparing a new edition; the index words have been compiled. Further, it is easy to add or delete words in this file. The problem is that every occurrence of 'syntax' or whatever will be indexed, including those which are not of relevance. We would then have to go through the file and check whether the particular highlighted 'syntax' was to be indexed. This method is a convenient way to compile an author index.

After the subject (or author) list has been completed, place the cursor where the index is to go (normally at the end of the file), go to Insert – Index and Tables – Automark – [type the name of the file: Bookidx]. All references or author names in this Bookidx file will now be marked with the XE field in the file. You can edit this index making any necessary refinements.

Problems

Inserting the index resulted only in a mysterious field code {INDEX \C "12"
\Z "1033"}. Just place the cursor on the field code, right click the mouse and
click 'Toggle Field Codes'. I found that I had to highlight this field first by
clicking twice on the left mouse, and then clicking the right mouse. You now
see the field results. Change this permanently under Tools – Options – Field
Codes (uncheck).

Calculations

Occasionally the non-fiction writer will need to calculate information from data
in his text. Consider the following: 'The ages of the ministers were 63, 62, 75,
29 and 48, a mean of 55.4 years.' Normally, we will use the pocket calculator
(where did I put it?). But there is a feature which may be included into Tools
called 'ToolsCalculate'. This is included using the following:

Tools – Customize – Commands tab – (Category List) – Select All Commands
– (Commands list) – go to ToolsCalculate. This is quite a long way down the
list. Click and drag this title to the Menu bar at the top of the screen, placing
it on 'Tools'. When the menu drops down, click to include it in the menu.
ToolsCalculate is now included.

How to use ToolsCalculate. Highlight the text, (sentence or paragraph) which
includes the numbers, here 63, 62, 75, 29 and 48. The text and commas will
be ignored except in numbers such as 2,325. The add sign is assumed. Then
click on ToolsCalculate. Place the cursor at an appropriate place, click
Ctrl + V and the sum will be given, here 277. (The results are stored in the
Edit memory). Alternatively edit the text (63, 62, 75, 29 and 48)/5. Carry out
the same procedure. You will, of course, have to edit the text removing
brackets and the /5.

Sometimes data is in a column:

Tories	2316
Labour	2429
Liberal	3112
Independent	916

Again, the total number of votes, 8773, is easily calculated. However, if the
list is numbered, we have to highlight just the numbers, otherwise the sum
would be increased by 10 (the sum of $1 + 2 + 3 + 4$).

1. Tories	2316
2. Labour	2429
3. Liberal	3112

4. Independent   916

The right-hand column is highlighted by holding Alt + Shift, placing the cursor at the top in front of the first '2', and dragging downwards and across.

The minus sign may be used for subtraction; single numbers to be subtracted may also be placed in parentheses. 2 (3) 5 and 2 -3 5 both give 4 as the result.

Multiplication is given by *. Symbols may be used but are ignored and will have to be typed in: $30.79*11 = 338.69. Division is given by /. 13/7 = 1.86. Results are rounded to 2 decimal places.

Two decimal places are given unless any number exceeds this: 2,367.265 /7.2 = 328.7868.

Powers are given by $4\hat{\ }4 = 256$. The fourth root is given by $64\hat{\ }(1/4) = 2.83$.

Percentages may also be given: $342*5\% = 17.1$.

Working with Tables

Word has quite a powerful table feature useful, among other things, for sorting data, whether typed in or imported from the Internet, for example. Let us say that we have registered the following and require to sort it according to a selected key or data. The numbers refer to 'incidents'.

England Bristol 5
England Liverpool 8
England Manchester 6
France Bordeaux 11
France Marseilles 9
France Paris 7

Go to Table – Convert – Text to table

Highlight the table with click and drag

Select Autofit behaviour: Autofit to Contents for this trial

Separate text at: Choose Other and type a blank in the box. This will create a table where each column is selected based on the spaces in the original data. Here is the result:

England	Bristol	5
England	Liverpool	8
England	Manchester	6
France	Bordeaux	11
France	Marseilles	9
France	Paris	7

We can sort on any column(s). Let us say that we wish to sort by country (col. 1) and number of incidents (col. 3). We highlight the table and select Table – Sort, Column 1 – Text – Ascending, Column 3 – Numbers – Ascending. No header row (i.e. no titles for columns). Here is the result.

England	Bristol	5
England	Manchester	6
England	Liverpool	8
France	Paris	7
France	Marseilles	9
France	Bordeaux	11

If we want, we can now convert the table to text, either preserving the table or reverting to the spaces as with the original:

Highlight table with Click and drag. Click Table (toolbar) – Convert – Table to Text.

Separate text with Tabs (as here) or Other (type in space).

Here is the final result:

England	Bristol	5
England	Manchester	6
England	Liverpool	8
France	Paris	7
France	Marseilles	9
France	Bordeaux	11

Any column may be deleted and the whole table imported into Excel, for example. This is often convenient if the order of the columns has to be changed. Just highlight the table, Copy, minimise or close Word, open a new sheet on Excel and paste. This can only be done if you have saved the original table in Word using tabs to delineate the columns, and not spaces. It is then also possible to make charts if required.

Sorting Your Own Records

Depending upon the nature of the data, records may be entered into a spreadsheet where they are easily sorted. But simple records of one line may also be sorted in Word under Table – Sort. Lines with a hard return at the end of the line are treated as separate paragraphs. This means that records containing hard returns, such as addresses, will need to be converted to single-line records, and then converted back again. We will see how to do this below.

Bibliographic references are usually easy to sort as these are written as a single string, the wrap-around at the end of the line being taken care of by the word processor. This means that a (concealed) paragraph mark is placed only at the end of each reference, and in all probability a second one to provide a blank line before the next reference. Line breaks and thus the end of the paragraph may be revealed by clicking the ¶ symbol on the 'Standard' toolbar.

The paragraph marks are referred to as 'hard returns', as opposed to 'soft returns' introduced casually by the word processor to wrap a line. This means that there is a problem in sorting addresses and similar lists where information for each record may occur on several lines. You may deliberately have chosen to register bibliographic records on several lines. The problem arises from the fact that there is a paragraph mark at the end of each line prohibiting effective sorting of a group of lines. Here are three records which will illustrate the procedure.

The problem with which one is faced is to sort records containing a hard return so as not to regard each line as a paragraph. In this event the lines would be sorted independently.

The original records: country and capital. The hard returns have been revealed by highlighting the table and clicking the ¶ icon on the Tools bar.

Norway¶
Oslo¶
¶
Lithuania¶
Vilnius¶
¶
Estonia¶
Tallinn¶

Sorting these by lines would produce the following. The blank lines between each record would appear at the top of the file and are not shown here.

Estonia¶
Lithuania¶
Norway¶
Oslo¶
Tallinn¶
Vilnius¶

But this is not what we want. Clearly we wish to retain the record lines (countries and capitals) together and a blank line between each record. This may be done using the following steps in the Search&Replace procedure. Each line concludes with a Paragraph Mark (revealed by clicking the ¶ symbol on the Standard Toolbar). It is not necessary to reveal these in order to sort, but they form part of the procedure. Note that a record is separated from the next by two Paragraph Marks, one at the end of the record followed by just a Paragraph Mark on the next line (this being a blank line, of course, separating the records). This is seen in the original file above.

When replacing the paragraph marks, we use 'Special' and then 'Paragraph Mark' on the Search&Replace screen. These appear as ˆp on the search and replace panels.

Stages 1 to 3 reconstruct the records as lines. Check that there is no blank line at the end of the file following the last record. Use ¶ to check this.

Stage	Replace	With
1	ˆpˆp	*
2	ˆp	+
3	*	*ˆp

The file now appears as follows:

Norway + Oslo*
Lithuania + Vilnius*
Estonia + Tallinn*

If records comprise long lines, these will wrap onto the next line and are essentially single line paragraphs, the ' + ' signs representing the former hard line breaks; the * sign represents end-of-record and the following blank line.

Stage 4
Using the Sort procedure under Tables, sort the lines (i.e. paragraphs) to give:

Estonia + Tallinn*
Lithuania + Vilnius*
Norway + Oslo*

The final stages reconstruct the records after the lines have been sorted using

Search&Replace.

Stage	Replace	With
5	*	ˆpˆp
6	+	ˆp

Remove any blank lines from the end of the file. The end result is:

Estonia
Tallinn
Lithuania
Vilnius

Norway
Oslo

Alternatively, you could just replace the + sign with a colon and space, and delete the * to give:

Estonia: Tallinn
Lithuania: Vilnius
Norway: Oslo

This method works even if records have different numbers of lines, e.g. addresses. You may find a way to refine this procedure or, ideally, record the steps as a macro.

A Couple of Tips

It is amazing what a slip of the thumb can do. Did you really mean to hit Alt + and the F key? Strange things can happen, one of the visually drastic disasters being the disappearance of the Table of Contents to be replaced by a code of apparent gibberish, e.g. {HYPERLINK, "_Toc8123388}" This really can cause a sweat the first time it is encountered. Just highlight the code, then Shift + F9 and the Table reappears.

Many things which appear to go wrong can be corrected by going to Tools – Options. Then look at View, General, Spelling and Grammar. Here are a host of things which can be changed. Just check/uncheck the boxes required. There are a few more under Tools – Customize. Look at Toolbars if you have too many on start-up, for example. I had trouble with typing MSc where the double capitals was reduced to Msc. Go to Tools – AutoCorrect. Here are a number of other useful options.

Trouble with line spacing? Go to Format – Paragraph. Here you can include a half or whole-line between paragraphs as well as indent. You can also adjust line spacing so that addresses fit labels, for example.

More Help

Clearly, there are thousands of questions which even the 'bibles' do not mention, let alone answer. This is where the Microsoft User Groups are a godsend. Go to www.mvps.org/word Here you will find a range of user-groups. If you have a question, send it and you will get a reply from an expert within 24 hours. Here also are a number of excellent articles such as 'Customizing Word', 'Crashes and Hang-ups' and so forth. Try 'General Word Usage' for starters. All articles may be downloaded or printed directly.

www.mvps.org/word/FAQs/General/CommandsList.htm yields a comprehensive summary of all Word shortcut commands as an Excel file.

How many times have you tried to intercept a Save or Print command? The answer is here: www.mvps.org/word/FAQs/MacrosVBA/InterceptSavePrint.htm You might find this easier than switching off the printer and then cancelling the file on the Printer and faxes menu (Start menu).

19
Spreadsheet Basics – Excel

42.7% of all statistics are made up on the spot. – Steven Wright
Using Excel, it may be calculated that 53.7% are not. – J. Taylor

This is a brief introduction to Excel which even a ten-year old will manage. (Parents, seek assistance from your child!) Again, this is a hands-on chapter, but if you have never used Excel before, you will learn how to carry out basic operations. You do not need to read this chapter in order to able to make charts and diagrams using Excel (See Chapter 6).

Excel is a *spreadsheet*: it is primarily used for calculations. It is generally not a convenient tool for constructing tables to be transferred into Word. The reason for this is that Excel normally does not wrap titles which exceed the width of the column designated. They become hidden behind the next column. It's no good using Enter to go to a new line; that will only place the cursor on the cell below. So if you are just typing in data use the Word Table function. When I say 'normally', it is possible to format the cells to wrap, but I find this a tiresome and not always a satisfactory procedure.

Excel nevertheless has a number of advantages and the spreadsheet may be easily imported into Word using the Insert – File command. Alternatively, highlight that portion of the spreadsheet to be copied which is particularly useful when only part of the sheet is to be copied. Click and drag from the top left cell of the portion to be copied (here B2) to the bottom right cell (E4). This is now highlighted.

	A	B	C	D	E	F	G	H
1	1	8	1	4	3	5	4	6
2	3	5	6	7	4	7	6	8
3	4	6	4	7	4	6	3	5
4	4	4	9	7	8	6	7	5
5	6	5	7	6	6	4	3	2

Copy into memory using Ctrl-C. Swap to the Word file and use Ctrl-V to copy the Excel table (in the memory) or the extract, as here, into the Word file. Generally you will find all the assistance you need under the Excel 'Help' feature.

Some adjustment will have to be made to column widths and left margin justification when importing. Place the cursor on a column or row boundary. When you see the double line, click and drag the boundary to the required width/height. (More information on adjusting column widths is given in Chapter 18.) Here is an example. Note that the column widths may conceal the full column title in Excel, but which will be revealed after the column widths have been adjusted.

Excel file (showing column/rows references)

	A	B	C	D	E
1	Shares:	Number	Purchas	Total val	Total val
2	IBM	1345	2.5		
3	South	6134	3.25		

Of course, adjusting the column width in Excel might seem to be the answer to the 'hidden' text. Try this by clicking and dragging the column boundaries and you will see the problem when you import the file.

Imported or copied into Word using one of the procedures mentioned above:

Shares: Company	Number of shares	Purchase price (USD)	Total Value: (GBP)	Total Value: (Euros)
IBM	1345	2.5		
South Sea Bubble Soap	6134	3.25		

Some clicking and dragging on the cell borders in Word gives us the following. Columns 'centred'. (You may delete gridlines.)

Shares: Company	Number of shares	Purchase price (USD)	Total Value: (GBP)	Total Value: (Euros)
IBM	1345	2.5		
South Sea Bubble Soap	6134	3.25		

It is when we wish to make calculations that Excel is particularly useful. Indeed, entire company finances, wage sheets, tax deductions, active and passive accounts may all be entered into a large worksheet. But it is frequently small tables involving calculations for which readers of this book may have use, and a few simple instructions will enable you to carry out quite complex operations using simple formula. Once the principle of entering a formula and the way in which this is copied into other cells and columns is understood, you will be able to use a worksheet effectively.

Imagine that we wish to keep an account of the value of the purchased shares. I have not entered the *total* price paid for the shares in USD, only the individual share price. Let us assume that we wish to know the total value of our investments in GBP and Euros. I choose to enter the conversion rates for USD into GBP and Euros in columns F and G. Note again the effect of no wrapping when entering this information yourself. Unless we increase the column width we cannot see that column D relates to GBP and column E to Euros.

	A	B	C	D	E	F	G
1	Shares:	Number of shares	Purchase price (USD)	Total Value (GBP)	Total Value (Euros)	USD = GBP	0.65
2	IBM	1345	2.5			USD = EU	1.125
3	South S.	6134	3.25				

Let us assume that we require cell D2 to show the value in GBP. This is the total number of IBM shares (1345) times the purchase price ($2.5) times the conversion rate of USD to GBP (0.65). We have to enter a formula to make this calculation. In cell E2 we show the value in Euros. We will also need formulas for cells D3 and E3 to show the value of South Sea Bubble Soap in both currencies. We don't have to write these formulas in each individual cell as we can copy them once we have written the formula for D2.

Further, if and when the conversion rate changes we can just enter the new conversion rates into H1 and H2 and the new values will be given automatically in columns D and E.

Writing a formula

If, at this point you have not got Excel up and running, you should now do so and enter the details above, 'cos we're hands-on again.

We should know that the four basic calculations (add, subtract, multiply, divide) are + − */.

Immediately above the spreadsheet is the formula line. The first element shows the cell where the cursor is located, here D2 as this is where we will write the formula. The grey field shows an equals sign [=]. Click this. In the long white field – the formula field – an equals sign now appears. We write the formula into this: = B2*C2*G1 then Enter. The value 2182.625 appears in cell D2.

Moving and copying formulas

There is an essential difference between these two procedures. *Moving* the formula will retain references to specific cells. We will see what this is below. If we *copy* a formula then all references become relative, i.e. these will all change. For example, copying the formula in cell D2 [B2*C2*G1] into cell D3 would give the formula for this cell as B3*C3*G2. Clearly this is wrong as H2 refers to Euro conversion. We still require the reference to cell G1, the GBP conversion rate. We need to 'fix' this reference to cell G1 when we copy the formula into other cells in columns D and E.

A fixed cell reference is preceded by the $ sign. Thus, G1 will 'fix' this reference in the formula to cell G1. The formula in cell D2 must be = B2*C2*G1. We do not need to type the formula in D3; we can copy it using Ctrl-C and Ctrl-V. This will automatically give: B3*C3*G1.

Indeed, if we had many different shares instead of just two, then we would want to copy the formula into all the cells in column D. To do this, click to highlight cell D2. The formula appears in the formula field at the top. If you clicked twice, the formula also appears in the cell (D2). In that case, hit Esc to show the value again, and then highlight cell D2. When this cell is highlighted, use Ctrl-C to copy it into the memory. The cell frame 'blinks'. This copies the formula, not the value shown in the cell, into the memory. Now move the cursor to D3 and hold down the Ctrl key while extending the highlighted area downwards through the cells into which the formula is to be copied (here cells D4 and below) using the down arrow. Press Esc if any cells are still blinking.

Now go to cell G2. Click the ' = ' sign to the left of the formula field and type in the formula after the = sign: B2*C2*G2. Enter. Highlight E2; Ctrl-C; move cursor to E3: Ctrl-V. All the values are now shown.

Go to cell G2 and change the rate of exchange to 0.66 for example. The new values are now shown. But we want to know the total value of our shares. Go to C4; write Sum or Total for example.

Go to cell D4. Click ' = ' and in the formula field write SUM(D2:D3). this means the sum of the cells in the range D2 to D3. Again use the copy command. Highlight D4; Ctrl-C; Highlight E4; Ctrl-V. The sums are now shown. But as a further exercise let us standardise the cells to two decimal points.

Ctrl-A to highlight the entire worksheet. Format – Number – select Number – Decimal places 2. Highlight the area A1 to E4 using click and drag; Ctrl-C; switch to the Word file; Ctrl-V to paste. Make some alignments (centering, for example), add some footnotes about rates of exchange, and we are now ready for the world of high finance.

Shares: Company	Number of shares	Purchase price (USD)	Value: GBP	Value (Euros)
IBM	1345.00	2.50	2252.88	3866.88
South Sea Bubble Soap	6134.00	3.25	13356.79	22925.83
		Sum	15609.66	26792.70

Importing Excel Tables into Word

It is often convenient to compile lists such as translations or records in an Excel file. I have several special term lists in such files with, for example, English in one column and Norwegian in the other. As I add new terms I can sort the table. Further, by swapping columns I can make either an English–Norwegian, or a Norwegian–English list. While much of this can be done using the Word Table feature, I find Excel easier as I do not have to keep adding extra rows or columns or changing the table dimensions. I could add that my CD-collection is also registered using Excel.

There are a few refinements which are useful when importing such an Excel file into Word. Here is part of my Excel file:

ENGLISH	NORWEGIAN
town	by
county	fylke
municipality	kommune

You may want to experiment using the French terms, for example, these being *ville, département, municipalite*, respectively.

In Word you may find it preferable to import your table into a new file first and then transfer it to your main text file later, if required. Using 'Insert file', click on the Excel file to be imported. (Make sure that the Open file screen shows 'All files' – not just 'All Word Documents'.) The imported file will probably look like this, i.e. right margin justified.

ENGLISH	NORWEGIAN
town	by
county	fylke
municipality	kommune

If the table grid lines are not shown, it may be convenient to display these. Click 'Table' then 'Show gridlines'.

Click and drag from the top left to bottom right to highlight the whole table, click the left justify text button to left-justify the text. A little refinement: click and drag the Norwegian (or French text), but not the column heading: click the *I* button to italicise the text in that column.

Highlight the table once again: click Table – Convert – Table to Text. Use the Tabs delimiter, or as I prefer, select 'other' and type a single space. We should now have the following:

ENGLISH – NORWEGIAN
town *by*
county *fylke*
municipality *kommune*

Highlight the text (except the heading) and use Format – Paragraph – Spacing After [0]; Single line spacing.

If you want more space between the English and Norwegian text, select the Tabs delimiter and then use Search and Replace (Ctrl-H) replacing tabs with three spaces for example.

ENGLISH – NORWEGIAN
county *fylke*
municipality *kommune*
town *by*

Finally select 2 or 3 columns on a page as layout if required.

Another example is an address book. This is the 'Inserted' file but left margin justified.

John Smith	6 Charley Street	Chester CH1 6YE
Fred. Crudley-Smyth	Flat 3, The Mansion	Dagenham LN2 2UP
Timmy Riddle	23 The Maze	Watford Gap AV1 2PP

To produce labels: Table – Convert – Table to Text – Separate with tabs. You can highlight and sort the table by paragraphs if required. Now, while highlighted, replace the end-of-line paragraph marks with two paragraph marks using Ctrl-H – More – Special. You can reveal these by clicking the ¶ symbol. Unclick afterwards. This puts an extra line between the addresses.

Single space the lines if necessary.

Fred. Crudley-Smyth	Flat 3, The Mansion	Dagenham LN2 2UP
John Smith	6 Charley Street	Chester CH1 6YE
Timmy Riddle	23 The Maze	Watford Gap AV1 2PP

Highlight the table again and using Ctrl-H replace the tab character with a single paragraph mark. Here is the result.

Fred. Crudley-Smyth
Flat 3 The Mansion
Dagenham LN2 2UP

John Smith
6 Charley Street
Chester CH1 6YE

Timmy Riddle
23 The Maze
Watford Gap AV1 2PP

If some addresses contain more than one line, insert an extra column, but always keep the postal codes in the same column. Further, if you buy labels on A4 paper, you can always adjust the line spacing so that the addresses fit the labels. Use Format – Paragraph – Line Spacing – Exactly *xx* point. Select 14 or 15 point for example.

Useful guides: Dorling-Kindersley publishers have a useful series *Essential Computers* of which the following are cheap and excellent: *Creating Worksheets,* and Dinwiddie, Robert, *Excel Formulas and Functions.*

20
Foreign Terms and Phrases

Omne ignotum pro magnifico[1]

Latin was compulsory in grammar schools in England well into the 1950s. By the school it was considered necessary as a sign of quality, standing and education: by the average pupil it was considered a bloody waste of time. Pupil power seems to have been exerted in the late 1960s and early 1970s and Latin largely became a 'free choice' subject. Not so French!

It is those little pieces of resistance which can add a some *couleur* to a jaded text. But check your French first so as to avoid writing *égout* when you really mean *égalité*. I am not convinced that translating the occasional phrase is the same as adding a single gem. For example, in his book *The Fourth Man*, Sutherland writes: 'Blackburn argued that whilst Nunn May's conviction and sentence was necessary, if only *pour décourager les autres*, he should not go down in history as a spy or a traitor but rather as an idealist.' We do not need any more than O-level French to understand that, but *soit qui se donne un air de sage* might be understood by some as meaning that he smelt of sage (and no onions).

Many dictionaries, especially of the pre-war era, frequently contained a supplement with Latin terms, although I am not aware of any such general dictionary today containing these gems of wisdom. It may scarcely be denied that the occasional foreign term adds a little *épice* to the text even though we have a sneaking feeling that the author was not quite as familiar with French as he would have us believe. Do not let your manuscript become tainted with use and over-use of foreign terms – it may all too soon be misunderstood as being *langage des halles*.[2] Neither is it advisable to give 'humorous' translations to your French quotations (e.g. *coup de grace* – lawnmower).

Foreign terms and phrases are *normally placed in italics* except where these have now become standard usage (et al., ad infinitum, etc.). The following includes a variety of expressions including a number of Latin terms encountered in law.[3]

---

1 That which is unknown is thought to be magnificent!
2 Language of the fish market!
3 A comprehensive overview of Latin legal terms is to be found in *Osborn's Concise Dictionary of Law*, Sweet and Maxwell, London.

a fortiori	with stronger reason *(Lat.)*
a posteriori	by induction; from the effect to the cause *(Lat.)*
a priori	by deduction; from the cause to the effect *(Lat.)*
à couvert	under cover *(Fr.)*
à la mode	according to fashion *(Fr.)*
à point	precisely to the point *(Fr.)*
à tout prix	at any price *(Fr.)*
à votre santé	to your health *(Fr.)*
ab initio	from the beginning *(Lat.)*
ad gustum	to one's taste *(Lat.)*
ad infinitum	to infinity *(Lat.)*
ad interim	meanwhile *(Lat.)*
ad literum	to the letter *(Lat.)*
ad nauseam	to a disgusting extent *(Lat.)*
ad referendum	for further consideration *(Lat.)*
ad valorem	according to the value *(Lat.)*
affaire de rien	a matter of nothing *(Fr.)*
anno domini	in the year of our Lord *(Lat.)*
argumentum ad judicium	an appeal to common sense *(Lat.)*
bon vivant	one who lives well *(Fr.)*
bona fide	in good faith *(Lat.)*
c'est à dire	that is to say *(Fr.)*
caveat emptor	let the buyer beware *(Lat.)*
certiorari	order a record from a lower court for presentation in a higher court *(Lat.)*
circa	about *(Lat.)*
cogito, ergo sum	I think, therefore I am *(Lat.)*
comme il faut	as it should be *(Fr.)*
compos mentis	of sane mind *(Lat.)*
conseil d'état	Privy Council *(Fr.)*
coram	in the presence of *(Lat.)*
corpus delicti	the material evidence of the offence *(Lat.)*
coup de grace	the finishing stroke *(Fr.)*
Das Beste ist gut genug	The best is good enough *(Ger.)*
de facto	in fact *(Lat.)*
de jure	by right *(Lat.)*
de rigeur	by custom *(Fr.)*
Dei gratia	by the grace of God *(Lat.)*
démenti	official denial *(Fr.)*
dies iræ	Day of Judgement *(Lat.)*
Dieu et mon droit	God and my right *(Fr.)*
dramatis personæ	characters represented *(Lat.)*
editio princeps	original edition *(Lat.)*

ex æquo	by right *(Lat.)*
ex curia	out of court *(Lat.)*
ex officio	by virtue of his office; as his position allows *(Lat.)*
ex post facto	after the event *(Lat.)*
exempli gratia	by way of example *(Lat.)*
fait accompli	something completed *(Fr.)*
faux pas	a false step/wrong move *(Fr.)*
genes de guerre	soldiers *(Fr.)*
gens d'église	people of the church *(Fr.)*
gens de condition	people of rank *(Fr.)*
gens de lettres	people of letters/literary people *(Fr.)*
habeas corpus	a writ to oppose detention of a person *(Lat.)*
hoc loco	in this place *(Lat.)*
hors de saison	out of season *(Fr.)*
ibidem	in the same place *(Lat.)*
id est	that is *(Lat.)*
impasse	an insoluble problem *(Fr.)*
imprimatur	let it be printed *(Lat.)*
in curia	in the court *(Lat.)*
in extenso	in its entirety *(Lat.)*
in loco parentis	in the place of a parent *(Lat.)*
in memoriam	in memory of *(Lat.)*
in nomine	in the name of *(Lat.)*
in puris naturalibus	stark naked *(Lat.)*
in reum natura	in the nature of things *(Lat.)*
in situ	in its original situation *(Lat.)*
in statu quo	in its original state *(Lat.)*
in toto	entirely *(Lat.)*
inter alia	among other matters *(Lat.)*
ipso facto	by the fact itself *(Lat.)*
ipso jure	by the law itself *(Lat.)*
jour de fête	festival *(Fr.)*
Juge de paix	Justice of the peace *(Fr.)*
jure divino	by divine law *(Lat.)*
jure humano	by human law *(Lat.)*
lapsus calami	a slip of the pen *(Lat.)*
lapsus linguæ	a slip of the tongue *(Lat.)*
lapsus memoriæ	a slip of the memory *(Lat.)*
Le roi et l'état	The King and The State *(Fr.)*
lex non scripta	the common law *(Lat.)*
lex terræ	the law of the land *(Lat.)*
loco citato	in the place quoted *(Lat.)*
mal à propos	ill-timed *(Fr.)*
mala fide	in bad faith *(Lat.)*

manu propria	with one's own hand *(Lat.)*
me judice	as I judge it *(Lat.)*
meo periculo	at my own risk *(Lat.)*
modo et forma	in manner and form *(Lat.)*
modo præscripto	in the manner prescribed *(Lat.)*
modus operandi	the manner of working *(Lat.)*
mon ami	my friend *(Fr.)*
Mon Dieu!	My God! *(Fr.)*
more suo	after his own manner *(Lat.)*
mos pro lege	custom for law *(Lat.)*
mot à mot	word for word *(Fr.)*
mot juste	the correct word *(Fr.)*
mots d'usage	common expressions *(Fr.)*
né *(m.)*, née *(fem.)*	born *(Fr.)*
necessitas non habat legem	necessity has no law *(Lat.)*
Nicht wahr?	Is that not so? *(Ger.)*
nihil ad rem	nothing to the purpose *(Lat.)*
nom du guerre	an assumed name *(Fr.)*
non compos mentis	of unsound mind *(Lat.)*
non sequitur	it does not follow *(Lat.)*
nota bene	mark well *(Lat.)*
nouveau riche	the new rich *(Fr.)*
nulli secundus	second to none *(Lat.)*
nunc aut nunquam	now or never *(Lat.)*
omnia vincit amor	love conquers all *(Lat.)*
omnia vincit labor	work conquers all *(Lat.)*
onus probandi	the weight of the proof *(Lat.)*
pace tua	by your leave *(Lat.)*
pacta conventa	on the agreed terms *(Lat.)*
pas dans le train	not up to date *(Fr.)*
passe-partout	a master key *(Fr.)*
passez-moi ce mot-là	excuse the expression *(Fr.)*
pax vobiscum	peace be with you *(Lat.)*
peccavi	I acknowledge the error *(Lat.)*
pendent lite	pending the litigation *(Lat.)*
per contra	on the contrary *(Lat.)*
per diem	by the day *(Lat.)*
per se	by itself *(Lat.)*
pièce bien faite	something well done *(Fr.)*
pièce de résistance	(Prev. used for food – the main joint at meals) *(Fr.)*
pleno jure	by full authority *(Lat.)*
pluries	on several occasions *(Lat.)*
poco à poco	little by little *(It.)*
post meridiem	after noon *(Lat.)*

post mortem	after death *(Lat.)*
pour ainsi dire	so to say *(Fr.)*
præmontius, præmunitus	forewarned, forearmed *(Lat.)*
primus inter pares	first among equals *(Lat.)*
pro et con	for and against *(Lat.)*
pro patria	for our country *(Lat.)*
pro rata	at the same rate; in proportion *(Lat.)*
pro tanto	as far as it goes *(Lat.)*
pro tempore	for the time being *(Lat.)*
probatum est	thus proved *(Lat.)*
projet de loi	a legislative bill *(Fr.)*
proximo	next month *(Lat.)*
pur et simple	purely and simply *(Fr.)*
quand même	all the same *(Fr.)*
quantum sufficit	as much as is required *(Lat.)*
quantum volueris	as much as you please *(Lat.)*
quo warranto?	by what warrant (legal writ)? *(Lat.)*
quoad hoc	to this extent *(Lat.)*
quondam	former *(Lat.)*
raison d'état	by reason of state *(Fr.)*
raison d'être	by reason of being *(Fr.)*
regium donum	a royal grant/decree *(Lat.)*
rente viagère	an anuuity *(Fr.)*
repetatur	let it be repeated *(Lat.)*
répondez, s'il vous plait	please reply (RSVP or R.S.V.P.) *(Fr.)*
res judicata	the case is already determined *(Lat.)*
ruse de guerre	a strategem *(Fr.)*
s'il vous plait	if you please *(Fr.)*
salus populi suprema est lex	the supreme law is the welfare of the people *(Lat.)*
salvo jure	saving the right *(Lat.)*
salvo pudore	without offence to modesty *(Lat.)*
sang-froid	indifference *(Fr.)*
savoir faire	with tact *(Fr.)*
savoir vivre	with good manners *(Fr.)*
secunda artum	according to the rule *(Lat.)*
seriatim	in a series *(Lat.)*
sic passim	so everywhere *(Lat.)*
simel et simul	once and at the same time *(Lat.)*
sine die	without a day being appointed/indefinitely *(Lat.)*
sine qua non	that which is indispensable *(Lat.)*
soit dit entre nous	between ourselves *(Fr.)*
sous tous les rapports	in all respects *(Fr.)*
stet	let it stand *(Lat.)*

sub judice	under consideration *(Lat.)*
sub pœna	under a penalty *(Lat.)*
sub rosa	in secret *(Lat.)*
sub silentio	in silence *(Lat.)*
sufficit	it is enough *(Lat.)*
sumendus	to be taken *(Lat.)*
suppressio veri	suppression of truth *(Lat.)*
talis pater, qualis filius	like father, like son *(Lat.)*
tant bien que mal	it is the same to us *(Fr.)*
tant mieux	so much the better *(Fr.)*
tant pis	so much the worse *(Fr.)*
telle vie, telle fin	as they live, so they die *(Fr.)*
terminus ad quem	the goal *(Lat.)*
tête-à-tête	confidential conversation *(Fr.)*
tiers État	The Third Estate *(Fr.)*
totidem verbis	in so many words *(Lat.)*
toties quoties	as often as *(Lat.)*
tout-à-fait	altogether; quite *(Fr.)*
tout bien ou rien	all or nothing *(Fr.)*
tout ensemble	the general effect *(Fr.)*
touts frais faits	all costs paid *(Fr.)*
tutte quanti	et cetera *(It.)*
ubi supra	where above mentioned *(Lat.)*
una voce	unanimously; with one voice *(Lat.)*
unum et idem	one and the same *(Lat.)*
ut infra	as below *(Lat.)*
ut supra	as above stated *(Lat.)*
vaille-que-vaille	at all events *(Fr.)*
valiorum notae	notes of various authors *(Lat.)*
variæ lectiones	various readings *(Lat.)*
vendre en gros et en detail	wholesaler and retailer *(Fr.)*
verba volant, scripta manent	words fly, the written word remains *(Lat.)*
via media	the middle course *(Lat.)*
vice	in place of *(Lat.)*
vide ut supra	see preceeding statement *(Lat.)*
vis-à-vis	opposite; as opposed to *(Fr.)*
voilà tout	that's all *(Fr.)*
vulgo	popularly *(Lat.)*
Wie gewonnen, so zerrinnen	Easy come, easy go *(Ger.)*
zum Beispiel	For example *(Ger.)*

Quod scripsi, scripsi[4]

---

4   What I have written, I have written.

Strange how much you've got to know before you know how little you know. – Anon.

Researching material for this book I was inspired not so much by my own interests as by the writings of others. By this I mean articles, papers, theses and so forth sent to me for, well, '... could you just glance through this when you have a moment ...'. And there I encounter 'a business of ferrets'. A business? Well, how right the author was. I'm glad he didn't ask me about the group name for skunks, or choir-masters. I couldn't find those. Might even be the same!

My curiosity was also aroused by a number of other things: Was Roosevelt a Democrat or a Republican? And when, precisely, was the 'Ming Dynasty'. I don't suggest for a minute that your paper will be peppered with gems of nature, history or politics, but one day you may have the need to feel enlightened about the group name for dotterel (assuming you have heard of dotterel, of course).

Group Names

Four legs good, two legs bad. – George Orwell (1903–1950). *Animal Farm.*

I often feel that the richness of the English language is particularly illustrated by hyperbole (def.: the use of an overstatement or exaggeration for effect – *Longmans Dictionary*), alliteration (repetitive sounds) or onomatopoeia (look it up in the dictionary). There is, however, one area where mistakes are often made but where a mastery of English can manifest itself – group names. These are included here for that reason, plus the fact that these are among the gems of the English language. Again, these may be found on the web, but save yourself the effort.

Birds

Birds in general: flight (in the air), flock (on the ground), volary, (race generally for gamebirds or waterfowl, referring to a pair or couple killed by hunter), dissimulation.

Bitterns: sedge, siege
Buzzards: wake
Bobolinks: chain
Chicks (of many species): brood; clutch
Coots: cover
Cormorants: gulp, flight
Cranes: sedge
Crows: murder, horde
Curlews: herd
Dotterel: trip
Doves: dule, pitying (specific to turtle doves), bevy, cote, dole, dule, paddling, piteousness, flight
Ducks: brace, flock (in flight), raft (on water) team, paddling (on water), paddling
Eagles: convocation
Eggs: clutch
Emus: mob
Falcons: cast; kettle (riding a thermal)
Finches: charm
Flamingos: stand
Geese: flock, gaggle (on the ground), skein (in flight)
Grouse: pack (in late season)
Gulls: colony
Hawks: cast, kettle (flying in large numbers), boil (two or more spiralling in flight)
Hens: brood
Herons: hedge, sedge, siege
Jays: party, scold
Lapwings: deceit
Larks: ascension, exaltation
Mallards: sord (in flight), brace
Magpies: tiding, gulp, murder, charm
Martens: richness
Nightingales: watch
Owls: parliament
Parrots: company
Partridge: covey
Peacocks: muster, ostentation
Penguins: colony, huddle, crèche (nursery group)

Pigeons: flight, flock
Pipers: poverty
Pheasant: nest, nide (a brood, on the ground), nye, bouquet (when flushed)
Plovers: congregation, wing (in flight)
Ptarmigans: covey
Quail: bevy, covey
Ravens: unkindness
Rooks: colony, building
Snipe: walk, wisp
Sparrows: host
Starlings: murmuration
Storks: muster, mustering
Swallows: flight
Swans: bevy, herd, wedge (in flight)
Swifts: flock
Teal: spring
Turkeys: raft, rafter, gang
Turtledoves: pitying
Widgeons: company
Wildfowl: plump
Woodcocks: fall
Woodpeckers: descent

Fish

Fish in general: draft or draught, haul, nest, run, school, shoal (some authors claim that the common 'school' is a corruption of shoal, and therefore incorrect).

Bass: shoal
Dolphins: pod
Goldfish: glint
Herring: army
Jellyfish: smack
Pilchards: shoal
Porpoises: herd, pod, occ. school
Sharks: shiver
Trout: hover

Insects

Ants: army, colony, swarm
Bacteria: culture
Bees: grist, hive, swarm
Caterpillars: army
Cockroaches: intrustion
Flies: swarm, business
Gnats: cloud, horde, swarm
Grasshoppers: cloud
Hornets: nest
Locusts: plague

Invertebrates

Clams: bed
Oysters: bed

Mammals

Antelope: herd
Apes: shrewdness
Asses: pace, herd
Badgers: cete, colony
Bats: colony
Bears: sloth, sleuth
Beavers: colony
Boars: sounder, singular
Buffalo: gang: obstinacy (I suspect
    these refer to old world buffalo;
    use 'herd' for American bison)
Cats: clowder, pounce; for kittens ...
    kindle, litter, intrigue
Cattle: drove, herd
Coyote: band
Deer: herd, hide, bevy (refers only to
    roe deer)
Dogs: litter (young), pack (wild),
    cowardice (of curs); specific to
    hounds – cry, mute, pack, kennel,
    litter (pups)
Donkeys: drove, herd, pace
Elephant seals: (weaner = pod, i.e.
    yearling elephant seals)
Elephants: herd

Elk: gang
Ferrets: business, cast, fesnying
Foxes: leash, skulk, earth
Frogs: army, colony, knot
Giraffes: tower
Gnu: implausibility
Goats: tribe, trip
Gorillas: band
Greyhounds: leash
Hares: down, husk
Hippopotamuses: bloat
Hogs: drift, parcel
Horses: team, harras, stable, rag (for
    colts), stud (a group of horses
    belonging to a single owner,
    string (ponies)
Hounds: cry, mute, pack
Housecats: clowder, cluster, dout,
    nuisance
Hyenas: cackle
Jackrabbits: husk
Kangaroos: herd, mob, troop
Kittens: litter, kindle
Leopards: leap
Lions: pride
Lizards: lounge
Mares: stud
Martens: richness
Moles: company, labour, movement
Monkeys: barrel, cartload, troop
Mules: rake, pack, span
Otters: family, romp, frolic
Oxen: drove, herd, team, yoke
Pigs: drift, drove, litter (young),
    sounder (of swine), team, passel
    (of hogs), singular (refers to:
    group of boars)
Piglets: farrow
Pigs: herd, litter, sounder
Polecats: chine
Ponies: string
Porcupines: prickle
Pups: litter
Rabbits: bury, colony, husk, leash,
    trace, trip, warren, nest, herd

(domestic only), litter, nest (young); specific to hares – down, husk

Raccoons: gaze

Rats: colony, pack, plague, swarm

Rattlesnakes: rhumba

Rhinoceroses: crash

Roebucks: bevy

Seals: colony, crash, harem, pod, herd, team

Sheep: drove, flock, herd, down, fold, hurtle, trip

Snakes: den, nest, pit

Squirrels: dray, scurry

Swine: drift, sounder

Tigers: streak, ambush

Toads: knot

Vipers: generation, nest

Walruses: ugly, herd, pod

Whales: school, pod, gam, herd

Wild cats: destruction

Wolves: herd, pack, rout or route (when in movement)

Zebras: crossing, herd

People

Boys: rascal (Some might call them a pest of boys)

Cuckolds: incredulity

Fishermen: drift

Ghosts: fraid

Girls: giggle

Jugglers: neverthriving

Lecturers, a drift

Linguists: babble

Nuns: superfluity

Oarsmen: row

Painters: illusion

Peddlers: impertinence

People: congregation

Priests, congregation

Servants: obeisance

Soldiers: boast

Stalkers: following

Thieves: skulk

Tourists: glaze

Undertakers: unction

Wives: impatience

Reptiles and Amphibians

Crocodiles: bask

Frogs: army

Toads: knot

Turtles: bale, nest

Sharks: shiver

Snakes, vipers: nest

Kings and Queens of England

I left England when I was four because I found out that I could never be King. – Bob Hope (1903–2003) (American comedian, born in the U.K.)

Somehow, it is always interesting to know about the history of England, not to mention Scotland. Here is a summary. And for you who already know your history, Alfred, *the Great*, was not a good cook. Perhaps he should have been known as Alfred the Cake!

House of Wessex
Egbert (802–839)
Aethelwulf (839–585)

Aethelbald (855–860)
Aethelbert (860–866)
Aethelred (866–871)
Alfred, the Great (871–899)
Edward, the Elder (899–925)
Athelstan (925–940)
Edmund, the Magnificent (940–946)
Eadred (946–955)
Eadwig (Edwy), All–Fair (955–959)
Edgar, the Peaceable (959–975)
Edward, the Martyr (975–978)
Aethelred, the Unready (978–1016)
Edmund, Ironside (1016)

Danish line
Svein, Forkbeard (1016)
Canute, the Great (1016–1035)
Harald, Harefoot (1035–1040)
Hardicanute (1040–1042)

House of Wessex, Restored
Edward, the Confessor (1042–1066)
Harold II (1066)

Norman line
William I, the Conqueror (14 Oct. 1066–9 Sept. 1087)
William II, Rufus (26 Sept. 1087–2 Aug. 1100)
Henry I, Beauclerc (5 Aug. 1100–1 Dec. 1135)
Stephen (26 Dec. 1135–25 Oct. 1154)
Empress Matilda (1141)

Plantagenet, Angevin line
Henry II, Curtmantle (19 Dec. 1154–6 July 1189)
Richard I the Lionheart (3 Sept. 1189–6 April 1199)
John, Lackland (27 May 1199–19 Oct. 1216)
Henry III (28 Oct. 1216–16 Nov. 1272)
Edward I, Longshanks (20 Nov. 1272–7 July 1307)
Edward II (8 July 1307–20 Jan. 1327)
Edward III (25 Jan. 1327–21 June 1377)
Richard II (22 June 1377–29 Sept. 1399)

Plantagenet, Lancastrian line
Henry IV, Bolingbroke (30 Sept. 1399–20 March 1413)
Henry V (21 March 1413–31 Aug. 1422)
Henry VI (1 Sept. 1422–4 March 1461)

Plantagenet, Yorkist line
Edward IV (4 March 1461–9 Oct. 1470, 1471–9 April 83)
Edward V (9 April 1483–25 June 1483)
Richard III, Crookback (26 June 1483–22 Aug. 1485)

House of Tudor
Henry VII, Tudor (22 Aug. 1485–21 April 1509)
Henry VIII (22 April 1509–28 Jan. 1547)
Edward VI (28 Jan. 1547–6 July 1553)
Lady Jane Grey (6 July 1553–17 July 1553)
Mary I, Tudor (6 July 1553–17 Nov. 1558)
Elizabeth I (17 Nov. 1558–24 March 1603)

House of Stuart
James I (24 March 1603–27 March 1625)
Charles I (27 March 1625–30 Jan. 1649)

The Commonwealth
Oliver Cromwell (1649–58)
Richard Cromwell (1658–59)

House of Stuart, Restored
Charles II (30 Jan. 1660–6 Feb. 1685). *De facto* king from 29 May 1660.
James II (6 Feb. 1685–11 Dec. 1688)

House of Orange and Stuart
William III, Mary II (13 Feb. 1689–8 March 1702). Mary died 27 Dec. 1694.

House of Stuart
Anne (8 March 1702–1 Aug. 1714)
House of Brunswick, Hanover Line
George I (1 Aug. 1714–11 June 1727)
George II (11 June 1727–25 Oct. 1760)
George III (25 Oct. 1760–29 Jan. 1820). Regency from 5 Feb. 1811.
George IV (29 Jan. 1820–26 June 1830)

William IV (26 June 1830–20 June 1837)
Victoria (20 June 1837–22 Jan. 1901)

House of Saxe–Coburg–Gotha
Edward VII (22 Jan. 1901–6 May 10)

House of Windsor
George V (6 May 1910–20 Jan. 36)
Edward VIII (20 Jan. 1936–10 Dec. 1936) Abdicated
George VI (11 Dec. 1936–6 Feb. 1952)
Elizabeth II (6 Feb. 1952–present)

Prime Ministers, Great Britain

I am extraordinarily patient, provided I get my own way in the end.
– Margaret Thatcher in the *Observer*, 4. April 1989.

Period	Prime Minister (Party)
1715–42	Sir Robert Walpole (Whig)
1742–43	Spencer Compton, Earl of Wilmington (Whig)
1743–54	Henry Pelham (Whig)
1754–56	Thomas Pelham–Holles, Duke of Newcastle (Whig)
1756–57	William Cavendish, Duke of Devonshire (Whig)
1757–62	Thomas Pelham-Holles, Duke of Newcastle (Whig)
1762–63	Stuart, Earl of Bute (Tory)
1763–65	George Grenville (Whig)
1765–66	Charles Watson–Wentworth, Marquess of Rockingham (Whig)
1766–67	William Pitt the Elder, Earl of Chatham (Whig)
1767–70	Augustus Fitzroy, Duke of Grafton (Whig)
1770–82	Frederick North, Lord North (Tory)
1782	Charles Watson–Wentworth, Marquess of Rockingham (Whig)
1782–83	William FitzMaurice, Earl of Shelburne (Whig)
1783	William Bentinck, Duke of Portland (Tory)
1783–181	William Pitt, the Younger (Tory)
1801–04	Henry Addington (Tory)
1804–06	William Pitt, the Younger (Tory)
1806–07	William Grenville, Lord Grenville (Whig)
1807–09	William Bentinck, Duke of Portland (Tory)
1809–12	Spencer Perceval (Tory)
1812–27	Robert Jenkinson, Earl of Liverpool (Tory)
1827	Frederick Robinson, Viscount Goderich (Tory)
1827–28	George Canning (Tory)
1828–30	Arthur Wellesley, Duke of Wellington (Tory)

1830–34	Charles Grey, Earl Grey (Whig)
1834	Arthur Wellesley, Duke of Wellington (Tory)
1834	William Lamb, Viscount Melbourne (Whig)
1834–35	Sir Robert Peel (Tory)
1835–41	William Lamb, Viscount Melbourne (Whig)
1841–46	Sir Robert Peel (Tory)
1846–52	Lord John Russell (Whig)
1852	Edward Stanley, Earl of Derby (Conservative)
1852–55	George Hamilton–Gordon, Earl of Aberdeen (Conservative)
1855–58	Viscount Palmerston (Liberal)
1858	Edward Stanley, Earl of Derby (Conservative)
1859–65	Viscount Palmerston (Liberal)
1865–66	John Russell, Earl Russell (Liberal)
1866–68	Edward Stanley, Earl of Derby (Conservative)
1868	Benjamin Disraeli (Conservative)
1868–74	William Ewart Gladstone (Liberal)
1874–80	Benjamin Disraeli (Conservative)
1880–85	William Ewart Gladstone (Liberal)
1885–86	Marquess of Salisbury (Conservative)
1886	William Ewart Gladstone (Liberal)
1886–92	Marquess of Salisbury (Conservative)
1892–94	William Ewart Gladstone (Liberal)
1894–95	Earl of Rosebery (Liberal)
1895–02	Marquess of Salisbury (Conservative)
1902–05	Arthur Balfour (Conservative)
1905–08	Henry Campbell–Bannerman (Liberal)
1908–1916	Herbert H. Asquith (Liberal)
1916–22	David Lloyd George (Liberal)
1922–23	Andrew Bonar Law (Conservative)
1923–24	Stanley Baldwin (Conservative)
1924	James Ramsay MacDonald (Labour)
1924–29	Stanley Baldwin (Conservative)
1929–31	James Ramsay MacDonald (Labour)
1931–35	James Ramsay MacDonald (National)
1935–37	Stanley Baldwin (Conservative)
1937–40	Neville Chamberlain (Conservative)
1940–45	Winston Churchill (Conservative)
1945–51	Clement Attlee (Labour)
1951–55	Winston Churchill (Conservative)
1955–57	Sir Anthony Eden (Conservative)
1957–63	Harold Macmillan (Conservative)
1963–64	Sir Alec Douglas-Home (Conservative)
1964–70	Harold Wilson (Labour)
1970–74	Edward Heath (Conservative)
1974–76	Harold Wilson (Labour)

1976–79	James Callaghan (Labour)
1979–90	Margaret Thatcher (Conservative)
1990–97	John Major (Conservative)
1997	Tony Blair (Labour)

Presidents of the USA

A hard dog to keep on the porch. – Hilary Rodham Clinton. (*On her husband.*)

President, (born-died)	Party	Period	Vice-president(s)
1. George Washington (1732–1799)	None, Federalist	1789–1797	John Adams
2. John Adams (1735–1826)	Federalist	1797–1801	Thomas Jefferson
3. Thomas Jefferson (1743–1826)	Dem.-Rep.	1801–1809	Aaron Burr, George Clinton
4. James Madison (1751–1836)	Dem.-Rep.	1809–1817	George Clinton, Elbridge Gerry
5. James Monroe (1758–1831)	Dem.-Rep.	1817–1825	Daniel Tompkins
6. John Quincy Adams (1767–1848)	Dem.-Rep.	1825–1829	John Calhoun
7. Andrew Jackson (1767–1845)	Democrat	1829–1837	John Calhoun, Martin van Buren
8. Martin van Buren (1782–1862)	Democrat	1837–1841	Richard Johnson
9. William H. Harrison (1773–1841)	Whig	1841	John Tyler
10. John Tyler (1790–1862)	Whig	1841–1845	
11. James K. Polk (1795–1849)	Democrat	1845–1849	George Dallas
12. Zachary Taylor (1784–1850)	Whig	1849–1850	Millard Fillmore
13. Millard Fillmore (1800–1874)	Whig	1850–1853	
14. Franklin Pierce (1804–1869)	Democrat	1853–1857	William King
15. James Buchanan (1791–1868)	Democrat	1857–1861	John Breckinridge
16. Abraham Lincoln (1809–1865)	Republican	1861–1865	Hannibal Hamlin, Andrew Johnson
17. Andrew Johnson (1808–1875)	National Union	1865–1869	
18. Ulysses S. Grant (1822–1885)	Republican	1869–1877	Schuyler Colfax
19. Rutherford Hayes (1822–1893)	Republican	1877–1881	William Wheeler
20. James Garfield (1831–1881)	Republican	1881	Chester Arthur
21. Chester Arthur (1829–1886)	Republican	1881–1885	
22. Grover Cleveland (1837–1908)	Democrat	1885–1889	Thomas Hendriks
23. Benjamin Harrison (1833–1901)	Republican	1889–1893	Levi Morton
24. Grover Cleveland (1837–1908)	Democrat	1893–1897	Adlai Stevenson
25. William McKinley (1843–1901)	Republican	1897–1901	Garret Hobart, Theodore Roosevelt
26. Theodore Roosevelt (1858–1919)	Republican	1901–1909	Charles Fairbanks
27. William Taft (1857–1930)	Republican	1909–1913	James Sherman
28. Woodrow Wilson (1856–1924)	Democrat	1913–1921	Thomas Marshall
29. Warren Harding (1865–1923)	Republican	1921–1923	Calvin Coolidge
30. Calvin Coolidge (1872–1933)	Republican	1923–1929	Charles Dawes
31. Herbert C. Hoover (1874–1964)	Republican	1929–1933	Charles Curtis
32. Franklin D. Roosevelt (1882–1945)	Democrat	1933–1945	John Garner, Henry Wallace, Harry S. Truman
33. Harry S. Truman (1884–1972)	Democrat	1945–1953	Alben Barkley

34.	Dwight D. Eisenhower (1890–1969)	Republican	1953–1961	Richard Milhous Nixon
35.	John F. Kennedy (1917–1963)	Democrat	1961–1963	Lyndon Johnson
36.	Lyndon B. Johnson (1908–1973)	Democrat	1963–1969	Hubert Humphrey
37.	Richard M. Nixon (1913–1994)	Republican	1969–1974	Spiro Agnew, Gerald R. Ford
38.	Gerald R. Ford (1913–)	Republican	1974–1977	Nelson Rockefeller
39.	James (Jimmy) Earl Carter, Jr. (1924–)	Democrat	1977–1981	Walter Mondale
40.	Ronald W. Reagan (1911–)	Republican	1981–1989	George H. W. Bush
41.	George H. W. Bush (1924–)	Republican	1989–1993	James Danforth (Dan) Quayle
42.	William (Bill) J. Clinton (1946–)	Democrat	1993–2001	Al Gore
43.	George W. Bush (1946–)	Republican	2001–	Richard Cheney

French Kings, Emperors and Presidents

France is an absolute monarchy, tempered by songs. – Nicolas-Sébastian Chamfort (17141–1794). French writer.

Later Carolingian transition

814–840 Louis I (not a king of 'France')
840–877 Charles II (the Bald)
877–879 Louis II (the Stammerer)
879–882 Louis III (joint with Carloman below)
879–884 Carloman (joint with Louis III above, until 882)
884–888 Charles the Fat
888–898 Eudes (also Odo) of Paris (non-Carolingian)
898–922 Charles III (the Simple)
922–923 Robert I (non-Carolingian)
923–936 Raoul (also Rudolf, non-Carolingian)
936–954 Louis IV (d'Outremer or The Foreigner)
954–986 Lothar (also Lothaire)
986–987 Louis V (the Do-Nothing)

Capetian dynasty

987–996 Hugh Capet
996–1031 Robert II (the Pious)
1031–1060 Henry I
1060–1108 Philip I
1108–1137 Louis VI (the Fat)
1137–1180 Louis VII (the Young)
1180–1223 Philip II Augustus
1223–1226 Louis VIII (the Lion)
1226–1270 Louis IX (St. Louis)
1270–1285 Philip III (the Bold)

1285–1314 Philip IV (the Fair)
1314–1316 Louis X (the Stubborn)
1316   John I
1316–1322 Philip V (the Tall)
1322–1328 Charles IV (the Fair)

Valois dynasty
1328–1350 Philip VI
1350–1364 John II (the Good)
1364–1380 Charles V (the Wise)
1380–1422 Charles VI (the Mad, Well-Beloved, or Foolish)
1422–1461 Charles VII (the Well-Served or Victorious)
1461–1483 Louis XI (the Spider)
1483–1498 Charles VIII (Father of his People)
1498–1515 Louis XII
1515–1547 Francis I
1547–1559 Henry II
1559–1560 Francis II
1560–1574 Charles IX
1574–1589 Henry III

Bourbon dynasty
1589–1610 Henry IV
1610–1643 Louis XIII
1643–1715 Louis XIV (the Sun King)
1715–1774 Louis XV
1774–1792 Louis XVI

First Republic
1792–1795   National Convention
1795–1799   Directory (Directors)
          1795–99   Paul François Jean Nicolas de Barras
          1795–99   Jean-François Reubell
          1795–99   Louis Marie La Revellíere-Lépeaux
          1795–97   Lazare Nicolas Marguerite Carnot
          1795–97   Etienne Le Tourneur
          1797   François Marquis de Barthélemy
          1797–99   Philippe Antoine Merlin de Douai
          1797–98   François de Neufchâteau
          1798–99   Jean Baptiste Comte de Treilhard
          1799   Emmanuel Joseph Comte de Sieyés
          1799   Roger Comte de Ducos
          1799   Jean François Auguste Moulins

	1799	Louis Gohier	
1799–1804	Consulate		
	1st Consul:	1799–1804	Napoleon Bonaparte
	2nd Consul:	1799	Emmanuel Joseph Comte de Sieyés,
		1799–1804	Jean-Jacques Régis Cambacérès
	3rd Consul:	1799–1799	Pierre-Roger Ducos
		1799–1804	Charles François Lebrun

First Empire (emperors)
1804–1814 Napoleon I
1814–1815 Louis XVIII (king)
1815   Napoleon I (2nd time)

Bourbons (restored)
1814–1824 Louis XVIII
1824–1830 Charles X

Orleans
1830–1848 Louis Philippe

Second Republic (presidents)
1848   Louis Eugéne Cavaignac
1848–1852 Louis Napoleon (later Napoleon III)

Second Empire (emperors)
1852–1870 (Louis) Napoleon III

Third Republic (presidents)
1870–1871 Louis Jules Trochu (provisional)
1871–1873 Adolphe Thiers
1873–1879 Patrice de MacMahon
1879–1887 Jules Grévy
1887–1894 Sadi Carnot
1894–1895 Jean Casimir-Périer
1895–1899 Félix Faure
1899–1906 Emile Loubet
1906–1913 Armand Fallières
1913–1920 Raymond Poincaré
1920   Paul Deschanel
1920–1924 Alexandre Millerand
1924–1931 Gaston Doumergue

1931–1932 Paul Doumer
1932–1940 Albert Lebrun

Vichy Government (Chief of State)
1940–1944 Henri Philippe Petain

Provisional Government (presidents)
1944–1946 Charles de Gaulle
1946   Félix Gouin
1946   Georges Bidault
1946   Leon Blum

Fourth Republic (presidents)
1947–1954 Vincent Auriol
1954–1959 René Coty

Fifth Republic (Presidents)
1959–1969 Charles de Gaulle
1969–1974 Georges Pompidou
1974–1981 Valéry Giscard d'Estaing
1981–1995 François Mitterand
1995–   Jacques Chirac

Popes Since AD 32

It often happens that I wake at night and begin to think about a serious problem and decide that I just have tell the Pope about it. Then I wake up completely and remember I am the Pope. – Pope John XXIII

St. Peter (32–67)
St. Linus (67–76)
St. Anacletus (Cletus) (76–88)
St. Clement I (88–97)
St. Evaristus (97–105)
St. Alexander I (105–115)
St. Sixtus I (115–125) – also called Xystus I
St. Telesphorus (125–136)
St. Hyginus (136–140)
St. Pius I (140–155)
St. Anicetus (155–166)

St. Soter (166–175)
St. Eleutherius (175–189)
St. Victor I (189–199)
St. Zephyrinus (199–217)
St. Callistus I (217–22)
St. Urban I (222–30)
St. Pontain (230–35)
St. Anterus (235–36)
St. Fabian (236–50)
St. Cornelius (251–53)
St. Lucius I (253–54)
St. Stephen I (254–257)

St. Sixtus II (257–258)
St. Dionysius (260–268)
St. Felix I (269–274)
St. Eutychian (275–283)
St. Caius (283–296) – also called
    Gaius
St. Marcellinus (296–304)
St. Marcellus I (308–309)
St. Eusebius (309 or 310)
St. Miltiades (311–14)
St. Sylvester I (314–35)
St. Marcus (336)
St. Julius I (337–52)
Liberius (352–66)
St. Damasus I (366–83)
St. Siricius (384–99)
St. Anastasius I (399–401)
St. Innocent I (401–17)
St. Zosimus (417–18)
St. Boniface I (418–22)
St. Celestine I (422–32)
St. Sixtus III (432–40)
St. Leo I (the Great) (440–61)
St. Hilarius (461–68)
St. Simplicius (468–83)
St. Felix III (II) (483–92)
St. Gelasius I (492–96)
Anastasius II (496–98)
St. Symmachus (498–514)
St. Hormisdas (514–23)
St. John I (523–26)
St. Felix IV (III) (526–30)
Boniface II (530–32)
John II (533–35)
St. Agapetus I (535–36)
also called Agapitus I
St. Silverius (536–37)
Vigilius (537–55)
Pelagius I (556–61)
John III (561–74)
Benedict I (575–79)
Pelagius II (579–90)
St. Gregory I (the Great) (590–604)
Sabinian (604–606)
Boniface III (607)

St. Boniface IV (608–15)
St. Deusdedit (Adeodatus I) (615–18)
Boniface V (619–25)
Honorius I (625–38)
Severinus (640)
John IV (640–42)
Theodore I (642–49)
St. Martin I (649–55)
St. Eugene I (655–57)
St. Vitalian (657–72)
Adeodatus (II) (672–76)
Donus (676–78)
St. Agatho (678–81)
St. Leo II (682–83)
St. Benedict II (684–85)
John V (685–86)
Conon (686–87)
St. Sergius I (687–701)
John VI (701–05)
John VII (705–07)
Sisinnius (708)
Constantine (708–15)
St. Gregory II (715–31)
St. Gregory III (731–41)
St. Zachary (741–52)
Stephen II (752)
Stephen III (752–57)
St. Paul I (757–67)
Stephen IV (767–72)
Adrian I (772–95)
St. Leo III (795–816)
Stephen V (816–17)
St. Paschal I (817–24)
Eugene II (824–27)
Valentine (827)
Gregory IV (827–44)
Sergius II (844–47)
St. Leo IV (847–55)
Benedict III (855–58)
St. Nicholas I (the Great) (858–67)
Adrian II (867–72)
John VIII (872–82)
Marinus I (882–84)
St. Adrian III (884–85)
Stephen VI (885–91)

Formosus (891–96)
Boniface VI (896)
Stephen VII (896–97)
Romanus (897)
Theodore II (897)
John IX (898–900)
Benedict IV (900–03)
Leo V (903)
Sergius III (904–11)
Anastasius III (911–13)
Lando (913–14)
John X (914–28)
Leo VI (928)
Stephen VIII (929–31)
John XI (931–35)
Leo VII (936–39)
Stephen IX (939–42)
Marinus II (942–46)
Agapetus II (946–55)
John XII (955–63)
Leo VIII (963–64)
Benedict V (964)
John XIII (965–72)
Benedict VI (973–74)
Benedict VII (974–83)
John XIV (983–84)
John XV (985–96)
Gregory V (996–99)
Sylvester II (999–1003)
John XVII (1003)
John XVIII (1003–09)
Sergius IV (1009–12)
Benedict VIII (1012–24)
John XIX (1024–32)
Benedict IX (1032–45)
Sylvester III (1045)
Benedict IX (1045)
Gregory VI (1045–46)
Clement II (1046–47)
Benedict IX (1047–48)
Damasus II (1048)
St. Leo IX (1049–54)
Victor II (1055–57)
Stephen X (1057–58)
Nicholas II (1058–61)

Alexander II (1061–73)
St. Gregory VII (1073–85)
Blessed Victor III (1086–87)
Blessed Urban II (1088–99)
Paschal II (1099–1118)
Gelasius II (1118–19)
Callistus II (1119–24)
Honorius II (1124–30)
Innocent II (1130–43)
Celestine II (1143–44)
Lucius II (1144–45)
Blessed Eugene III (1145–53)
Anastasius IV (1153–54)
Adrian IV (1154–59)
Alexander III (1159–81)
Lucius III (1181–85)
Urban III (1185–87)
Gregory VIII (1187)
Clement III (1187–91)
Celestine III (1191–98)
Innocent III (1198–1216)
Honorius III (1216–27)
Gregory IX (1227–41)
Celestine IV (1241)
Innocent IV (1243–54)
Alexander IV (1254–61)
Urban IV (1261–64)
Clement IV (1265–68)
Blessed Gregory X (1271–76)
Blessed Innocent V (1276)
Adrian V (1276)
John XXI (1276–77)
Nicholas III (1277–80)
Martin IV (1281–85)
Honorius IV (1285–87)
Nicholas IV (1288–92)
St. Celestine V (1294)
Boniface VIII (1294–1303)
Blessed Benedict XI (1303–04)
Clement V (1305–14)
John XXII (1316–34)
Benedict XII (1334–42)
Clement VI (1342–52)
Innocent VI (1352–62)
Blessed Urban V (1362–70)

Gregory XI (1370–78)
Urban VI (1378–89)
Boniface IX (1389–1404)
Innocent VII (1404–06)
Gregory XII (1406–15)
Martin V (1417–31)
Eugene IV (1431–47)
Nicholas V (1447–55)
Callistus III (1455–58)
Pius II (1458–64)
Paul II (1464–71)
Sixtus IV (1471–84)
Innocent VIII (1484–92)
Alexander VI (1492–1503)
Pius III (1503)
Julius II (1503–13)
Leo X (1513–21)
Adrian VI (1522–23)
Clement VII (1523–34)
Paul III (1534–49)
Julius III (1550–55)
Marcellus II (1555)
Paul IV (1555–59)
Pius IV (1559–65)
St. Pius V (1566–72)
Gregory XIII (1572–85)
Sixtus V (1585–90)
Urban VII (1590)
Gregory XIV (1590–91)
Innocent IX (1591)
Clement VIII (1592–1605)
Leo XI (1605)
Paul V (1605–21)

Gregory XV (1621–23)
Urban VIII (1623–44)
Innocent X (1644–55)
Alexander VII (1655–67)
Clement IX (1667–69)
Clement X (1670–76)
Blessed Innocent XI (1676–89)
Alexander VIII (1689–91)
Innocent XII (1691–1700)
Clement XI (1700–21)
Innocent XIII (1721–24)
Benedict XIII (1724–30)
Clement XII (1730–40)
Benedict XIV (1740–58)
Clement XIII (1758–69)
Clement XIV (1769–74)
Pius VI (1775–99)
Pius VII (1800–23)
Leo XII (1823–29)
Pius VIII (1829–30)
Gregory XVI (1831–46)
Blessed Pius IX (1846–78)
Leo XIII (1878–1903)
St. Pius X (1903–14)
Benedict XV (1914–22)
Pius XI (1922–39)
Pius XII (1939–58)
Blessed John XXIII (1958–63)
Paul VI (1963–78)
John Paul I (1978)
John Paul II (1978–2005)
Benedict XVI (2005–)

Russian Leaders Since 1462

In Russia they treated me like a Czar and you know how they treated the Czar. – Bob Hope (1903–2003) (American Comedian).

House of Rurik
Ivan III (the Great), 1462–1505
Vasily III, 1505–33
Ivan IV (the Terrible), 1533–84
Feodor I, 1584–98

House of Godunov
Boris Godunov, 1598–1605
Feodor II, 1605
Usurpers
Dmitri, 1605–6
Vasily IV, 1606–10 Interregnum, 1610–13

House of Romanov
Michael, 1613–45
Alexis, 1645–76
Feodor III, 1676–82
Ivan V and Peter I (the Great), 1682–96

The Imperial period, 1689–1917
1689–1725 Peter I, The Great
1725–1727 Catherine I Skavronska
1727–1730 Peter II Romanov
1730–1740 Anna Romanova
1740–1741 Ivan VI Romanov
1741–1762 Elizabeth Romanova
1761–1762 Peter III Romanov
1762–1796 Catherine II The Great Von Anhalt–Zerbst
1796–1801 Paul I Romanov
1801–1825 Alexander I Romanov
1825–1855 Nicholas I Romanov
1855–1881 Alexander II Romanov
1881–1894 Alexander III Romanov
1894–1917 Nicholas II Romanov
October 17 1905 Revolution: General Strike

The Soviet period, 1917–1991
1917   Revolutions (February 23/March 8)
1918–1924 Vladimir Ilyich Lenin
1927–1953 Josif Vissarionovich Stalin
1958–1964 Nikita Khrushchev
1964–1982 Leonid Ilyich Brezhnev
1983–1984 Yuri Andropov
1984–1985 Konstantin Chernenko
1985–1991 Mikhail Gorbachev

The Post–Soviet period, 1991–
1991–2000 Boris Nikolaevich Yeltsin

2000 –   Vladimir Putin

Rulers of the Roman Empire

The Roman Conquest was, however, a Good Thing, *since the Britons were only natives at the time.* –W.C. Sellar and R.J. Yeatman. *1066 and All That* (1930).

The Principate/Julian line
Augustus (27 BC–AD 14)
Tiberius (14–37)
Gaius Caligula (37–41)
Claudius (41–54)
Nero (54–68)
Galba (68–69)
Otho (69)
Vitellius (69)

Flavian Dynasty
Vespasian (69–79)
Titus Flavius (79–81)
Domitian (81–96)

Nervan-Antonian Dynasty
Nerva (96–98)
Trajan (98–117)
Hadrian (117–138)
Antoninus Pius (138–161)
Marcus Aurelius (161–180) (co-emperor Lucius Verus 161–169; throne
    claimed by Avidius Cassius 175)
Commodus (180–193)
Pertinax (193) (recognized as emperor by Septimius Severus)
Septimius Severus (193–211) (throne was also claimed by Didius Julianus 193,
    Pescennius Niger 193–194, and Clodius Albinus 193–197)
Caracalla (211–217)
Macrinus (217–218)
Heliogabalus (218–222) (throne claimed by Verus 219, and Uranius c.221)
Alexander Severus (222–235) (throne claimed by Taurinus)

Rulers during the crisis of the third century
Maximinus Thrax (235–238) (throne claimed by Quartinus 235)
Gordian I and Gordian II (238)

Pupienus and Balbinus (238)

Gordian III (238–244) (throne claimed by Sabinianus 240)

Philip the Arab (244–249) (throne claimed by Pacantius 248, Iotapianus 248, and Silbannacus)

Decius (249–251) (throne claimed by Priscus 249–252, and Licinianus 250)

Herennius Etruscus (251)

Hostilian (251)

Trebonianus Gallus (251–253)

Aemilianus (253)

Valerian I (253–260)

Gallienus (260–268) (throne claimed by Ingenuus 260; Regalianus 260; Macrianus Major, Macrianus Minor and Quietus 260–261; Memor 261; Mussius Aemilianus 261–262; and Aureolus 265)

Claudius II Gothicus (268–270)

Quintillus (270)

Aurelian (270–275) (throne claimed by Domitianus 270–271, Felicissimus 271, and Septimius 271)

Tacitus (275–276)

Florianus (276)

Probus (276-282) (throne claimed by Saturninus 280, Proculus 280, and Bonosus 280)

Carus (282-283)

Carinus (283-285) (co-emperor Numerian; throne claimed by M. Aurelius Julianus 283)

Tetrarchy

Diocletian (284–305) (co-emperor Maximian 286–305)

Constantius Chlorus (305-306) (co-emperor Galerius 305–311)

Constantine I, the Great (306–337) (co-emperors Galerius, Licinius 308–324, and Maximinus Daia 308–313; throne claimed by Maxentius 306–312, and Domitius Alexander 308–309)

House of Constantine

Constantius II (337–361) (together with Constantine II 337–340, and Constans 337–350; throne claimed by Magnentius 350–353)

Julian (361–363). Also known as 'the Apostate'

Jovian (363–364)

Valentinian Dynasty

Valentinian I (364–375) (co-emperor Valens 364–378; throne claimed by Procopius 364–365)

Gratianus (375–383) (co-emperor Valentinian II, 375–392; throne claimed by Magnus Maximus, 383–388)

House of Theodosius

Theodosius I (379–395) (throne claimed by Eugenius 392–394)

Western Empire

Honorius (395–423) (co-emperor Constantius III 421; throne claimed by
    Priscus Attalus 409–410 and again in 414–415, Constantine III 409–411,
    and Jovinus, 411–412)
Valentinian III (423–455) (throne also claimed by Joannes 423–425)
Petronius Maximus (455)
Avitus (456–457)
Majorian (457–461)
Libius Severus (461–465)
Anthemius (467–472)
Olybrius (472)
Glycerius (473–474)
Julius Nepos–(474–475/480)
Romulus Augustus (a.k.a. Romulus Augustulus) 'last' western emperor (475–
    476) continuation: Barbarian kings of Rome

Eastern Empire

Arcadius (395–408)
Theodosius II (408–450)
Marcian (450–457)
Leo I (457–474)
Leo II (474)
Zeno (474–491)
Basiliscus (475–476)
Zeno (restored) (476–491)

Brief History of Egypt

British Occupation Period	(1883–1945)
French Occupation Period	(1798–1882)
Islamic Period	(ca. 750–1796)
Ottoman Turk Period	(1517–1796)
Burgi Mameluke Period	(1382–1517)
Bahri Mameluke Period	(1250–1381)
Mameluke Period	(ca.1250)
Ayyubid Period	(1171–1250)
Fatimid Period	(969–1171)
Abbasid Period	(ca. 750–969
Roman Period	(ca. 31 BC – ca. AD 636)
Byzantine Period	
Roman Period	

The Dynasties (All dates are B.C.E. (Before Common Era)

	Period (B.C.E.)	Dynasty	Famous people
Greek Dynasty	(332–30)	XXXII	Cleopatra VII
			Ptolemy I
			Arsinoe II
			Pompey
			Alexander
			Augustus Caesar
Persian Period II	(342–332)	XXXI	Darius III
			Artaxerxes III
Late Period II	(425–342)	XXX	Nectanebo I
		XXIX	Amyrteos
Persian Period I	(517–425)	XXVII	Artaxeres
			Xerxes
			Darius I
			Cambyses
Late Period I	(1069–517)	XXVI	Necho II
			Herodotus
		XXV	Shabaka
		XXIV	Tefnakht
		XXIII	
		XXII	Osoraken I
			Shoshenk I
		XXI	Psusennes I
New Kingdom	(1550–1069)	XX	Ramses III
		XIX	Ramses II
		XVIII	Nefertiti
			Princess Ankhesenaton
			Tutankhamun
			Hatshepsut
			Tuthmosis I II III IV
			Ahmose I
			Rekhmire
Intermediate Period II	(1650–1550)	XVII	
		XV	Khyan
	Period (B.C.E.)	**Dynasty**	**Famous people**
		XIV	
		XIII	
Middle Kingdom	(2125–1650)	XII	Senusret I II III
			Amenemhet I II III
Intermediate Period I	(2181–2125)	XI	Mentuhotep I
		X	

		IX	Achthoes
		VIII	
		VII	
Old Kingdom	(3100–2181)	VI	Pepi II
			Pepi I
			Weni
			VSahure
		IV	Chepheren
			Khufu
			Sneferu
		III	Huni
			Imhotep
			Dzoser
Archaic Period	(3414–3100)	II	
		I	Menes
Predynastic Period	(ca. 5464–3414)	Late	
		Middle	
		Early	

An excellent web site on Egyptian history is www.touregypt.net

Chinese Dynasties

Dates	Dynasty
ca. 2000–1500 BC	Xia
1700–1027 BC	Shang
1027–771 BC	Western Zhou
770–221 BC	Eastern Zhou
770–476 BC	– *Spring and Autumn period*
475–221 BC	– *Warring States period*
221–207 BC	Qin
206 BC–AD 9	Western Han
AD 9–24	Xin (Wang Mang interregnum)
AD 25–220	Eastern Han
AD 220–280	Three Kingdoms
220–265	*– Wei*
221–263	*– Shu*
229–280	*– Wu*
AD 265–316	Western Jin
AD 317–420	Eastern Jin
AD 420–588	Southern and Northern Dynasties
420–588	*Southern Dynasties*
420–478	*– Song*
479–501	*– Qi*
502–556	*– Liang*

557–588	*– Chen*
386–588	*Northern Dynasties*
386–533	*– Northern Wei*
534–549	*– Eastern Wei*
535–557	*– Western Wei*
550–577	*– Northern Qi*
557–588	*– Northern Zhou*
AD 581–617	Sui
AD 618–907	Tang
AD 907–960	Five Dynasties
907–923	*– Later Liang*
923–936	*– Later Tang*
936–946	*– Later Han*
951–960	*– Later Zhou*
AD 907–979	Ten Kingdoms
AD 960–1279	Song
960–1127	*– Northern Song*
1127–1279	*– Southern Song*
AD 916–1125	Liao
AD 1038–1227	Western Xia
AD 1115–1234	Jin
AD 1279–1368	Yuan
AD 1368 – 1644	Ming
AD 1644 – 1911	Qing
AD 1911 – 1949	Republic of China (in mainland China)
AD 1949 –	Republic of China (in Taiwan)
AD 1949 –	People's Republic of China

Geological Time Scale

Hadean time (4500 to 3800 million years ago)

Archaean Era	**(3800 to 2500 million years ago)**
Proterozoic Era	**(2500 to 544 million years ago)**
Ediacaran Period	(650 to 544 million years ago) (prev. called Vendian period)

Phanerozoic eon (544 million years ago to present)

Paleozoic Era	**(544 to 248 million years ago)**
Cambrian Period	(544 to 505 million years ago)
Ordovician Period	(505 to 440 million years ago)
Silurian Period	(440 to 410 million years ago)
Devonian Period	(410 to 360 million years ago)
Mississippian Period	(360 to 325 million years ago)
Pennsylvanian Period	(325 to 286 million years ago)

Carboniferous Period	(360 to 286 million years ago)
Permian Period	(286 to 248 million years ago)
Mesozoic Era	**(248 to 65 million years ago)**
Triassic Period	(248 to 213 million years ago)
Jurassic Period	(213 to 145 million years ago)
Cretaceous Period	(145 to 65 million years ago)
Cenozoic Era (65 million	**years ago to present)**
Tertiary Period	(65 to 1.8 million years ago)
Paleocene Epoch	(65 to 55.5 million years ago)
Eocene Epoch	(5.5 to 33.7 million years ago)
Oligocene Epoch	(33.7 to 23.8 million years ago)
Miocene Epoch	(23.8 to 5.3 million years ago)
Pliocene Epoch	(5.3 to 1.8 million years ago)
Quaternary Period	(1.8 million years ago to present)
Pleistocene Epoch	(1.8 million to 8,000 years ago)
Holocene Epoch	(8,000 years ago to present)

Ice ages

Late Proterozoic (between about 800 and 600 million years ago).

Lesser extensive glaciations during parts of the Ordovician and Silurian (between about 460 and 430 million years ago).

Pennsylvanian and Permian (between about 350 and 250 million years ago)

Late Neogene to Quaternary (the last 4 million years) especially the Pleistocene Ice Ages (1,600,000 to 10,000 years ago).

The 'Little Ice Age' commenced in the 16th c. with a maximum about 1750.

The Ages of Mankind

Note that these differ between Europe and America.

Stone Age. Europe: 2 million years ago until about 4000 BC. In the Americas from 30,000 BC (arrival of the first human beings) until 2500 BC.

Eolithic

    Paleolithic (Old (or Early) Stone Age). 2 million BC until end of last Ice Age, ca. 13,000 BC.

    Mesolithic (Middle Stone Age). From ca. 13,000 BC

Neolothic (New Stone Age). 6000 BC – 3000 BC in Europe and Western Asia. This was the Second part of the Stone Age.

    Chaclithic Period (from Greek, copper + stone). Transiton from Neolithic to Bronze Ages

Bronze Age. About 1500 BC in Europe.

Iron Age. About 1000 BC in Europe

    Hallstatt Cuture. Early Iron Age period: From about 750 to 450 BC.

    La Tène Culture. Latter Iron Age: Central and northwestern Europe from about 450 to 58 BC.

Books of the Bible

And God said unto Moses 'Go forth' – but he came in fifth and lost his deposit.

Old Testament
Genesis
Exodus
Leviticus
Numbers
Deuteronomy
Joshua
Judges
Ruth
1 Samuel
2 Samuel
1 Kings
2 Kings
1 Chronicles
2 Chronicles
Ezra
Nehemiah
Esther
Job
Psalms
Proverbs
Ecclesiastes
Song of Solomon

Isaiah
Jeremiah
Lamentations
Ezekiel
Daniel
Hosea
Joel
Amos
Obadiah
Jonah
Micah
Nahum
Habakkuk
Zephaniah
Haggai
Zechariah
Malachi

New Testament
Matthew
Mark
Luke
John

Acts
Romans
1 Corinthians
2 Corinthians
Galatians
Ephesians
Philippians
Colossians
1 Thessalonians
2 Thessalonians
1 Timothy
2 Timothy
Titus
Philemon
Hebrews
James
1 Peter
2 Peter
1 John
2 John
3 John
Jude
Revelation

Useful websites: biblegateway.com

The British Isles: Counties

England

Bedfordshire
Berkshire
Buckinghamshire
Cambridgeshire
Cornwall
Cumberland
Derbyshire
Devon
Dorset

Durham
Essex
Gloucestershire
Hampshire
Herefordshire
Hertfordshire
Huntingdonshire
Kent
Lancashire

Leicestershire
Lincolnshire
Middlesex
Norfolk
Northamptonshire
Northumberland
Nottinghamshire
Oxfordshire
Rutland

Shropshire	Sussex	Yorkshire
Somerset	Warwickshire	North Riding
Staffordshire	Westmoreland	East Riding
Suffolk	Wiltshire	West Riding
Surrey	Worcestershire	York (within the Walls)

The 'Home counties' usually refers to Surrey, Kent, Essex and Middlesex, sometimes including Hertfordshire, Buckinghamshire, Berkshire and occasionally Sussex.

Wales (including Monmouthshire)

Anglesey/Sir Fon	Cardiganshire/	Monmouthshire/Sir
Brecknockshire/Sir	Ceredigion	Fynwy
Frycheiniog	Denbighshire/Sir	Montgomeryshire/Sir
Caernarfonshire/Sir	Ddinbych	Drefaldwyn
Gaernarfon	Flintshire/Sir Fflint	Pembrokeshire/Sir
Carmarthenshire/Sir	Glamorgan/Morgannwg	Benfro
Gaerfyrddin	Merioneth/Meirionnydd	Radnorshire/Sir
		Faesyfed

Scotland

Aberdeenshire	East Lothian/	Peeblesshire
Angus/Forfarshire	Haddingtonshire	Perthshire
Argyllshire	Fife	Renfrewshire
Ayrshire	Inverness-shire	Ross-shire
Banffshire	Kincardineshire	Roxburghshire
Berwickshire	Kinross-shire	Selkirkshire
Buteshire	Kirkcudbrightshire	Shetland
Cromartyshire	Lanarkshire	Stirlingshire
Caithness	Midlothian/	Sutherland
Clackmannanshire	Edinburghshire	West Lothian/
Dumfriesshire	Morayshire	Linlithgowshire
Dunbartonshire/	Nairnshire	Wigtownshire
Dumbartonshire	Orkney	

Ireland

	Down	Limerick
Ulster:	Fermanagh	Tipperary
Antrim	Monaghan	*Leinster:*
Armagh	Tyrone	Carlow
Cavan	*Munster:*	Dublin
Derry	Clare	Kildare
Donegal	Cork	Kilkenny
	Kerry	Laois

Longford	Offaly	*Connaught:*	Mayo
Louth	Westmeath	Galway	Roscommon
Meath	Wexford	Leitrim	Silgo

Useful website: The Association of British Counties has an excellent website with many links on www.abcounties.co.uk

London Postal Districts

'Do you know if there's any insanity in her family?'
'Insanity?, No, I never heard of any. Her father lives in West
Kensington, but I believe he's sane on all other points.' – Saki (1870–
1916).

More a curiosity for most rather than an aid to your paper, the origins of London Postal Districts date back to the mid-nineteenth century. Consequently the districts do not coincide with modern administrative boundaries. While now being incorporated into modern postal codes, the initials are still retained. So where did that pop group 'East 17' come from? And the EastEnders? The London Borough of Walford is E20, but that is fictitious (believe it or not).

East London

E1	Whitechapel, Stepney, Mile End	E11	Leytonstone (also covers Wanstead)
E2	Bethnal Green, Shoreditch	E12	Manor Park
E3	Bow, Bromley-by-Bow	E13	Plaistow
E4	Chingford, Highams Park	E14	Poplar, Millwall (also covers Isle of Dogs)
E5	Clapton	E15	Stratford, West Ham
E6	East Ham (also covers Beckton)	E16	Victoria Docks & North Woolwich (also covers Canning Town)
E7	Forest Gate, Upton Park	E17	Walthamstow
E8	Hackney, Dalston	E18	Woodford and South Woodford (in reality only South Woodford is covered by
E9	Hackney, Homerton (includes South Hackney)		
E10	Leyton		

E18; most of Woodford itself is covered by postcode area IG8, outside the London postal districts)

East Central London

EC1 covers the Clerkenwell, Finsbury,

Barbican area
EC2 covers the north eastern (Moorgate, Liverpool Street) area of The City
EC3 covers the south eastern (Monument, Aldgate, Fenchurch St, Tower Hill) area of The City
EC4 covers the western (Fleet Street, Temple, Blackfriars, St Paul's) area of The City

North London

N1 covers the Islington, Barnsbury, Canonbury area
N2 East Finchley (includes eastern part of Hampstead Garden Suburb)
N3 Finchley Central, Finchley Church End (central Finchley)
N4 Finsbury Park, Manor House
N5 Highbury
N6 Highgate
N7 Holloway (includes Lower Holloway)
N8 Hornsey (also covers Crouch End)
N9 Lower Edmonton
N10 Muswell Hill
N11 New Southgate (also covers Friern Barnet)
N12 North Finchley, Woodside Park
N13 Palmers Green
N14 Southgate
N15 South Tottenham, Seven Sisters
N16 Stoke Newington, Stamford Hill
N17 Tottenham
N18 Upper Edmonton
N19 Upper Holloway, Archway, Tufnell Park
N20 Whetstone (also covers Totteridge)
N21 Winchmore Hill
N22 Wood Green, Alexandra Palace

North West London

NW1 covers the Camden Town, Regent's Park, north Marylebone area
NW2 Cricklewood, Neasden (also covers Dollis Hill)
NW3 Hampstead, Swiss Cottage (also covers Belsize Park)
NW4 Hendon, Brent Cross
NW5 Kentish Town
NW6 Kilburn, Queens Park (also covers South and West Hampstead, Brondesbury Park)
NW7 Mill Hill
NW8 St John's Wood
NW9 The Hyde (also covers Kingsbury and Colindale)
NW10 Willesden (also covers Harlesden and Kensal Green)
NW11 Golders Green (includes western part of Hampstead Garden Suburb)

South East London

SE1 covers the Waterloo, Bermondsey, Southwark (South Bank and Borough) and north Lambeth area
SE2 Abbey Wood (includes Thamesmead South)
SE3 Blackheath, Westcombe Park (also covers Kidbrooke)
SE4 Brockley, Crofton Park, Honor Oak Park
SE5 Camberwell
SE6 Catford, Hither Green (also covers Bellingham)
SE7 Charlton
SE8 Deptford
SE9 Eltham (also covers Mottingham)
SE10 Greenwich (Town)
SE11 Lambeth, Kennington
SE12 Lee, Grove Park

SE13   Hither Green, Lewisham (Town)
SE14   New Cross, New Cross Gate
SE15   Peckham, Nunhead
SE16   Rotherhithe, South Bermonsey, Surrey Docks
SE17   Walworth, Elephant and Castle
SE18   Woolwich (also covers Plumstead)
SE19   Crystal Palace, Norwood (central Norwood: Upper Norwood and Norwood New Town)
SE20   Anerley (also covers Penge)
SE21   Dulwich (includes West Dulwich)
SE22   East Dulwich
SE23   Forest Hill
SE24   Herne Hill
SE25   South Norwood
SE26   Sydenham
SE27   West Norwood, Tulse Hill
SE28   Thamesmead (NB small parts of Thamesmead are in SE2, and in DA18 Dartford which is not in London Postal Districts)

South West London

SW1   covers the Westminster, Belgravia, Pimlico, Victoria area
SW2   Brixton (central and southern Brixton, includes Streatham Hill)
SW3   Chelsea, Brompton
SW4   Clapham
SW5   Earl's Court
SW6   Fulham, Parson's Green
SW7   South Kensington
SW8   South Lambeth (also covers Vauxhall, Nine Elms)
SW9   Stockwell (includes northern Brixton)
SW10   World's End, West Brompton (NB Brompton is covered by SW7, SW3 and SW1)
SW11   Battersea, Clapham Junction

SW12   Balham
SW13   Barnes, Castelnau
SW14   Mortlake (also covers East Sheen)
SW15   Putney (also covers Roehampton)
SW16   Streatham, Norbury
SW17   Tooting
SW18   Wandsworth (Town), Earlsfield
SW19   Wimbledon (also covers Merton (Town) and Collier's Wood)
SW20   South Wimbledon, West Wimbledon (also covers Raynes Park and Cottenham Park)

West London

W1   covers the West End, including Mayfair, Soho and south Marylebone
W2   covers the Paddington, Bayswater, Hyde Park area
W3   Acton
W4   Chiswick
W5   Ealing
W6   Hammersmith
W7   Hanwell
W8   Kensington (central Kensington)
W9   Warwick Avenue, Maida Hill (also covers Maida Vale)
W10   Ladbroke Grove, North Kensington
W11   Notting Hill, Holland Park
W12   Shepherd's Bush
W13   West Ealing
W14   West Kensington

West Central London

WC1   covers the Bloomsbury and Gray's Inn area
WC2   covers the Holborn/Strand/ Covent Garden area

Postcodes

Post code	Post town
AB	Aberdeen
AL	St. Albans
B	Birmingham
BA	Bath
BB	Blackburn
BD	Bradford
BH	Bournemouth
BL	Bolton
BN	Brighton
BR	Bromley
BS	Bristol
BT	Belfast
CA	Carlisle
CB	Cambridge
CF	Cardiff
CH	Chester
CM	Chelmsford
CO	Colchester
CR	Croydon
CT	Canterbury
CV	Coventry
CW	Crewe
DA	Dartford
DD	Dundee
DE	Derby
DG	Dumfries
DH	Durham
DL	Darlington
DN	Doncaster
DT	Dorchester
DY	Dudley
E	London East
EC	London East Central
EH	Edinburgh
EN	Enfield
EX	Exeter
FK	Falkirk
FY	Fylde (Blackpool)
G	Glasgow
GL	Gloucester
GU	Guildford
GY	Guernsey & Alderney
HA	Harrow
HD	Huddersfield
HG	Harrogate
HP	Hemel Hempstead
HR	Hereford
HS	Hebrides
HU	Hull
HX	Halifax
IG	Ilford
IM	Isle of Man
IP	Ipswich
IV	Inverness
JE	Jersey
KA	Kilmarnock
KT	Kingston Upon Thames
KW	Kirkwall
KY	Kirkcaldy
L	Liverpool
LA	Lancaster
LD	Llandridnod Wells
LE	Leicester
LL	Llandudno
LN	Lincoln
LS	Leeds
LU	Luton
M	Manchester
ME	Medway (Rochester)
MK	Milton Keynes
ML	Motherwell
N	London North
NE	Newcastle on Tyne
NG	Nottingham
NN	Northampton
NP	Newport
NR	Norwich
NW	London North West
OL	Oldham
OX	Oxford
PA	Paisley
PE	Peterborough
PH	Perth
PL	Plymouth
PO	Portsmouth
PR	Preston
RG	Reading
RH	Redhill
RM	Romford
S	Sheffield
SA	Swansea
SE	London South East
SG	Stevenage
SK	Stockport
SL	Slough
SM	Sutton
SN	Swindon
SO	Southampton
SP	Salisbury
SR	Sunderland
SS	Southend-on-Sea
ST	Stoke On Trent
SW	London South West
SY	Shrewsbury
TA	Taunton
TD	Berwick upon Tweed
TF	Telford
TN	Tunbridge Wells
TQ	Torquay
TR	Truro
TS	Teesside (Middlesbrough)
TW	Twickenham
UB	Uxbridge
W	London West
WA	Warrington
WC	London West Central
WD	Watford
WF	Wakefield
WN	Wigan
WR	Worcester
WS	Walsall
WV	Wolverhampton
YO	York
ZE	Lerwick

22
Style

I have never read a book before reviewing it; it prejudices one so.
–Sydney Smith, 1771–1845, English clergyman, essayist, and wit.

Let's go in at the deep end. Here is an extract from a paper I was asked to comment on:

> In the following pages an attempt is made to identify and put together events and features that may be potential building-blocks for the comparative identification and characterisation of some key aspects of the social and political processes in Norwegian society that has emerged in response to the many complex and controversial issues raised by the new genetic technologies. While the characteristics that are highlighted are in often obvious ways linked to specific, entrenched aspects of Norwegian social and political culture, the nature of the shaping influences of a unique national context is not one of a stable cultural 'identity' that remains stable and identical with itself throughout the many-faceted, conflictual, and hence, and not least, open-ended processes involved. Rather, such identities are at the same time both shaping, and put at stake in, these processes, one essential feature of which is their being experimental and innovative in terms of institutional structures, socio-political relations, and cultural identities. Thus, this is an account of yet another variety of social and political innovation in coping with the challenges of genetic technology within the specific configuration which defines the Norwegian industrial structure and political culture.

The above comprises: Words, 191; sentences, 4 (mean length 48); commas, 13 (4 + per sentence); semicolons, 0; colons 0; dashes 0; grammatical errors, excessive. OK, but at least we understood what the article is about – didn't we? All of which reminds us of Oscar Wilde who once said: 'Nowadays to be intelligble is to be found out.'

Did this arouse your interest? Did the author ask herself if this aroused *her* interest? So, what is it that arouses, retains, stimulates and satisfies (apart from Madonna)? The art of stimulating (in a literary context, of course) is dependent upon a variety of techniques; it is the art and mastery of presenting a text which encompasses all these elements, something which may be summarised as *style*.

So what do we really mean by 'style'? Here is the *OED* definition:

style (noun)

1   a manner of doing something – a way of painting, writing, etc., characteristic of a particular period, person, etc.
2   a distinctive appearance, design, or arrangement.
3   elegance and sophistication.

Now you will appreciate my allusions to Madonna – elegance and sophistication. But isn't this the keynote of Shakespeare as well? Not all of our prose will reflect the genius of William, but neither should it leave us fumbling to find an interpretation. And then the punctuation. We should not be doused in redundant commas, suspect semicolons and questionable colons, to the extent that we become focused on the punctuation rather than the content of the text. Next, the layout. Page after page of long paragraphs causes us to doze off. That second point in the *OED* definition: distinctive arrangement. We (at least our readers) might have been rescued by a systematic numbering of sections whereby we know that we are in Chapter 6, section 3, sub-section 4, segment 2, point (i), as indicated by 6.3.4.2 (i)

There are many books on the market which are intended as a guide to style. Some are excellent; others less so. One failing appears to be that authors of such books seem to wish to impose rules upon others reflecting their own style. My approach is different. Rather than provide instruction on how to acquire style I find it more constructive to examine some of the pitfalls which we may all encounter. Don't think that I haven't been at the receiving end. I remember well: 'Taylor, you lack style.' My professor at the time (Wise by name!) was not referring to my dinner jacket but to my Master's thesis. Here was judgement and sentence (not the literary kind). His brusque remark made me think, and even though this was aeons ago, it stuck, and I woke up to the authority and power of the English language as well as to the authority and power of the professor, whose own style was to reject any thesis first and foremost on the absence of style in his students' writings: 'Never mind the academic content. Can I understand it?'

It is now fitting that we disentangle our thoughts and examine some of the basic elements which when considered as a whole determine style.

What is the Theme?

On the 'classic formula' for a novel: *A beginning, a muddle and an end.* Philip Larkin (1922–85). English poet.

What is the theme? Don't we know what we are writing about? Probably, yes. But do we always make this clear – from the outset? It is surprising how many authors fail to do so. You don't need me to tell you that. You have probably read enough books and articles to know that some authors are not too clear about their subject matter. They cope with this in two ways. The first is excessive punctuation: when in doubt add a comma; when in severe doubt use a semicolon; when they've lost the plot, a colon.

A second weakness is that the author uses an excessive amount of space and time informing the reader (a) what he is going to read in the next chapter, and (b) what he has read in the previous chapter. And all this after a six-page introductory chapter summarising the entire book. To be honest, my feelings are that when an author has to tell you what he has just been telling you, he really isn't sure whether he has told you at all.

What this all comes down to is being quite clear in the mind what one is going to do, how one is going to analyse the material and how one is going to present it. Many academic works are concerned with testing a hypothesis. An article might be concerned with presenting the results of an investigation. The theme should be stated quite clearly in the opening lines as should the approach and method used.

> This article concerns the control of chicken 'flu in the province of Ping Pong Poo in the autumn of 2003. It commences with the recognition of the outbreak, the identification of the strain and the measures that were introduced by the authorities to contain it. Of particular interest were the procedures invoked to ensure that farmers complied with the restrictions imposed.

Now that seems quite clear to me. The ensuing paragraph may briefly outline the structure of the article, but it is not necessary to go into detail about the methods used to evaluate the effectiveness of restrictions or how these were imposed and administered. If an important theme was how the 'flu affected the different breeds of hen (Rhode Island Red, Yangtze Yellow, etc.), then the introductory paragraph might mention 'The effect of the outbreak upon different breeds of hen is also discussed.'

Neither should it be forgotten that the Table of Contents usually provides a solid summary of the book. The prospective purchaser will almost certainly glance at the TOC before anything else. As such, it is important that the chapter titles are informative. Ambiguous titles such as 'Chicken farmers clucking at straws' might suit a popular version of the article, but are clearly not appropriate in a PhD thesis.

In summary: do not leave your reader in doubt about the message you are conveying in the particular chapter, section or paragraph.

The Target Group

The world may be full of fourth-rate writers, but it's also full of fourth-rate readers. – Stan Barstow (1928–)

An important point to remember is that you are writing for a specific group of persons – your audience. Who are these? Are these passengers on a train, undergraduate students, post-doctoral fellows, your work colleagues? Is this a subject entirely new to them – or do they have some background knowledge? Are they familiar with the jargon, the technical language, or shall we have to add some explanatory footnotes?

Nothing is more off-putting for the reader than to have to struggle with a vocabulary that he felt he should be familiar with. He likes to open the book prepared to absorb and even challenge the written word. But if after a few pages he is questioning his own academic ability to the extent that he develops an inferiority complex, you may be sure that communication will cease by Chapter 2.

I really feel that the opening extract in this chapter illustrates this point precisely. The author was so concerned with exhibiting her own command of the language that she forgot the subject of her paper and the target group.

The personal touch is sometimes used to establish contact with the target group. Both 'I' and 'we' can serve a purpose, but the first person singular can become overbearing, even conceited. A matter of style, but consider: 'We then interviewed the parents. The replies did not surprise us particularly.' And the more impersonal approach: 'The parents were then interviewed although the replies were as expected.' So far, so good. But when this is presented in the first person, the results may appear to be very definitive. 'I then interviewed the parents. Their replies did not surprise me.' This does not give the leeway for interpretation that the critical reader may be looking for. The author describing the results of a research project desires to produce convincing findings; the PhD student certainly does. But any hypothesis is set up so as to be proven or disproven. Nothing wrong with reaching the conclusion that there was sufficient evidence to support the hypothesis. The point being made here is that the direct, personal approach, rather than the indirect, may result in the reader feeling pressured into believing that the results were so conclusive as to question why it was necessary to test the hypothesis in the first place.

Style and Content

I just got out of hospital. I was in a speed-reading accident. I hit a bookmark. – Steven Wright. American comic.

Structuring the paper

In summary, style is a means by which material is presented, an argument communicated, and interest stimulated. But a single style is not applicable or appropriate to all material or all audiences. Further, different approaches may be made to the analytical and the descriptive article. The former is concerned with a sequence of events, for example hypothesis, testing, results, conclusions. The descriptive article does not possess the same natural structure. Consider an article entitled 'Hospital Reform: Budgeting processes and rationalisation'. This type of article needs particularly careful planning. Posing a number of questions may assist in the design of the article.

– What was the basis of the reform?

– What did the government directive state about budgeting?

– What was the reaction to this by the hospitals, unions, etc.?

– What changes were required in the existing budgeting routines?

– Did existing routines function satisfactorily? Where were they unsatisfactory and why?

– How was rationalisation defined? How was it to be measured?

Have we covered all the questions? What is the appropriate order for these to be taken up? What information is needed to be assembled in order that these can be answered? What are the sources of this information? For the undergraduate preparing his thesis, and indeed, for the post-graduate, there are numerous handbooks on preparing and writing a thesis. The more experienced writer will be familiar with the procedure of planning a paper. But common to both the student and the professional is the need to consider the following questions relating to the style and presentation of the material.

Preparation of the analytical paper is often more straightforward than the descriptive article such as that on hospital reform. The analytical paper will normally be based on a structure: problem–hypothesis–data–analysis–results. But the descriptive article may be constructed upon a more liberal framework. In consequence, particular care has to be taken in assigning material to the appropriate chapter such that each chapter presents a clear argument related to a specific theme. This emphasises the importance of the structure of the descriptive paper. Of course, this does not mean to say that the treatise is void of any analysis whatsoever. But I have noticed a tendency to apply terms such as 'analysis' to descriptive material where in fact no real analysis is found. Data collection and summary statistics hardly comprise an *analysis*. The Oxford English Dictionary defines analysis as: 'The resolution or breaking up of anything complex into its various simple elements.' *Collins*

Dictionary goes a stage further adding 'or using statistical methods to understand or explain it'. Note 'or using', not '*and* using' statistical methods. There are various approaches to analysis, but a key word in the *OED* is 'complex'. By complex we mean 'consisting of many different and connected parts' (*COD*).

Analysing your presentation

Whatever the subject matter, the style will be reflected in the final presentation of the material. I have mentioned the referee under 'Proofreading' in Part 1 of this book. While a referee or adjudication panel will be concentrating on the academic content, this cannot be divorced from its presentation. But a requirement to revise and resubmit a paper may not be due to a faulty argument: it is far more likely to be related to the presentation of the argument. A reader does not return your paper, of course, but he might well make a mental note not to purchase any more of your books. What are some of the pitfalls which every author should consider? What is it that consciously, or subconsciously, causes a reaction by the reader. These are just some of the points to be considered, but are not intended as a list of points to be checked at the end. Rather, these are points for on-going consideration.

► Are sentences generally too long?

► Is there sufficient variety between the thought-provoking sentence and the short snappy comment/reflection?

► Do the chapter headings reflect the course of development of the argument (from hypothesis to conclusion)?

► Do the sections and sub-sections have appropriate headings? Is the (sub-) section too short, or too long?

► Could bullets have contributed to clarity? Should these have been bulleted as this paragraph, or with numbers 1), 2)... or a), b)... etc.

► Did you drown your reader with references which were imprecise and of dubious interest, e.g. *(See Smith 1995)*? In other words, were you more concerned with impressing the reader with your broad knowledge of the field?

► Did you check the dictionary? Were technical terms self-explanatory or have you explained their meaning in your context? Did you construct words? Was the meaning of these clear (e.g. objectivated).

▶ Was the reader perfectly clear about the aim and purpose of the thesis or article? Did you repeatedly use phrases such as 'The aim is to...'; 'My intention is...'; 'I will show that...'? Did you conclude by telling the reader that 'I have shown that...'; 'It was seen that...'?

▶ Were the conclusions clear and concise.

Humour

From the moment I picked up your book until I laid it down I was convulsed with laughter. Someday I intend reading it. – Groucho Marx (1895–1977).

Generally, there is nothing wrong with the occasional touch of humour – a witty remark or play on words, an appropriate quote, even one of those dashed words '*****!', although only if this is a quote. Naturally, the emphasis of your paper is on the academic content and puns have little place in academic treatises. The paper on chicken flu is hardly enhanced by adding: 'The chicken farmer received only a poultry amount for his hens.' A thesis on sleeping problems will not be regarded as academically serious if you write: 'In order to stop his snoring she bestowed upon him a night-hood.'

However, even the PhD thesis should not be entirely immune to the occasional lighter stroke of the pen. As indicated above, a quotation may be incorporated into the text, not with the intention of reviving the reader's flagging interest, but even if not to stimulate it, to retain it. I remember reading a book on the legal system many years ago. I remember neither the author nor the title and little of the content, but I do remember reading it! The golden opportunity was missed when the author could have commenced: 'Laws are the basis of society: they serve and protect.' It may be that Oscar Wilde had not quite grasped this when he wrote 'Laws are made in order that people in authority may not remember them, just as marriages are made in order that the divorce court may not play about idly'.' Even that eminent Q.C., John Mortimer (creator of Rumpole), wrote in the introduction to his book *Famous Trials*: 'Murder, as is well known, like divorce and Christmas, mainly takes place in the family circle.'

But whatever the nature of the writing – article, thesis, book, review, or whatever, the aim has to be to retain the interest of the reader, to arouse his interest in the subject, to stimulate his curiosity, and to leave him as satisfied as though he had just seen Madonna's latest video. (I have not seen it myself, but I am informed...).

Phrasal Phrases

A few years ago everything became 'phrasal'. This was the 'in thing' to learn: phrasal verbs, phrasal auxiliary verbs, phrasal prepositional verbs, even phrasal genitives![1] I was not in the least surprised to read in the *Daily Telegraph* that an internet[2] poll had revealed the words and phrases that people wanted to get *rid* of. These included 'bling bling' – a term for ostentatious jewellery, 'smoking gun' (probably a Bushism) because voters considered that it was not obvious what it meant (except probably to Bush), and most of all 'metrosexual' – one of the most genitival phrases I've come across. (Definition: Urban, usually heterosexual men, with a keen interest in fashion, shopping, and men's beauty treatments. I must ask my wife about it.) Anyway, my choice would be to prohibit anything defined as phrasal.

One of the most distracting style faults (for the reader), yet unobtrusive (to the author), is the over-use of *sentence connectors*. Used considerately, they enhance the flow: if a flow becomes a flood we are all swept downstream. The most common sentence connectors are the following: although, but, consequently, even so, further, moreover, nevertheless, still, therefore, though, thus. There are others (see Chapter 3, Sentence connectors). All these *modify* the previous sentence by an apparent confirmation (consequently, therefore, thus), contradiction (but, even so, nevertheless, although, though), clarification (still), amplification (further, moreover). But when a modification is apparently modified the reader asks: 'What is the main argument of the author, what is he getting at?'

I am not stating that modifiers (or qualifiers) such as these are to be avoided. But consider:

> It was stated, **however**, that the sub-committee's decision was ill-founded and **thus**, the question of legitimacy was raised. The resolution, **therefore**, was unlikely to be approved by the AGM. **Nevertheless**, there was sufficient opposition to the resolution that a new debate was inevitable, **although** this opposition was less vociferous than hitherto. **Further**, the voting procedure was also in doubt. The constitution of the sub-committee was, **moreover**, questionable. **Even so**, it was considered that the subsequent debate would reach the same result, **but** the necessary two-thirds majority remained in doubt. **Consequently**, the committee's original decision appeared controvertible, **although** this question would be resolved in a subsequent debate. **Still**, the sub-committee remained confident. **Accordingly** a new debate was finally proposed.

---

1   All terms found in my grammar books.
2   Incidentally, *internet* is no longer capitalised in many contexts.

Point made! But it is not only the sentence connector which may provoke a break in the chain of thought. The comma is not only an elucidator, it is a confuser. It is the gateway to superfluous and irrelevant adverbial phases, noun clauses, interjections – and sentence connectors. Examples are to be found in all texts ranging from the Bible to Britain's national newspaper *The Sun.* But times are changing and there is a tendency to omit the formal, superfluous comma where the only consequence of its removal is improved readability.

Which Words?

Read over your compositions, and where ever you meet with a passage which you think is particularly fine, strike it out.– Samuel Johnson (1709–1784).

Diction – the choice and use of words in writing (*COD*). We all like to feel that we are masters of our own languages when we are more likely to be the mistress – subservient to the language. Remember the first essays we wrote at school? – how we loved to find new words to gain the admiration of Miss Buxom, the English teacher (supply, of course), only to be met with: 'Sorry, John. I don't think I can accept that word.' Of course, we are now more mature and selective in our choice of words. But do not make the fatal error of thinking that a few ritzy or up-market words will make your style admirable and lead your readers to assume that your IQ has been under-rated. Frequent use, or even an overdose of words like decontextualised, proletarianised, solidaristic and undogmatic – in fact even occasional use of those to which your spellchecker reacts, should be regarded with caution. As for those hyphenated terms such as anarcho-syndicalism, my advice is to watch your 'isms'. And even if it may appear to breach the rules, don't make matters worse by removing the hyphen: anarchosyndicalism. Now the spellchecker is not infallible and 'solidaristic' will be found in the *OED*, but not much elsewhere. We don't want to restrict our text to words with a maximum of two syllables, but, are these terms familiar to your readers? Might a footnote assist the first time such a term is used?

We should not overlook the value of the very occasional singular – selected – word or expression. As Linus said to Lucy: 'I always thought that opinions should have quality and not just quantity.' To which Lucy replied: 'That's because you don't know anything about opinionation!'[3]

We might think that 650,000 or so words to be found in the *Oxford English Dictionary* should be sufficient to meet most needs. But sometimes we just

---

3 I understand the Peanuts cartoons are still to be found in the national press in many countries.

cannot find that word we need. Consequently we make one up. Now there is nothing wrong with a constructed or invented word; the English language does not stand still and new words appear in the press every day. But the first time we use a word we should indicate that we are aware of the special nature of the term by placing it in inverted commas. Later in the text we do not need to do so: we have established it as part of our terminology. But do not sprinkle your text with gems of literary compilations, either words or phrases, such that the reader struggling with Einsteinian syntax loses sight of what you are saying. Here are some pearls (I won't call them gems) from just *one* chapter in a PhD I had to read: conscient individuals, generisibility, intersubjectivity, objectivated, normativity, objectivation, perspectivate; perspectivating, plurivocity. I could accept representativeness even without studying the context. Perhaps do we need the context in order that certain terms may be understood:

> the polysemic character of language; I abstended from prompting too strongly; the dichotomy between disembedding and reimbedding still remains the core piece of this thinking; is to produce generalisable knowledge; [making] it possible to perspectivate the verbal statements; may serve to preclude certain reductory readings.

– or even the entire sentence:

> In insisting on the link between the structured, objectivated text/action and contexts of lived experience, Ricoeur avoids the relativism that is ultimately furthered by structuralism and semiotics.

> The use of these five interviews within the thesis consists both of perspectivating the knowledge produced within the two cases, and in broadening the analysis of the connection between sense of community and individual features.

Even when not using constructed words, the alternate use of a specialist term can add a little spice:

> I was defined as a competent interlocutor who was apt to valorise the importance of offering training to people.

To valorise is to determine a stable price (as if we didn't know). Many would certainly put a price on this author's interloculation, I am sure. But the point of this paragraph is to remind you, the author, that your choice of phrasing, diction, must always take consideration of the target group. Don't over-estimate your target group, but don't under-estimate them either.

I did actually pick this author up on the term 'operationalise'. Now this sounded like a constructed word, but it seemed quite clear what was meant. It was more than 'to execute, to put into operation'; it was 'to plan, formulate and execute'. But sticking to my principle that if it is not found in the *OED* it does not exist, I made a comment on this. But when looking at

Encarta and *Random House dictionaries* I find 'operationalism = operational + ism'. Well, if you can add one suffix, you can add the other. After all, somebody has to invent new words.

Choice of words is not only an important element of style; it is a reflection on your command of the English language. We have already dismissed the x-form such as connexion for connection; we know the difference between sex and gender. We wish to be politically correct and use the term 'chairperson' and even 'person-years' rather than 'man-years'. But several readers might not yet be ready for such refinements.

Which and what

One area where familiarity has bred contempt is the distinction between *which* and *what*. There are many and varied articles in the literature on the distinction between *which* and *what*, but the most frequent mistakes appear to be when they are used as interrogative pronouns.

> Never mind the horsepower, which colour car would madam like?
> Never mind the horsepower, what colour car would madam like?

Which is used when there is a limited choice; *what* is non-specific. *Which* in the above might well imply which of two: lilac or puce. *What* indicates a choice: red, orange, yellow, blue, green, indigo, violet, or any colour of the rainbow (which these are).

Which and who

The distinction between *which* and *who* is less problematic as these relate to the impersonal and personal forms respectively, whether used interrogatively or as relative pronouns. 'Which of you said it?', or 'Who said that?'

Which and that

These words are largely interchangeable in sentences such as: Take the bus which (that) goes to Folkestone. If you are looking for a rule, then 'that' or 'which' may be used in what are called 'identifying clauses'. An identifying clause does not contain commas. The bus *that goes to Folkestone* leaves at 9.30. 'Which' or 'that' may be omitted when preceding a pronoun in an identifying clause: The document (that) he presented at the meeting was not new.

A non-identifying clause is separated by a comma and employs 'which': The document, which was not new, was now considered interesting material.

Who and whom

Blamires (2000)[4] refers to 'this relic of Anglo-Saxon differentiation...'. Nevertheless his discussion is not in conflict with *Collins Cobuild* where it is stated (in summary): *Whom* is used in formal or written English instead of 'who' when it is the object of a verb or preposition. It is used particularly after verbs and adjectives, to introduce a clause referring to a person or group of persons. It is also used at the beginning of a relative clause when specifying the person or group of people.

> The committee appointed Smith, whom they knew from previous experience.
> The member to whom the matter should be addressed is on vacation.

For example, it is correct to say: He is someone about whom I know little. *Whom* is the object of the verb *I know*. But it is incorrect to say: He is someone whom I know little about. In this case *whom* is not an object form of a verb or a preposition. Even worse: 'Whom do you think you are?' If you are in doubt, then do not be too proud to use *who*.

Which and whose

Distinctions between interrogatives such as *which* and *whose* are again associated with objects and persons:

- ✓ Which of you does this book belong to?
- ✓ Whose book is this?
- ✓ To whom does this book belong?
- ✗ Who of you does this belong to?

The subject of a sentence may be clear, but the pronoun should be unambiguous with respect to the subject:

> The committee revised the plans but they remained unclear in their objective.

Who or what remained unclear in their objectives? The committee or the plans?

> The budget was rejected and the chairman resigned, something which was regretted by the council.

What, specifically, was regretted? – the rejection, the resignation, or both?

As a general rule the pronoun should relate to the last subject (or object) referred to. The interpretation of the above would normally be that the

---

4   Blamires, H., (2000), *The Penguin Guide to Plain English*, London, Penguin, p. 156 ff.

council regretted the resignation rather than the rejection of the budget. Otherwise rewrite the sentence.

This problem particularly arises with the pronoun it, or the possessive form its (no apostrophe)

✗ The dog lost its' bone.

Although he had initially voiced opposition to the contract he admitted that he had agreed to amendment, but nevertheless voted against it.

Was it the amendment which he had voted against or the contract?

Ones

Somewhat akin to 'its', this plural substitute word is often to be found rather loosely used at the end of a sentence:

✗ In the subsequent vote these countries were joined by several other ones.

... several others is sufficient. Of course the sentence could have continued 'several others such as...'.

This brings me to another point:

Whether or not

Another vague expression.

The data does not show whether the level of living has improved or not.

Is 'or not' superfluous, or is it not? Quite possibly, but was the data gathered with the objective of proving something, or disproving something? It can't do both. In case you wondered, economists refer to the 'level of living'.

Probably having read around a thousand articles and at least a hundred theses, I have become aware of the main weaknesses in style, not least my own. Frequently, when I correct these the author rejects my proposal and appears to regard me as pedantic. But I feel that the author often forgets the reader's tenacity and his (or her) ability – or lack thereof – to concentrate on long sentences, long paragraphs and long sections.

Like, such as, including, comprising. Several countries like France were opposed to the war. 'Like' is vague. It means 'similar to' or 'resembling'. In the example given, 'like France' was probably intended to mean 'such as' or even 'including'. In other words, France was one of a number of countries opposing the war. 'Like' then means 'an example being'. The other countries may not have resembled France in any other way whatsoever, either in terms of size, area, geography, politics or language. We also have a problem with 'include/including'. Consider: The opponents, including France and Germany, were in conflict with the USA. This seems to imply that there were more opponents than just France and Germany, but what if we had written: The opponents included France and Germany. But this may not be exclusive. Were France and Germany included among several others, or did they comprise the sole opponents? It is for this reason that I frequently question authors whether they mean 'including among others,' or 'comprising', 'composed of', 'constituting'.

Concept, conception of

Here's a nice one. His conception of the module was that it was ground-breaking. But what if we had written: 'His concept of the module was that it was ground-breaking'? A concept is the way in which something is perceived in the mind (*COD*). A 'Conception' is an idea, a founding of an idea, a birth. The first sentence implies that 'he' was the one who had devised and planned the module; the second was someone's impression of the module. Some may argue that the distinction is not important. Others may well postulate that it is these niceties of the English language which make it such a challenge for the author (and the reader!).

All the above points, and hundreds more, will be found in almost any book on grammar, style, or *plain English*. As indicated in several places in the above I have no intention of entering the fray, but you may well find a handy companion to this text covering grammar and style in detail in your local bookshop. This is one area where I found the Internet to be of little use; you need to see the contents of the book first. A number of books incorporating 'style' into the title frequently contain lists of new words, hyphenated words, compound words, abbreviations, punctuation and proofing. *How* these are used and pieced together is what, in my mind, constitutes 'style'; how the sentences are composed, the paragraphs constructed, the appropriate phraseology, the adjustment to the target audience – which reminds me of a doctorate thesis on training centres. 'When asked, the member stated her reason for joining was to avoid getting flabby with a big bum!' I have no reason to believe that those were her actual words, but I would have thought that a more appropriate academic style was the use of square parentheses: 'to avoid getting flabby with a big [posterior]!' Leaving it open to the imagination will more likely lead to a wry smile.

Verbosity

The covers of this book are too far apart. – Ambrose Bierce (1842–1914). American journalist.

If you want to upset you reader, verbosity will do it. There are several aspects of verbosity worth mentioning. The first is those meaningless phrases we attach at the end of the sentence: The committee discussed the matter to and fro. Now what does 'to and fro' mean. Does it mean that it was discussed by those sitting on one side of the table, and then by those on the other; or did it mean that they kept repeating things which had been said earlier? In fact I almost wrote: those sitting on one side of the table, and then by those sitting on the other side of the table. But suffice it to write: The committee discussed the matter thoroughly.

The other irritating habit is to repeat something unnecessarily: He repeated it many times, over and over again. Of course, there are times when the objective is served: He emphasised what he was saying, stressing each individual point. But phrases such as: Also, it was stated *in addition...*, *Possibly*, the statement *may have been* too brief..., It was with *great pleasure* that he announced how *pleased* he was with the results...

The worst offence is to use several words when one or two will do: Well after the deadline and long after it should have been presented, the manager concluded that the provisional budget gave a deceptive and erroneous picture of the company's true financial situation and of necessity would have to be re-presented. (39 words). Alternatively: Belatedly, the manager concluded that the provisional budget was disingenuous, necessitating redrafting. (12 words). You may decide that the latter version was, in fact, too brief. This can be a dilemma: do we trim down the fat, or do we put some flesh on the skeleton? We immediately realise the importance and need for rewriting the text several times. Too frequently, I find that when rewriting my own material I divide a long sentence and rephrase both parts. The result is still the same – verbosity. For example: The deadline for presenting the budget had been long exceeded. The provisional budget now being considered by the manager was regarded as erroneous and deceptive. It was essential that it be redrafted. We have come back to the same thing, but possibly worse: a single sentence, possibly two, should be quite sufficient. Pick out the key words, including others if necessary: deadline, exceeded, provisional budget, manager, disingenuous. You may consider that one or more of these words could be substituted – your electronic thesaurus will be invaluable here. Try juggling the word order and draft some alternative sentences. One possible result is: Although the deadline had expired the manager considered the provisional budget misleading. It would have to be redrafted. Eighteen words have captured the essential points and presented these in a manner which can be immediately comprehended.

The above example illustrates the importance of rewriting a manuscript. This is a time-consuming task. Our first draft is invariably characterised by a degree of verbosity – the result of our thinking rate exceeding that of our typing. We endeavour to get all our thoughts down onto the hard disk. The problem is that when we re-read the material, we do this at the same velocity as our initial thoughts. In fact, checking your own material involves two stages. The first is to read through at normal speed to control that your message was presented, the order was logical, and nothing omitted or superfluous.

But it is the second stage that is most demanding. You have written the material; you remember what you were thinking when you applied pen to paper (read: fingers to keyboard); you recall what you had written when reading through the manuscript on the last stage. By now you are fed up with the whole thing. You are now being confronted with the tedious and demanding task of reading the *words* rather than the *meaning*. It is this stage where the manuscript may be doomed to failure on the launch pad, or projected into space, even though the destination may still be unclear.

When reading a manuscript I often find myself actually asking the author if this is the first draft or even the final draft. Replies frequently verge on the indignant, but I then point out that what may have been checked is the content and meaning, but not the presentation – the diction, the syntax the terminology, the phraseology, the verbosity, the *style*. But to this list we can add a further item – logic. Now this may go beyond rhetoric, the gentle art of persuasion; the absence of logic may be definitively unpersuasive. By logic, I mean not the logic of the content but the logic of the structure, often reflected in a 'circular sentence', a characteristic of several sociological works. A gem from one of these: 'One of the motivations for the design of incentive regulation is the perception of poor cost performance of regulated or public ally-owned firms due to a lack of incentives.' The mind boggles. If there is a lack of incentives, why should we be motivated to regulate them? – or did I miss the point?

Food for thought? But don't get indigestion over it – you may be one of those who are able to present their argument clearly and comprehensively at first sitting. And once we have all reached that stage we then look at our manuscript as a whole, this visual presentation – the *layout*. But first, a final reference to the sentence.

Style and the Sentence

In matters of grave importance, style, not sincerity, is the thing. – Oscar Wilde.

Whereas the mean length of paragraph measured in number of lines, words or sentences, is an indication of 'readability' (related to the reader), the same statistics applied to sentences provide an indication of clarity of thought (related to the author). I would question whether any sentence exceeding 40 words could not be divided so as to improve its comprehension: I would seriously question whether this should not be done with any sentence exceeding 60 words: I would deny that any sentence exceeding 75 words could not be divided into two, if not three, sentences. And yet I have read papers where words bubble forth like pigeon faeces in Trafalgar Square, and hardly a colon in sight. You believe me not! Example:

> While the unique balance between the functions and contending voices with which it has to juggle, is continually challenged, it has succeeded in retaining its role as a mini- and model, public sphere for biotechnology debate, providing a sufficiently broad framework and credible standards for debating biotechnology issues to secure a key role for its input to public debate and to the political process.

Did you, at first reading, grasp the message? Yes, because you are a person of average to high intelligence (otherwise you would not have bought this book). But you were prepared for this challenge. You might not have been if you had been reading the article from which this is taken and where the two previous sentences were 32 and 40 words respectively. If a *mean* length is 15 to 18 words, anything above 25 should be examined. And in case you were wondering, the mean length of sentence in this chapter hitherto (excluding the example) is 19.1 words.

At this point I have to add a comment about transcribing interviews. Many research studies are based on interviews and quotations from interviewed persons are often considered by authors to add credence to the material. This may be so, but transcribing recorded material word-for-word (and uh-for-uh) does not validate the argument. 'Well, I, er, am not too, mmm, sure about the, uh, actual, er, what should I say, signals coming from the, er, the White House, but, mmm, er, it is not an, ah, easy question.' Now, the authenticity of the interview is not increased by the fact that the author states the interview to have been transcribed from the original tapes by student research assistants. The ellipsis was derived as a symbol for the faint of heart when it comes to transcription: 'I'm not too sure about...what should I say? Signals coming from the White House...It's not an easy question.' I would suggest that this simplified transcription does more to emphasise the validity of the argument by at least reducing uncertainty and confusion in the original. Is the Ph.D. hypothesis (let alone the thesis) really enhanced and justified by a series of grunts and groans? Methinks not. Rather, methinks that the literal transcription has diverted attention away from the essential, even away from what in all possibility was a baseless argument to begin with. Incidentally, I wonder what this author would have done with someone who lithped!

Layout – In General

Layout comprises a number of elements. First of all, the general structure of the book. It is interesting to watch potential purchasers of a book in a bookshop (subject for a PhD?). First, they look at the cover. Those books with dark print on a dark background rendering the title difficult to read are less likely to be looked at. Next, they glance at the blurb on the back cover. Here are a few lines and quotes ('unrivalled in its coverage') and other meaningless expressions. But should a few bulleted comments arouse attention, they will then turn to the List of Contents. A quick glance at the price, a moment's thought, another glance at the contents ... sold!

But if the back cover blurb really failed to hit its mark then we falter at stage one. An article does not have this handicap, but that is all the more reason why the synopsis should be right to the point. The potential reader will then glance through the article looking at the subheadings.

The layout, so far, is focused on chapter and section headings. Are these clear and systematic? Do they follow a logical progression? In this computer age it is so much easier to juggle with titles, chapters, sections and to change the order of these at will. I have mentioned a very useful feature in this connection, the Outline tool in Word (see Chapter 18). But many may still prefer a system of hand-written index cards. Even this book was initially planned with coloured cards – red for chapters, green for sections. I was then able to juggle these at will before entering the essentials onto the PC.

The Word feature mentioned above is particularly useful where sections are numbered. Numbering can assist the author in his thoughts and the reader in his comprehension of the argument being developed. But paragraph numbering can also be confusing. Too many levels and too much numbering – as mentioned elsewhere in this book – can all too easily give the impression of a handbook for assembling a car engine.

Layout – In Particular

There is another aspect of layout which is important – the visual aspect. Books with predominantly long paragraphs and little variation *can* become tiresome to read. Of course, many short paragraphs can also divert our attention away from the main theme. This is the point: each paragraph should have an underlying theme. After twenty lines or so, we may have become confused by what the actual theme is at this point. Similarly, a short paragraph may also leave us questioning the point of an apparent intrusion into our thoughts. A media psychologist would be able to explain the importance of the visual layout, but take a glance at a book – any book. Does the layout appeal? Looking at a book, *Famous Trials*, I note that many paragraphs exceed thirty and even forty lines. Now this should have been an easy book to read as the breath of 'air' given by the occasional paragraph of a couple of lines gives us a chance to breathe. Another aspect of appearance is the use of the bullet. As has been pointed out, excessive use of bulleted lists is rather reminiscent of a school text book, but these should be seriously considered when summing up the main points of a chapter.

The Word Count feature under Tools in Word does state the number of paragraphs in your text, but it does not show the variation. We can calculate the mean number of lines per paragraph and the mean number of words per sentence, but we require one of the specialist programmes for a more detailed analysis. Indeed, this brings us to the question of sentences as part of the layout.

Style – In Summary

Bearing in mind the *OED* definition we can compile a number of points that the author should consider. These points have to be seen in the light of the reader – capturing his attention and retaining his interest until the last page.

▶ Read your own material back to yourself. Was it understandable? Was it enjoyable? Or was it characterised by your own prowess – the intention of impressing the reader with your extensive knowledge of the field, and that of others particularly by an epidemic of references?

▶ The references – were they precise? Did they contain the date and page of the source? Or were they just some vague reference such as 'See Smith, 1999'. What purpose do such general references serve? References in the text shall be specific; those in the bibliography shall be comprehensive in bibliographic detail.

▶ Did the introduction make it perfectly clear what the subject of your article, thesis or paper is? Don't cloud the issue with technical jargon. Just indicate that the article 'will take up issues of genetic technology'. That will be sufficient to enlighten the informed reader, or inform the unenlightened reader.

▶ When the going gets tough, did you repeatedly use phrases such as 'The aim is to...'; 'My intention is...'; 'I will show that...'? Did you conclude by telling the reader 'I have shown that...'; 'It was seen that...'? When the going gets really tough, there is a tendency to substitute 'I' by 'we'. (We then found that...) We now have someone else to blame for the confusing state of affairs.

▶ Sentences – varied length, mean of 13–17 words; any over 40 words? Sensibly punctuated with proper use of commas, semicolons and colons? Is there sufficient variety between the thought-provoking sentence and the short snappy comment/reflection?

▶ Paragraphs. Was the subject of each paragraph clear? Are there sufficient paragraphs? Are some too short or too long? Check the visual appearance. The concentration of some will wilt under long sessions. One Sage publication I have just looked at has many paragraphs of 30 lines and even more. Fine, except the book was concerned with Qualitative Research – not the lightest of subjects. Yes, some paragraphs can exceed twenty lines, but intersperse these with the occasional short-and-to-the-point paragraph. Nothing wrong with the *occasional* two-line paragraph.

▶ Sections and subsections. Does the subsection have an appropriate heading? Is the subsection too short, or too long?

▶ Could bullets have contributed to clarification? Should these have been bulleted as this paragraph, or with numbers 1), 2)... or a), b)... etc.?

▶ Could tables have been used for some of the information, even diagrams?

Did you commence a paragraph with an expression such as 'It is clear that this needs to be clarified'? A new paragraph has to be quite specific in references to 'this', 'that' and so forth. It is often desirable to restate the subject. The above opening sentence could thus be rewritten: 'It is clear that the question of what is meant by illegal immigration needs clarification.'

Style is more than a mastery of the language; it is also more than a presentation of ideas and development of an argument. It is a combination of all these and has to grip the reader and retain his interest. The very occasional touch of wry humour may have its place. If your book or article has not been accepted for publication, style may be the main culprit. The publishing house will be tolerant towards a few punctuation errors (your readers may not), providing these are not swarming like a plague of locusts; it will even assist in pointing out those few lapses in grammar. As Oscar Wilde once said: 'George Moore wrote brilliant English until he discovered grammar.' But style is your responsibility, and yours alone. It is not something which is learned from a book but rather *acquired* through writing, and reading and absorbing the style of others. But, as I have learnt, weaknesses in style have to be recognised, acknowledged and rectified. What better way than to have these pointed out? Your colleague will invariably be tactful and reserved in his comments; your proof-reader may not be and should not be. I remember reading one thesis which was well written with careful punctuation and clear paragraphing. But the style was best defined as 'woolly'. I had difficulty in following the argument – and said so. Instead of describing data in the text rather than providing a few simple tables or charts would have given some life to 300 pages of words, plain words. The response was that her colleagues had not commented on this and in any case my job was to check the grammar and punctuation; the content was hers. My approach is the 5-percent rule. 'If you believe that even 5 percent of your readers will query your text – a paragraph, a sentence, a phrase, or even a word, then consider rewriting it.'

Postlude

postlude [music]: a final or concluding piece or movement.[5]

Style is what you make it, or as the English clergyman Sydney Smith (1771–1845) once said: 'In composing, as a general rule, run your pen through every other word you have written; you have no idea what vigour it will give to your style.' His contemporary, [von] Goethe (1749–1832) commented that: 'If any man wishes to write a clear style, let him first be clear in his thoughts.' But Albert Camus probably summed it all up when he commented: 'Those who write clearly have readers; those who write obscurely have commentators.'

---

5   I had never heard of an 'afterword' until one of my clients used it. But the *COD* confirms she was right.

23
Internet Addresses

Q: What, exactly, is the Internet?
A: The Internet is a world-wide network of university, government, business and private computer systems.
Q: Who runs it?
A: A 13-year-old named Jason.
– Dave Barry

International Addresses

The following list shows the major national addresses on the Internet.

address *country*			
.at	Austria	.hk	Hong Kong
.au	Australia	.hr	Croatia
.ba	Bosnia, Herz.	.hu	Hungary
.be	Belgium	.ie	Ireland
.bg	Bulgaria	.il	Israel
.ca	Canada	.in	India
.cc	Cocos Islands	.iq	Iraq
.cn	China	.ir	Iran
.cs	Czechoslovakia	.is	Iceland
.cy	Cyprus	.it	Italy
.cz	Czech Republic	.jm	Jamaica
.de	Germany	.jo	Jordan
.dk	Denmark	.jp	Japan
.ee	Estonia	.kr	South Korea
.eg	Egypt	.li	Liechtenstein
.es	Spain	.lt	Lithuania
.fi	Finland	.lu	Luxembourg
.fo	Faeroe Islands	.lv	Latvia
.fr	France	.ly	Libya
.gb	Great Britain	.ma	Morocco
.gl	Greenland	.mc	Monaco
.gr	Greece	.mt	Malta
		.mx	Mexico
		.my	Malaysia

.nl	Netherlands	.se	Sweden	.vi	British Virgin
.no	Norway	.sg	Singapore		Islands
.nz	New Zealand	.si	Slovenia	*International and*	
.ph	Philippines	.sk	Slovak Republic	*national*	
.pk	Pakistan	.tn	Tunisia	.co.uk	
.pl	Poland	.tw	Taiwan	.com	
.pt	Portugal	.ua	Ukraine	.edu	
.py	Paraguay	.uk	United Kingdom	.gov	
.ro	Romania	.us	USA	.int	
.ru	Russian	.ve	Venezuela	.me	
	Federation	.vg	U.S. Virgin	.net	
.sa	Saudi Arabia		Islands	.org	

Hyperlinks

When writing an email address or the name of a website (www...), it is probable that the hyperlink will be automatically activated as the default setting. Frequently this means that the address will appear in blue and underlined, e.g. john@jgtaylor.com. What this means is that when the cursor is placed on the address, it changes so that by clicking on the address, your PC will automatically connect to the address or website, assuming you are connected to the Internet. You may not want this. Under 'Tools' in your word processor you will find 'Hyperlink' where you can activate/deactivate the link.

Information on the Internet

General information

Unquestionably, the Internet is an unrivalled source of information. When we search for information a search engine checks out sources of information. You may have noticed that a search on *Yahoo*, for example, will provide different results to another site. There are a number of search engines which link to others, thus broadening the field. For research purposes, **www.twics.com/takakuwa/search/** will enable you to locate the major search engines in most countries. The Internet is constantly changing, but try these for information:

www.askjeeves.com; www.just35.com; www.infoplease.com; www.dogpile.com, and one of the best, **www.goggle.com** (not to be confused with google.com).

Politics

Much of my work is concerned with political reports and I suspect that many readers of this book may have interests in this field. Here are some useful sites, and certainly interesting to others who may not be specialists.

www.parliament.uk contains the home pages of the Houses of Parliament and the House of Lords with full information on current bills etc.
www.uk.p.org – UK Politics Directory – contains similar material but more links to other government sites as well as historical summaries of parliamentary Acts since 1945. For those more interested in political theory and political science resources, **www.psr.keele.co.uk** will be a valuable site. Elections are covered on **www.election.demon.co.uk** for the UK (from 1885) and other countries. Historical material is also to be found on **www.spartacus.schoolnet.co.uk**, a site of especial value to teachers. **www.tic.mil/doctrine** contains DOD – Dictionary of Military and Associated terms.

Dictionaries

Amazon.co.uk or Amazon.com (for US readers) will yield full information about all available dictionaries. Search on keywords such as Dictionary; English; CD-ROM. Otherwise you may prefer to go directly to the publisher's site. (See Chapter 24).

24
References

I must admit to being something of a bibliophile regarding dictionaries. There are a number of superb dictionaries published in the 1920s and 1930s which may be purchased for a song, often at flea markets or boot sales! One of these, The *King's English Dictionary,* British Books Limited, 1927, is inscribed by my grandmother to her daughter (my mother): *'To Read, mark, learn, and inwardly digest'.* (I've read this before somewhere.)

Another gem is *Nuttall's Standard Dictionary of the English Language. Based upon the Labours of the most Eminent Lexicographers.* Warne & Co. 1929. This contains the following definition:

> GAY: in bright spirits; lively; mirthful; showy; devoted to pleasure; inflamed or merry with liquor.

Times have changed! (– or perhaps not!!) Nevertheless, these publications frequently contain appendixes of material and information seldom encountered. The latter publication contains, among other things:

- ▶ Phrases, Proverbs, Maxims, Quotations and Mottoes from the Latin and other languages
- ▶ Greek, Latin and Geographical Names and their pronunciation
- ▶ Etymology of place names
- ▶ Group terms
- ▶ Esperanto
- ▶ Forms of address
- ▶ Traffic signs!

The first-mentioned dictionary contains similar material plus:

- ▶ Pseudonyms and Pen-Names. (Did you know that Maxim Gorki's real name was Alexei Maximovitch Pyeshkov?)
- ▶ Glossary of terms used in Aviation and Motoring (empennage = tail plane)
- ▶ Glossary of Scottish words and phrases
- ▶ Not least – an atlas, in full colour.

Dictionaries and Handbooks

[*New books published since the first edition have been included. A number of older publications may be out of print. I have not checked this but have retained them in the list as useful texts which may still be found in 'remainder' bookshops. There are, of course, a large number of other texts which do not appear in my library. But search on the web with words such as grammar, punctuation, style, and so forth. A number of major dictionaries which have been consulted are not included in this list.*]

Aitchison, James (1994), *The Cassell Guide to Written English*. London: Cassell.

Allen, Robert (2001), *Punctuation. One step ahead series*. Oxford: OUP.

Amis, Kingsley (1997), *The King's English. A Guide to Modern Usage*. London: HarperCollins. [Excellent reading, entertaining]

Baugh, Sue L. (1991), *Essentials of English Grammar*. London: Guild Publishing.

Better Word Power. Oxford: OUP.

Bickerton, Anthea (1998), *American English – English American*. London: Abson Books.

Billingham, Jo (2002), *Editing and Revising Text*. Oxford: OUP.

Blamires, Harry (2000), *The Penguin Guide to Plain English*. London: Penguin.

Bowden, John (1997), *Writing a Report*. Oxford: How To Books.

Burt, Angela (2000), *The A to Z of Correct English*. Oxford: How To Books.

Burchfield, R.W. (Ed.), *New Fowler's Modern English Usage*. Oxford: OUP.

Butcher J. (1992), *Copy-Editing for Editors, Authors and Publishers*. Cambridge: CUP. [Standard guide for Cambridge University Press.]

Carey, G. V. (1976), *Mind the Stop. A Brief Guide to Punctuation with a Note on Proof-correction*. London: Penguin. [First published 1939. Very enjoyable reading.]

Chalker, S., and Weiner, E. (1994), *The Oxford Dictionary of English Grammar*. London: BCA

Chambers Good punctuation Guide (1996). Edinburgh: Chambers.

Chambers Dictionary of Spelling and Word Division (1995). Edinburgh: Chambers.

Chicago Manual of Style, The (2003). Univeristy of Chicago Press. [A seminal work in its 15th edition. Sub-title *The Essential Guide for Writers, Editors, and Publishers*. Essential it certainly is – especially if you are thinking of publishing in the USA.

Collins Cobuild English Guides, 1. Prepositions (1994). London: HarperCollins.

Collins English Spelling Dictionary (1993), London: HarperCollins. [Hyphenation guide.]

Concise Family Medical Handbook (1981), London: HarperCollins.

Cutts, Martin (1995), *The Plain English Guide*. Oxford: OUP.

Davis, Christopher. *Divided by a Common Language*. Sarasota, Florida: Mayflower Press. [Comprehensive comparison of UK/US English.]

Delahunty A., Weiner E.S. (1995), *The Oxford Guide to English Usage*. Oxford: OUP.

Devlin. J. A. (1961), *Dictionary of Synonyms and Antonyms*. New York: Popular Library Inc.

Dictionary of English Usage (1995). London: Brockhampton Press.

Dictionary of Philosophy (1979). London: Pan Books.

Encarta World English Dictionary (2000). Microsoft. [Also CD version. Probably the most comprehensive US dictionary with excellent computer dictionary]

English Dictionary (1969). London: Penguin.

Etherington, Mike (1999), *The Best of British. The American's Guide to Speaking English*. Basingstoke: Effingpot Productions Ltd.

Field, M. (2000), *Improving Your Spelling*. Oxford: How To Books.

Field, M. (2000), *Polish up your Punctuation and Grammar*. Oxford: How To Books.

Fowler, H.W. (1994), *A Dictionary of Modern English Usage*. London: Wordsworth.

Gibaldi, J. (1998), *MLA Style Manual and Guide to Scholarly Publishing*. New York: The Modern Language Association of America. [Valuable guide if you intend to publish in the USA.]

Grubb, P. and Reah, D. (1998), *Writing a Textbook*. Oxford: How To Books.

Gould, William (1991), *Harrap's English Punctuation and Hyphenation*. London: Harrap.

Greenbaum, S. (2000), *The Oxford Reference Grammar*. Oxford: OUP.

Hart's Rules for Compositors and Readers at the University Press, Oxford (1893) [39th edn 2000.] Oxford: OUP.

Hilton C., Hyder, M. (1992), *Getting to Grips with Punctuation and Grammar*. London: BPP (Letts Educational) Ltd.

King, Graham (2000), *Punctuation*. Glasgow: HarperCollins.

Kipfer, Barbara Ann (1993), *21st Century Manual of Style*. New York: Philip Lief Group.

Kirkman, John (1999), *Full marks. Advice on puncutation for scientific and technical writing*. Marlborough: Ramsbury Books. [A lot of useful information of value to other writers, not just to science and technical authors.]

Knowles E. and Elliot J. (1998), *The Oxford Dictionary of New Words*. Oxford: OUP.

Lang, L. B. (1994), *Letter Writing*. (Collins Pocket Reference). Glasgow: HarperCollins.

Langenscheidt's Pocket Merriam-Webster. Guide to Punctuation. (1995). Mass, USA: Merriam-Webster.

Lewis, N. (ed.) (1961), *Roget's Thesaurus in Dictionary Form.* New York: Berkeley Publishing Corp.

Longman Language Activator (1993). London: Longman.

Oxford Dictionary of Abbreviations (1998). Oxford: OUP.

Page, G. Terry (1991), *The Book of Spelling Rules.* Edinburgh: Harrap.

Parody, A. (2004). *Eats Shites & Leaves.* London: Michael O'Mara Books Limited. [One of the funniest books I have read in years.]

Partridge, Eric (1973), *Usage and Abusage. A Guide to Good English.* London: Penguin.

Partridge, Eric (1953), *You have a point there.* London: Routledge. [The ultimate in punctuation, somewhat overwhelming.]

Peck, J. and Coyle, M. (1999), *The Student's Guide to Writing.* UK: Palgrave. [Useful guide to writing and style for students and others.]

Penguin Dictionary of [Various titles: *Computers, Economics, English idioms, Literary terms and Literary theory, Psychology.* Several good reference books are published by Penguin.]

Phythian, B. A. (1985), *Correct English* ('Teach Yourself Series'). London: Hodder & Stoughton.

Phythian, B. A. (1980), *English Grammar* ('Teach Yourself Series'). London: Hodder & Stoughton.

Ritter, R. M. (ed.) (2000), *The Oxford Dictionary for Writers & Editors.* Oxford: OUP. [Superb handbook and reference.]

Roget's International Thesaurus. (1963), London: Collins. [There are many versions of this standard reference in different forms, such as the Penguin version. This is the classic version. If buying a 'dictionary version', check to see if antonyms are referred to.]

Rutherford, L., Bone, S. (eds) (1996), *Osborn's Concise Law Dictionary* 8 edn. London: Sweet & Maxwell.

Sabin, William A. (1999), *The Gregg Reference Manual.* 9. edn. New York: McGraw-Hill. [The standard guide to US style. Very comprehensive.]

Seely, John (2004), *Oxford A–Z of Grammar and Punctuation.* Oxford: OUP. [Comprehensive summary of all grammatical terms.]

Speake, Jennifer (ed.) (2000), *The Oxford Dictionary of Foreign Words and Phrases.* Oxford: OUP.

Sullivan, K. D. (1996), *Go Ahead...Proof It!* New York: Barron's. [Interesting reading – and useful.]

Swan, Michael (1991), *Practical English Usage.* Oxford: OUP.

Swan, Michael (1992), *Oxford Pocket Basic English Usage.* Oxford: OUP.

The Complete handy reference: Dictionary, Thesaurus, Guide to English Usage (1997). London: Chancellor Press.

The Concise Oxford Dictionary (1951). Oxford: Clarendon Press.

The Economist Style Guide (2000). London: Profile Books Ltd.

The New American Roget's College Thesaurus in Dictionary Form (1958). New York: Signet Books. [Certainly republished since, but an excellent version.]

The New Shorter Oxford English Dictionary. (1993). Oxford: OUP. [2 vols.].

[The ultimate in dictionaries, but many of the latest words missing. See below.]

The Oxford Dictionary of New Words (1998). Oxford: OUP. [Excellent supplement to the above.]

The Oxford Dictionary for Writers and Editors (2000). Oxford: OUP.

The Oxford Dictionary of English Grammar (1993). Oxford: OUP.

The Oxford Guide to Style (2002). Oxford: OUP. [Standard guide for Oxford University Press.]

The Oxford Reverse Dictionary (1999). Oxford: OUP. [Essentially a thesaurus, but where a variety of associated phrases and terms are given.]

The Universal Dictionary of the English language (1988). London: Wordsworth.

Todd, L. (1995), *The Cassell Guide to Punctuation.* London: Cassell.

Trask, R. L. (2000), *The Penguin Dictionary of English Grammar.* London: Penguin Books.

Trask, R. L. (1997), *The Penguin Guide to Punctuation.* London: Penguin Books.

Truss, Lynne (2003), *Eats, Shoots & Leaves.* London: Profile Books. [Best seller. Humorous approach to punctuation – subtitle *The zero tolerance approach to punctuation.*]

Wiener, E. S. C. and Delahunty, A. (1994). *The Oxford Guide to English Usage.* London: BCA.

Wood, F. T., Flavell, R. H., and Flavell, L. M. (1981). *The Macmillan Dictionary of Current English Usage.* London: Macmillan.

Writers' & Artists' Yearbook. London: A&C Black. [Annually.]

Youngson, Robert M., (1992), *Collins Dictionary of Medicine.* Glasgow: HarperCollins. [Nearly all the medical words not found in the spell-checker. The Oxford publication is very similar.]

[As this book does not cover grammar, only a few basic references are included. Use the power search on amazon.com and search for authors Quirk R., and Greenbaum S. for some of the major grammar texts.]

Humour

[Well worth considering at least one of these books for entertainment if not inspiration.]

Bentley N. and Esar E. (1962), *The Treasury of Humorous Quotations,* London: J.M.Dent. [Long out of print, but worth mentioning. You might pick it up at a book sale.]

Metcalf, F. (2001), *The Penguin Book of 'Modern Humorous Quotations',* London: Penguin.

Peter, L.J. (1977), *Peter's Quotations. Ideas for our time,* New York: Bantam Books. [Also out of print, but the most comprehensive collection.]

Rees N. (2003), *Cassell's humourous quotations,* London: Weidenfeld & Nicolson.

Sherrin, N. (2003), *The Oxford Dictionary of Humorous Quotations,* Oxford: Oxford University Press.

Electronic dictionaries

An electronic dictionary is the most important working aid to any serious writer. Gone are the days when we, as schoolboys, were told that a dictionary was used to show you the correct spelling of a word. But as we did not know how to spell chrysoberyl or strychnine, it was not a lot of help.

The modern electronic dictionary contains aids which assist even we who are semi-illiterate. But our needs may vary. Here are some of the features you may want to consider when purchasing an electronic dictionary. Most dictionaries have the option to be downloaded onto the hard disk but some require to be run from the CD or to have this in place at start-up. This is inconvenient if you are using more than one CD at a time unless you have a CD *and* a DVD player, for example.

The main entry. Are examples given? Some dictionaries contain phrases with the opportunity for a full text search across all entries. We are then able to see examples of 'compared to' and 'compared with'.

Is it possible to add new words into a User Dictionary? Does the dictionary suggest alternative spellings for misspelt words? Does it have phonetic search possibilities (sounds like...)? This feature is sometimes called a 'Spell help'.

Wild cards. [* = any number of alphabetic characters; ? = one character]. Using the *Oxford Concise Dictionary*, I found the following:

*ire   Result 129 hits: admire, acquire...
*ire? Result 25 hits. Example: unimpaired
??ire? Result 2 hits: soirée, spirea

Anagram: A word or phrase formed by reordering the letters of another word or phrase, such as *satin* to *stain*. Fun for Scrabble players. This feature seems to be increasingly popular on electronic dictionaries.

Can definitions be searched? Many dictionaries have Boolean operators enabling AND, OR and NOT to be used when searching definitions. Thus presupposes that the definitions are searchable.

Other inclusions? Abbreviations, synonyms, antonyms, proper nouns and names, Latin terms. Can the definitions be cross-referenced by highlighting a word so as then to be able to see the dictionary definition of that word. Can highlighted words be copied into your text file? – and more important, is a

	1. Lang.	2. Thes.; Syn.	3. Boolean Wildcard	4. Anag.	5. Sound Video Pict.	6. Phonetic spell.	7. Publisher's web site: www
American Heritage	US	T.	B,W	✓	SVP	–	bartleby.com
Cambridge	UK	–	–	–	S (UK, US)	–	cambridge.org
Cassell Concise Dict.	UK	-	W	✓*	-	-	-
Chambers 21st C.	UK	–	W	–	–	–	chambers.co.uk
Collins Cobuild	UK	T.,S.				–	collinsdictionaries.com
Collins English Dictionary and Thesaurus	UK	T	–	✓	–	✓	collinsdictionaries.com
Encarta	US	T., S.	B	–	–	–	[Microsoft product]
Longman Dictionary of Contemporary English	UK (US)	Phrase book	–	–	–	–	Longman.com/ldoce
McMillan English Dict.	UK (US)	–	–	–	–	–	mcmillandictionary.com
Merriam-Webster	US	T.,S.	B,W	✓		Spell help	Merriam-webstercollegiate.com m-w.com unabridged.Merriam-webster.com
New Oxford English	UK, US. Can. Aus.	T.	-	-	-	-	oup.com
Oxford (Full)	UK	-	-	-	-	-	oup.com
Oxford Concise	UK (US)	-	B,W	-	-	✓	oup.com
Penguin English Dictionary*	UK						penguin.co.uk
Random House Webster's Unabridged	US	–	–	–	S	-	randomhouse.com
The Chambers Dict.	UK	-	B.W.	-		✓	chambersharrap.co.uk
Webster's New World Dictionary	US	S.	?			✓	wiley.com

* Penguin English Dictionary – not currently available

highlighted word in your file automatically read into the dictionary? Tiresome when you have to retype the word. A 'History' feature, enabling you to recall previous entries seems to be standard on all dictionaries.

Does that word exist? A morphological search will show all inflections of a word. Thus, looking up synonym, *Collins English Dictionary and Thesaurus* gives synonymic *or* synonymical – adjective; synonymity – noun (none of which are accepted by the Word spellchecker). See if the dictionary contains this feature, it might be more useful than you think. Check also if Latin terms are given.

Some dictionaries now include UK and US spellings, and even the pronunciation in either language (requiring appropriate software and speakers).

Thesaurus. This is probably the most useful feature of any electronic dictionary, but not all have this feature. A list of synonyms (words with the same meaning) is not quite the same as a fully-fledged thesaurus which contains related words. It is here that cross-referencing is particularly useful so that the definitions of the individual terms may be accessed.

Other features. Some electronic dictionaries, such as *Encarta Dictionary* include an almanac. A few dictionaries link this feature to an on-line encyclopaedia, which is not always as convenient as it sounds. It is the 'extras' which I find particularly appealing. *Encarta Dictionary*, for instance, includes several thousand quotations from many sources. It also includes a style guide. These are more entertaining than educational.

Finally, is technical support available? I have needed this from time to time, especially when trying to install an older version on the latest OS. Not only was I informed that the program was not suited to XP, I was sent a free upgrade, but only because I had registered the purchase of the original CD.

The foregoing table is a brief synopsis of some of the features in my collection of electronic dictionaries. It is not comprehensive and I may even have missed one or two features. Check the publisher's web site for more details. Availability and price may vary from one supplier to another, often the most expensive when ordering from the publisher. The registration card will still be supplied (if registration is possible).

Which dictionary? I had intended to summarise the features of the above but will post these on my web site (www.jgtaylor.com) at a later date. A word of caution. You may find some CD dictionaries at PC fairs at 'bargain prices'. These are often older versions which run successfully on Windows 95 and 98 but not at all on later systems. XP dated one of my best thesauruses (*Oxford*). Finally, check the publisher's website as new and improved versions appear quite regularly.

Searching for Reference Books

Note to this edition

Many new dictionaries and handbooks have appeared since the previous edition of this book. Many of those previously listed are no longer available. Using the advanced search on **amazon.co.uk** (US **amazon.com**), and Barnes and Noble site at **bn.co.uk**, all recent publications may be found, frequently with reviews. Search using Dictionary; English; CD – and you will find most of the dictionaries and thesauruses available on CD-ROM. Prices may vary, so try: **www.books.co.uk/index.html** and you will be able to see which of the major bookshops have the publication in stock together with the price (+p&p). You may be in for some surprises.

While I find the Amazon and bn sites excellent, more details may be found on the publishers' own sites. Here, you will also find 'tips for authors'. Try Oxford University Press on **oup.co.uk** or Cambridge University Press on **cup.org**

Dictionaries and glossaries

While an electronic dictionary is extremely useful, there is always something extra you may need. Try **www.xrefer.com** As their site says: *'xrefer contains encyclopaedias, dictionaries, thesauri & books of quotations from the world's leading publishers. All cross-referenced, all in one place – providing you with a single source for reliable factual information.'* I have found this to be indispensable. Another superb site: **www.yourdictionary.com** with 1800 dictionaries in 230 languages. Here are dozens of lists of acronyms, synonyms and so forth. This site is really fun – and educational! You can supplement this via a link to **www.britannica.com** where you may not only utilise the Merriam-Webster Dictionary and Thesaurus, but gain access to millions of articles. Another link goes to **www.foreignword.com** where you can translate between several foreign languages. This site also has links to many other useful sites for people working with languages and translators. Of course, you do not need to use the links – just go direct to your chosen www site. You may find that you want to register these under 'Favourites'.

An excellent site for new words: **www.worldwidewords.org** – and asking about them is **www.quinion.com/words** Michael Quinion is an authority. His site will lead you to many others (use *Other words sites*), one of which is exceptionally useful – **www.zilker.net**, covering 1700 glossaries listed by subject and compiled by Frank Dietz. Almost 1000 of these are in English (the others are in German). Here, you will find Education Measurement Terms, London Slang (and Rhyming slang), Telecom Terms, Cargo Acronyms,

Rubber Glossary, Cricket Dictionary as well as a whole range of more 'standard' dictionaries, lists and glossaries.

Grammar and more

Grammar is well covered under **www.englishplus.com** and then link to the 'grammar slammar'. But if you want an advanced book on the English Grammar, then see Greenbaum, S., *The Oxford Reference Grammar*.

What is that acronym? Try **www.acronymfinder.com**

Maps

If you want to include a map in your paper or article, look at **www.expedia.com** Select 'Site Map', then 'Maps', and 'Find a Map'. The *Encarta Atlas* on CD-ROM is certainly worth looking at. This came packaged with some editions of Microsoft Works.

Weights and measures

A brilliant program is available on **www.accelware.com** This contains conversions covering more than fifty fields including, distance, volume, mass, radiation, velocity etc. in metric, UK, US, international and biblical units. Download the trial version. *Cassells Dictionary of Weights and Measures* may be a useful alternative.

For the specialist, the *National Bureau of Standards,* Special Publication 330, provides information on the International System of Units (SI).British Standards Institute Publications. BSI has published a number of pamphlets, one of which, *Copy preparation and proof correction*, has been widely reproduced. However, those concerned with documents which have to comply with specific BSI standards will find the following useful:

BS 1629:1989 *Recommendations for references to published materials*
BS 4148:1985 *Specification for abbreviation of title words and titles of publications*
BS 5261-1:2000 *Copy preparation and proof correction. Part 1: Design and layout of documents*
BS 5261-2:2000 *Copy preparation and proof correction. Part 2: Specification for typographic requirements, marks for copy preparation and proof correction, proofing procedure*
BS 5261-3:2000 *Copy preparation and proof correction.* Part 3: *Specification marks for mathematical copy preparation and mathematical proof correction and their use*

BS 5605:1990 *Recommendations for citing and referencing published material*

BS 5848:1980 Numbering of divisions and subdivisions in written documents (point-numbering)

Useful websites

In compiling material for this book I have noted a number of useful websites. But on returning to some of these a year or so later I find that they have either disappeared or become a nesting site for those irritating messages inviting me to renew my mortgage, or that I have won a prize. More than once I have had to give up using a site. There are a considerable number of books on the market with titles like *1500 useful websites*. But the same problems arise, and further, new sites are arising all the time. My advice is therefore to use a search engine. You can make Google, Yahoo or whatever, your opening page every time you start the Internet. If you are using a search engine that came with the PC, just enter www.Google.com (for example), and you will be asked if you want this to be your Home Page. If you are not asked, it is a simple task to change this.

Get used to advanced search techniques using Boolean operators in your search terms, e.g. Cops AND Robbers; Crime NOT murder; Police OR Coppers; (Males AND females) NOT children. However, Google has an Advanced Search link where you can enter the words you want as well (AND, OR) as those to be excluded (NOT), simplifying the process. I expect other search engines do this as well.

Useful website: http://library.albany.edu/internet/boolean.html

As with any site address, this is the full address, but the basic http:// library.albany.edu will start you, i.e. the address as far as the first forward slash, thereby reducing the chances of a typing error.

A final note as this book goes to press, a really useful program for writers, students, linguists and others – Wordweb. Just search for Wordweb and this will be the first site shown. The free version is excellent, the cheap program is brilliant.

Appendix

It was not my intention that you should struggle through this book. I hope that you realised that it was a reference guide! Language is living, rules are flexible (there to be broken) and times change as the following (modified) from the Internet explains:

The European Union Commissioners have announced that agreement has been reached to adopt ENGLISH as the preferred language for European communications, rather than GERMAN, which was the other possibility.

As part of the negotiations, the British government conceded that English spelling had some room for improvement and has accepted a five-year phased plan for what will be known as EuroEnglish (Euro € for short). In the first year, 's' will be used instead of the soft 'c'. Sertainly, sivil servants will resieve this news with joy. Also, the hard 'c' will be replaced with 'k'. Not only will this klear up konfusion, but typewriters kan have one letter less.

There will be growing publik enthusiasm in the sekond year, when the troublesome 'ph' will be replaced by 'f'. This will make words like 'fotograf' 20 per sent shorter. Confusion between 'ir' and 'er' will be standardised. In the therd year, publik akseptanse of the new spelling kan be expekted to reach the stage where more komplikated changes are possible.

Guvernments will enkurage the removal of double letters, which have always ben a deterent to akurate speling. Also, al wil agre that the horible mes of silent 'e's in the languag is disgrasful, and they would go. Where 'our' is pronounced as 'or' (as in 'your'), the u will no longer be rekwird.

By the forth year, peopl wil be reseptiv to steps such as replasing 'th' by 'z', and 'w' by 'v'. Trublsum 'er' will be standardizd to 'ur' and 'ai' to just 'a'. ('ear' will now bekum 'er'). As for 'tion' the natral speling of 'shon' will be used.

During ze fifz year, ze unesesary 'o' kan be dropd from vords kontaning 'ou', and similar changes vud of kors be aplid to uzur kombinashons of leturs.

After zis fifz yer, ve vil hav a reli sensibl riten styl. Kapital letr E vil be riten as ___. ___vrivun vil find it ezi tu understand ech uzur. Zer vil be no mor trubls or difikultis. Ze drem vil finali hav kum tru!

Of kors, yor speling cheker ma not be abl to korekt evry inakurasi but riters vil be abl to expres zemselvs freli wizout ani inhibishon. Publish and be damd.

Mi publisher ses that i am alredi!

(A kopi of zis tekst is avalibl in gurman, rushan and sevrl uzur langwigis). Correction: 2nd Edition. The last sentence should read: *A kopi of this tekst is avalibl in jerman langwijis (not langwigis). Yor komentz are welkm. We ar wurkin on common punktuashon for orl Yuropian langwijis. This mai mayk a furthr edishon of this buk superfloous.*

Index

If you want to know how ... to find out more about our greatest writers

'We have in the British Isles a wonderfully rich store of literature. The purpose of this book is to offer a guide to that inheritance and to invite exploration of the great writers. You will find help towards understanding each writer's work, key biographical detail, extracts from the literature, and suggestions for further reading. The body of our literature is not a territory that we need feel obliged to map out in systematic and comprehensive detail. We can enjoy it inconsequentially, dipping into its random pleasures. I hope this book will encourage that.'

John Carrington

Our Greatest Writers
and their major works
John Carrington

'A perfect tool for upping your literary IQ.' – *The Good Book Guide*

'Excellent.' – *The Teacher*

This book will take you to the heart of the great literature of the English language, to discover or rediscover the best that has been written. In concise and clearly structured sections, all the major writers are presented in order of their birth, giving a strong sense of the unfolding history of English literature from *Beowulf* to Seamus Heaney.

ISBN 1 84528 037 7

If you want to know how ... to improve your spelling

'English spelling is extremely complex because it owes so much to other languages. There *are* rules but unfortunately there are just as many exceptions to the rules. This book has been written to help you sort out the problems. It gives examples of spelling variations and lists frequently misspelled words as well as providing you with some fascinating background information on the origin of certain words.'

Marion Field

Spell Well
Boost your word power and your confidence
Marion Field

A well-written letter is taken far more seriously that one using misspelt words. People will automatically assume you're more intelligent, and they'll take notice of you in a way they never did before. Now, with the help of this exciting book, you too can discover the power of words. Simply follow the clear steps and checklists throughout and you'll soon be writing with much greater confidence.

ISBN 1 84528 069 5

If you want to know how ... to learn another language

Gill James has published several collections of teaching materials, which emphasise the students' control of their own language learning. In the course of offering private tuition she discovered ways, outlined in this book, of making the learning of language easier.

'If only I had known all this sooner! When I first started on my own language learning for instance, or when I first started teaching others. We would have attained our goals more rapidly. I hope this will offer you a short cut.'

Gill James

The Complete Guide to Learning a Language
How to learn a language with the least amount of difficulty and the most amount of fun
Gill James

'Language expert James injects the learning process with a mega-dose of fun, giving us this book filled with tips and tactics to pluck up our courage and get us mingling with the natives in no time at all.' – *The Good Book Guide*

ISBN 1 85703 903 3

If you want to know how ... to become a touch typist

'Almost everyone today has to use a keyboard. Of course it is possible to use two fingers, or even three and stumble along making lots of mistakes and taking an age to type a single document. But there is a better way. Why not learn to touch type? Just think, a few hours now will teach you a skill that will be with you for life. What have you got to lose? Take the book home and start working through it today. By this time next week your hard work will be paying off.'

Ann Dobson

Touch Typing in Ten Hours
Spend a few hours now and gain a valuable skill for life
Ann Dobson

'It works! Even if you are a two-fingered, search-and-hunt, typist you can learn to touch type if you follow the ten one-hour exercises.' – *Writers' News*

'This is a very useful book indeed.' – *Reach*

'Liberate your fingers with this easy to follow book. The lessons are split into one hour chunks and, if you master one a week (easy), you'll be competent in less than three months.' – *Writers' Bulletin*

ISBN 1 85703 827 4

If you want to know how ... to write with confidence

'This book will offer practical help and guidance to all who lack confidence when faced with everyday writing tasks, whether it is having to reply to a formal wedding invitation, compiling a CV, or completing a job application form. Everyday situations are discussed and sample responses provided. This book shows you what to do, so you can go away and do it yourself.'

Angela Burt

Write with Confidence
Solutions and examples for everyday writing needs
Angela Burt

'Everyday writing has its own rules. It needs to be framed in a conventional way, so you need to know the conventions; it needs to be set out in a formal manner, so you need to know the construction. Angela Burt shows just how it should be done.' – *Writers' News*

'A very useful book, no matter what your problem.' – *Expos'd*

'A very useful guide to getting it right!' – *Changes*

ISBN 1 85703 894 0

If you want to know how ... to become more self-reliant in your writing

'Once, in an evening class, one of my adult students said, 'If there's a right way to spell a word, I want to know it.' On another occasion, at the end of a punctuation session on possessive apostrophes, a college student said rather angrily. 'Why wasn't I told this years ago?'

'This book has been written to answer all the questions my students over the years have needed to ask. I hope all who now use it will have their questions answered also and enjoy the confidence and mastery that this will bring.'

Angela Burt

Quick Solutions to Common Errors in English
An A-Z guide to spelling, punctuation and grammar
Angela Burt

'You will never doubt your written English again.' – *Evening Standard*

'A straightforward and accessible handbook for anyone who ever has a query about correct English – and that's all of us.' – *Freelance News*

'This is an excellent book; good value and useful .. buy it!' – *V. Tilbury, Cranfield University*

ISBN 1 85703 947 5

How To Books are available through all good bookshops, or you can order direct from us through Grantham Book Services.

Tel: +44 (0)1476 541080
Fax: +44 (0)1476 541061
Email: *orders@gbs.tbs-ltd.co.uk*

Or via our website

www.howtobooks.co.uk

To order via any of these methods please quote the title(s) of the book(s) and your credit card number together with its expiry date.

For further information about our books and catalogue, please contact:

How To Books
3 Newtec Place
Magdalen Road
Oxford OX4 1RE

Visit our web site at

www.howtobooks.co.uk

Or you can contact us by email at info@howtobooks.co.uk